Apache HTTP Server 2.4 Reference Manual 3/3

A catalogue record for this book is available from the Hong Kong Public Libraries.

Published in Hong Kong by Samurai Media Limited.

Email: info@samuraimedia.org

ISBN 978-988-8381-81-4

Contents

10.71   Apache Module mod_macro

Description:	Provides macros within apache httpd runtime configuration files
Status:	Base
ModuleIdentifier:	macro_module
SourceFile:	mod_macro.c

Summary

Provides macros within Apache httpd runtime configuration files, to ease the process of creating numerous similar configuration blocks. When the server starts up, the macros are expanded using the provided parameters, and the result is processed as along with the rest of the configuration file.

Directives

- <Macro>
- UndefMacro
- Use

Usage

Macros are defined using <MACRO> blocks, which contain the portion of your configuration that needs to be repeated, complete with variables for those parts that will need to be substituted.

For example, you might use a macro to define a <VIRTUALHOST> block, in order to define multiple similar virtual hosts:

```
<Macro VHost $name $domain>
<VirtualHost *:80>
    ServerName $domain
    ServerAlias www.$domain

    DocumentRoot "/var/www/vhosts/$name"
    ErrorLog "/var/log/httpd/$name.error_log"
    CustomLog "/var/log/httpd/$name.access_log" combined
</VirtualHost>
</Macro>
```

Macro names are case-insensitive, like httpd configuration directives. However, variable names are case sensitive.

You would then invoke this macro several times to create virtual hosts:

```
Use VHost example example.com
Use VHost myhost hostname.org
Use VHost apache apache.org

UndefMacro VHost
```

At server startup time, each of these USE invocations would be expanded into a full virtualhost, as described by the MACRO definition.

The UNDEFMACRO directive is used so that later macros using the same variable names don't result in conflicting definitions.

A more elaborate version of this example may be seen below in the Examples section.

Tips

Parameter names should begin with a sigil such as $, %, or @, so that they are clearly identifiable, and also in order to help deal with interactions with other directives, such as the core DEFINE directive. Failure to do so will result in a warning. Nevertheless, you are encouraged to have a good knowledge of your entire server configuration in order to avoid reusing the same variables in different scopes, which can cause confusion.

Parameters prefixed with either $ or % are not escaped. Parameters prefixes with @ are escaped in quotes.

Avoid using a parameter which contains another parameter as a prefix, (For example, $win and $winter) as this may cause confusion at expression evaluation time. In the event of such confusion, the longest possible parameter name is used.

If you want to use a value within another string, it is useful to surround the parameter in braces, to avoid confusion:

```
<Macro DocRoot ${docroot}>
    DocumentRoot "/var/www/${docroot}/htdocs"
</Macro>
```

Examples

Virtual Host Definition

A common usage of MOD_MACRO is for the creation of dynamically-generated virtual hosts.

```
## Define a VHost Macro for repetitive configurations

<Macro VHost $host $port $dir>
  Listen $port
  <VirtualHost *:$port>

    ServerName $host
    DocumentRoot "$dir"

    # Public document root
    <Directory "$dir">
        Require all granted
    </Directory>

    # limit access to intranet subdir.
    <Directory "$dir/intranet">
      Require ip 10.0.0.0/8
    </Directory>
  </VirtualHost>
</Macro>

## Use of VHost with different arguments.

Use VHost www.apache.org 80 /vhosts/apache/htdocs
Use VHost example.org 8080 /vhosts/example/htdocs
Use VHost www.example.fr 1234 /vhosts/example.fr/htdocs
```

Removal of a macro definition

It's recommended that you undefine a macro once you've used it. This avoids confusion in a complex configuration file where there may be conflicts in variable names.

```
<Macro DirGroup $dir $group>
  <Directory "$dir">
    Require group $group
  </Directory>
</Macro>

Use DirGroup /www/apache/private private
Use DirGroup /www/apache/server  admin

UndefMacro DirGroup
```

Macro Directive

Description:	Define a configuration file macro
Syntax:	`<Macro name [par1 .. parN> ... </Macro>`
Context:	server config, virtual host, directory
Status:	Base
Module:	mod_macro

The MACRO directive controls the definition of a macro within the server runtime configuration files. The first argument is the name of the macro. Other arguments are parameters to the macro. It is good practice to prefix parameter names with any of '$%@', and not macro names with such characters.

```
<Macro LocalAccessPolicy>
    Require ip 10.2.16.0/24
</Macro>

<Macro RestrictedAccessPolicy $ipnumbers>
    Require ip $ipnumbers
</Macro>
```

UndefMacro Directive

Description:	Undefine a macro
Syntax:	`UndefMacro name`
Context:	server config, virtual host, directory
Status:	Base
Module:	mod_macro

The UNDEFMACRO directive undefines a macro which has been defined before hand.

```
UndefMacro LocalAccessPolicy
UndefMacro RestrictedAccessPolicy
```

Use Directive

Description:	Use a macro
Syntax:	Use name [value1 ... valueN]
Context:	server config, virtual host, directory
Status:	Base
Module:	mod_macro

The USE directive controls the use of a macro. The specified macro is expanded. It must be given the same number of arguments as in the macro definition. The provided values are associated to their corresponding initial parameters and are substituted before processing.

```
Use LocalAccessPolicy
...
Use RestrictedAccessPolicy "192.54.172.0/24 192.54.148.0/24"
```

is equivalent, with the macros defined above, to:

```
Require ip 10.2.16.0/24
...
Require ip 192.54.172.0/24 192.54.148.0/24
```

10.72   Apache Module mod_mime

Description:	Associates the requested filename's extensions with the file's behavior (handlers and filters) and content (mime-type, language, character set and encoding)
Status:	Base
ModuleIdentifier:	mime_module
SourceFile:	mod_mime.c

Summary

This module is used to assign content metadata to the content selected for an HTTP response by mapping patterns in the URI or filenames to the metadata values. For example, the filename extensions of content files often define the content's Internet media type, language, character set, and content-encoding. This information is sent in HTTP messages containing that content and used in content negotiation when selecting alternatives, such that the user's preferences are respected when choosing one of several possible contents to serve. See MOD_NEGOTIATION for more information about content negotiation (p. 68).

The directives ADDCHARSET, ADDENCODING, ADDLANGUAGE and ADDTYPE are all used to map file extensions onto the metadata for that file. Respectively they set the character set, content-encoding, content-language, and media-type (content-type) of documents. The directive TYPESCONFIG is used to specify a file which also maps extensions onto media types.

In addition, MOD_MIME may define the handler (p. 98) and filters (p. 100) that originate and process content. The directives ADDHANDLER, ADDOUTPUTFILTER, and ADDINPUTFILTER control the modules or scripts that serve the document. The MULTIVIEWSMATCH directive allows MOD_NEGOTIATION to consider these file extensions to be included when testing Multiviews matches.

While MOD_MIME associates metadata with filename extensions, the CORE server provides directives that are used to associate all the files in a given container (*e.g.*, <LOCATION>, <DIRECTORY>, or <FILES>) with particular metadata. These directives include FORCETYPE, SETHANDLER, SETINPUTFILTER, and SETOUTPUTFILTER. The core directives override any filename extension mappings defined in MOD_MIME.

Note that changing the metadata for a file does not change the value of the Last-Modified header. Thus, previously cached copies may still be used by a client or proxy, with the previous headers. If you change the metadata (language, content type, character set or encoding) you may need to 'touch' affected files (updating their last modified date) to ensure that all visitors are receive the corrected content headers.

Directives

- AddCharset
- AddEncoding
- AddHandler
- AddInputFilter
- AddLanguage
- AddOutputFilter
- AddType
- DefaultLanguage
- ModMimeUsePathInfo
- MultiviewsMatch
- RemoveCharset
- RemoveEncoding

- RemoveHandler

- RemoveInputFilter

- RemoveLanguage

- RemoveOutputFilter

- RemoveType

- TypesConfig

See also

- MIMEMAGICFILE

- ADDDEFAULTCHARSET

- FORCETYPE

- SETHANDLER

- SETINPUTFILTER

- SETOUTPUTFILTER

Files with Multiple Extensions

Files can have more than one extension; the order of the extensions is *normally* irrelevant. For example, if the file `welcome.html.fr` maps onto content type `text/html` and language French then the file `welcome.fr.html` will map onto exactly the same information. If more than one extension is given that maps onto the same type of meta-data, then the one to the right will be used, except for languages and content encodings. For example, if `.gif` maps to the media-type `image/gif` and `.html` maps to the media-type `text/html`, then the file `welcome.gif.html` will be associated with the media-type `text/html`.

Languages and content encodings are treated accumulative, because one can assign more than one language or encoding to a particular resource. For example, the file `welcome.html.en.de` will be delivered with `Content-Language: en, de` and `Content-Type: text/html`.

Care should be taken when a file with multiple extensions gets associated with both a media-type and a handler. This will usually result in the request being handled by the module associated with the handler. For example, if the `.imap` extension is mapped to the handler `imap-file` (from MOD_IMAGEMAP) and the `.html` extension is mapped to the media-type `text/html`, then the file `world.imap.html` will be associated with both the `imap-file` handler and `text/html` media-type. When it is processed, the `imap-file` handler will be used, and so it will be treated as a MOD_IMAGEMAP imagemap file.

If you would prefer only the last dot-separated part of the filename to be mapped to a particular piece of meta-data, then do not use the `Add*` directives. For example, if you wish to have the file `foo.html.cgi` processed as a CGI script, but not the file `bar.cgi.html`, then instead of using `AddHandler cgi-script .cgi`, use

Configure handler based on final extension only

```
<FilesMatch "[^.]+\.cgi$">
  SetHandler cgi-script
</FilesMatch>
```

Content encoding

A file of a particular media-type can additionally be encoded a particular way to simplify transmission over the Internet. While this usually will refer to compression, such as `gzip`, it can also refer to encryption, such a `pgp` or to an encoding such as UUencoding, which is designed for transmitting a binary file in an ASCII (text) format.

The HTTP/1.1 RFC[47], section 14.11 puts it this way:

> The Content-Encoding entity-header field is used as a modifier to the media-type. When present, its value indicates what additional content codings have been applied to the entity-body, and thus what decoding mechanisms must be applied in order to obtain the media-type referenced by the Content-Type header field. Content-Encoding is primarily used to allow a document to be compressed without losing the identity of its underlying media type.

By using more than one file extension (see section above about multiple file extensions), you can indicate that a file is of a particular *type*, and also has a particular *encoding*.

For example, you may have a file which is a Microsoft Word document, which is pkzipped to reduce its size. If the `.doc` extension is associated with the Microsoft Word file type, and the `.zip` extension is associated with the pkzip file encoding, then the file `Resume.doc.zip` would be known to be a pkzip'ed Word document.

Apache sends a `Content-encoding` header with the resource, in order to tell the client browser about the encoding method.

```
Content-encoding: pkzip
```

Character sets and languages

In addition to file type and the file encoding, another important piece of information is what language a particular document is in, and in what character set the file should be displayed. For example, the document might be written in the Vietnamese alphabet, or in Cyrillic, and should be displayed as such. This information, also, is transmitted in HTTP headers.

The character set, language, encoding and mime type are all used in the process of content negotiation (See MOD_NEGOTIATION) to determine which document to give to the client, when there are alternative documents in more than one character set, language, encoding or mime type. All filename extensions associations created with ADDCHARSET, ADDENCODING, ADDLANGUAGE and ADDTYPE directives (and extensions listed in the MIMEMAGICFILE) participate in this select process. Filename extensions that are only associated using the ADDHANDLER, ADDINPUTFILTER or ADDOUTPUTFILTER directives may be included or excluded from matching by using the MULTIVIEWSMATCH directive.

Charset

To convey this further information, Apache optionally sends a `Content-Language` header, to specify the language that the document is in, and can append additional information onto the `Content-Type` header to indicate the particular character set that should be used to correctly render the information.

```
Content-Language:  en, fr Content-Type:  text/plain;
charset=ISO-8859-1
```

The language specification is the two-letter abbreviation for the language. The `charset` is the name of the particular character set which should be used.

---

[47]http://www.ietf.org/rfc/rfc2616.txt

AddCharset Directive

Description:	Maps the given filename extensions to the specified content charset
Syntax:	`AddCharset charset extension [extension] ...`
Context:	server config, virtual host, directory, .htaccess
Override:	FileInfo
Status:	Base
Module:	mod_mime

The ADDCHARSET directive maps the given filename extensions to the specified content charset (the Internet registered name for a given character encoding). *charset* is the media type's charset parameter[18] for resources with filenames containing *extension*. This mapping is added to any already in force, overriding any mappings that already exist for the same *extension*.

Example

```
AddLanguage ja .ja
AddCharset EUC-JP .euc
AddCharset ISO-2022-JP .jis
AddCharset SHIFT_JIS .sjis
```

Then the document `xxxx.ja.jis` will be treated as being a Japanese document whose charset is `ISO-2022-JP` (as will the document `xxxx.jis.ja`). The ADDCHARSET directive is useful for both to inform the client about the character encoding of the document so that the document can be interpreted and displayed appropriately, and for content negotiation (p. 68) , where the server returns one from several documents based on the client's charset preference.

The *extension* argument is case-insensitive and can be specified with or without a leading dot. Filenames may have multiple extensions and the *extension* argument will be compared against each of them.

See also

- MOD_NEGOTIATION
- ADDDEFAULTCHARSET

AddEncoding Directive

Description:	Maps the given filename extensions to the specified encoding type
Syntax:	`AddEncoding encoding extension [extension] ...`
Context:	server config, virtual host, directory, .htaccess
Override:	FileInfo
Status:	Base
Module:	mod_mime

The ADDENCODING directive maps the given filename extensions to the specified HTTP content-encoding. *encoding* is the HTTP content coding to append to the value of the Content-Encoding header field for documents named with the *extension*. This mapping is added to any already in force, overriding any mappings that already exist for the same *extension*.

Example

```
AddEncoding x gzip .gz
AddEncoding x-compress .Z
```

---

[48]http://www.iana.org/assignments/character-sets

This will cause filenames containing the `.gz` extension to be marked as encoded using the `x-gzip` encoding, and filenames containing the `.Z` extension to be marked as encoded with `x-compress`.

Old clients expect `x-gzip` and `x-compress`, however the standard dictates that they're equivalent to `gzip` and `compress` respectively. Apache does content encoding comparisons by ignoring any leading `x-`. When responding with an encoding Apache will use whatever form (*i.e.*, `x-foo` or `foo`) the client requested. If the client didn't specifically request a particular form Apache will use the form given by the `AddEncoding` directive. To make this long story short, you should always use `x-gzip` and `x-compress` for these two specific encodings. More recent encodings, such as `deflate`, should be specified without the `x-`.

The *extension* argument is case-insensitive and can be specified with or without a leading dot. Filenames may have multiple extensions and the *extension* argument will be compared against each of them.

AddHandler Directive

Description:	Maps the filename extensions to the specified handler
Syntax:	`AddHandler handler-name extension [extension] ...`
Context:	server config, virtual host, directory, .htaccess
Override:	FileInfo
Status:	Base
Module:	mod_mime

Files having the name *extension* will be served by the specified *handler-name (p. 98)* . This mapping is added to any already in force, overriding any mappings that already exist for the same *extension*. For example, to activate CGI scripts with the file extension `.cgi`, you might use:

```
AddHandler cgi-script .cgi
```

Once that has been put into your httpd.conf file, any file containing the `.cgi` extension will be treated as a CGI program.

The *extension* argument is case-insensitive and can be specified with or without a leading dot. Filenames may have multiple extensions and the *extension* argument will be compared against each of them.

See also

- SETHANDLER

AddInputFilter Directive

Description:	Maps filename extensions to the filters that will process client requests
Syntax:	`AddInputFilter filter[;filter...]  extension [extension] ...`
Context:	server config, virtual host, directory, .htaccess
Override:	FileInfo
Status:	Base
Module:	mod_mime

ADDINPUTFILTER maps the filename extension *extension* to the filters (p. 100) which will process client requests and POST input when they are received by the server. This is in addition to any filters defined elsewhere, including the SETINPUTFILTER directive. This mapping is merged over any already in force, overriding any mappings that already exist for the same *extension*.

If more than one *filter* is specified, they must be separated by semicolons in the order in which they should process the content. The *filter* is case-insensitive.

The *extension* argument is case-insensitive and can be specified with or without a leading dot. Filenames may have multiple extensions and the *extension* argument will be compared against each of them.

See also

- REMOVEINPUTFILTER
- SETINPUTFILTER

AddLanguage Directive

Description:	Maps the given filename extension to the specified content language
Syntax:	`AddLanguage language-tag extension [extension] ...`
Context:	server config, virtual host, directory, .htaccess
Override:	FileInfo
Status:	Base
Module:	mod_mime

The ADDLANGUAGE directive maps the given filename extension to the specified content language. Files with the filename *extension* are assigned an HTTP Content-Language value of *language-tag* corresponding to the language identifiers defined by RFC 3066. This directive overrides any mappings that already exist for the same *extension*.

Example

```
AddEncoding x-compress .Z
AddLanguage en .en
AddLanguage fr .fr
```

Then the document `xxxx.en.Z` will be treated as being a compressed English document (as will the document `xxxx.Z.en`). Although the content language is reported to the client, the browser is unlikely to use this information. The ADDLANGUAGE directive is more useful for content negotiation (p. 68) , where the server returns one from several documents based on the client's language preference.

If multiple language assignments are made for the same extension, the last one encountered is the one that is used. That is, for the case of:

```
AddLanguage en .en
AddLanguage en-gb .en
AddLanguage en-us .en
```

documents with the extension `.en` would be treated as being `en-us`.

The *extension* argument is case-insensitive and can be specified with or without a leading dot. Filenames may have multiple extensions and the *extension* argument will be compared against each of them.

See also

- MOD_NEGOTIATION

AddOutputFilter Directive

Description:	Maps filename extensions to the filters that will process responses from the server
Syntax:	`AddOutputFilter filter[;filter...] extension [extension] ...`
Context:	server config, virtual host, directory, .htaccess
Override:	FileInfo
Status:	Base
Module:	mod_mime

The ADDOUTPUTFILTER directive maps the filename extension *extension* to the filters (p. 100) which will process responses from the server before they are sent to the client. This is in addition to any filters defined elsewhere, including SETOUTPUTFILTER and ADDOUTPUTFILTERBYTYPE directive. This mapping is merged over any already in force, overriding any mappings that already exist for the same *extension*.

For example, the following configuration will process all .shtml files for server-side includes and will then compress the output using MOD_DEFLATE.

```
AddOutputFilter INCLUDES;DEFLATE shtml
```

If more than one filter is specified, they must be separated by semicolons in the order in which they should process the content. The *filter* argument is case-insensitive.

The *extension* argument is case-insensitive and can be specified with or without a leading dot. Filenames may have multiple extensions and the *extension* argument will be compared against each of them.

Note that when defining a set of filters using the ADDOUTPUTFILTER directive, any definition made will replace any previous definition made by the ADDOUTPUTFILTER directive.

```
# Effective filter "DEFLATE"
AddOutputFilter DEFLATE shtml
<Location "/foo">
  # Effective filter "INCLUDES", replacing "DEFLATE"
  AddOutputFilter INCLUDES shtml
</Location>
<Location "/bar">
  # Effective filter "INCLUDES;DEFLATE", replacing "DEFLATE"
  AddOutputFilter INCLUDES;DEFLATE shtml
</Location>
<Location "/bar/baz">
  # Effective filter "BUFFER", replacing "INCLUDES;DEFLATE"
  AddOutputFilter BUFFER shtml
</Location>
<Location "/bar/baz/buz">
  # No effective filter, replacing "BUFFER"
  RemoveOutputFilter shtml
</Location>
```

See also

- REMOVEOUTPUTFILTER
- SETOUTPUTFILTER

AddType Directive

Description:	Maps the given filename extensions onto the specified content type
Syntax:	`AddType media-type extension [extension] ...`
Context:	server config, virtual host, directory, .htaccess
Override:	FileInfo
Status:	Base
Module:	mod_mime

The ADDTYPE directive maps the given filename extensions onto the specified content type. *media-type* is the media type to use for filenames containing *extension*. This mapping is added to any already in force, overriding any mappings that already exist for the same *extension*.

It is recommended that new media types be added using the ADDTYPE directive rather than changing the TYPESCONFIG file.

Example

```
AddType image/gif .gif
```

Or, to specify multiple file extensions in one directive:

Example

```
AddType image/jpeg jpeg jpg jpe
```

The *extension* argument is case-insensitive and can be specified with or without a leading dot. Filenames may have multiple extensions and the *extension* argument will be compared against each of them.

A simmilar effect to MOD_NEGOTIATION's LANGUAGEPRIORITY can be achieved by qualifying a *media-type* with qs:

Example

```
AddType application/rss+xml;qs=0.8 .xml
```

This is useful in situations, *e.g.* when a client requesting `Accept: */*` can not actually processes the content returned by the server.

This directive primarily configures the content types generated for static files served out of the filesystem. For resources other than static files, where the generator of the response typically specifies a Content-Type, this directive has no effect.

Note
> If no handler is explicitly set for a request, the specified content type will also be used as the handler name.
> When explicit directives such as SETHANDLER or ADDHANDLER do not apply to the current request, the internal handler name normally set by those directives is instead set to the content type specified by this directive.
> This is a historical behavior that may be used by some third-party modules (such as mod_php) for taking responsibility for the matching request.
> Configurations that rely on such "synthetic" types should be avoided. Additionally, configurations that restrict access to SETHANDLER or ADDHANDLER should restrict access to this directive as well.

See also

- FORCETYPE
- MOD_NEGOTIATION

DefaultLanguage Directive

Description:	Defines a default language-tag to be sent in the Content-Language header field for all resources in the current context that have not been assigned a language-tag by some other means.
Syntax:	`DefaultLanguage language-tag`
Context:	server config, virtual host, directory, .htaccess
Override:	FileInfo
Status:	Base
Module:	mod_mime

The DEFAULTLANGUAGE directive tells Apache that all resources in the directive's scope (*e.g.*, all resources covered by the current <DIRECTORY> container) that don't have an explicit language extension (such as .fr or .de as configured by ADDLANGUAGE) should be assigned a Content-Language of *language-tag*. This allows entire directory trees to be marked as containing Dutch content, for instance, without having to rename each file. Note that unlike using extensions to specify languages, DEFAULTLANGUAGE can only specify a single language.

If no DEFAULTLANGUAGE directive is in force and a file does not have any language extensions as configured by ADDLANGUAGE, then no Content-Language header field will be generated.

Example

```
DefaultLanguage en
```

See also

- MOD_NEGOTIATION

ModMimeUsePathInfo Directive

Description:	Tells MOD_MIME to treat path_info components as part of the filename
Syntax:	ModMimeUsePathInfo On|Off
Default:	ModMimeUsePathInfo Off
Context:	directory
Status:	Base
Module:	mod_mime

The MODMIMEUSEPATHINFO directive is used to combine the filename with the path_info URL component to apply MOD_MIME's directives to the request. The default value is Off - therefore, the path_info component is ignored.

This directive is recommended when you have a virtual filesystem.

Example

```
ModMimeUsePathInfo On
```

If you have a request for /index.php/foo.shtml MOD_MIME will now treat the incoming request as /index.php/foo.shtml and directives like AddOutputFilter INCLUDES .shtml will add the INCLUDES filter to the request. If MODMIMEUSEPATHINFO is not set, the INCLUDES filter will not be added. This will work analogously for virtual paths, such as those defined by <LOCATION>

See also

- ACCEPTPATHINFO

MultiviewsMatch Directive

Description:	The types of files that will be included when searching for a matching file with MultiViews
Syntax:	MultiviewsMatch Any|NegotiatedOnly|Filters|Handlers [Handlers|Filters]
Default:	MultiviewsMatch NegotiatedOnly
Context:	server config, virtual host, directory, .htaccess
Override:	FileInfo
Status:	Base
Module:	mod_mime

MULTIVIEWSMATCH permits three different behaviors for mod_negotiation (p. 721)'s Multiviews feature. Multiviews allows a request for a file, *e.g.* `index.html`, to match any negotiated extensions following the base request, *e.g.* `index.html.en`, `index.html.fr`, or `index.html.gz`.

The `NegotiatedOnly` option provides that every extension following the base name must correlate to a recognized MOD_MIME extension for content negotiation, *e.g.* Charset, Content-Type, Language, or Encoding. This is the strictest implementation with the fewest unexpected side effects, and is the default behavior.

To include extensions associated with Handlers and/or Filters, set the MULTIVIEWSMATCH directive to either `Handlers`, `Filters`, or both option keywords. If all other factors are equal, the smallest file will be served, *e.g.* in deciding between `index.html.cgi` of 500 bytes and `index.html.pl` of 1000 bytes, the `.cgi` file would win in this example. Users of `.asis` files might prefer to use the Handler option, if `.asis` files are associated with the `asis-handler`.

You may finally allow `Any` extensions to match, even if MOD_MIME doesn't recognize the extension. This can cause unpredictable results, such as serving .old or .bak files the webmaster never expected to be served.

For example, the following configuration will allow handlers and filters to participate in Multviews, but will exclude unknown files:

```
MultiviewsMatch Handlers Filters
```

MULTIVIEWSMATCH is not allowed in a <LOCATION> or <LOCATIONMATCH> section.

See also

- OPTIONS
- MOD_NEGOTIATION

RemoveCharset Directive

Description:	Removes any character set associations for a set of file extensions
Syntax:	`RemoveCharset extension [extension] ...`
Context:	virtual host, directory, .htaccess
Override:	FileInfo
Status:	Base
Module:	mod_mime

The REMOVECHARSET directive removes any character set associations for files with the given extensions. This allows `.htaccess` files in subdirectories to undo any associations inherited from parent directories or the server config files.

The *extension* argument is case-insensitive and can be specified with or without a leading dot.

Example

```
RemoveCharset .html .shtml
```

RemoveEncoding Directive

Description:	Removes any content encoding associations for a set of file extensions
Syntax:	`RemoveEncoding extension [extension] ...`
Context:	virtual host, directory, .htaccess
Override:	FileInfo
Status:	Base
Module:	mod_mime

The REMOVEENCODING directive removes any encoding associations for files with the given extensions. This allows
.htaccess files in subdirectories to undo any associations inherited from parent directories or the server config files.
An example of its use might be:

/foo/.htaccess:

```
AddEncoding x-gzip .gz
AddType text/plain .asc
<Files "*.gz.asc">
    RemoveEncoding .gz
</Files>
```

This will cause foo.gz to be marked as being encoded with the gzip method, but foo.gz.asc as an unencoded
plaintext file.

Note

> REMOVEENCODING directives are processed *after* any ADDENCODING directives, so it is
> possible they may undo the effects of the latter if both occur within the same directory config-
> uration.

The *extension* argument is case-insensitive and can be specified with or without a leading dot.

RemoveHandler Directive

Description:	Removes any handler associations for a set of file extensions
Syntax:	RemoveHandler extension [extension] ...
Context:	virtual host, directory, .htaccess
Override:	FileInfo
Status:	Base
Module:	mod_mime

The REMOVEHANDLER directive removes any handler associations for files with the given extensions. This allows
.htaccess files in subdirectories to undo any associations inherited from parent directories or the server config files.
An example of its use might be:

/foo/.htaccess:

```
AddHandler server-parsed .html
```

/foo/bar/.htaccess:

```
RemoveHandler .html
```

This has the effect of returning .html files in the /foo/bar directory to being treated as normal files, rather than
as candidates for parsing (see the MOD_INCLUDE module).

The *extension* argument is case-insensitive and can be specified with or without a leading dot.

RemoveInputFilter Directive

Description:	Removes any input filter associations for a set of file extensions
Syntax:	RemoveInputFilter extension [extension] ...
Context:	virtual host, directory, .htaccess
Override:	FileInfo
Status:	Base
Module:	mod_mime

The REMOVEINPUTFILTER directive removes any input filter (p. 100) associations for files with the given extensions. This allows .htaccess files in subdirectories to undo any associations inherited from parent directories or the server config files.

The *extension* argument is case-insensitive and can be specified with or without a leading dot.

See also

- ADDINPUTFILTER
- SETINPUTFILTER

RemoveLanguage Directive

Description:	Removes any language associations for a set of file extensions
Syntax:	`RemoveLanguage extension [extension] ...`
Context:	virtual host, directory, .htaccess
Override:	FileInfo
Status:	Base
Module:	mod_mime

The REMOVELANGUAGE directive removes any language associations for files with the given extensions. This allows .htaccess files in subdirectories to undo any associations inherited from parent directories or the server config files.

The *extension* argument is case-insensitive and can be specified with or without a leading dot.

RemoveOutputFilter Directive

Description:	Removes any output filter associations for a set of file extensions
Syntax:	`RemoveOutputFilter extension [extension] ...`
Context:	virtual host, directory, .htaccess
Override:	FileInfo
Status:	Base
Module:	mod_mime

The REMOVEOUTPUTFILTER directive removes any output filter (p. 100) associations for files with the given extensions. This allows .htaccess files in subdirectories to undo any associations inherited from parent directories or the server config files.

The *extension* argument is case-insensitive and can be specified with or without a leading dot.

Example

```
RemoveOutputFilter shtml
```

See also

- ADDOUTPUTFILTER

RemoveType Directive

Description:	Removes any content type associations for a set of file extensions
Syntax:	`RemoveType extension [extension] ...`
Context:	virtual host, directory, .htaccess
Override:	FileInfo
Status:	Base
Module:	mod_mime

The REMOVETYPE directive removes any media type associations for files with the given extensions. This allows `.htaccess` files in subdirectories to undo any associations inherited from parent directories or the server config files. An example of its use might be:

/foo/.htaccess:

```
RemoveType .cgi
```

This will remove any special handling of `.cgi` files in the `/foo/` directory and any beneath it, causing responses containing those files to omit the HTTP Content-Type header field.

Note

REMOVETYPE directives are processed *after* any ADDTYPE directives, so it is possible they may undo the effects of the latter if both occur within the same directory configuration.

The *extension* argument is case-insensitive and can be specified with or without a leading dot.

TypesConfig Directive

Description:	The location of the `mime.types` file
Syntax:	`TypesConfig file-path`
Default:	`TypesConfig conf/mime.types`
Context:	server config
Status:	Base
Module:	mod_mime

The TYPESCONFIG directive sets the location of the media types configuration file. *File-path* is relative to the SERVERROOT. This file sets the default list of mappings from filename extensions to content types. Most administrators use the `mime.types` file provided by their OS, which associates common filename extensions with the official list of IANA registered media types maintained at http://www.iana.org/assignments/media-types/index.html as well as a large number of unofficial types. This simplifies the `httpd.conf` file by providing the majority of media-type definitions, and may be overridden by ADDTYPE directives as needed. You should not edit the `mime.types` file, because it may be replaced when you upgrade your server.

The file contains lines in the format of the arguments to an ADDTYPE directive:

```
media-type [extension] ...
```

The case of the extension does not matter. Blank lines, and lines beginning with a hash character (#) are ignored. Empty lines are there for completeness (of the mime.types file). Apache httpd can still determine these types with MOD_MIME_MAGIC.

Please do **not** send requests to the Apache HTTP Server Project to add any new entries in the distributed `mime.types` file unless (1) they are already registered with IANA, and (2) they use widely accepted, non-conflicting filename extensions across platforms. `category/x-subtype` requests will be automatically rejected, as will any new two-letter extensions as they will likely conflict later with the already crowded language and character set namespace.

See also

- MOD_MIME_MAGIC

10.73 Apache Module mod_mime_magic

Description:	Determines the MIME type of a file by looking at a few bytes of its contents
Status:	Extension
ModuleIdentifier:	mime_magic_module
SourceFile:	mod_mime_magic.c

Summary

This module determines the MIME type of files in the same way the Unix file(1) command works: it looks at the first few bytes of the file. It is intended as a "second line of defense" for cases that MOD_MIME can't resolve.

This module is derived from a free version of the file(1) command for Unix, which uses "magic numbers" and other hints from a file's contents to figure out what the contents are. This module is active only if the magic file is specified by the MIMEMAGICFILE directive.

Directives

- MimeMagicFile

Format of the Magic File

The contents of the file are plain ASCII text in 4-5 columns. Blank lines are allowed but ignored. Commented lines use a hash mark (#). The remaining lines are parsed for the following columns:

Column	Description	
1	byte number to begin checking from	
	">" indicates a dependency upon the previous non-">" line	
2	type of data to match	
	byte	single character
	short	machine-order 16-bit integer
	long	machine-order 32-bit integer
	string	arbitrary-length string
	date	long integer date (seconds since Unix epoch/1970)
	beshort	big-endian 16-bit integer
	belong	big-endian 32-bit integer
	bedate	big-endian 32-bit integer date
	leshort	little-endian 16-bit integer
	lelong	little-endian 32-bit integer
	ledate	little-endian 32-bit integer date
3	contents of data to match	
4	MIME type if matched	
5	MIME encoding if matched (optional)	

For example, the following magic file lines would recognize some audio formats:

```
# Sun/NeXT audio data
0       string     .snd
>12     belong     1         audio/basic
>12     belong     2         audio/basic
>12     belong     3         audio/basic
>12     belong     4         audio/basic
>12     belong     5         audio/basic
>12     belong     6         audio/basic
>12     belong     7         audio/basic
>12     belong     23        audio/x-adpcm
```

Or these would recognize the difference between *.doc files containing Microsoft Word or FrameMaker documents. (These are incompatible file formats which use the same file suffix.)

```
# Frame
0   string  \<MakerFile        application/x-frame
0   string  \<MIFFile          application/x-frame
0   string  \<MakerDictionary  application/x-frame
0   string  \<MakerScreenFon   application/x-frame
0   string  \<MML              application/x-frame
0   string  \<Book             application/x-frame
0   string  \<Maker            application/x-frame

# MS-Word
0   string  \376\067\0\043           application/msword
0   string  \320\317\021\340\241\261 application/msword
0   string  \333\245-\0\0\0          application/msword
```

An optional MIME encoding can be included as a fifth column. For example, this can recognize gzipped files and set the encoding for them.

```
# gzip (GNU zip, not to be confused with
#       [Info-ZIP/PKWARE] zip archiver)

0   string  \037\213  application/octet-stream  x-gzip
```

Performance Issues

This module is not for every system. If your system is barely keeping up with its load or if you're performing a web server benchmark, you may not want to enable this because the processing is not free.

However, an effort was made to improve the performance of the original file(1) code to make it fit in a busy web server. It was designed for a server where there are thousands of users who publish their own documents. This is probably very common on intranets. Many times, it's helpful if the server can make more intelligent decisions about a file's contents than the file name allows ...even if just to reduce the "why doesn't my page work" calls when users improperly name their own files. You have to decide if the extra work suits your environment.

Notes

The following notes apply to the MOD_MIME_MAGIC module and are included here for compliance with contributors' copyright restrictions that require their acknowledgment.

mod_mime_magic: MIME type lookup via file magic numbers

Copyright (c) 1996-1997 Cisco Systems, Inc.

This software was submitted by Cisco Systems to the Apache Group in July 1997. Future revisions and derivatives of this source code must acknowledge Cisco Systems as the original contributor of this module. All other licensing and usage conditions are those of the Apache Group.

Some of this code is derived from the free version of the file command originally posted to comp.sources.unix. Copyright info for that program is included below as required.

 - Copyright (c) Ian F. Darwin, 1987. Written by Ian F. Darwin.

This software is not subject to any license of the American Telephone and Telegraph Company or of the Regents of the University of California.

Permission is granted to anyone to use this software for any purpose on any computer system, and to alter it and redistribute it freely, subject to the following restrictions:

1. The author is not responsible for the consequences of use of this software, no matter how awful, even if they arise from flaws in it.

2. The origin of this software must not be misrepresented, either by explicit claim or by omission. Since few users ever read sources, credits must appear in the documentation.

3. Altered versions must be plainly marked as such, and must not be misrepresented as being the original software. Since few users ever read sources, credits must appear in the documentation.

4. This notice may not be removed or altered.

For compliance with Mr Darwin's terms: this has been very significantly modified from the free "file" command.

- all-in-one file for compilation convenience when moving from one version of Apache to the next.

- Memory allocation is done through the Apache API's pool structure.

- All functions have had necessary Apache API request or server structures passed to them where necessary to call other Apache API routines. (*i.e.*, usually for logging, files, or memory allocation in itself or a called function.)

- struct magic has been converted from an array to a single-ended linked list because it only grows one record at a time, it's only accessed sequentially, and the Apache API has no equivalent of `realloc()`.

- Functions have been changed to get their parameters from the server configuration instead of globals. (It should be reentrant now but has not been tested in a threaded environment.)

- Places where it used to print results to stdout now saves them in a list where they're used to set the MIME type in the Apache request record.

- Command-line flags have been removed since they will never be used here.

MimeMagicFile Directive

Description:	Enable MIME-type determination based on file contents using the specified magic file
Syntax:	`MimeMagicFile file-path`
Context:	server config, virtual host
Status:	Extension
Module:	mod_mime_magic

The MIMEMAGICFILE directive can be used to enable this module, the default file is distributed at `conf/magic`. Non-rooted paths are relative to the SERVERROOT. Virtual hosts will use the same file as the main server unless a more specific setting is used, in which case the more specific setting overrides the main server's file.

Example

```
MimeMagicFile conf/magic
```

10.74 Apache Module mod_negotiation

Description:	Provides for content negotiation (p. 68)
Status:	Base
ModuleIdentifier:	negotiation_module
SourceFile:	mod_negotiation.c

Summary

Content negotiation, or more accurately content selection, is the selection of the document that best matches the clients capabilities, from one of several available documents. There are two implementations of this.

- A type map (a file with the handler `type-map`) which explicitly lists the files containing the variants.
- A Multiviews search (enabled by the `Multiviews` OPTIONS), where the server does an implicit filename pattern match, and choose from amongst the results.

Directives

- CacheNegotiatedDocs
- ForceLanguagePriority
- LanguagePriority

See also

- OPTIONS
- MOD_MIME
- Content Negotiation (p. 68)
- Environment Variables (p. 82)

Type maps

A type map has a format similar to RFC822 mail headers. It contains document descriptions separated by blank lines, with lines beginning with a hash character ('#') treated as comments. A document description consists of several header records; records may be continued on multiple lines if the continuation lines start with spaces. The leading space will be deleted and the lines concatenated. A header record consists of a keyword name, which always ends in a colon, followed by a value. Whitespace is allowed between the header name and value, and between the tokens of value. The headers allowed are:

Content-Encoding: The encoding of the file. Apache only recognizes encodings that are defined by an AD-DENCODING directive. This normally includes the encodings `x-compress` for compress'd files, and `x-gzip` for gzip'd files. The `x-` prefix is ignored for encoding comparisons.

Content-Language: The language(s) of the variant, as an Internet standard language tag (RFC 1766[49]). An example is `en`, meaning English. If the variant contains more than one language, they are separated by a comma.

Content-Length: The length of the file, in bytes. If this header is not present, then the actual length of the file is used.

---

[49]http://www.ietf.org/rfc/rfc1766.txt

Content-Type: The MIME media type of the document, with optional parameters. Parameters are separated from the media type and from one another by a semi-colon, with a syntax of `name=value`. Common parameters include:

level an integer specifying the version of the media type. For `text/html` this defaults to 2, otherwise 0.

qs a floating-point number with a value in the range 0[.000] to 1[.000], indicating the relative 'quality' of this variant compared to the other available variants, independent of the client's capabilities. For example, a jpeg file is usually of higher source quality than an ascii file if it is attempting to represent a photograph. However, if the resource being represented is ascii art, then an ascii file would have a higher source quality than a jpeg file. All `qs` values are therefore specific to a given resource.

```
Example
Content-Type:   image/jpeg; qs=0.8
```

URI: uri of the file containing the variant (of the given media type, encoded with the given content encoding). These are interpreted as URLs relative to the map file; they must be on the same server, and they must refer to files to which the client would be granted access if they were to be requested directly.

Body: The actual content of the resource may be included in the type-map file using the Body header. This header must contain a string that designates a delimiter for the body content. Then all following lines in the type map file will be considered part of the resource body until the delimiter string is found.

```
Example:
Body:----xyz----
<html>
<body>
<p>Content of the page.</p>
</body>
</html>
----xyz----
```

Consider, for example, a resource called `document.html` which is available in English, French, and German. The files for each of these are called `document.html.en`, `document.html.fr`, and `document.html.de`, respectively. The type map file will be called `document.html.var`, and will contain the following:

```
URI: document.html

Content-language:  en
Content-type:  text/html
URI: document.html.en

Content-language:  fr
Content-type:  text/html
URI: document.html.fr

Content-language:  de
Content-type:  text/html
URI: document.html.de
```

All four of these files should be placed in the same directory, and the `.var` file should be associated with the `type-map` handler with an ADDHANDLER directive:

```
AddHandler type-map .var
```

A request for `document.html.var` in this directory will result in choosing the variant which most closely matches the language preference specified in the user's `Accept-Language` request header.

If `Multiviews` is enabled, and MULTIVIEWSMATCH is set to "handlers" or "any", a request to `document.html` will discover `document.html.var` and continue negotiating with the explicit type map.

Other configuration directives, such as ALIAS can be used to map `document.html` to `document.html.var`.

Multiviews

A Multiviews search is enabled by the `Multiviews` OPTIONS. If the server receives a request for `/some/dir/foo` and `/some/dir/foo` does *not* exist, then the server reads the directory looking for all files named `foo.*`, and effectively fakes up a type map which names all those files, assigning them the same media types and content-encodings it would have if the client had asked for one of them by name. It then chooses the best match to the client's requirements, and returns that document.

The MULTIVIEWSMATCH directive configures whether Apache will consider files that do not have content negotiation meta-information assigned to them when choosing files.

CacheNegotiatedDocs Directive

Description:	Allows content-negotiated documents to be cached by proxy servers
Syntax:	`CacheNegotiatedDocs On|Off`
Default:	`CacheNegotiatedDocs Off`
Context:	server config, virtual host
Status:	Base
Module:	mod_negotiation

If set, this directive allows content-negotiated documents to be cached by proxy servers. This could mean that clients behind those proxys could retrieve versions of the documents that are not the best match for their abilities, but it will make caching more efficient.

This directive only applies to requests which come from HTTP/1.0 browsers. HTTP/1.1 provides much better control over the caching of negotiated documents, and this directive has no effect in responses to HTTP/1.1 requests.

ForceLanguagePriority Directive

Description:	Action to take if a single acceptable document is not found
Syntax:	`ForceLanguagePriority None|Prefer|Fallback [Prefer|Fallback]`
Default:	`ForceLanguagePriority Prefer`
Context:	server config, virtual host, directory, .htaccess
Override:	FileInfo
Status:	Base
Module:	mod_negotiation

The FORCELANGUAGEPRIORITY directive uses the given LANGUAGEPRIORITY to satisfy negotiation where the server could otherwise not return a single matching document.

`ForceLanguagePriority Prefer` uses `LanguagePriority` to serve a one valid result, rather than returning an HTTP result 300 (MULTIPLE CHOICES) when there are several equally valid choices. If the directives below were given, and the user's `Accept-Language` header assigned `en` and `de` each as quality `.500` (equally acceptable) then the first matching variant, `en`, will be served.

```
LanguagePriority en fr de
ForceLanguagePriority Prefer
```

ForceLanguagePriority Fallback uses LANGUAGEPRIORITY to serve a valid result, rather than returning an HTTP result 406 (NOT ACCEPTABLE). If the directives below were given, and the user's Accept-Language only permitted an es language response, but such a variant isn't found, then the first variant from the LANGUAGEPRIORITY list below will be served.

```
LanguagePriority en fr de
ForceLanguagePriority Fallback
```

Both options, Prefer and Fallback, may be specified, so either the first matching variant from LANGUAGEPRIORITY will be served if more than one variant is acceptable, or first available document will be served if none of the variants matched the client's acceptable list of languages.

See also

- ADDLANGUAGE

LanguagePriority Directive

Description:	The precendence of language variants for cases where the client does not express a preference
Syntax:	LanguagePriority MIME-lang [MIME-lang] ...
Context:	server config, virtual host, directory, .htaccess
Override:	FileInfo
Status:	Base
Module:	mod_negotiation

The LANGUAGEPRIORITY sets the precedence of language variants for the case where the client does not express a preference, when handling a Multiviews request. The list of *MIME-lang* are in order of decreasing preference.

```
LanguagePriority en fr de
```

For a request for foo.html, where foo.html.fr and foo.html.de both existed, but the browser did not express a language preference, then foo.html.fr would be returned.

Note that this directive only has an effect if a 'best' language cannot be determined by any other means or the FORCE-LANGUAGEPRIORITY directive is not None. In general, the client determines the language preference, not the server.

See also

- ADDLANGUAGE

10.75 Apache Module mod_nw_ssl

Description:	Enable SSL encryption for NetWare
Status:	Base
ModuleIdentifier:	nwssl_module
SourceFile:	mod_nw_ssl.c
Compatibility:	NetWare only

Summary

This module enables SSL encryption for a specified port. It takes advantage of the SSL encryption functionality that is built into the NetWare operating system.

Directives

- NWSSLTrustedCerts
- NWSSLUpgradeable
- SecureListen

NWSSLTrustedCerts Directive

Description:	List of additional client certificates
Syntax:	`NWSSLTrustedCerts filename [filename] ...`
Context:	server config
Status:	Base
Module:	mod_nw_ssl

Specifies a list of client certificate files (DER format) that are used when creating a proxied SSL connection. Each client certificate used by a server must be listed separately in its own `.der` file.

NWSSLUpgradeable Directive

Description:	Allows a connection to be upgraded to an SSL connection upon request
Syntax:	`NWSSLUpgradeable [IP-address:]portnumber`
Context:	server config
Status:	Base
Module:	mod_nw_ssl

Allow a connection that was created on the specified address and/or port to be upgraded to an SSL connection upon request from the client. The address and/or port must have already be defined previously with a LISTEN directive.

SecureListen Directive

Description:	Enables SSL encryption for the specified port
Syntax:	`SecureListen [IP-address:]portnumber Certificate-Name [MUTUAL]`
Context:	server config
Status:	Base
Module:	mod_nw_ssl

Specifies the port and the eDirectory based certificate name that will be used to enable SSL encryption. An optional third parameter also enables mutual authentication.

10.76   Apache Module mod_privileges

Description:	Support for Solaris privileges and for running virtual hosts under different user IDs.
Status:	Experimental
ModuleIdentifier:	privileges_module
SourceFile:	mod_privileges.c
Compatibility:	Available in Apache 2.3 and up, on Solaris 10 and OpenSolaris platforms

Summary

This module enables different Virtual Hosts to run with different Unix *User* and *Group* IDs, and with different Solaris Privileges[50]. In particular, it offers a solution to the problem of privilege separation between different Virtual Hosts, first promised by the abandoned perchild MPM. It also offers other security enhancements.

Unlike perchild, MOD_PRIVILEGES is not itself an MPM. It works *within* a processing model to set privileges and User/Group *per request* in a running process. It is therefore not compatible with a threaded MPM, and will refuse to run under one.

MOD_PRIVILEGES raises security issues similar to those of suexec (p. 105) . But unlike suexec, it applies not only to CGI programs but to the entire request processing cycle, including in-process applications and subprocesses. It is ideally suited to running PHP applications under **mod_php**, which is also incompatible with threaded MPMs. It is also well-suited to other in-process scripting applications such as **mod_perl**, **mod_python**, and **mod_ruby**, and to applications implemented in C as apache modules where privilege separation is an issue.

Directives

- DTracePrivileges
- PrivilegesMode
- VHostCGIMode
- VHostCGIPrivs
- VHostGroup
- VHostPrivs
- VHostSecure
- VHostUser

Security Considerations

MOD_PRIVILEGES introduces new security concerns in situations where **untrusted code** may be run **within the web-server process**. This applies to untrusted modules, and scripts running under modules such as mod_php or mod_perl. Scripts running externally (e.g. as CGI or in an appserver behind mod_proxy or mod_jk) are NOT affected.

The basic security concerns with mod_privileges are:

- Running as a system user introduces the same security issues as mod_suexec, and near-equivalents such as cgiwrap and suphp.

- A privileges-aware malicious user extension (module or script) could escalate its privileges to anything available to the httpd process in any virtual host. This introduces new risks if (and only if) mod_privileges is compiled with the *BIG_SECURITY_HOLE* option.

---

[50]http://sosc-dr.sun.com/bigadmin/features/articles/least_privilege.jsp

- A privileges-aware malicious user extension (module or script) could escalate privileges to set its user ID to another system user (and/or group).

The PRIVILEGESMODE directive allows you to select either *FAST* or *SECURE* mode. You can mix modes, using *FAST* mode for trusted users and fully-audited code paths, while imposing SECURE mode where an untrusted user has scope to introduce code.

Before describing the modes, we should also introduce the target use cases: Benign vs Hostile. In a benign situation, you want to separate users for their convenience, and protect them and the server against the risks posed by honest mistakes, but you trust your users are not deliberately subverting system security. In a hostile situation - e.g. commercial hosting - you may have users deliberately attacking the system or each other.

FAST mode In *FAST* mode, requests are run in-process with the selected uid/gid and privileges, so the overhead is negligible. This is suitable for benign situations, but is not secure against an attacker escalating privileges with an in-process module or script.

SECURE mode A request in *SECURE* mode forks a subprocess, which then drops privileges. This is a very similar case to running CGI with suexec, but for the entire request cycle, and with the benefit of fine-grained control of privileges.

You can select different PRIVILEGESMODEs for each virtual host, and even in a directory context within a virtual host. *FAST* mode is appropriate where the user(s) are trusted and/or have no privilege to load in-process code. *SECURE* mode is appropriate to cases where untrusted code might be run in-process. However, even in *SECURE* mode, there is no protection against a malicious user who is able to introduce privileges-aware code running *before the start of the request-processing cycle.*

DTracePrivileges Directive

Description:	Determines whether the privileges required by dtrace are enabled.
Syntax:	`DTracePrivileges On|Off`
Default:	`DTracePrivileges Off`
Context:	server config
Status:	Experimental
Module:	mod_privileges
Compatibility:	Available on Solaris 10 and OpenSolaris with non-threaded MPMs (PREFORK or custom MPM).

This server-wide directive determines whether Apache will run with the privileges[51] required to run dtrace[52]. Note that *DTracePrivileges On* will not in itself activate DTrace, but *DTracePrivileges Off* will prevent it working.

PrivilegesMode Directive

Description:	Trade off processing speed and efficiency vs security against malicious privileges-aware code.
Syntax:	`PrivilegesMode FAST|SECURE|SELECTIVE`
Default:	`PrivilegesMode FAST`
Context:	server config, virtual host, directory
Status:	Experimental
Module:	mod_privileges
Compatibility:	Available on Solaris 10 and OpenSolaris with non-threaded MPMs (PREFORK or custom MPM).

---

[51]http://sosc-dr.sun.com/bigadmin/features/articles/least_privilege.jsp
[52]http://sosc-dr.sun.com/bigadmin/content/dtrace/

This directive trades off performance vs security against malicious, privileges-aware code. In *SECURE* mode, each request runs in a secure subprocess, incurring a substantial performance penalty. In *FAST* mode, the server is not protected against escalation of privileges as discussed above.

This directive differs slightly between a `<Directory>` context (including equivalents such as Location/Files/If) and a top-level or `<VirtualHost>`.

At top-level, it sets a default that will be inherited by virtualhosts. In a virtual host, FAST or SECURE mode acts on the entire HTTP request, and any settings in a `<Directory>` context will be **ignored**. A third pseudo-mode SELECTIVE defers the choice of FAST vs SECURE to directives in a `<Directory>` context.

In a `<Directory>` context, it is applicable only where SELECTIVE mode was set for the VirtualHost. Only FAST or SECURE can be set in this context (SELECTIVE would be meaningless).

 Warning

Where SELECTIVE mode is selected for a virtual host, the activation of privileges must be deferred until *after* the mapping phase of request processing has determined what `<Directory>` context applies to the request. This might give an attacker opportunities to introduce code through a REWRITEMAP running at top-level or `<VirtualHost>` context *before* privileges have been dropped and userid/gid set.

VHostCGIMode Directive

Description:	Determines whether the virtualhost can run subprocesses, and the privileges available to sub-processes.
Syntax:	`VHostCGIMode On|Off|Secure`
Default:	`VHostCGIMode On`
Context:	virtual host
Status:	Experimental
Module:	mod_privileges
Compatibility:	Available on Solaris 10 and OpenSolaris with non-threaded MPMs (PREFORK or custom MPM).

Determines whether the virtual host is allowed to run fork and exec, the privileges[53] required to run subprocesses. If this is set to *Off* the virtualhost is denied the privileges and will not be able to run traditional CGI programs or scripts under the traditional MOD_CGI, nor similar external programs such as those created by MOD_EXT_FILTER or REWRITEMAP *prog*. Note that it does not prevent CGI programs running under alternative process and security models such as mod_fcgid[54], which is a recommended solution in Solaris.

If set to *On* or *Secure*, the virtual host is permitted to run external programs and scripts as above. Setting VHOSTCGI-MODE *Secure* has the effect of denying privileges to the subprocesses, as described for VHOSTSECURE.

---

[53] http://sosc-dr.sun.com/bigadmin/features/articles/least_privilege.jsp
[54] http://fastcgi.coremail.cn

VHostCGIPrivs Directive

Description:	Assign arbitrary privileges to subprocesses created by a virtual host.
Syntax:	`VHostPrivs [+-]?privilege-name [[+-]?privilege-name] ...`
Default:	`None`
Context:	virtual host
Status:	Experimental
Module:	mod_privileges
Compatibility:	Available on Solaris 10 and OpenSolaris with non-threaded MPMs (`PREFORK` or custom MPM) and when `MOD_PRIVILEGES` is compiled with the *BIG_SECURITY_HOLE* compile-time option.

VHOSTCGIPRIVS can be used to assign arbitrary privileges[55] to subprocesses created by a virtual host, as discussed under VHOSTCGIMODE. Each *privilege-name* is the name of a Solaris privilege, such as *file_setid* or *sys_nfs*.

A *privilege-name* may optionally be prefixed by + or -, which will respectively allow or deny a privilege. If used with neither + nor -, all privileges otherwise assigned to the virtualhost will be denied. You can use this to override any of the default sets and construct your own privilege set.

 Security

This directive can open huge security holes in apache subprocesses, up to and including running them with root-level powers. Do not use it unless you fully understand what you are doing!

VHostGroup Directive

Description:	Sets the Group ID under which a virtual host runs.
Syntax:	`VHostGroup unix-groupid`
Default:	`Inherits the group id specified in GROUP`
Context:	virtual host
Status:	Experimental
Module:	mod_privileges
Compatibility:	Available on Solaris 10 and OpenSolaris with non-threaded MPMs (`PREFORK` or custom MPM).

The VHOSTGROUP directive sets the Unix group under which the server will process requests to a virtualhost. The group is set before the request is processed and reset afterwards using Solaris Privileges[56]. Since the setting applies to the *process*, this is not compatible with threaded MPMs.

Unix-group is one of:

A group name Refers to the given group by name.

 # followed by a group number. Refers to a group by its number.

 Security

This directive cannot be used to run apache as root! Nevertheless, it opens potential security issues similar to those discussed in the suexec (p. 105) documentation.

See also

- GROUP

---

[55]http://sosc-dr.sun.com/bigadmin/features/articles/least_privilege.jsp
[56]http://sosc-dr.sun.com/bigadmin/features/articles/least_privilege.jsp

- SUEXECUSERGROUP

VHostPrivs Directive

Description:	Assign arbitrary privileges to a virtual host.
Syntax:	`VHostPrivs [+-]?privilege-name [[+-]?privilege-name] ...`
Default:	`None`
Context:	virtual host
Status:	Experimental
Module:	mod_privileges
Compatibility:	Available on Solaris 10 and OpenSolaris with non-threaded MPMs (PREFORK or custom MPM) and when MOD_PRIVILEGES is compiled with the *BIG_SECURITY_HOLE* compile-time option.

VHOSTPRIVS can be used to assign arbitrary privileges[57] to a virtual host. Each *privilege-name* is the name of a Solaris privilege, such as *file_setid* or *sys_nfs*.

A *privilege-name* may optionally be prefixed by + or -, which will respectively allow or deny a privilege. If used with neither + nor -, all privileges otherwise assigned to the virtualhost will be denied. You can use this to override any of the default sets and construct your own privilege set.

 Security

This directive can open huge security holes in apache, up to and including running requests with root-level powers. Do not use it unless you fully understand what you are doing!

VHostSecure Directive

Description:	Determines whether the server runs with enhanced security for the virtualhost.
Syntax:	`VHostSecure On|Off`
Default:	`VHostSecure On`
Context:	virtual host
Status:	Experimental
Module:	mod_privileges
Compatibility:	Available on Solaris 10 and OpenSolaris with non-threaded MPMs (PREFORK or custom MPM).

Determines whether the virtual host processes requests with security enhanced by removal of Privileges[58] that are rarely needed in a webserver, but which are available by default to a normal Unix user and may therefore be required by modules and applications. It is recommended that you retain the default (On) unless it prevents an application running. Since the setting applies to the *process*, this is not compatible with threaded MPMs.

Note

If VHOSTSECURE prevents an application running, this may be a warning sign that the application should be reviewed for security.

---

[57]http://sosc-dr.sun.com/bigadmin/features/articles/least_privilege.jsp
[58]http://sosc-dr.sun.com/bigadmin/features/articles/least_privilege.jsp

VHostUser Directive

Description:	Sets the User ID under which a virtual host runs.
Syntax:	`VHostUser unix-userid`
Default:	`Inherits the userid specified in USER`
Context:	virtual host
Status:	Experimental
Module:	mod_privileges
Compatibility:	Available on Solaris 10 and OpenSolaris with non-threaded MPMs (PREFORK or custom MPM).

The VHOSTUSER directive sets the Unix userid under which the server will process requests to a virtualhost. The userid is set before the request is processed and reset afterwards using Solaris Privileges[59]. Since the setting applies to the *process*, this is not compatible with threaded MPMs.

Unix-userid is one of:

A username Refers to the given user by name.

 # followed by a user number. Refers to a user by its number.

 Security

This directive cannot be used to run apache as root! Nevertheless, it opens potential security issues similar to those discussed in the suexec (p. 105) documentation.

See also

- USER
- SUEXECUSERGROUP

---

[59]http://sosc-dr.sun.com/bigadmin/features/articles/least_privilege.jsp

10.77   Apache Module mod_proxy

Description:	Multi-protocol proxy/gateway server
Status:	Extension
ModuleIdentifier:	proxy_module
SourceFile:	mod_proxy.c

Summary

 Warning

Do not enable proxying with PROXYREQUESTS until you have secured your server. Open proxy servers are dangerous both to your network and to the Internet at large.

MOD_PROXY and related modules implement a proxy/gateway for Apache HTTP Server, supporting a number of popular protocols as well as several different load balancing algorithms. Third-party modules can add support for additional protocols and load balancing algorithms.

A set of modules must be loaded into the server to provide the necessary features. These modules can be included statically at build time or dynamically via the LOADMODULE directive). The set must include:

- MOD_PROXY, which provides basic proxy capabilities

- MOD_PROXY_BALANCER and one or more balancer modules if load balancing is required.   (See MOD_PROXY_BALANCER for more information.)

- one or more proxy scheme, or protocol, modules:

Protocol	Module
AJP13 (Apache JServe Protocol version 1.3)	MOD_PROXY_AJP
CONNECT (for SSL)	MOD_PROXY_CONNECT
FastCGI	MOD_PROXY_FCGI
ftp	MOD_PROXY_FTP
HTTP/0.9, HTTP/1.0, and HTTP/1.1	MOD_PROXY_HTTP
SCGI	MOD_PROXY_SCGI
WS and WSS (Web-sockets)	MOD_PROXY_WSTUNNEL

In addition, extended features are provided by other modules. Caching is provided by MOD_CACHE and related modules. The ability to contact remote servers using the SSL/TLS protocol is provided by the SSLProxy* directives of MOD_SSL. These additional modules will need to be loaded and configured to take advantage of these features.

Directives

- BalancerGrowth
- BalancerInherit
- BalancerMember
- BalancerPersist
- NoProxy
- <Proxy>
- ProxyAddHeaders
- ProxyBadHeader
- ProxyBlock

- ProxyDomain
- ProxyErrorOverride
- ProxyIOBufferSize
- <ProxyMatch>
- ProxyMaxForwards
- ProxyPass
- ProxyPassInherit
- ProxyPassInterpolateEnv
- ProxyPassMatch
- ProxyPassReverse
- ProxyPassReverseCookieDomain
- ProxyPassReverseCookiePath
- ProxyPreserveHost
- ProxyReceiveBufferSize
- ProxyRemote
- ProxyRemoteMatch
- ProxyRequests
- ProxySet
- ProxySourceAddress
- ProxyStatus
- ProxyTimeout
- ProxyVia

See also

- MOD_CACHE
- MOD_PROXY_AJP
- MOD_PROXY_CONNECT
- MOD_PROXY_FCGI
- MOD_PROXY_FTP
- MOD_PROXY_HTTP
- MOD_PROXY_SCGI
- MOD_PROXY_WSTUNNEL
- MOD_PROXY_BALANCER
- MOD_SSL

Forward Proxies and Reverse Proxies/Gateways

Apache HTTP Server can be configured in both a *forward* and *reverse* proxy (also known as *gateway*) mode.

An ordinary *forward proxy* is an intermediate server that sits between the client and the *origin server*. In order to get content from the origin server, the client sends a request to the proxy naming the origin server as the target. The proxy then requests the content from the origin server and returns it to the client. The client must be specially configured to use the forward proxy to access other sites.

A typical usage of a forward proxy is to provide Internet access to internal clients that are otherwise restricted by a firewall. The forward proxy can also use caching (as provided by MOD_CACHE) to reduce network usage.

The forward proxy is activated using the PROXYREQUESTS directive. Because forward proxies allow clients to access arbitrary sites through your server and to hide their true origin, it is essential that you secure your server so that only authorized clients can access the proxy before activating a forward proxy.

A *reverse proxy* (or *gateway*), by contrast, appears to the client just like an ordinary web server. No special configuration on the client is necessary. The client makes ordinary requests for content in the namespace of the reverse proxy. The reverse proxy then decides where to send those requests and returns the content as if it were itself the origin.

A typical usage of a reverse proxy is to provide Internet users access to a server that is behind a firewall. Reverse proxies can also be used to balance load among several back-end servers or to provide caching for a slower back-end server. In addition, reverse proxies can be used simply to bring several servers into the same URL space.

A reverse proxy is activated using the PROXYPASS directive or the [P] flag to the REWRITERULE directive. It is **not** necessary to turn PROXYREQUESTS on in order to configure a reverse proxy.

Basic Examples

The examples below are only a very basic idea to help you get started. Please read the documentation on the individual directives.

In addition, if you wish to have caching enabled, consult the documentation from MOD_CACHE.

Reverse Proxy

```
ProxyPass "/foo" "http://foo.example.com/bar"
ProxyPassReverse "/foo" "http://foo.example.com/bar"
```

Forward Proxy

```
ProxyRequests On
ProxyVia On

<Proxy "*">
  Require host internal.example.com
</Proxy>
```

Access via Handler

You can also force a request to be handled as a reverse-proxy request, by creating a suitable Handler pass-through. The example configuration below will pass all requests for PHP scripts to the specified FastCGI server using reverse proxy:

Reverse Proxy PHP scripts

```
<FilesMatch "\.php$">
    # Unix sockets require 2.4.7 or later
    SetHandler  "proxy:unix:/path/to/app.sock|fcgi://localhost/"
</FilesMatch>
```

This feature is available in Apache HTTP Server 2.4.10 and later.

Workers

The proxy manages the configuration of origin servers and their communication parameters in objects called *workers*. There are two built-in workers: the default forward proxy worker and the default reverse proxy worker. Additional workers can be configured explicitly.

The two default workers have a fixed configuration and will be used if no other worker matches the request. They do not use HTTP Keep-Alive or connection pooling. The TCP connections to the origin server will instead be opened and closed for each request.

Explicitly configured workers are identified by their URL. They are usually created and configured using PROXYPASS or PROXYPASSMATCH when used for a reverse proxy:

```
ProxyPass "/example" "http://backend.example.com" connectiontimeout=5 timeout=3
```

This will create a worker associated with the origin server URL http://backend.example.com that will use the given timeout values. When used in a forward proxy, workers are usually defined via the PROXYSET directive:

```
ProxySet "http://backend.example.com" connectiontimeout=5 timeout=30
```

or alternatively using PROXY and PROXYSET:

```
<Proxy "http://backend.example.com">
  ProxySet connectiontimeout=5 timeout=30
</Proxy>
```

Using explicitly configured workers in the forward mode is not very common, because forward proxies usually communicate with many different origin servers. Creating explicit workers for some of the origin servers can still be useful if they are used very often. Explicitly configured workers have no concept of forward or reverse proxying by themselves. They encapsulate a common concept of communication with origin servers. A worker created by PROXYPASS for use in a reverse proxy will also be used for forward proxy requests whenever the URL to the origin server matches the worker URL, and vice versa.

The URL identifying a direct worker is the URL of its origin server including any path components given:

```
ProxyPass "/examples" "http://backend.example.com/examples"
ProxyPass "/docs" "http://backend.example.com/docs"
```

This example defines two different workers, each using a separate connection pool and configuration.

Worker Sharing

Worker sharing happens if the worker URLs overlap, which occurs when the URL of some worker is a leading substring of the URL of another worker defined later in the configuration file. In the following example

```
ProxyPass "/apps" "http://backend.example.com/" timeout=60
ProxyPass "/examples" "http://backend.example.com/examples" timeout=10
```

the second worker isn't actually created. Instead the first worker is used. The benefit is, that there is only one connection pool, so connections are more often reused. Note that all configuration attributes given explicitly for the later worker will be ignored. This will be logged as a warning. In the above example, the resulting timeout value for the URL /examples will be 60 instead of 10!

If you want to avoid worker sharing, sort your worker definitions by URL length, starting with the longest worker URLs. If you want to maximize worker sharing, use the reverse sort order. See also the related warning about ordering PROXYPASS directives.

Explicitly configured workers come in two flavors: *direct workers* and *(load) balancer workers*. They support many important configuration attributes which are described below in the PROXYPASS directive. The same attributes can also be set using PROXYSET.

The set of options available for a direct worker depends on the protocol which is specified in the origin server URL. Available protocols include `ajp`, `fcgi`, `ftp`, `http` and `scgi`.

Balancer workers are virtual workers that use direct workers known as their members to actually handle the requests. Each balancer can have multiple members. When it handles a request, it chooses a member based on the configured load balancing algorithm.

A balancer worker is created if its worker URL uses `balancer` as the protocol scheme. The balancer URL uniquely identifies the balancer worker. Members are added to a balancer using BALANCERMEMBER.

Controlling Access to Your Proxy

You can control who can access your proxy via the <PROXY> control block as in the following example:

```
<Proxy "*">
  Require ip 192.168.0
</Proxy>
```

For more information on access control directives, see MOD_AUTHZ_HOST.

Strictly limiting access is essential if you are using a forward proxy (using the PROXYREQUESTS directive). Otherwise, your server can be used by any client to access arbitrary hosts while hiding his or her true identity. This is dangerous both for your network and for the Internet at large. When using a reverse proxy (using the PROXYPASS directive with `ProxyRequests Off`), access control is less critical because clients can only contact the hosts that you have specifically configured.

See Also the Proxy-Chain-Auth (p. 789) environment variable.

Slow Startup

If you're using the PROXYBLOCK directive, hostnames' IP addresses are looked up and cached during startup for later match test. This may take a few seconds (or more) depending on the speed with which the hostname lookups occur.

Intranet Proxy

An Apache httpd proxy server situated in an intranet needs to forward external requests through the company's firewall (for this, configure the PROXYREMOTE directive to forward the respective *scheme* to the firewall proxy). However, when it has to access resources within the intranet, it can bypass the firewall when accessing hosts. The NOPROXY directive is useful for specifying which hosts belong to the intranet and should be accessed directly.

Users within an intranet tend to omit the local domain name from their WWW requests, thus requesting "http://somehost/" instead of `http://somehost.example.com/`. Some commercial proxy servers let them get away with this and simply serve the request, implying a configured local domain. When the PROXYDOMAIN directive is used and the server is configured for proxy service, Apache httpd can return a redirect response and send the client to the correct, fully qualified, server address. This is the preferred method since the user's bookmark files will then contain fully qualified hosts.

Protocol Adjustments

For circumstances where MOD_PROXY is sending requests to an origin server that doesn't properly implement keepalives or HTTP/1.1, there are two environment variables (p. 82) that can force the request to use HTTP/1.0 with no keepalive. These are set via the SETENV directive.

These are the `force-proxy-request-1.0` and `proxy-nokeepalive` notes.

```
<Location "/buggyappserver/">
  ProxyPass "http://buggyappserver:7001/foo/"
  SetEnv force-proxy-request-1.0 1
  SetEnv proxy-nokeepalive 1
</Location>
```

Request Bodies

Some request methods such as POST include a request body. The HTTP protocol requires that requests which include a body either use chunked transfer encoding or send a `Content-Length` request header. When passing these requests on to the origin server, MOD_PROXY_HTTP will always attempt to send the `Content-Length`. But if the body is large and the original request used chunked encoding, then chunked encoding may also be used in the upstream request. You can control this selection using environment variables (p. 82) . Setting `proxy-sendcl` ensures maximum compatibility with upstream servers by always sending the `Content-Length`, while setting `proxy-sendchunked` minimizes resource usage by using chunked encoding.

Under some circumstances, the server must spool request bodies to disk to satisfy the requested handling of request bodies. For example, this spooling will occur if the original body was sent with chunked encoding (and is large), but the administrator has asked for backend requests to be sent with Content-Length or as HTTP/1.0. This spooling can also occur if the request body already has a Content-Length header, but the server is configured to filter incoming request bodies.

LIMITREQUESTBODY only applies to request bodies that the server will spool to disk

Reverse Proxy Request Headers

When acting in a reverse-proxy mode (using the PROXYPASS directive, for example), MOD_PROXY_HTTP adds several request headers in order to pass information to the origin server. These headers are:

X-Forwarded-For The IP address of the client.

X-Forwarded-Host The original host requested by the client in the Host HTTP request header.

X-Forwarded-Server The hostname of the proxy server.

Be careful when using these headers on the origin server, since they will contain more than one (comma-separated) value if the original request already contained one of these headers. For example, you can use `%{X-Forwarded-For}i` in the log format string of the origin server to log the original clients IP address, but you may get more than one address if the request passes through several proxies.

See also the PROXYPRESERVEHOST and PROXYVIA directives, which control other request headers.

Note: If you need to specify custom request headers to be added to the forwarded request, use the REQUESTHEADER directive.

BalancerGrowth Directive

Description:	Number of additional Balancers that can be added Post-configuration
Syntax:	`BalancerGrowth #`
Default:	`BalancerGrowth 5`
Context:	server config, virtual host
Status:	Extension
Module:	mod_proxy
Compatibility:	BalancerGrowth is only available in Apache HTTP Server 2.3.13 and later.

This directive allows for growth potential in the number of Balancers available for a virtualhost in addition to the number pre-configured. It only takes effect if there is at least one pre-configured Balancer.

BalancerInherit Directive

Description:	Inherit ProxyPassed Balancers/Workers from the main server
Syntax:	`BalancerInherit On|Off`
Default:	`BalancerInherit On`
Context:	server config, virtual host
Status:	Extension
Module:	mod_proxy
Compatibility:	BalancerInherit is only available in Apache HTTP Server 2.4.5 and later.

This directive will cause the current server/vhost to "inherit" ProxyPass Balancers and Workers defined in the main server. This can cause issues and inconsistent behavior if using the Balancer Manager and so should be disabled if using that feature.

The setting in the global server defines the default for all vhosts.

BalancerMember Directive

Description:	Add a member to a load balancing group
Syntax:	`BalancerMember [balancerurl] url [key=value [key=value ...]]`
Context:	directory
Status:	Extension
Module:	mod_proxy
Compatibility:	BalancerMember is only available in Apache HTTP Server 2.2 and later.

This directive adds a member to a load balancing group. It can be used within a `<Proxy balancer://...>` container directive and can take any of the key value pair parameters available to PROXYPASS directives.

One additional parameter is available only to BALANCERMEMBER directives: *loadfactor*. This is the member load factor - a number between 1 (default) and 100, which defines the weighted load to be applied to the member in question.

The *balancerurl* is only needed when not within a `<Proxy balancer://...>` container directive. It corresponds to the url of a balancer defined in PROXYPASS directive.

The path component of the balancer URL in any `<Proxy balancer://...>` container directive is ignored.

Trailing slashes should typically be removed from the URL of a BALANCERMEMBER.

BalancerPersist Directive

Description:	Attempt to persist changes made by the Balancer Manager across restarts.
Syntax:	`BalancerPersist On|Off`
Default:	`BalancerPersist Off`
Context:	server config, virtual host
Status:	Extension
Module:	mod_proxy
Compatibility:	BalancerPersist is only available in Apache HTTP Server 2.4.4 and later.

This directive will cause the shared memory storage associated with the balancers and balancer members to be persisted across restarts. This allows these local changes to not be lost during the normal restart/graceful state transitions.

NoProxy Directive

Description:	Hosts, domains, or networks that will be connected to directly
Syntax:	`NoProxy host [host] ...`
Context:	server config, virtual host
Status:	Extension
Module:	mod_proxy

This directive is only useful for Apache httpd proxy servers within intranets. The NOPROXY directive specifies a list of subnets, IP addresses, hosts and/or domains, separated by spaces. A request to a host which matches one or more of these is always served directly, without forwarding to the configured PROXYREMOTE proxy server(s).

Example

```
ProxyRemote   "*"   "http://firewall.example.com:81"
NoProxy           ".example.com" "192.168.112.0/21"
```

The *host* arguments to the NOPROXY directive are one of the following type list:

Domain A *Domain* is a partially qualified DNS domain name, preceded by a period. It represents a list of hosts which logically belong to the same DNS domain or zone (*i.e.*, the suffixes of the hostnames are all ending in *Domain*).

Examples
`.com .example.org.`

To distinguish *Domain*s from *Hostname*s (both syntactically and semantically; a DNS domain can have a DNS A record, too!), *Domain*s are always written with a leading period.

Note

> Domain name comparisons are done without regard to the case, and *Domain*s are always assumed to be anchored in the root of the DNS tree; therefore, the two domains `.ExAmple.com` and `.example.com.` (note the trailing period) are considered equal. Since a domain comparison does not involve a DNS lookup, it is much more efficient than subnet comparison.

SubNet A *SubNet* is a partially qualified internet address in numeric (dotted quad) form, optionally followed by a slash and the netmask, specified as the number of significant bits in the *SubNet*. It is used to represent a subnet of hosts which can be reached over a common network interface. In the absence of the explicit net mask it is assumed that omitted (or zero valued) trailing digits specify the mask. (In this case, the netmask can only be multiples of 8 bits wide.) Examples:

192.168 or 192.168.0.0 the subnet 192.168.0.0 with an implied netmask of 16 valid bits (sometimes used in the netmask form `255.255.0.0`)

192.168.112.0/21 the subnet `192.168.112.0/21` with a netmask of 21 valid bits (also used in the form `255.255.248.0`)

As a degenerate case, a *SubNet* with 32 valid bits is the equivalent to an *IPAddr*, while a *SubNet* with zero valid bits (*e.g.*, 0.0.0.0/0) is the same as the constant *_Default_*, matching any IP address.

IPAddr A *IPAddr* represents a fully qualified internet address in numeric (dotted quad) form. Usually, this address represents a host, but there need not necessarily be a DNS domain name connected with the address.

> **Example**
> `192.168.123.7`

Note

> An *IPAddr* does not need to be resolved by the DNS system, so it can result in more effective apache performance.

Hostname A *Hostname* is a fully qualified DNS domain name which can be resolved to one or more *IPAddrs* via the DNS domain name service. It represents a logical host (in contrast to *Domain*s, see above) and must be resolvable to at least one *IPAddr* (or often to a list of hosts with different *IPAddrs*).

> **Examples**
> `prep.ai.example.edu`
> `www.example.org`

Note

> In many situations, it is more effective to specify an *IPAddr* in place of a *Hostname* since a DNS lookup can be avoided. Name resolution in Apache httpd can take a remarkable deal of time when the connection to the name server uses a slow PPP link.
>
> *Hostname* comparisons are done without regard to the case, and *Hostname*s are always assumed to be anchored in the root of the DNS tree; therefore, the two hosts `WWW.ExAmple.com` and `www.example.com.` (note the trailing period) are considered equal.

See also

- DNS Issues (p. 111)

Proxy Directive

Description:	Container for directives applied to proxied resources
Syntax:	`<Proxy wildcard-url> ...</Proxy>`
Context:	server config, virtual host
Status:	Extension
Module:	mod_proxy

Directives placed in <PROXY> sections apply only to matching proxied content. Shell-style wildcards are allowed.

For example, the following will allow only hosts in `yournetwork.example.com` to access content via your proxy server:

```
<Proxy "*">
  Require host yournetwork.example.com
</Proxy>
```

The following example will process all files in the `foo` directory of `example.com` through the `INCLUDES` filter when they are sent through the proxy server:

```
<Proxy "http://example.com/foo/*">
  SetOutputFilter INCLUDES
</Proxy>
```

Differences from the Location configuration section

A backend URL matches the configuration section if it begins with the the *wildcard-url* string, even if the last path segment in the directive only matches a prefix of the backend URL. For example, <Proxy "http://example.com/foo"> matches all of http://example.com/foo, http://example.com/foo/bar, and http://example.com/foobar. The matching of the final URL differs from the behavior of the <LOCATION> section, which for purposes of this note treats the final path component as if it ended in a slash.

For more control over the matching, see <PROXYMATCH>.

See also

- <PROXYMATCH>

ProxyAddHeaders Directive

Description:	Add proxy information in X-Forwarded-* headers
Syntax:	`ProxyAddHeaders Off|On`
Default:	`ProxyAddHeaders On`
Context:	server config, virtual host, directory
Status:	Extension
Module:	mod_proxy
Compatibility:	Available in version 2.3.10 and later

This directive determines whether or not proxy related information should be passed to the backend server through X-Forwarded-For, X-Forwarded-Host and X-Forwarded-Server HTTP headers.

**Effectiveness**

This option is of use only for HTTP proxying, as handled by MOD_PROXY_HTTP.

ProxyBadHeader Directive

Description:	Determines how to handle bad header lines in a response
Syntax:	`ProxyBadHeader IsError|Ignore|StartBody`
Default:	`ProxyBadHeader IsError`
Context:	server config, virtual host
Status:	Extension
Module:	mod_proxy

The PROXYBADHEADER directive determines the behavior of MOD_PROXY if it receives syntactically invalid response header lines (*i.e.* containing no colon) from the origin server. The following arguments are possible:

IsError Abort the request and end up with a 502 (Bad Gateway) response. This is the default behavior.

Ignore Treat bad header lines as if they weren't sent.

StartBody When receiving the first bad header line, finish reading the headers and treat the remainder as body. This helps to work around buggy backend servers which forget to insert an empty line between the headers and the body.

ProxyBlock Directive

Description:	Words, hosts, or domains that are banned from being proxied
Syntax:	`ProxyBlock *|word|host|domain [word|host|domain] ...`
Context:	server config, virtual host
Status:	Extension
Module:	mod_proxy

The PROXYBLOCK directive specifies a list of words, hosts and/or domains, separated by spaces. HTTP, HTTPS, and FTP document requests to sites whose names contain matched words, hosts or domains are *blocked* by the proxy server. The proxy module will also attempt to determine IP addresses of list items which may be hostnames during startup, and cache them for match test as well. That may slow down the startup time of the server.

Example

```
ProxyBlock "news.example.com" "auctions.example.com" "friends.example.com"
```

Note that `example` would also be sufficient to match any of these sites.

Hosts would also be matched if referenced by IP address.

Note also that

```
ProxyBlock "*"
```

blocks connections to all sites.

ProxyDomain Directive

Description:	Default domain name for proxied requests
Syntax:	`ProxyDomain Domain`
Context:	server config, virtual host
Status:	Extension
Module:	mod_proxy

This directive is only useful for Apache httpd proxy servers within intranets. The PROXYDOMAIN directive specifies the default domain which the apache proxy server will belong to. If a request to a host without a domain name is encountered, a redirection response to the same host with the configured *Domain* appended will be generated.

Example

```
ProxyRemote  "*"   "http://firewall.example.com:81"
NoProxy          ".example.com" "192.168.112.0/21"
ProxyDomain      ".example.com"
```

ProxyErrorOverride Directive

Description:	Override error pages for proxied content
Syntax:	`ProxyErrorOverride On|Off`
Default:	`ProxyErrorOverride Off`
Context:	server config, virtual host, directory
Status:	Extension
Module:	mod_proxy

This directive is useful for reverse-proxy setups where you want to have a common look and feel on the error pages seen by the end user. This also allows for included files (via MOD_INCLUDE's SSI) to get the error code and act accordingly. (Default behavior would display the error page of the proxied server. Turning this on shows the SSI Error message.)

This directive does not affect the processing of informational (1xx), normal success (2xx), or redirect (3xx) responses.

ProxyIOBufferSize Directive

Description:	Determine size of internal data throughput buffer
Syntax:	`ProxyIOBufferSize bytes`
Default:	`ProxyIOBufferSize 8192`
Context:	server config, virtual host
Status:	Extension
Module:	mod_proxy

The PROXYIOBUFFERSIZE directive adjusts the size of the internal buffer which is used as a scratchpad for the data between input and output. The size must be at least `512`.

In almost every case, there's no reason to change that value.

If used with AJP, this directive sets the maximum AJP packet size in bytes. Values larger than 65536 are set to 65536. If you change it from the default, you must also change the `packetSize` attribute of your AJP connector on the Tomcat side! The attribute `packetSize` is only available in Tomcat `5.5.20+` and `6.0.2+`

Normally it is not necessary to change the maximum packet size. Problems with the default value have been reported when sending certificates or certificate chains.

ProxyMatch Directive

Description:	Container for directives applied to regular-expression-matched proxied resources
Syntax:	`<ProxyMatch regex> ...</ProxyMatch>`
Context:	server config, virtual host
Status:	Extension
Module:	mod_proxy

The <PROXYMATCH> directive is identical to the <PROXY> directive, except that it matches URLs using regular expressions.

From 2.4.8 onwards, named groups and backreferences are captured and written to the environment with the corresponding name prefixed with "MATCH_" and in upper case. This allows elements of URLs to be referenced from within expressions (p. 89) and modules like MOD_REWRITE. In order to prevent confusion, numbered (unnamed) backreferences are ignored. Use named groups instead.

```
<ProxyMatch "^http://(?<sitename>[^/]+)">
    Require ldap-group cn=%{env:MATCH_SITENAME},ou=combined,o=Example
</ProxyMatch>
```

See also

- <PROXY>

ProxyMaxForwards Directive

Description:	Maximum number of proxies that a request can be forwarded through
Syntax:	`ProxyMaxForwards number`
Default:	`ProxyMaxForwards -1`
Context:	server config, virtual host
Status:	Extension
Module:	mod_proxy
Compatibility:	Default behaviour changed in 2.2.7

The PROXYMAXFORWARDS directive specifies the maximum number of proxies through which a request may pass if there's no `Max-Forwards` header supplied with the request. This may be set to prevent infinite proxy loops or a DoS attack.

Example

```
ProxyMaxForwards 15
```

Note that setting PROXYMAXFORWARDS is a violation of the HTTP/1.1 protocol (RFC2616), which forbids a Proxy setting `Max-Forwards` if the Client didn't set it. Earlier Apache httpd versions would always set it. A negative PROXYMAXFORWARDS value, including the default -1, gives you protocol-compliant behavior but may leave you open to loops.

ProxyPass Directive

Description:	Maps remote servers into the local server URL-space
Syntax:	`ProxyPass [path] !|url [key=value [key=value ...]]  [nocanon]` `[interpolate] [noquery]`
Context:	server config, virtual host, directory
Status:	Extension
Module:	mod_proxy
Compatibility:	Unix Domain Socket (UDS) support added in 2.4.7

This directive allows remote servers to be mapped into the space of the local server. The local server does not act as a proxy in the conventional sense but appears to be a mirror of the remote server. The local server is often called a *reverse proxy* or *gateway*. The *path* is the name of a local virtual path; *url* is a partial URL for the remote server and cannot include a query string.

⟹ **Note:** This directive cannot be used within a `<Directory>` context.

⚠ The PROXYREQUESTS directive should usually be set **off** when using PROXYPASS.

In 2.4.7 and later, support for using a Unix Domain Socket is available by using a target which prepends `unix:/path/lis.sock|`. For example, to proxy HTTP and target the UDS at /home/www/socket, you would use `unix:/home/www.socket|http://localhost/whatever/`.

⟹ **Note:** The path associated with the `unix:` URL is DEFAULTRUNTIMEDIR aware.

When used inside a `<LOCATION>` section, the first argument is omitted and the local directory is obtained from the `<LOCATION>`. The same will occur inside a `<LOCATIONMATCH>` section; however, ProxyPass does not interpret the regexp as such, so it is necessary to use PROXYPASSMATCH in this situation instead.

Suppose the local server has address `http://example.com/`; then

```
<Location "/mirror/foo/">
    ProxyPass "http://backend.example.com/"
</Location>
```

will cause a local request for `http://example.com/mirror/foo/bar` to be internally converted into a proxy request to `http://backend.example.com/bar`.

The ProxyPass directive is not supported in <DIRECTORY> or <FILES> sections.

If you require a more flexible reverse-proxy configuration, see the REWRITERULE directive with the [P] flag.

The following alternative syntax is possible; however, it can carry a performance penalty when present in very large numbers. The advantage of the below syntax is that it allows for dynamic control via the Balancer Manager (p. 768) interface:

```
ProxyPass "/mirror/foo/" "http://backend.example.com/"
```

 If the first argument ends with a trailing /, the second argument should also end with a trailing /, and vice versa. Otherwise, the resulting requests to the backend may miss some needed slashes and do not deliver the expected results.

The ! directive is useful in situations where you don't want to reverse-proxy a subdirectory, *e.g.*

```
<Location "/mirror/foo/">
    ProxyPass "http://backend.example.com/"
</Location>
<Location "/mirror/foo/i">
    ProxyPass "!"
</Location>
```

```
ProxyPass "/mirror/foo/i" "!"
ProxyPass "/mirror/foo" "http://backend.example.com"
```

will proxy all requests to `/mirror/foo` to `backend.example.com` *except* requests made to `/mirror/foo/i`.

 Ordering ProxyPass Directives
The configured PROXYPASS and PROXYPASSMATCH rules are checked in the order of configuration. The first rule that matches wins. So usually you should sort conflicting PROXYPASS rules starting with the longest URLs first. Otherwise, later rules for longer URLS will be hidden by any earlier rule which uses a leading substring of the URL. Note that there is some relation with worker sharing. In contrast, only one PROXYPASS directive can be placed in a LOCATION block, and the most specific location will take precedence.
For the same reasons, exclusions must come *before* the general PROXYPASS directives.

ProxyPass `key=value` Parameters

In Apache HTTP Server 2.1 and later, mod_proxy supports pooled connections to a backend server. Connections created on demand can be retained in a pool for future use. Limits on the pool size and other settings can be coded on the PROXYPASS directive using `key=value` parameters, described in the tables below.

By default, mod_proxy will allow and retain the maximum number of connections that could be used simultaneously by that web server child process. Use the `max` parameter to reduce the number from the default. Use the `ttl` parameter to set an optional time to live; connections which have been unused for at least `ttl` seconds will be closed. `ttl` can be used to avoid using a connection which is subject to closing because of the backend server's keep-alive timeout.

The pool of connections is maintained per web server child process, and `max` and other settings are not coordinated among all child processes, except when only one child process is allowed by configuration or MPM design.

Example

```
ProxyPass "/example" "http://backend.example.com" max=20 ttl=120 retry=300
```

BalancerMember parameters		

Parameter	Default	Description
min	0	Minimum number of connection pool entries, unrelated to the actual number of connections. This only needs to be modified from the default for special circumstances where heap memory associated with the backend connections should be preallocated or retained.
max	1...n	Maximum number of connections that will be allowed to the backend server. The default for this limit is the number of threads per process in the active MPM. In the Prefork MPM, this is always 1, while with other MPMs, it is controlled by the THREADSPERCHILD directive.
smax	max	Retained connection pool entries above this limit are freed during certain operations if they have been unused for longer than the time to live, controlled by the `ttl` parameter. If the connection pool entry has an associated connection, it will be closed. This only needs to be modified from the default for special circumstances where connection pool entries and any associated connections which have exceeded the time to live need to be freed or closed more aggressively.
acquire	-	If set, this will be the maximum time to wait for a free connection in the connection pool, in milliseconds. If there are no free connections in the pool, the Apache httpd will return SERVER_BUSY status to the client.
connectiontimeout	timeout	Connect timeout in seconds. The number of seconds Apache httpd waits for the creation of a connection to the backend to complete. By adding a postfix of ms, the timeout can be also set in milliseconds.

disablereuse	Off	This parameter should be used when you want to force mod_proxy to immediately close a connection to the backend after being used, and thus, disable its persistent connection and pool for that backend. This helps in various situations where a firewall between Apache httpd and the backend server (regardless of protocol) tends to silently drop connections or when backends themselves may be under round- robin DNS. To disable connection pooling reuse, set this property value to On.
enablereuse	On	This is the inverse of 'disablereuse' above, provided as a convenience for scheme handlers that require opt-in for connection reuse (such as MOD_PROXY_FCGI). 2.4.11 and later only.
flushpackets	off	Determines whether the proxy module will auto-flush the output brigade after each "chunk" of data. 'off' means that it will flush only when needed; 'on' means after each chunk is sent; and 'auto' means poll/wait for a period of time and flush if no input has been received for 'flushwait' milliseconds. Currently, this is in effect only for AJP.
flushwait	10	The time to wait for additional input, in milliseconds, before flushing the output brigade if 'flushpackets' is 'auto'.
iobuffersize	8192	Adjusts the size of the internal scratchpad IO buffer. This allows you to override the PROXYIOBUFFERSIZE for a specific worker. This must be at least 512 or set to 0 for the system default of 8192.
keepalive	Off	This parameter should be used when you have a firewall between your Apache httpd and the backend server, which tends to drop inactive connections. This flag will tell the Operating System to send KEEP_ALIVE messages on inactive connections and thus prevent the firewall from dropping the connection. To enable keepalive, set this property value to On. The frequency of initial and subsequent TCP keepalive probes depends on global OS settings, and may be as high as 2 hours. To be useful, the frequency configured in the OS must be smaller than the threshold used by the firewall.
lbset	0	Sets the load balancer cluster set that the worker is a member of. The load balancer will try all members of a lower numbered lbset before trying higher numbered ones

ping	0	Ping property tells the webserver to "test" the connection to the backend before forwarding the request. For AJP it causes MOD_PROXY_AJP to send a CPING request on the ajp13 connection (implemented on Tomcat 3.3.2+ 4.1.28+ and 5.0.13+). For HTTP, it causes MOD_PROXY_HTTP to send a 100-Continue to the backend (only valid for HTTP/1.1 - for non HTTP/1.1 backends, this property has no effect). In both cases, the parameter is the delay in seconds to wait for the reply. This feature has been added to avoid problems with hung and busy backends. This will increase the network traffic during the normal operation which could be an issue but it will lower the traffic in case some of the cluster nodes are down or busy. By adding a postfix of ms, the delay can be also set in milliseconds.
receivebuffersize	0	Adjusts the size of the explicit (TCP/IP) network buffer size for proxied connections. This allows you to override the PROXYRECEIVEBUFFERSIZE for a specific worker. This must be at least 512 or set to 0 for the system default.
redirect	-	Redirection Route of the worker. This value is usually set dynamically to enable safe removal of the node from the cluster. If set, all requests without session id will be redirected to the BalancerMember that has route parameter equal to this value.
retry	60	Connection pool worker retry timeout in seconds. If the connection pool worker to the backend server is in the error state, Apache httpd will not forward any requests to that server until the timeout expires. This enables to shut down the backend server for maintenance and bring it back online later. A value of 0 means always retry workers in an error state with no timeout.
route	-	Route of the worker when used inside load balancer. The route is a value appended to session id.

status	-	Single letter value defining the initial status of this worker D: Worker is disabled and will not accept any requests. S: Worker is administratively stopped. I: Worker is in ignore-errors mode and will always be considered available. H: Worker is in hot-standby mode and will only be used if no other viable workers are available. E: Worker is in an error state. N: Worker is in drain mode and will only accept existing sticky sessions destined for itself and ignore all other requests. Status can be set (which is the default) by prepending with '+' or cleared by prepending with '-'. Thus, a setting of 'S-E' sets this worker to Stopped and clears the in-error flag.
timeout	PROXYTIMEOUT	Connection timeout in seconds. The number of seconds Apache httpd waits for data sent by / to the backend.
ttl	-	Time to live for inactive connections and associated connection pool entries, in seconds. Once reaching this limit, a connection will not be used again; it will be closed at some later time.

If the Proxy directive scheme starts with the `balancer://` (eg: `balancer://cluster`, any path information is ignored), then a virtual worker that does not really communicate with the backend server will be created. Instead, it is responsible for the management of several "real" workers. In that case, the special set of parameters can be added to this virtual worker. See MOD_PROXY_BALANCER for more information about how the balancer works.

Balancer parameters

Parameter	Default	Description
lbmethod	byrequests	Balancer load-balance method. Select the load-balancing scheduler method to use. Either `byrequests` to perform weighted request counting `bytraffic`, to perform weighted traffic byte count balancing; or `bybusyness` to perform pending request balancing The default is `byrequests`.
maxattempts	One less than the number of workers, or 1 with a single worker.	Maximum number of failover attempts before giving up.
nofailover	Off	If set to `On`, the session will break if the worker is in error state or disabled. Set this value to `On` if backend servers do not support session replication.
stickysession	-	Balancer sticky session name. The value is usually set to something like `JSESSIONID` or `PHPSESSIONID`, and it depends on the backend application server that support sessions. If the backend application server uses different name for cookies and url encoded id (like servlet containers) use — to separate them. The first part is for the cookie the second for the path. Available in Apache HTTP Server 2.4.4 and later.
stickysessionsep	"."	Sets the separation symbol in the session cookie. Some backend application servers do not use the '.' as the symbol. For example, the Oracle Weblogic server uses '!'. The correct symbol can be set using this option. The setting of 'Off' signifies that no symbol is used.
scolonpathdelim	Off	If set to `On`, the semi-colon character ';' will be used as an additional sticky session path delimiter/separator. This is mainly used to emulate mod_jk's behavior when dealing with paths such as `JSESSIONID=6736bcf34;foo=aa`
timeout	0	Balancer timeout in seconds. If set, this will be the maximum time to wait for a free worker. The default is to not wait.
failonstatus	-	A single or comma-separated list of HTTP status codes. If set, this will force the worker into error state when the backend returns any status code in the list Worker recovery behaves the same as other worker errors.
failontimeout	Off	If set, an IO read timeout after a request is sent to the backend will force the worker into error state. Worker recovery behaves the same as other worker errors. Available in Apache HTTP Server 2.4.5 and later.
nonce	\<auto\>	The protective nonce used in the `balancer-manager` application page. The default is to use an automatically determined UUID-based nonce to provide for further protection for the page. If set, then the nonce is set to that value. A setting of `None` disables all nonce checking.

> **Note**
>
> In addition to the nonce, `balancer-manager` pa should be protected via an AC

A sample balancer setup:

```
ProxyPass "/special-area" "http://special.example.com" smax=5 max=10
ProxyPass "/" "balancer://mycluster/" stickysession=JSESSIONID|jsessionid nofai
<Proxy "balancer://mycluster">
    BalancerMember "ajp://1.2.3.4:8009"
    BalancerMember "ajp://1.2.3.5:8009" loadfactor=20
    # Less powerful server, don't send as many requests there,
    BalancerMember "ajp://1.2.3.6:8009" loadfactor=5
</Proxy>
```

Setting up a hot-standby that will only be used if no other members are available:

```
ProxyPass "/" "balancer://hotcluster/"
<Proxy "balancer://hotcluster">
    BalancerMember "ajp://1.2.3.4:8009" loadfactor=1
    BalancerMember "ajp://1.2.3.5:8009" loadfactor=2
    # The server below is on hot standby
    BalancerMember "ajp://1.2.3.6:8009" status=+H
    ProxySet lbmethod=bytraffic
</Proxy>
```

Additional ProxyPass Keywords

Normally, mod_proxy will canonicalise ProxyPassed URLs. But this may be incompatible with some backends, particularly those that make use of *PATH_INFO*. The optional *nocanon* keyword suppresses this and passes the URL path "raw" to the backend. Note that this keyword may affect the security of your backend, as it removes the normal limited protection against URL-based attacks provided by the proxy.

Normally, mod_proxy will include the query string when generating the *SCRIPT_FILENAME* environment variable. The optional *noquery* keyword (available in httpd 2.4.1 and later) prevents this.

The optional *interpolate* keyword, in combination with PROXYPASSINTERPOLATEENV, causes the ProxyPass to interpolate environment variables, using the syntax ${*VARNAME*}. Note that many of the standard CGI-derived environment variables will not exist when this interpolation happens, so you may still have to resort to MOD_REWRITE for complex rules. Also note that interpolation is not supported within the scheme portion of a URL. Dynamic determination of the scheme can be accomplished with MOD_REWRITE as in the following example.

```
RewriteEngine On

RewriteCond "%{HTTPS}" =off
RewriteRule "." "-" [E=protocol:http]
RewriteCond "%{HTTPS}" =on
RewriteRule "." "-" [E=protocol:https]

RewriteRule "^/mirror/foo/(.*)" "%{ENV:protocol}://backend.example.com/$1" [P]
ProxyPassReverse  "/mirror/foo/" "http://backend.example.com/"
ProxyPassReverse  "/mirror/foo/" "https://backend.example.com/"
```

ProxyPassInherit Directive

Description:	Inherit ProxyPass directives defined from the main server
Syntax:	`ProxyPassInherit On|Off`
Default:	`ProxyPassInherit On`
Context:	server config, virtual host
Status:	Extension
Module:	mod_proxy
Compatibility:	ProxyPassInherit is only available in Apache HTTP Server 2.4.5 and later.

This directive will cause the current server/vhost to "inherit" PROXYPASS directives defined in the main server. This can cause issues and inconsistent behavior if using the Balancer Manager for dynamic changes and so should be disabled if using that feature.

The setting in the global server defines the default for all vhosts.

Disabling ProxyPassInherit also disables BALANCERINHERIT.

ProxyPassInterpolateEnv Directive

Description:	Enable Environment Variable interpolation in Reverse Proxy configurations
Syntax:	`ProxyPassInterpolateEnv On|Off`
Default:	`ProxyPassInterpolateEnv Off`
Context:	server config, virtual host, directory
Status:	Extension
Module:	mod_proxy
Compatibility:	Available in httpd 2.2.9 and later

This directive, together with the *interpolate* argument to PROXYPASS, PROXYPASSREVERSE, PROXYPASSREVERSECOOKIEDOMAIN, and PROXYPASSREVERSECOOKIEPATH, enables reverse proxies to be dynamically configured using environment variables which may be set by another module such as MOD_REWRITE. It affects the PROXYPASS, PROXYPASSREVERSE, PROXYPASSREVERSECOOKIEDOMAIN, and PROXYPASSREVERSECOOKIEPATH directives and causes them to substitute the value of an environment variable `varname` for the string `${varname}` in configuration directives if the *interpolate* option is set.

Keep this turned off (for server performance) unless you need it!

ProxyPassMatch Directive

Description:	Maps remote servers into the local server URL-space using regular expressions
Syntax:	`ProxyPassMatch [regex] !|url [key=value [key=value ...]]`
Context:	server config, virtual host, directory
Status:	Extension
Module:	mod_proxy

This directive is equivalent to PROXYPASS but makes use of regular expressions instead of simple prefix matching. The supplied regular expression is matched against the *url*, and if it matches, the server will substitute any parenthesized matches into the given string and use it as a new *url*.

Note: This directive cannot be used within a `<Directory>` context.

Suppose the local server has address `http://example.com/`; then

```
ProxyPassMatch "^/(.*\.gif)$" "http://backend.example.com/$1"
```

will cause a local request for `http://example.com/foo/bar.gif` to be internally converted into a proxy request to `http://backend.example.com/foo/bar.gif`.

Note

> The URL argument must be parsable as a URL *before* regexp substitutions (as well as after). This limits the matches you can use. For instance, if we had used
>
> ```
> ProxyPassMatch "^(/.*\.gif)$" "http://backend.example.com:8000$1"
> ```
>
> in our previous example, it would fail with a syntax error at server startup. This is a bug (PR 46665 in the ASF bugzilla), and the workaround is to reformulate the match:
>
> ```
> ProxyPassMatch "^/(.*\.gif)$" "http://backend.example.com:8000/$1"
> ```

The `!` directive is useful in situations where you don't want to reverse-proxy a subdirectory.

When used inside a <LOCATIONMATCH> section, the first argument is omitted and the regexp is obtained from the <LOCATIONMATCH>.

If you require a more flexible reverse-proxy configuration, see the REWRITERULE directive with the [P] flag.

**Default Substitution**

> When the URL parameter doesn't use any backreferences into the regular expression, the original URL will be appended to the URL parameter.

> ! **Security Warning**

> Take care when constructing the target URL of the rule, considering the security impact from allowing the client influence over the set of URLs to which your server will act as a proxy. Ensure that the scheme and hostname part of the URL is either fixed or does not allow the client undue influence.

ProxyPassReverse Directive

Description:	Adjusts the URL in HTTP response headers sent from a reverse proxied server
Syntax:	`ProxyPassReverse [path] url [interpolate]`
Context:	server config, virtual host, directory
Status:	Extension
Module:	mod_proxy

This directive lets Apache httpd adjust the URL in the `Location`, `Content-Location` and `URI` headers on HTTP redirect responses. This is essential when Apache httpd is used as a reverse proxy (or gateway) to avoid bypassing the reverse proxy because of HTTP redirects on the backend servers which stay behind the reverse proxy.

Only the HTTP response headers specifically mentioned above will be rewritten. Apache httpd will not rewrite other response headers, nor will it by default rewrite URL references inside HTML pages. This means that if the proxied content contains absolute URL references, they will bypass the proxy. To rewrite HTML content to match the proxy, you must load and enable MOD_PROXY_HTML.

path is the name of a local virtual path; *url* is a partial URL for the remote server. These parameters are used the same way as for the PROXYPASS directive.

For example, suppose the local server has address `http://example.com/`; then

```
ProxyPass         "/mirror/foo/" "http://backend.example.com/"
ProxyPassReverse  "/mirror/foo/" "http://backend.example.com/"
```

```
ProxyPassReverseCookieDomain  "backend.example.com"  "public.example.com"
ProxyPassReverseCookiePath  "/"  "/mirror/foo/"
```

will not only cause a local request for the `http://example.com/mirror/foo/bar` to be internally converted into a proxy request to `http://backend.example.com/bar` (the functionality which `ProxyPass` provides here). It also takes care of redirects which the server `backend.example.com` sends when redirecting `http://backend.example.com/bar` to `http://backend.example.com/quux`. Apache httpd adjusts this to `http://example.com/mirror/foo/quux` before forwarding the HTTP redirect response to the client. Note that the hostname used for constructing the URL is chosen in respect to the setting of the USECANONICALNAME directive.

Note that this PROXYPASSREVERSE directive can also be used in conjunction with the proxy feature (`RewriteRule ... [P]`) from MOD_REWRITE because it doesn't depend on a corresponding PROXYPASS directive.

The optional *interpolate* keyword, used together with PROXYPASSINTERPOLATEENV, enables interpolation of environment variables specified using the format *${VARNAME}*. Note that interpolation is not supported within the scheme portion of a URL.

When used inside a <LOCATION> section, the first argument is omitted and the local directory is obtained from the <LOCATION>. The same occurs inside a <LOCATIONMATCH> section, but will probably not work as intended, as ProxyPassReverse will interpret the regexp literally as a path; if needed in this situation, specify the ProxyPassReverse outside the section or in a separate <LOCATION> section.

This directive is not supported in <DIRECTORY> or <FILES> sections.

ProxyPassReverseCookieDomain Directive

Description:	Adjusts the Domain string in Set-Cookie headers from a reverse- proxied server
Syntax:	`ProxyPassReverseCookieDomain internal-domain public-domain [interpolate]`
Context:	server config, virtual host, directory
Status:	Extension
Module:	mod_proxy

Usage is basically similar to PROXYPASSREVERSE, but instead of rewriting headers that are a URL, this rewrites the `domain` string in `Set-Cookie` headers.

ProxyPassReverseCookiePath Directive

Description:	Adjusts the Path string in Set-Cookie headers from a reverse- proxied server
Syntax:	`ProxyPassReverseCookiePath internal-path public-path [interpolate]`
Context:	server config, virtual host, directory
Status:	Extension
Module:	mod_proxy

Useful in conjunction with PROXYPASSREVERSE in situations where backend URL paths are mapped to public paths on the reverse proxy. This directive rewrites the `path` string in `Set-Cookie` headers. If the beginning of the cookie path matches *internal-path*, the cookie path will be replaced with *public-path*.

In the example given with PROXYPASSREVERSE, the directive:

```
ProxyPassReverseCookiePath  "/"  "/mirror/foo/"
```

will rewrite a cookie with backend path `/` (or `/example` or, in fact, anything) to `/mirror/foo/`.

ProxyPreserveHost Directive

Description:	Use incoming Host HTTP request header for proxy request
Syntax:	`ProxyPreserveHost On|Off`
Default:	`ProxyPreserveHost Off`
Context:	server config, virtual host, directory
Status:	Extension
Module:	mod_proxy
Compatibility:	Usable in directory context in 2.3.3 and later.

When enabled, this option will pass the Host: line from the incoming request to the proxied host, instead of the hostname specified in the PROXYPASS line.

This option should normally be turned Off. It is mostly useful in special configurations like proxied mass name-based virtual hosting, where the original Host header needs to be evaluated by the backend server.

ProxyReceiveBufferSize Directive

Description:	Network buffer size for proxied HTTP and FTP connections
Syntax:	`ProxyReceiveBufferSize bytes`
Default:	`ProxyReceiveBufferSize 0`
Context:	server config, virtual host
Status:	Extension
Module:	mod_proxy

The PROXYRECEIVEBUFFERSIZE directive specifies an explicit (TCP/IP) network buffer size for proxied HTTP and FTP connections, for increased throughput. It has to be greater than 512 or set to 0 to indicate that the system's default buffer size should be used.

Example

```
ProxyReceiveBufferSize 2048
```

ProxyRemote Directive

Description:	Remote proxy used to handle certain requests
Syntax:	`ProxyRemote match remote-server`
Context:	server config, virtual host
Status:	Extension
Module:	mod_proxy

This defines remote proxies to this proxy. *match* is either the name of a URL-scheme that the remote server supports, or a partial URL for which the remote server should be used, or * to indicate the server should be contacted for all requests. *remote-server* is a partial URL for the remote server. Syntax:

```
remote-server = scheme://hostname[:port]
```

scheme is effectively the protocol that should be used to communicate with the remote server; only `http` and `https` are supported by this module. When using `https`, the requests are forwarded through the remote proxy using the HTTP CONNECT method.

Example

```
ProxyRemote "http://goodguys.example.com/" "http://mirrorguys.example.com:8000"
ProxyRemote "*" "http://cleverproxy.localdomain"
ProxyRemote "ftp" "http://ftpproxy.mydomain:8080"
```

In the last example, the proxy will forward FTP requests, encapsulated as yet another HTTP proxy request, to another proxy which can handle them.

This option also supports reverse proxy configuration; a backend webserver can be embedded within a virtualhost URL space even if that server is hidden by another forward proxy.

ProxyRemoteMatch Directive

Description:	Remote proxy used to handle requests matched by regular expressions
Syntax:	`ProxyRemoteMatch regex remote-server`
Context:	server config, virtual host
Status:	Extension
Module:	mod_proxy

The PROXYREMOTEMATCH is identical to the PROXYREMOTE directive, except that the first argument is a regular expression match against the requested URL.

ProxyRequests Directive

Description:	Enables forward (standard) proxy requests
Syntax:	`ProxyRequests On|Off`
Default:	`ProxyRequests Off`
Context:	server config, virtual host
Status:	Extension
Module:	mod_proxy

This allows or prevents Apache httpd from functioning as a forward proxy server. (Setting ProxyRequests to `Off` does not disable use of the PROXYPASS directive.)

In a typical reverse proxy or gateway configuration, this option should be set to `Off`.

In order to get the functionality of proxying HTTP or FTP sites, you need also MOD_PROXY_HTTP or MOD_PROXY_FTP (or both) present in the server.

In order to get the functionality of (forward) proxying HTTPS sites, you need MOD_PROXY_CONNECT enabled in the server.

 Warning

Do not enable proxying with PROXYREQUESTS until you have secured your server. Open proxy servers are dangerous both to your network and to the Internet at large.

See also

- Forward and Reverse Proxies/Gateways

ProxySet Directive

Description:	Set various Proxy balancer or member parameters
Syntax:	`ProxySet url key=value [key=value ...]`
Context:	directory
Status:	Extension
Module:	mod_proxy
Compatibility:	ProxySet is only available in Apache HTTP Server 2.2 and later.

This directive is used as an alternate method of setting any of the parameters available to Proxy balancers and workers normally done via the PROXYPASS directive. If used within a `<Proxy balancer url|worker url>` container directive, the *url* argument is not required. As a side effect the respective balancer or worker gets created. This can be useful when doing reverse proxying via a REWRITERULE instead of a PROXYPASS directive.

```
<Proxy "balancer://hotcluster">
    BalancerMember "http://www2.example.com:8080" loadfactor=1
    BalancerMember "http://www3.example.com:8080" loadfactor=2
    ProxySet lbmethod=bytraffic
</Proxy>
```

```
<Proxy "http://backend">
    ProxySet keepalive=On
</Proxy>
```

```
ProxySet "balancer://foo" lbmethod=bytraffic timeout=15
```

```
ProxySet "ajp://backend:7001" timeout=15
```

⚠ **Warning**

Keep in mind that the same parameter key can have a different meaning depending whether it is applied to a balancer or a worker, as shown by the two examples above regarding timeout.

ProxySourceAddress Directive

Description:	Set local IP address for outgoing proxy connections
Syntax:	`ProxySourceAddress address`
Context:	server config, virtual host
Status:	Extension
Module:	mod_proxy
Compatibility:	Available in version 2.3.9 and later

This directive allows to set a specific local address to bind to when connecting to a backend server.

ProxyStatus Directive

Description:	Show Proxy LoadBalancer status in mod_status
Syntax:	`ProxyStatus Off|On|Full`
Default:	`ProxyStatus Off`
Context:	server config, virtual host
Status:	Extension
Module:	mod_proxy
Compatibility:	Available in version 2.2 and later

This directive determines whether or not proxy loadbalancer status data is displayed via the MOD_STATUS server-status page.

⟹ **Note**

Full is synonymous with **On**

ProxyTimeout Directive

Description:	Network timeout for proxied requests
Syntax:	`ProxyTimeout seconds`
Default:	`Value of TIMEOUT`
Context:	server config, virtual host
Status:	Extension
Module:	mod_proxy

This directive allows a user to specifiy a timeout on proxy requests. This is useful when you have a slow/buggy appserver which hangs, and you would rather just return a timeout and fail gracefully instead of waiting however long it takes the server to return.

ProxyVia Directive

Description:	Information provided in the `Via` HTTP response header for proxied requests
Syntax:	`ProxyVia On|Off|Full|Block`
Default:	`ProxyVia Off`
Context:	server config, virtual host
Status:	Extension
Module:	mod_proxy

This directive controls the use of the `Via:` HTTP header by the proxy. Its intended use is to control the flow of proxy requests along a chain of proxy servers. See RFC 2616[60] (HTTP/1.1), section 14.45 for an explanation of `Via:` header lines.

- If set to `Off`, which is the default, no special processing is performed. If a request or reply contains a `Via:` header, it is passed through unchanged.

- If set to `On`, each request and reply will get a `Via:` header line added for the current host.

- If set to `Full`, each generated `Via:` header line will additionally have the Apache httpd server version shown as a `Via:` comment field.

- If set to `Block`, every proxy request will have all its `Via:` header lines removed. No new `Via:` header will be generated.

---

[60]http://www.ietf.org/rfc/rfc2616.txt

10.78 Apache Module mod_proxy_ajp

Description:	AJP support module for MOD_PROXY
Status:	Extension
ModuleIdentifier:	proxy_ajp_module
SourceFile:	mod_proxy_ajp.c
Compatibility:	Available in version 2.1 and later

Summary

This module *requires* the service of MOD_PROXY. It provides support for the Apache JServ Protocol version 1.3 (hereafter *AJP13*).

Thus, in order to get the ability of handling AJP13 protocol, MOD_PROXY and MOD_PROXY_AJP have to be present in the server.

 Warning
Do not enable proxying until you have secured your server (p. 732) . Open proxy servers are dangerous both to your network and to the Internet at large.

Directives This module provides no directives.

See also

- MOD_PROXY
- Environment Variable documentation (p. 82)

Usage

This module is used to reverse proxy to a backend application server (e.g. Apache Tomcat) using the AJP13 protocol. The usage is similar to an HTTP reverse proxy, but uses the ajp:// prefix:

Simple Reverse Proxy

```
ProxyPass "/app" "ajp://backend.example.com:8009/app"
```

Balancers may also be used:

Balancer Reverse Proxy

```
<Proxy "balancer://cluster">
    BalancerMember "ajp://app1.example.com:8009" loadfactor=1
    BalancerMember "ajp://app2.example.com:8009" loadfactor=2
    ProxySet lbmethod=bytraffic
</Proxy>
ProxyPass "/app" "balancer://cluster/app"
```

Note that usually no PROXYPASSREVERSE directive is necessary. The AJP request includes the original host header given to the proxy, and the application server can be expected to generate self-referential headers relative to this host, so no rewriting is necessary.

The main exception is when the URL path on the proxy differs from that on the backend. In this case, a redirect header can be rewritten relative to the original host URL (not the backend ajp:// URL), for example:

Rewriting Proxied Path

```
ProxyPass "/apps/foo" "ajp://backend.example.com:8009/foo"
ProxyPassReverse "/apps/foo" "http://www.example.com/foo"
```

However, it is usually better to deploy the application on the backend server at the same path as the proxy rather than to take this approach.

Environment Variables

Environment variables whose names have the prefix AJP_ are forwarded to the origin server as AJP request attributes (with the AJP_ prefix removed from the name of the key).

Overview of the protocol

The AJP13 protocol is packet-oriented. A binary format was presumably chosen over the more readable plain text for reasons of performance. The web server communicates with the servlet container over TCP connections. To cut down on the expensive process of socket creation, the web server will attempt to maintain persistent TCP connections to the servlet container, and to reuse a connection for multiple request/response cycles.

Once a connection is assigned to a particular request, it will not be used for any others until the request-handling cycle has terminated. In other words, requests are not multiplexed over connections. This makes for much simpler code at either end of the connection, although it does cause more connections to be open at once.

Once the web server has opened a connection to the servlet container, the connection can be in one of the following states:

- Idle
  No request is being handled over this connection.

- Assigned
  The connection is handling a specific request.

Once a connection is assigned to handle a particular request, the basic request information (e.g. HTTP headers, etc) is sent over the connection in a highly condensed form (e.g. common strings are encoded as integers). Details of that format are below in Request Packet Structure. If there is a body to the request (content-length > 0), that is sent in a separate packet immediately after.

At this point, the servlet container is presumably ready to start processing the request. As it does so, it can send the following messages back to the web server:

- SEND_HEADERS
  Send a set of headers back to the browser.

- SEND_BODY_CHUNK
  Send a chunk of body data back to the browser.

- GET_BODY_CHUNK
  Get further data from the request if it hasn't all been transferred yet. This is necessary because the packets have a fixed maximum size and arbitrary amounts of data can be included the body of a request (for uploaded files, for example). (Note: this is unrelated to HTTP chunked transfer).

- END_RESPONSE
  Finish the request-handling cycle.

Each message is accompanied by a differently formatted packet of data. See Response Packet Structures below for details.

Basic Packet Structure

There is a bit of an XDR heritage to this protocol, but it differs in lots of ways (no 4 byte alignment, for example).

AJP13 uses network byte order for all data types.

There are four data types in the protocol: bytes, booleans, integers and strings.

Byte A single byte.

Boolean A single byte, 1 = `true`, 0 = `false`. Using other non-zero values as true (i.e. C-style) may work in some places, but it won't in others.

Integer A number in the range of 0 to 2^16 (32768). Stored in 2 bytes with the high-order byte first.

String A variable-sized string (length bounded by 2^16). Encoded with the length packed into two bytes first, followed by the string (including the terminating '\0'). Note that the encoded length does **not** include the trailing '\0' – it is like `strlen`. This is a touch confusing on the Java side, which is littered with odd autoincrement statements to skip over these terminators. I believe the reason this was done was to allow the C code to be extra efficient when reading strings which the servlet container is sending back – with the terminating \0 character, the C code can pass around references into a single buffer, without copying. if the \0 was missing, the C code would have to copy things out in order to get its notion of a string.

Packet Size

According to much of the code, the max packet size is `8 * 1024 bytes (8K)`. The actual length of the packet is encoded in the header.

Packet Headers

Packets sent from the server to the container begin with `0x1234`. Packets sent from the container to the server begin with AB (that's the ASCII code for A followed by the ASCII code for B). After those first two bytes, there is an integer (encoded as above) with the length of the payload. Although this might suggest that the maximum payload could be as large as 2^16, in fact, the code sets the maximum to be 8K.

Packet Format (Server->Container)					
Byte	0	1	2	3	4...(n+3)
Contents	0x12	0x34	Data Length (n)	Data	

Packet Format (Container->Server)					
Byte	0	1	2	3	4...(n+3)
Contents	A	B	Data Length (n)	Data	

For most packets, the first byte of the payload encodes the type of message. The exception is for request body packets sent from the server to the container – they are sent with a standard packet header (`0x1234` and then length of the packet), but without any prefix code after that.

The web server can send the following messages to the servlet container:

Code	Type of Packet	Meaning
2	Forward Request	Begin the request-processing cycle with the following data
7	Shutdown	The web server asks the container to shut itself down.
8	Ping	The web server asks the container to take control (secur phase).
10	CPing	The web server asks the container to respond quickly CPong.
none	Data	Size (2 bytes) and corresponding body data.

To ensure some basic security, the container will only actually do the Shutdown if the request comes from the same machine on which it's hosted.

The first Data packet is send immediately after the Forward Request by the web server.

The servlet container can send the following types of messages to the webserver:

Code	Type of Packet	Meaning
3	Send Body Chunk	Send a chunk of the body from the servlet container to tl server (and presumably, onto the browser).
4	Send Headers	Send the response headers from the servlet container to tl server (and presumably, onto the browser).
5	End Response	Marks the end of the response (and thus the request-handl cle).
6	Get Body Chunk	Get further data from the request if it hasn't all been tran yet.
9	CPong Reply	The reply to a CPing request

Each of the above messages has a different internal structure, detailed below.

Request Packet Structure

For messages from the server to the container of type *Forward Request*:

```
AJP13_FORWARD_REQUEST :=
    prefix_code       (byte) 0x02 = JK_AJP13_FORWARD_REQUEST
    method            (byte)
    protocol          (string)
    req_uri           (string)
    remote_addr       (string)
    remote_host       (string)
    server_name       (string)
    server_port       (integer)
    is_ssl            (boolean)
    num_headers       (integer)
    request_headers  *(req_header_name req_header_value)
    attributes       *(attribut_name attribute_value)
    request_terminator (byte) 0xFF
```

The request_headers have the following structure:

```
req_header_name :=
    sc_req_header_name | (string)  [see below for how this is parsed]

sc_req_header_name := 0xA0xx (integer)

req_header_value := (string)
```

The `attributes` are optional and have the following structure:

```
attribute_name := sc_a_name | (sc_a_req_attribute string)

attribute_value := (string)
```

Not that the all-important header is `content-length`, because it determines whether or not the container looks for another packet immediately.

Detailed description of the elements of Forward Request

Request prefix

For all requests, this will be 2. See above for details on other Prefix codes.

Method

The HTTP method, encoded as a single byte:

Command Name	Code
OPTIONS	1
GET	2
HEAD	3
POST	4
PUT	5
DELETE	6
TRACE	7
PROPFIND	8
PROPPATCH	9
MKCOL	10
COPY	11
MOVE	12
LOCK	13
UNLOCK	14
ACL	15
REPORT	16
VERSION-CONTROL	17
CHECKIN	18
CHECKOUT	19
UNCHECKOUT	20
SEARCH	21
MKWORKSPACE	22
UPDATE	23
LABEL	24
MERGE	25
BASELINE_CONTROL	26
MKACTIVITY	27

Later version of ajp13, will transport additional methods, even if they are not in this list.

protocol, req_uri, remote_addr, remote_host, server_name, server_port, is_ssl

These are all fairly self-explanatory. Each of these is required, and will be sent for every request.

Headers

The structure of `request_headers` is the following: First, the number of headers `num_headers` is encoded. Then, a series of header name `req_header_name` / value `req_header_value` pairs follows. Common header names are encoded as integers, to save space. If the header name is not in the list of basic headers, it is encoded normally (as a string, with prefixed length). The list of common headers `sc_req_header_name` and their codes is as follows (all are case-sensitive):

Name	Code value	Code name
accept	0xA001	SC_REQ_ACCEPT
accept-charset	0xA002	SC_REQ_ACCEPT_CHARSET
accept-encoding	0xA003	SC_REQ_ACCEPT_ENCODING
accept-language	0xA004	SC_REQ_ACCEPT_LANGUAGE
authorization	0xA005	SC_REQ_AUTHORIZATION
connection	0xA006	SC_REQ_CONNECTION
content-type	0xA007	SC_REQ_CONTENT_TYPE
content-length	0xA008	SC_REQ_CONTENT_LENGTH
cookie	0xA009	SC_REQ_COOKIE
cookie2	0xA00A	SC_REQ_COOKIE2
host	0xA00B	SC_REQ_HOST
pragma	0xA00C	SC_REQ_PRAGMA
referer	0xA00D	SC_REQ_REFERER
user-agent	0xA00E	SC_REQ_USER_AGENT

The Java code that reads this grabs the first two-byte integer and if it sees an '0xA0' in the most significant byte, it uses the integer in the second byte as an index into an array of header names. If the first byte is not 0xA0, it assumes that the two-byte integer is the length of a string, which is then read in.

This works on the assumption that no header names will have length greater than 0x9FFF (==0xA000 - 1), which is perfectly reasonable, though somewhat arbitrary.

Note:

> The `content-length` header is extremely important. If it is present and non-zero, the container assumes that the request has a body (a POST request, for example), and immediately reads a separate packet off the input stream to get that body.

Attributes

The attributes prefixed with a ? (e.g. ?context) are all optional. For each, there is a single byte code to indicate the type of attribute, and then its value (string or integer). They can be sent in any order (though the C code always sends them in the order listed below). A special terminating code is sent to signal the end of the list of optional attributes. The list of byte codes is:

Information	Code Value	Type Of Value	Note
?context	0x01	-	Not currently implemented
?servlet_path	0x02	-	Not currently implemented
?remote_user	0x03	String	
?auth_type	0x04	String	
?query_string	0x05	String	
?jvm_route	0x06	String	
?ssl_cert	0x07	String	
?ssl_cipher	0x08	String	
?ssl_session	0x09	String	
?req_attribute	0x0A	String	Name (the name of the tribute follows)
?ssl_key_size	0x0B	Integer	
are_done	0xFF	-	request_terminator

The `context` and `servlet_path` are not currently set by the C code, and most of the Java code completely ignores whatever is sent over for those fields (and some of it will actually break if a string is sent along after one of those codes). I don't know if this is a bug or an unimplemented feature or just vestigial code, but it's missing from both sides of the connection.

The `remote_user` and `auth_type` presumably refer to HTTP-level authentication, and communicate the remote user's username and the type of authentication used to establish their identity (e.g. Basic, Digest).

The `query_string`, `ssl_cert`, `ssl_cipher`, and `ssl_session` refer to the corresponding pieces of HTTP and HTTPS.

The `jvm_route`, is used to support sticky sessions – associating a user's sesson with a particular Tomcat instance in the presence of multiple, load-balancing servers.

Beyond this list of basic attributes, any number of other attributes can be sent via the `req_attribute` code 0x0A. A pair of strings to represent the attribute name and value are sent immediately after each instance of that code. Environment values are passed in via this method.

Finally, after all the attributes have been sent, the attribute terminator, `0xFF`, is sent. This signals both the end of the list of attributes and also then end of the Request Packet.

Response Packet Structure

for messages which the container can send back to the server.

```
AJP13_SEND_BODY_CHUNK :=
  prefix_code    3
  chunk_length  (integer)
  chunk         *(byte)
  chunk_terminator (byte) 0x00


AJP13_SEND_HEADERS :=
  prefix_code       4
  http_status_code  (integer)
  http_status_msg   (string)
  num_headers       (integer)
  response_headers *(res_header_name header_value)

res_header_name :=
    sc_res_header_name | (string)   [see below for how this is parsed]

sc_res_header_name := 0xA0 (byte)

header_value := (string)

AJP13_END_RESPONSE :=
  prefix_code    5
  reuse          (boolean)


AJP13_GET_BODY_CHUNK :=
  prefix_code    6
  requested_length  (integer)
```

Details:

Send Body Chunk

The chunk is basically binary data, and is sent directly back to the browser.

Send Headers

The status code and message are the usual HTTP things (e.g. 200 and OK). The response header names are encoded the same way the request header names are. See header_encoding above for details about how the codes are distinguished from the strings.

The codes for common headers are:

Name	Code value
Content-Type	0xA001
Content-Language	0xA002
Content-Length	0xA003
Date	0xA004
Last-Modified	0xA005
Location	0xA006
Set-Cookie	0xA007
Set-Cookie2	0xA008
Servlet-Engine	0xA009
Status	0xA00A
WWW-Authenticate	0xA00B

After the code or the string header name, the header value is immediately encoded.

End Response

Signals the end of this request-handling cycle. If the `reuse` flag is true (`anything other than 0 in the actual C code`), this TCP connection can now be used to handle new incoming requests. If `reuse` is false (==0), the connection should be closed.

Get Body Chunk

The container asks for more data from the request (If the body was too large to fit in the first packet sent over or when the request is chunked). The server will send a body packet back with an amount of data which is the minimum of the `request_length`, the maximum send body size (`8186 (8 Kbytes - 6)`), and the number of bytes actually left to send from the request body.

If there is no more data in the body (i.e. the servlet container is trying to read past the end of the body), the server will send back an *empty* packet, which is a body packet with a payload length of 0. (`0x12,0x34,0x00,0x00`)

10.79   Apache Module mod_proxy_balancer

Description:	MOD_PROXY extension for load balancing
Status:	Extension
ModuleIdentifier:	proxy_balancer_module
SourceFile:	mod_proxy_balancer.c
Compatibility:	Available in version 2.1 and later

Summary

This module *requires* the service of MOD_PROXY. It provides load balancing support for HTTP, FTP and AJP13 protocols

Load balancing scheduler algorithm is provided by not this module but other modules such as: MOD_LBMETHOD_BYREQUESTS, MOD_LBMETHOD_BYTRAFFIC, MOD_LBMETHOD_BYBUSYNESS and MOD_LBMETHOD_HEARTBEAT.

Thus, in order to get the ability of load balancing, MOD_PROXY, MOD_PROXY_BALANCER and at least one of load balancing scheduler algorithm modules have to be present in the server.

 Warning

Do not enable proxying until you have secured your server (p. 732) . Open proxy servers are dangerous both to your network and to the Internet at large.

Directives This module provides no directives.

See also

- MOD_PROXY

Load balancer scheduler algorithm

At present, there are 3 load balancer scheduler algorithms available for use: Request Counting, Weighted Traffic Counting and Pending Request Counting. These are controlled via the lbmethod value of the Balancer definition. See the PROXYPASS directive for more information, especially regarding how to configure the Balancer and Balancer-Members.

Load balancer stickyness

The balancer supports stickyness. When a request is proxied to some back-end, then all following requests from the same user should be proxied to the same back-end. Many load balancers implement this feature via a table that maps client IP addresses to back-ends. This approach is transparent to clients and back-ends, but suffers from some problems: unequal load distribution if clients are themselves hidden behind proxies, stickyness errors when a client uses a dynamic IP address that changes during a session and loss of stickyness, if the mapping table overflows.

The module MOD_PROXY_BALANCER implements stickyness on top of two alternative means: cookies and URL encoding. Providing the cookie can be either done by the back-end or by the Apache web server itself. The URL encoding is usually done on the back-end.

Examples of a balancer configuration

Before we dive into the technical details, here's an example of how you might use MOD_PROXY_BALANCER to provide load balancing between two back-end servers:

```
<Proxy "balancer://mycluster">
    BalancerMember "http://192.168.1.50:80"
    BalancerMember "http://192.168.1.51:80"
</Proxy>
ProxyPass "/test" "balancer://mycluster"
ProxyPassReverse "/test" "balancer://mycluster"
```

Another example of how to provide load balancing with stickyness using MOD_HEADERS, even if the back-end server does not set a suitable session cookie:

```
Header add Set-Cookie "ROUTEID=.%{BALANCER_WORKER_ROUTE}e; path=/" env=BALANCER
<Proxy "balancer://mycluster">
    BalancerMember "http://192.168.1.50:80" route=1
    BalancerMember "http://192.168.1.51:80" route=2
    ProxySet stickysession=ROUTEID
</Proxy>
ProxyPass "/test" "balancer://mycluster"
ProxyPassReverse "/test" "balancer://mycluster"
```

Exported Environment Variables

At present there are 6 environment variables exported:

BALANCER_SESSION_STICKY This is assigned the *stickysession* value used for the current request. It is the name of the cookie or request parameter used for sticky sessions

BALANCER_SESSION_ROUTE This is assigned the *route* parsed from the current request.

BALANCER_NAME This is assigned the name of the balancer used for the current request. The value is something like balancer://foo.

BALANCER_WORKER_NAME This is assigned the name of the worker used for the current request. The value is something like http://hostA:1234.

BALANCER_WORKER_ROUTE This is assigned the *route* of the worker that will be used for the current request.

BALANCER_ROUTE_CHANGED This is set to 1 if the session route does not match the worker route (BALANCER_SESSION_ROUTE != BALANCER_WORKER_ROUTE) or the session does not yet have an established route. This can be used to determine when/if the client needs to be sent an updated route when sticky sessions are used.

Enabling Balancer Manager Support

This module *requires* the service of MOD_STATUS. Balancer manager enables dynamic update of balancer members. You can use balancer manager to change the balance factor of a particular member, or put it in the off line mode.

Thus, in order to get the ability of load balancer management, MOD_STATUS and MOD_PROXY_BALANCER have to be present in the server.

To enable load balancer management for browsers from the example.com domain add this code to your httpd.conf configuration file

```
<Location "/balancer-manager">
    SetHandler balancer-manager
    Require host example.com
</Location>
```

You can now access load balancer manager by using a Web browser to access the page `http://your.server.name/balancer-manager`. Please note that only Balancers defined outside of `<Location ...>` containers can be dynamically controlled by the Manager.

Details on load balancer stickyness

When using cookie based stickyness, you need to configure the name of the cookie that contains the information about which back-end to use. This is done via the *stickysession* attribute added to either PROXYPASS or PROXYSET. The name of the cookie is case-sensitive. The balancer extracts the value of the cookie and looks for a member worker with *route* equal to that value. The *route* must also be set in either PROXYPASS or PROXYSET. The cookie can either be set by the back-end, or as shown in the above example by the Apache web server itself.

Some back-ends use a slightly different form of stickyness cookie, for instance Apache Tomcat. Tomcat adds the name of the Tomcat instance to the end of its session id cookie, separated with a dot (.) from the session id. Thus if the Apache web server finds a dot in the value of the stickyness cookie, it only uses the part behind the dot to search for the route. In order to let Tomcat know about its instance name, you need to set the attribute `jvmRoute` inside the Tomcat configuration file `conf/server.xml` to the value of the *route* of the worker that connects to the respective Tomcat. The name of the session cookie used by Tomcat (and more generally by Java web applications based on servlets) is `JSESSIONID` (upper case) but can be configured to something else.

The second way of implementing stickyness is URL encoding. The web server searches for a query parameter in the URL of the request. The name of the parameter is specified again using *stickysession*. The value of the parameter is used to lookup a member worker with *route* equal to that value. Since it is not easy to extract and manipulate all URL links contained in responses, generally the work of adding the parameters to each link is done by the back-end generating the content. In some cases it might be feasible doing this via the web server using MOD_SUBSTITUTE or MOD_SED. This can have negative impact on performance though.

The Java standards implement URL encoding slightly different. They use a path info appended to the URL using a semicolon (;) as the separator and add the session id behind. As in the cookie case, Apache Tomcat can include the configured `jvmRoute` in this path info. To let Apache find this sort of path info, you neet to set `scolonpathdelim` to On in PROXYPASS or PROXYSET.

Finally you can support cookies and URL encoding at the same time, by configuring the name of the cookie and the name of the URL parameter separated by a vertical bar (|) as in the following example:

```
ProxyPass "/test" "balancer://mycluster" stickysession=JSESSIONID|jsessionid sc
<Proxy "balancer://mycluster">
    BalancerMember "http://192.168.1.50:80" route=node1
    BalancerMember "http://192.168.1.51:80" route=node2
</Proxy>
```

If the cookie and the request parameter both provide routing information for the same request, the information from the request parameter is used.

Troubleshooting load balancer stickyness

If you experience stickyness errors, e.g. users lose their application sessions and need to login again, you first want to check whether this is because the back-ends are sometimes unavailable or whether your configuration is wrong. To find out about possible stability problems with the back-ends, check your Apache error log for proxy error messages.

To verify your configuration, first check, whether the stickyness is based on a cookie or on URL encoding. Next step would be logging the appropriate data in the access log by using an enhanced LOGFORMAT. The following fields are useful:

%{MYCOOKIE}C The value contained in the cookie with name MYCOOKIE. The name should be the same given in the *stickysession* attribute.

%{Set-Cookie}o This logs any cookie set by the back-end. You can track, whether the back-end sets the session cookie you expect, and to which value it is set.

%{BALANCER_SESSION_STICKY}e The name of the cookie or request parameter used to lookup the routing information.

%{BALANCER_SESSION_ROUTE}e The route information found in the request.

%{BALANCER_WORKER_ROUTE}e The route of the worker chosen.

%{BALANCER_ROUTE_CHANGED}e Set to 1 if the route in the request is different from the route of the worker, i.e. the request couldn't be handled sticky.

Common reasons for loss of session are session timeouts, which are usually configurable on the back-end server.

The balancer also logs detailed information about handling stickyness to the error log, if the log level is set to debug or higher. This is an easy way to troubleshoot stickyness problems, but the log volume might be to high for production servers under high load.

10.80   Apache Module mod_proxy_connect

Description:	MOD_PROXY extension for CONNECT request handling
Status:	Extension
ModuleIdentifier:	proxy_connect_module
SourceFile:	mod_proxy_connect.c

Summary

This module *requires* the service of MOD_PROXY. It provides support for the CONNECT HTTP method. This method is mainly used to tunnel SSL requests through proxy servers.

Thus, in order to get the ability of handling CONNECT requests, MOD_PROXY and MOD_PROXY_CONNECT have to be present in the server.

CONNECT is also used when the server needs to send an HTTPS request through a forward proxy. In this case the server acts as a CONNECT client. This functionality is part of MOD_PROXY and MOD_PROXY_CONNECT is not needed in this case.

 Warning

Do not enable proxying until you have secured your server (p. 732). Open proxy servers are dangerous both to your network and to the Internet at large.

Directives

- AllowCONNECT

See also

- MOD_PROXY

Request notes

MOD_PROXY_CONNECT creates the following request notes for logging using the %{VARNAME}n format in LOGFOR-MAT or ERRORLOGFORMAT:

proxy-source-port The local port used for the connection to the backend server.

AllowCONNECT Directive

Description:	Ports that are allowed to CONNECT through the proxy
Syntax:	AllowCONNECT port[-port] [port[-port]] ...
Default:	AllowCONNECT 443 563
Context:	server config, virtual host
Status:	Extension
Module:	mod_proxy_connect
Compatibility:	Moved from MOD_PROXY in Apache 2.3.5. Port ranges available since Apache 2.3.7.

The ALLOWCONNECT directive specifies a list of port numbers or ranges to which the proxy CONNECT method may connect. Today's browsers use this method when a https connection is requested and proxy tunneling over HTTP is in effect.

By default, only the default https port (443) and the default snews port (563) are enabled. Use the ALLOWCON-NECT directive to override this default and allow connections to the listed ports only.

10.81 Apache Module mod_proxy_express

Description:	Dynamic mass reverse proxy extension for MOD_PROXY
Status:	Extension
ModuleIdentifier:	proxy_express_module
SourceFile:	mod_proxy_express.c

Summary

This module creates dynamically configured mass reverse proxies, by mapping the Host: header of the HTTP request to a server name and backend URL stored in a DBM file. This allows for easy use of a huge number of reverse proxies with no configuration changes. It is much less feature-full than MOD_PROXY_BALANCER, which also provides dynamic growth, but is intended to handle much, much larger numbers of backends. It is ideally suited as a front-end HTTP switch.

This module *requires* the service of MOD_PROXY.

 Warning
Do not enable proxying until you have secured your server (p. 732) . Open proxy servers are dangerous both to your network and to the Internet at large.

**Limitations**

- This module is not intended to replace the dynamic capability of MOD_PROXY_BALANCER. Instead, it is intended to be mostly a lightweight and fast alternative to using MOD_REWRITE with REWRITEMAP and the [P] flag for mapped reverse proxying.

- It does not support regex or pattern matching at all.

- It emulates:

```
<VirtualHost *:80>
    ServerName front.end.server
    ProxyPass "/" "back.end.server:port"
    ProxyPassReverse "/" "back.end.server:port"
</VirtualHost>
```

  That is, the entire URL is appended to the mapped backend URL. This is in keeping with the intent of being a simple but fast reverse proxy switch.

Directives

- ProxyExpressDBMFile
- ProxyExpressDBMType
- ProxyExpressEnable

See also

- MOD_PROXY·

ProxyExpressDBMFile Directive

Description:	Pathname to DBM file.
Syntax:	`ProxyExpressDBMFile <pathname>`
Default:	`None`
Context:	server config, virtual host
Status:	Extension
Module:	mod_proxy_express
Compatibility:	Available in Apache 2.3.13 and later

The PROXYEXPRESSDBMFILE directive points to the location of the Express map DBM file. This file serves to map the incoming server name, obtained from the Host: header, to a backend URL.

Note

The file is constructed from a plain text file format using the `httxt2dbm` `(p. 315)` utility.

ProxyExpress map file
```
##
##express-map.txt:
##
www1.example.com http://192.168.211.2:8080
www2.example.com http://192.168.211.12:8088
www3.example.com http://192.168.212.10
```

Create DBM file
```
httxt2dbm -i express-map.txt -o emap
```

Configuration
```
ProxyExpressEnable on
ProxyExpressDBMFile emap
```

ProxyExpressDBMType Directive

Description:	DBM type of file.
Syntax:	`ProxyExpressDBMFile <type>`
Default:	`"default"`
Context:	server config, virtual host
Status:	Extension
Module:	mod_proxy_express
Compatibility:	Available in Apache 2.3.13 and later

The PROXYEXPRESSDBMTYPE directive controls the DBM type expected by the module. The default is the default DBM type created with `httxt2dbm` `(p. 315)` .

Possible values are (not all may be available at run time):

Value	Description
db	Berkeley DB files
gdbm	GDBM files
ndbm	NDBM files
sdbm	SDBM files (always available)
default	default DBM type

ProxyExpressEnable Directive

Description:	Enable the module functionality.
Syntax:	ProxyExpressEnable [on|off]
Default:	off
Context:	server config, virtual host
Status:	Extension
Module:	mod_proxy_express
Compatibility:	Available in Apache 2.3.13 and later

The PROXYEXPRESSENABLE directive controls whether the module will be active.

10.82   Apache Module mod_proxy_fcgi

Description:	FastCGI support module for MOD_PROXY
Status:	Extension
ModuleIdentifier:	proxy_fcgi_module
SourceFile:	mod_proxy_fcgi.c
Compatibility:	Available in version 2.3 and later

Summary

This module *requires* the service of MOD_PROXY. It provides support for the FastCGI[61] protocol.

Thus, in order to get the ability of handling the FastCGI protocol, MOD_PROXY and MOD_PROXY_FCGI have to be present in the server.

Unlike mod_fcgid[62] and mod_fastcgi[63], MOD_PROXY_FCGI has no provision for starting the application process; fcgistarter is provided (on some platforms) for that purpose. Alternatively, external launching or process management may be available in the FastCGI application framework in use.

 Warning

Do not enable proxying until you have secured your server (p. 732) . Open proxy servers are dangerous both to your network and to the Internet at large.

Directives This module provides no directives.

See also

- fcgistarter
- MOD_PROXY
- MOD_AUTHNZ_FCGI

Examples

Remember, in order to make the following examples work, you have to enable MOD_PROXY and MOD_PROXY_FCGI.

Single application instance

```
ProxyPass "/myapp/" "fcgi://localhost:4000/"
```

MOD_PROXY_FCGI disables connection reuse by default, so after a request has been completed the connection will NOT be held open by that httpd child process and won't be reused. If the FastCGI application is able to handle concurrent connections from httpd, you can opt-in to connection reuse as shown in the following example:

Single application instance, connection reuse (2.4.11 and later)

```
ProxyPass "/myapp/" "fcgi://localhost:4000/" enablereuse=on
```

The following example passes the request URI as a filesystem path for the PHP-FPM daemon to run. The request URL is implicitly added to the 2nd parameter. The hostname and port following fcgi:// are where PHP-FPM is listening. Connection pooling is enabled.

---

[61]http://www.fastcgi.com/
[62]http://httpd.apache.org/mod_fcgid/
[63]http://www.fastcgi.com/

PHP-FPM

```
ProxyPassMatch "^/myapp/.*\.php(/.*)?$" "fcgi://localhost:9000/var/www/" enable
```

The following example passes the request URI as a filesystem path for the PHP-FPM daemon to run. In this case, PHP-FPM is listening on a unix domain socket (UDS). Requires 2.4.9 or later. With this syntax, the hostname and optional port following fcgi:// are ignored.

PHP-FPM with UDS

```
# UDS does not currently support connection reuse
ProxyPassMatch "^/(.*\.php(/.*)?)$" "unix:/var/run/php5-fpm.sock|fcgi://l
```

The balanced gateway needs MOD_PROXY_BALANCER and at least one load balancer algorithm module, such as MOD_LBMETHOD_BYREQUESTS, in addition to the proxy modules listed above. MOD_LBMETHOD_BYREQUESTS is the default, and will be used for this example configuration.

Balanced gateway to multiple application instances

```
ProxyPass "/myapp/" "balancer://myappcluster/"
<Proxy "balancer://myappcluster/">
    BalancerMember "fcgi://localhost:4000"
    BalancerMember "fcgi://localhost:4001"
</Proxy>
```

You can also force a request to be handled as a reverse-proxy request, by creating a suitable Handler pass-through. The example configuration below will pass all requests for PHP scripts to the specified FastCGI server using reverse proxy. This feature is available in Apache HTTP Server 2.4.10 and later. For performance reasons, you will want to define a worker (p. 732) representing the same fcgi:// backend. The benefit of this form is that it allows the normal mapping of URI to filename to occur in the server, and the local filesystem result is passed to the backend. When FastCGI is configured this way, the server can calculate the most accurate PATH_INFO.

Proxy via Handler

```
<FilesMatch "\.php$">
    # Note: The only part that varies is /path/to/app.sock
    SetHandler  "proxy:unix:/path/to/app.sock|fcgi://localhost/"
</FilesMatch>
    # Define a matching worker.
    # The part that is matched to the SetHandler is the part that
    # follows the pipe. If you need to distinguish, "localhost; can
    # be anything unique.
    <Proxy "fcgi://localhost/" enablereuse=on max=10>
    </Proxy>

<FilesMatch ...>
    SetHandler  "proxy:fcgi://localhost:9000"
</FilesMatch>

<FilesMatch ...>
    SetHandler  "proxy:balancer://myappcluster/"
</FilesMatch>
```

Environment Variables

In addition to the configuration directives that control the behaviour of MOD_PROXY, there are a number of *environment variables* that control the FCGI protocol provider:

proxy-fcgi-pathinfo When configured via PROXYPASS or PROXYPASSMATCH, MOD_PROXY_FCGI will not set the *PATH_INFO* environment variable. This allows the backend FCGI server to correctly determine *SCRIPT_NAME* and *Script-URI* and be compliant with RFC 3875 section 3.3. If instead you need MOD_PROXY_FCGI to generate a "best guess" for *PATH_INFO*, set this env-var. This is a workaround for a bug in some FCGI implementations. This variable can be set to multiple values to tweak at how the best guess is chosen (In 2.4.11 and later only):

> **first-dot** PATH_INFO is split from the slash following the *first* "." in the URL.
>
> **last-dot** PATH_INFO is split from the slash following the *last* "." in the URL.
>
> **full** PATH_INFO is calculated by an attempt to map the URL to the local filesystem.
>
> **unescape** PATH_INFO is the path component of the URL, unescaped / decoded.
>
> **any other value** PATH_INFO is the same as the path component of the URL. Originally, this was the only proxy-fcgi-pathinfo option.

10.83 Apache Module mod_proxy_fdpass

Description:	fdpass external process support module for MOD_PROXY
Status:	Extension
ModuleIdentifier:	proxy_fdpass_module
SourceFile:	mod_proxy_fdpass.c
Compatibility:	Available for unix in version 2.3 and later

Summary

This module *requires* the service of MOD_PROXY. It provides support for the passing the socket of the client to another process.

mod_proxy_fdpass uses the ability of AF_UNIX domain sockets to pass an open file descriptor[64] to allow another process to finish handling a request.

The module has a proxy_fdpass_flusher provider interface, which allows another module to optionally send the response headers, or even the start of the response body. The default flush provider disables keep-alive, and sends the response headers, letting the external process just send a response body.

At this time the only data passed to the external process is the client socket. To receive a client socket, call recvfrom with an allocated struct cmsghdr[65]. Future versions of this module may include more data after the client socket, but this is not implemented at this time.

Directives This module provides no directives.

See also

- MOD_PROXY

---

[64] http://www.freebsd.org/cgi/man.cgi?query=recv
[65] http://www.kernel.org/doc/man-pages/online/pages/man3/cmsg.3.html

10.84   Apache Module mod_proxy_ftp

Description:	FTP support module for MOD_PROXY
Status:	Extension
ModuleIdentifier:	proxy_ftp_module
SourceFile:	mod_proxy_ftp.c

Summary

This module *requires* the service of MOD_PROXY. It provides support for the proxying FTP sites. Note that FTP support is currently limited to the GET method.

Thus, in order to get the ability of handling FTP proxy requests, MOD_PROXY and MOD_PROXY_FTP have to be present in the server.

 Warning

Do not enable proxying until you have secured your server (p. 732) . Open proxy servers are dangerous both to your network and to the Internet at large.

Directives

- ProxyFtpDirCharset
- ProxyFtpEscapeWildcards
- ProxyFtpListOnWildcard

See also

- MOD_PROXY

Why doesn't file type *xxx* download via FTP?

You probably don't have that particular file type defined as application/octet-stream in your proxy's mime.types configuration file. A useful line can be

```
application/octet-stream   bin dms lha lzh exe class tgz taz
```

Alternatively you may prefer to default everything to binary:

```
ForceType application/octet-stream
```

How can I force an FTP ASCII download of File *xxx*?

In the rare situation where you must download a specific file using the FTP ASCII transfer method (while the default transfer is in binary mode), you can override MOD_PROXY's default by suffixing the request with ;type=a to force an ASCII transfer. (FTP Directory listings are always executed in ASCII mode, however.)

How can I do FTP upload?

Currently, only GET is supported for FTP in mod_proxy. You can of course use HTTP upload (POST or PUT) through an Apache proxy.

How can I access FTP files outside of my home directory?

An FTP URI is interpreted relative to the home directory of the user who is logging in. Alas, to reach higher directory levels you cannot use /../, as the dots are interpreted by the browser and not actually sent to the FTP server. To address this problem, the so called *Squid %2f hack* was implemented in the Apache FTP proxy; it is a solution which is also used by other popular proxy servers like the Squid Proxy Cache[66]. By prepending /%2f to the path of your request, you can make such a proxy change the FTP starting directory to / (instead of the home directory). For example, to retrieve the file /etc/motd, you would use the URL:

```
ftp://user@host/%2f/etc/motd
```

How can I hide the FTP cleartext password in my browser's URL line?

To log in to an FTP server by username and password, Apache uses different strategies. In absence of a user name and password in the URL altogether, Apache sends an anonymous login to the FTP server, *i.e.*,

```
user:  anonymous
password:  apache_proxy@
```

This works for all popular FTP servers which are configured for anonymous access.

For a personal login with a specific username, you can embed the user name into the URL, like in:

```
ftp://username@host/myfile
```

If the FTP server asks for a password when given this username (which it should), then Apache will reply with a 401 (Authorization required) response, which causes the Browser to pop up the username/password dialog. Upon entering the password, the connection attempt is retried, and if successful, the requested resource is presented. The advantage of this procedure is that your browser does not display the password in cleartext (which it would if you had used

```
ftp://username:password@host/myfile
```

in the first place).

Note
> The password which is transmitted in such a way is not encrypted on its way. It travels between your browser and the Apache proxy server in a base64-encoded cleartext string, and between the Apache proxy and the FTP server as plaintext. You should therefore think twice before accessing your FTP server via HTTP (or before accessing your personal files via FTP at all!) When using insecure channels, an eavesdropper might intercept your password on its way.

---

[66]http://www.squid-cache.org/

Why do I get a file listing when I expected a file to be downloaded?

In order to allow both browsing the directories on an FTP server and downloading files, Apache looks at the request URL. If it looks like a directory, or contains wildcard characters ("*?[{~"), then it guesses that a listing is wanted instead of a download.

You can disable the special handling of names with wildcard characters. See the PROXYFTPLISTONWILDCARD directive.

ProxyFtpDirCharset Directive

Description:	Define the character set for proxied FTP listings
Syntax:	`ProxyFtpDirCharset character set`
Default:	`ProxyFtpDirCharset ISO-8859-1`
Context:	server config, virtual host, directory
Status:	Extension
Module:	mod_proxy_ftp
Compatibility:	Available in Apache 2.2.7 and later. Moved from MOD_PROXY in Apache 2.3.5.

The PROXYFTPDIRCHARSET directive defines the character set to be set for FTP directory listings in HTML generated by MOD_PROXY_FTP.

ProxyFtpEscapeWildcards Directive

Description:	Whether wildcards in requested filenames are escaped when sent to the FTP server
Syntax:	`ProxyFtpEscapeWildcards [on|off]`
Default:	`on`
Context:	server config, virtual host, directory
Status:	Extension
Module:	mod_proxy_ftp
Compatibility:	Available in Apache 2.3.3 and later

The PROXYFTPESCAPEWILDCARDS directive controls whether wildcard characters ("*?[{~") in requested filenames are escaped with backslash before sending them to the FTP server. That is the default behavior, but many FTP servers don't know about the escaping and try to serve the literal filenames they were sent, including the backslashes in the names.

Set to "off" to allow downloading files with wildcards in their names from FTP servers that don't understand wildcard escaping.

ProxyFtpListOnWildcard Directive

Description:	Whether wildcards in requested filenames trigger a file listing
Syntax:	`ProxyFtpListOnWildcard [on|off]`
Default:	`on`
Context:	server config, virtual host, directory
Status:	Extension
Module:	mod_proxy_ftp
Compatibility:	Available in Apache 2.3.3 and later

The PROXYFTPLISTONWILDCARD directive controls whether wildcard characters ("*?[{~") in requested filenames cause MOD_PROXY_FTP to return a listing of files instead of downloading a file. By default (value on), they do. Set to "off" to allow downloading files even if they have wildcard characters in their names.

10.85 Apache Module mod_proxy_html

Description:	Rewrite HTML links in to ensure they are addressable from Clients' networks in a proxy context.
Status:	Base
ModuleIdentifier:	proxy_html_module
SourceFile:	mod_proxy_html.c
Compatibility:	Version 2.4 and later. Available as a third-party module for earlier 2.x versions

Summary

This module provides an output filter to rewrite HTML links in a proxy situation, to ensure that links work for users outside the proxy. It serves the same purpose as Apache's ProxyPassReverse directive does for HTTP headers, and is an essential component of a reverse proxy.

For example, if a company has an application server at `appserver.example.com` that is only visible from within the company's internal network, and a public webserver `www.example.com`, they may wish to provide a gateway to the application server at `http://www.example.com/appserver/`. When the application server links to itself, those links need to be rewritten to work through the gateway. mod_proxy_html serves to rewrite `<a href="http://appserver.example.com/foo/bar.html">foobar</a>` to `<a href="http://www.example.com/appserver/foo/bar.html">foobar</a>` making it accessible from outside.

mod_proxy_html was originally developed at Webing, whose extensive documentation[67] may be useful to users.

Directives

- ProxyHTMLBufSize
- ProxyHTMLCharsetOut
- ProxyHTMLDocType
- ProxyHTMLEnable
- ProxyHTMLEvents
- ProxyHTMLExtended
- ProxyHTMLFixups
- ProxyHTMLInterp
- ProxyHTMLLinks
- ProxyHTMLMeta
- ProxyHTMLStripComments
- ProxyHTMLURLMap

ProxyHTMLBufSize Directive

Description:	Sets the buffer size increment for buffering inline scripts and stylesheets.
Syntax:	`ProxyHTMLBufSize bytes`
Context:	server config, virtual host, directory
Status:	Base
Module:	mod_proxy_html
Compatibility:	Version 2.4 and later; available as a third-party for earlier 2.x versions

---

[67]http://apache.webthing.com/mod_proxy_html/

In order to parse non-HTML content (stylesheets and scripts) embedded in HTML documents, mod_proxy_html has to read the entire script or stylesheet into a buffer. This buffer will be expanded as necessary to hold the largest script or stylesheet in a page, in increments of *bytes* as set by this directive.

The default is 8192, and will work well for almost all pages. However, if you know you're proxying pages containing stylesheets and/or scripts bigger than 8K (that is, for a single script or stylesheet, NOT in total), it will be more efficient to set a larger buffer size and avoid the need to resize the buffer dynamically during a request.

ProxyHTMLCharsetOut Directive

Description:	Specify a charset for mod_proxy_html output.
Syntax:	`ProxyHTMLCharsetOut Charset	*`
Context:	server config, virtual host, directory
Status:	Base
Module:	mod_proxy_html
Compatibility:	Version 2.4 and later; available as a third-party for earlier 2.x versions

This selects an encoding for mod_proxy_html output. It should not normally be used, as any change from the default `UTF-8` (Unicode - as used internally by libxml2) will impose an additional processing overhead. The special token `ProxyHTMLCharsetOut *` will generate output using the same encoding as the input.

Note that this relies on MOD_XML2ENC being loaded.

ProxyHTMLDocType Directive

Description:	Sets an HTML or XHTML document type declaration.
Syntax:	`ProxyHTMLDocType HTML|XHTML [Legacy]`
	OR
	`ProxyHTMLDocType fpi [SGML|XML]`
Context:	server config, virtual host, directory
Status:	Base
Module:	mod_proxy_html
Compatibility:	Version 2.4 and later; available as a third-party for earlier 2.x versions

In the first form, documents will be declared as HTML 4.01 or XHTML 1.0 according to the option selected. This option also determines whether HTML or XHTML syntax is used for output. Note that the format of the documents coming from the backend server is immaterial: the parser will deal with it automatically. If the optional second argument is set to "Legacy", documents will be declared "Transitional", an option that may be necessary if you are proxying pre-1998 content or working with defective authoring/publishing tools.

In the second form, it will insert your own FPI. The optional second argument determines whether SGML/HTML or XML/XHTML syntax will be used.

The default is changed to omitting any FPI, on the grounds that no FPI is better than a bogus one. If your backend generates decent HTML or XHTML, set it accordingly.

If the first form is used, mod_proxy_html will also clean up the HTML to the specified standard. It cannot fix every error, but it will strip out bogus elements and attributes. It will also optionally log other errors at LOGLEVEL Debug.

ProxyHTMLEnable Directive

Description:	Turns the proxy_html filter on or off.
Syntax:	`ProxyHTMLEnable On|Off`
Default:	`ProxyHTMLEnable Off`
Context:	server config, virtual host, directory
Status:	Base
Module:	mod_proxy_html
Compatibility:	Version 2.4 and later; available as a third-party module for earlier 2.x versions.

A simple switch to enable or disable the proxy_html filter. If MOD_XML2ENC is loaded it will also automatically set up internationalisation support.

Note that the proxy_html filter will only act on HTML data (Content-Type text/html or application/xhtml+xml) and when the data are proxied. You can override this (at your own risk) by setting the *PROXY_HTML_FORCE* environment variable.

ProxyHTMLEvents Directive

Description:	Specify attributes to treat as scripting events.
Syntax:	`ProxyHTMLEvents attribute [attribute ...]`
Context:	server config, virtual host, directory
Status:	Base
Module:	mod_proxy_html
Compatibility:	Version 2.4 and later; available as a third-party for earlier 2.x versions

Specifies one or more attributes to treat as scripting events and apply PROXYHTMLURLMAPs to where enabled. You can specify any number of attributes in one or more `ProxyHTMLEvents` directives.

Normally you'll set this globally. If you set ProxyHTMLEvents in more than one scope so that one overrides the other, you'll need to specify a complete set in each of those scopes.

A default configuration is supplied in *proxy-html.conf* and defines the events in standard HTML 4 and XHTML 1.

ProxyHTMLExtended Directive

Description:	Determines whether to fix links in inline scripts, stylesheets, and scripting events.
Syntax:	`ProxyHTMLExtended On|Off`
Default:	`ProxyHTMLExtended Off`
Context:	server config, virtual host, directory
Status:	Base
Module:	mod_proxy_html
Compatibility:	Version 2.4 and later; available as a third-party for earlier 2.x versions

Set to `Off`, HTML links are rewritten according to the PROXYHTMLURLMAP directives, but links appearing in Javascript and CSS are ignored.

Set to `On`, all scripting events (as determined by PROXYHTMLEVENTS) and embedded scripts or stylesheets are also processed by the PROXYHTMLURLMAP rules, according to the flags set for each rule. Since this requires more parsing, performance will be best if you only enable it when strictly necessary.

You'll also need to take care over patterns matched, since the parser has no knowledge of what is a URL within an embedded script or stylesheet. In particular, extended matching of / is likely to lead to false matches.

ProxyHTMLFixups Directive

Description:	Fixes for simple HTML errors.
Syntax:	`ProxyHTMLFixups [lowercase] [dospath] [reset]`
Context:	server config, virtual host, directory
Status:	Base
Module:	mod_proxy_html
Compatibility:	Version 2.4 and later; available as a third-party for earlier 2.x versions

This directive takes one to three arguments as follows:

- `lowercase` Urls are rewritten to lowercase

- `dospath` Backslashes in URLs are rewritten to forward slashes.

- `reset` Unset any options set at a higher level in the configuration.

Take care when using these. The fixes will correct certain authoring mistakes, but risk also erroneously fixing links that were correct to start with. Only use them if you know you have a broken backend server.

ProxyHTMLInterp Directive

Description:	Enables per-request interpolation of PROXYHTMLURLMAP rules.
Syntax:	`ProxyHTMLInterp On|Off`
Default:	`ProxyHTMLInterp Off`
Context:	server config, virtual host, directory
Status:	Base
Module:	mod_proxy_html
Compatibility:	Version 2.4 and later; available as a third-party for earlier 2.x versions

This enables per-request interpolation in PROXYHTMLURLMAP to- and from- patterns.

If interpolation is not enabled, all rules are pre-compiled at startup. With interpolation, they must be re-compiled for every request, which implies an extra processing overhead. It should therefore be enabled only when necessary.

ProxyHTMLLinks Directive

Description:	Specify HTML elements that have URL attributes to be rewritten.
Syntax:	`ProxyHTMLLinks element attribute [attribute2 ...]`
Context:	server config, virtual host, directory
Status:	Base
Module:	mod_proxy_html
Compatibility:	Version 2.4 and later; available as a third-party for earlier 2.x versions

Specifies elements that have URL attributes that should be rewritten using standard PROXYHTMLURLMAPs. You will need one ProxyHTMLLinks directive per element, but it can have any number of attributes.

Normally you'll set this globally. If you set ProxyHTMLLinks in more than one scope so that one overrides the other, you'll need to specify a complete set in each of those scopes.

A default configuration is supplied in *proxy-html.conf* and defines the HTML links for standard HTML 4 and XHTML 1.

ProxyHTMLMeta Directive

Description:	Turns on or off extra pre-parsing of metadata in HTML <head> sections.
Syntax:	`ProxyHTMLMeta On|Off`
Default:	`ProxyHTMLMeta Off`
Context:	server config, virtual host, directory
Status:	Base
Module:	mod_proxy_html
Compatibility:	Version 2.4 and later; available as a third-party module for earlier 2.x versions.

This turns on or off pre-parsing of metadata in HTML <head> sections.

If not required, turning ProxyHTMLMeta Off will give a small performance boost by skipping this parse step. However, it is sometimes necessary for internationalisation to work correctly.

ProxyHTMLMeta has two effects. Firstly and most importantly it enables detection of character encodings declared in the form

```
<meta http-equiv="Content-Type" content="text/html;charset=foo">
```

or, in the case of an XHTML document, an XML declaration. It is NOT required if the charset is declared in a real HTTP header (which is always preferable) from the backend server, nor if the document is *utf-8* (unicode) or a subset such as ASCII. You may also be able to dispense with it where documents use a default declared using XML2ENCDEFAULT, but that risks propagating an incorrect declaration. A PROXYHTMLCHARSETOUT can remove that risk, but is likely to be a bigger processing overhead than enabling ProxyHTMLMeta.

The other effect of enabling ProxyHTMLMeta is to parse all <meta http-equiv=...> declarations and convert them to real HTTP headers, in keeping with the original purpose of this form of the HTML <meta> element.

ProxyHTMLStripComments Directive

Description:	Determines whether to strip HTML comments.
Syntax:	`ProxyHTMLStripComments On|Off`
Default:	`ProxyHTMLStripComments Off`
Context:	server config, virtual host, directory
Status:	Base
Module:	mod_proxy_html
Compatibility:	Version 2.4 and later; available as a third-party for earlier 2.x versions

This directive will cause mod_proxy_html to strip HTML comments. Note that this will also kill off any scripts or styles embedded in comments (a bogosity introduced in 1995/6 with Netscape 2 for the benefit of then-older browsers, but still in use today). It may also interfere with comment-based processors such as SSI or ESI: be sure to run any of those *before* mod_proxy_html in the filter chain if stripping comments!

ProxyHTMLURLMap Directive

Description:	Defines a rule to rewrite HTML links
Syntax:	`ProxyHTMLURLMap from-pattern to-pattern [flags] [cond]`
Context:	server config, virtual host, directory
Status:	Base
Module:	mod_proxy_html
Compatibility:	Version 2.4 and later; available as a third-party module for earlier 2.x versions.

This is the key directive for rewriting HTML links. When parsing a document, whenever a link target matches *from-pattern*, the matching portion will be rewritten to *to-pattern*, as modified by any flags supplied and by the PROXY-HTMLEXTENDED directive.

The optional third argument may define any of the following **Flags**. Flags are case-sensitive.

h Ignore HTML links (pass through unchanged)

e Ignore scripting events (pass through unchanged)

c Pass embedded script and style sections through untouched.

L Last-match. If this rule matches, no more rules are applied (note that this happens automatically for HTML links).

l Opposite to L. Overrides the one-change-only default behaviour with HTML links.

R Use Regular Expression matching-and-replace. `from-pattern` is a regexp, and `to-pattern` a replacement string that may be based on the regexp. Regexp memory is supported: you can use brackets () in the `from-pattern` and retrieve the matches with $1 to $9 in the `to-pattern`.

If R is not set, it will use string-literal search-and-replace. The logic is *starts-with* in HTML links, but *contains* in scripting events and embedded script and style sections.

x Use POSIX extended Regular Expressions. Only applicable with R.

i Case-insensitive matching. Only applicable with R.

n Disable regexp memory (for speed). Only applicable with R.

s Line-based regexp matching. Only applicable with R.

^ Match at start only. This applies only to string matching (not regexps) and is irrelevant to HTML links.

$ Match at end only. This applies only to string matching (not regexps) and is irrelevant to HTML links.

V Interpolate environment variables in `to-pattern`. A string of the form `${varname|default}` will be replaced by the value of environment variable `varname`. If that is unset, it is replaced by `default`. The `|default` is optional.

NOTE: interpolation will only be enabled if PROXYHTMLINTERP is *On*.

v Interpolate environment variables in `from-pattern`. Patterns supported are as above.

NOTE: interpolation will only be enabled if PROXYHTMLINTERP is *On*.

The optional fourth **cond** argument defines a condition that will be evaluated per Request, provided PROXYHTMLINTERP is *On*. If the condition evaluates FALSE the map will not be applied in this request. If TRUE, or if no condition is defined, the map is applied.

A **cond** is evaluated by the Expression Parser (p. 89) . In addition, the simpler syntax of conditions in mod_proxy_html 3.x for HTTPD 2.0 and 2.2 is also supported.

10.86 Apache Module mod_proxy_http

Description:	HTTP support module for MOD_PROXY
Status:	Extension
ModuleIdentifier:	proxy_http_module
SourceFile:	mod_proxy_http.c

Summary

This module *requires* the service of MOD_PROXY. It provides the features used for proxying HTTP and HTTPS requests. MOD_PROXY_HTTP supports HTTP/0.9, HTTP/1.0 and HTTP/1.1. It does *not* provide any caching abilities. If you want to set up a caching proxy, you might want to use the additional service of the MOD_CACHE module.

Thus, in order to get the ability of handling HTTP proxy requests, MOD_PROXY and MOD_PROXY_HTTP have to be present in the server.

Warning
Do not enable proxying until you have secured your server (p. 732) . Open proxy servers are dangerous both to your network and to the Internet at large.

Directives This module provides no directives.

See also

- MOD_PROXY
- MOD_PROXY_CONNECT

Environment Variables

In addition to the configuration directives that control the behaviour of MOD_PROXY, there are a number of *environment variables* that control the HTTP protocol provider. Environment variables below that don't specify specific values are enabled when set to any value.

proxy-sendextracrlf Causes proxy to send an extra CR-LF newline on the end of a request. This is a workaround for a bug in some browsers.

force-proxy-request-1.0 Forces the proxy to send requests to the backend as HTTP/1.0 and disables HTTP/1.1 features.

proxy-nokeepalive Forces the proxy to close the backend connection after each request.

proxy-chain-auth If the proxy requires authentication, it will read and consume the proxy authentication credentials sent by the client. With *proxy-chain-auth* it will *also* forward the credentials to the next proxy in the chain. This may be necessary if you have a chain of proxies that share authentication information. **Security Warning:** Do not set this unless you know you need it, as it forwards sensitive information!

proxy-sendcl HTTP/1.0 required all HTTP requests that include a body (e.g. POST requests) to include a *Content-Length* header. This environment variable forces the Apache proxy to send this header to the backend server, regardless of what the Client sent to the proxy. It ensures compatibility when proxying for an HTTP/1.0 or unknown backend. However, it may require the entire request to be buffered by the proxy, so it becomes very inefficient for large requests.

proxy-sendchunks or proxy-sendchunked This is the opposite of *proxy-sendcl*. It allows request bodies to be sent to the backend using chunked transfer encoding. This allows the request to be efficiently streamed, but requires that the backend server supports HTTP/1.1.

proxy-interim-response This variable takes values `RFC` (the default) or `Suppress`. Earlier httpd versions would suppress HTTP interim (1xx) responses sent from the backend. This is technically a violation of the HTTP protocol. In practice, if a backend sends an interim response, it may itself be extending the protocol in a manner we know nothing about, or just broken. So this is now configurable: set `proxy-interim-response RFC` to be fully protocol compliant, or `proxy-interim-response Suppress` to suppress interim responses.

proxy-initial-not-pooled If this variable is set, no pooled connection will be reused if the client request is the initial request on the frontend connection. This avoids the `"proxy: error reading status line from remote server"` error message caused by the race condition that the backend server closed the pooled connection after the connection check by the proxy and before data sent by the proxy reached the backend. It has to be kept in mind that setting this variable downgrades performance, especially with HTTP/1.0 clients.

Request notes

MOD_PROXY_HTTP creates the following request notes for logging using the `%{VARNAME}n` format in LOGFORMAT or ERRORLOGFORMAT:

proxy-source-port The local port used for the connection to the backend server.

proxy-status The HTTP status received from the backend server.

10.87 Apache Module mod_proxy_scgi

Description:	SCGI gateway module for MOD_PROXY
Status:	Extension
ModuleIdentifier:	proxy_scgi_module
SourceFile:	mod_proxy_scgi.c
Compatibility:	Available in version 2.2.14 and later

Summary

This module *requires* the service of MOD_PROXY. It provides support for the SCGI protocol, version 1[68].

Thus, in order to get the ability of handling the SCGI protocol, MOD_PROXY and MOD_PROXY_SCGI have to be present in the server.

 Warning

Do not enable proxying until you have secured your server (p. 732) . Open proxy servers are dangerous both to your network and to the Internet at large.

Directives

- ProxySCGIInternalRedirect
- ProxySCGISendfile

See also

- MOD_PROXY
- MOD_PROXY_BALANCER

Examples

Remember, in order to make the following examples work, you have to enable MOD_PROXY and MOD_PROXY_SCGI.

Simple gateway

```
ProxyPass /scgi-bin/ scgi://localhost:4000/
```

The balanced gateway needs MOD_PROXY_BALANCER and at least one load balancer algorithm module, such as MOD_LBMETHOD_BYREQUESTS, in addition to the proxy modules listed above. MOD_LBMETHOD_BYREQUESTS is the default, and will be used for this example configuration.

Balanced gateway

```
ProxyPass "/scgi-bin/" "balancer://somecluster/"
<Proxy "balancer://somecluster">
    BalancerMember "scgi://localhost:4000"
    BalancerMember "scgi://localhost:4001"
</Proxy>
```

---

[68]http://python.ca/scgi/protocol.txt

Environment Variables

In addition to the configuration directives that control the behaviour of MOD_PROXY, an *environment variable* may also control the SCGI protocol provider:

proxy-scgi-pathinfo By default MOD_PROXY_SCGI will neither create nor export the *PATH_INFO* environment variable. This allows the backend SCGI server to correctly determine *SCRIPT_NAME* and *Script-URI* and be compliant with RFC 3875 section 3.3. If instead you need MOD_PROXY_SCGI to generate a "best guess" for *PATH_INFO*, set this env-var. The variable must be set before SETENV is effective. SETENVIF can be used instead: `SetEnvIf Request_URI . proxy-scgi-pathinfo`

ProxySCGIInternalRedirect Directive

Description:	Enable or disable internal redirect responses from the backend
Syntax:	`ProxySCGIInternalRedirect On|Off|Headername`
Default:	`ProxySCGIInternalRedirect On`
Context:	server config, virtual host, directory
Status:	Extension
Module:	mod_proxy_scgi
Compatibility:	The *Headername* feature is available in version 2.4.13 and later

The PROXYSCGIINTERNALREDIRECT enables the backend to internally redirect the gateway to a different URL. This feature originates in MOD_CGI, which internally redirects the response if the response status is OK (200) and the response contains a `Location` (or configured alternate header) and its value starts with a slash (/). This value is interpreted as a new local URL that Apache httpd internally redirects to.

MOD_PROXY_SCGI does the same as MOD_CGI in this regard, except that you can turn off the feature or specify the use of a header other than `Location`.

Example

```
ProxySCGIInternalRedirect Off

# Django and some other frameworks will fully qualify "local URLs"
# set by the application, so an alternate header must be used.
<Location /django-app/>
    ProxySCGIInternalRedirect X-Location
</Location>
```

ProxySCGISendfile Directive

Description:	Enable evaluation of *X-Sendfile* pseudo response header
Syntax:	`ProxySCGISendfile On|Off|Headername`
Default:	`ProxySCGISendfile Off`
Context:	server config, virtual host, directory
Status:	Extension
Module:	mod_proxy_scgi

The PROXYSCGISENDFILE directive enables the SCGI backend to let files be served directly by the gateway. This is useful for performance purposes - httpd can use `sendfile` or other optimizations, which are not possible if the file comes over the backend socket. Additionally, the file contents are not transmitted twice.

The PROXYSCGISENDFILE argument determines the gateway behaviour:

Off No special handling takes place.

On The gateway looks for a backend response header called `X-Sendfile` and interprets the value as the filename to serve. The header is removed from the final response headers. This is equivalent to `ProxySCGISendfile X-Sendfile`.

anything else Similar to `On`, but instead of the hardcoded header name `X-Sendfile`, the argument is used as the header name.

Example

```
# Use the default header (X-Sendfile)
ProxySCGISendfile On

# Use a different header
ProxySCGISendfile X-Send-Static
```

10.88   Apache Module mod_proxy_wstunnel

Description:	Websockets support module for MOD_PROXY
Status:	Extension
ModuleIdentifier:	proxy_wstunnel_module
SourceFile:	mod_proxy_wstunnel.c
Compatibility:	Available in httpd 2.4.5 and later

Summary

This module *requires* the service of MOD_PROXY. It provides support for the tunnelling of web socket connections to a backend websockets server. The connection is automagically upgraded to a websocket connection:

```
Upgrade: WebSocket
Connection: Upgrade
```

Proxying requests to websockets server

```
ProxyPass "/ws2/"  "ws://echo.websocket.org/"
ProxyPass "/wss2/" "wss://echo.websocket.org/"
```

Directives This module provides no directives.

See also

- MOD_PROXY

10.89   Apache Module mod_ratelimit

Description:	Bandwidth Rate Limiting for Clients
Status:	Extension
ModuleIdentifier:	ratelimit_module
SourceFile:	mod_ratelimit.c

Summary

Provides a filter named RATE_LIMIT to limit client bandwidth. The connection speed to be simulated is specified, in KiB/s, using the environment variable rate-limit.

Example Configuration

```
<Location "/downloads">
    SetOutputFilter RATE_LIMIT
    SetEnv rate-limit 400
</Location>
```

Directives This module provides no directives.

10.90   Apache Module mod_reflector

Description:	Reflect a request body as a response via the output filter stack.
Status:	Base
ModuleIdentifier:	reflector_module
SourceFile:	mod_reflector.c
Compatibility:	Version 2.3 and later

Summary

This module allows request bodies to be reflected back to the client, in the process passing the request through the output filter stack. A suitably configured chain of filters can be used to transform the request into a response. This module can be used to turn an output filter into an HTTP service.

Directives

- ReflectorHeader

Examples

Compression service Pass the request body through the DEFLATE filter to compress the body. This request requires a Content-Encoding request header containing "gzip" for the filter to return compressed data.

```
<Location "/compress">
    SetHandler reflector
    SetOutputFilter DEFLATE
</Location>
```

Image downsampling service Pass the request body through an image downsampling filter, and reflect the results to the caller.

```
<Location "/downsample">
    SetHandler reflector
    SetOutputFilter DOWNSAMPLE
</Location>
```

ReflectorHeader Directive

Description:	Reflect an input header to the output headers
Syntax:	`ReflectorHeader inputheader [outputheader]`
Context:	server config, virtual host, directory, .htaccess
Override:	Options
Status:	Base
Module:	mod_reflector

This directive controls the reflection of request headers to the response. The first argument is the name of the request header to copy. If the optional second argument is specified, it will be used as the name of the response header, otherwise the original request header name will be used.

10.91 Apache Module mod_remoteip

Description:	Replaces the original client IP address for the connection with the useragent IP address list presented by a proxies or a load balancer via the request headers.
Status:	Base
ModuleIdentifier:	remoteip_module
SourceFile:	mod_remoteip.c

Summary

This module is used to treat the useragent which initiated the request as the originating useragent as identified by httpd for the purposes of authorization and logging, even where that useragent is behind a load balancer, front end server, or proxy server.

The module overrides the client IP address for the connection with the useragent IP address reported in the request header configured with the REMOTEIPHEADER directive.

Once replaced as instructed, this overridden useragent IP address is then used for the MOD_AUTHZ_HOST REQUIRE IP feature, is reported by MOD_STATUS, and is recorded by MOD_LOG_CONFIG %a and CORE %a format strings. The underlying client IP of the connection is available in the %{c}a format string.

> ! It is critical to only enable this behavior from intermediate hosts (proxies, etc) which are trusted by this server, since it is trivial for the remote useragent to impersonate another useragent.

Directives

- RemoteIPHeader
- RemoteIPInternalProxy
- RemoteIPInternalProxyList
- RemoteIPProxiesHeader
- RemoteIPTrustedProxy
- RemoteIPTrustedProxyList

See also

- MOD_AUTHZ_HOST
- MOD_STATUS
- MOD_LOG_CONFIG

Remote IP Processing

Apache by default identifies the useragent with the connection's client_ip value, and the connection remote_host and remote_logname are derived from this value. These fields play a role in authentication, authorization and logging and other purposes by other loadable modules.

mod_remoteip overrides the client IP of the connection with the advertised useragent IP as provided by a proxy or load balancer, for the duration of the request. A load balancer might establish a long lived keepalive connection with the server, and each request will have the correct useragent IP, even though the underlying client IP address of the load balancer remains unchanged.

When multiple, comma delimited useragent IP addresses are listed in the header value, they are processed in Right-to-Left order. Processing halts when a given useragent IP address is not trusted to present the preceding IP address. The header field is updated to this remaining list of unconfirmed IP addresses, or if all IP addresses were trusted, this header is removed from the request altogether.

In overriding the client IP, the module stores the list of intermediate hosts in a remoteip-proxy-ip-list note, which MOD_LOG_CONFIG can record using the %{remoteip-proxy-ip-list}n format token. If the administrator needs to store this as an additional header, this same value can also be recording as a header using the directive REMOTEIPPROXIESHEADER.

 IPv4-over-IPv6 Mapped Addresses
As with httpd in general, any IPv4-over-IPv6 mapped addresses are recorded in their IPv4 representation.

Internal (Private) Addresses
All internal addresses 10/8, 172.16/12, 192.168/16, 169.254/16 and 127/8 blocks (and IPv6 addresses outside of the public 2000::/3 block) are only evaluated by mod_remoteip when REMOTEIPINTERNALPROXY internal (intranet) proxies are registered.

RemoteIPHeader Directive

Description:	Declare the header field which should be parsed for useragent IP addresses
Syntax:	RemoteIPHeader header-field
Context:	server config, virtual host
Status:	Base
Module:	mod_remoteip

The REMOTEIPHEADER directive triggers MOD_REMOTEIP to treat the value of the specified *header-field* header as the useragent IP address, or list of intermediate useragent IP addresses, subject to further configuration of the REMOTEIPINTERNALPROXY and REMOTEIPTRUSTEDPROXY directives. Unless these other directives are used, MOD_REMOTEIP will trust all hosts presenting a REMOTEIPHEADER IP value.

Internal (Load Balancer) Example

```
RemoteIPHeader X-Client-IP
```

Proxy Example

```
RemoteIPHeader X-Forwarded-For
```

RemoteIPInternalProxy Directive

Description:	Declare client intranet IP addresses trusted to present the RemoteIPHeader value
Syntax:	RemoteIPInternalProxy proxy-ip|proxy-ip/subnet|hostname ...
Context:	server config, virtual host
Status:	Base
Module:	mod_remoteip

The REMOTEIPINTERNALPROXY directive adds one or more addresses (or address blocks) to trust as presenting a valid RemoteIPHeader value of the useragent IP. Unlike the REMOTEIPTRUSTEDPROXY directive, any IP address presented in this header, including private intranet addresses, are trusted when passed from these proxies.

Internal (Load Balancer) Example

```
RemoteIPHeader X-Client-IP
RemoteIPInternalProxy 10.0.2.0/24
RemoteIPInternalProxy gateway.localdomain
```

RemoteIPInternalProxyList Directive

Description:	Declare client intranet IP addresses trusted to present the RemoteIPHeader value
Syntax:	`RemoteIPInternalProxyList filename`
Context:	server config, virtual host
Status:	Base
Module:	mod_remoteip

The REMOTEIPINTERNALPROXYLIST directive specifies a file parsed at startup, and builds a list of addresses (or address blocks) to trust as presenting a valid RemoteIPHeader value of the useragent IP.

The '#' hash character designates a comment line, otherwise each whitespace or newline separated entry is processed identically to the REMOTEIPINTERNALPROXY directive.

Internal (Load Balancer) Example

```
RemoteIPHeader X-Client-IP
RemoteIPInternalProxyList conf/trusted-proxies.lst
```

conf/trusted-proxies.lst contents

```
# Our internally trusted proxies;
10.0.2.0/24         #Everyone in the testing group
gateway.localdomain #The front end balancer
```

RemoteIPProxiesHeader Directive

Description:	Declare the header field which will record all intermediate IP addresses
Syntax:	`RemoteIPProxiesHeader HeaderFieldName`
Context:	server config, virtual host
Status:	Base
Module:	mod_remoteip

The REMOTEIPPROXIESHEADER directive specifies a header into which MOD_REMOTEIP will collect a list of all of the intermediate client IP addresses trusted to resolve the useragent IP of the request. Note that intermediate REMOTEIPTRUSTEDPROXY addresses are recorded in this header, while any intermediate REMOTEIPINTERNALPROXY addresses are discarded.

Example

```
RemoteIPHeader X-Forwarded-For
RemoteIPProxiesHeader X-Forwarded-By
```

RemoteIPTrustedProxy Directive

Description:	Declare client intranet IP addresses trusted to present the RemoteIPHeader value
Syntax:	`RemoteIPTrustedProxy proxy-ip|proxy-ip/subnet|hostname ...`
Context:	server config, virtual host
Status:	Base
Module:	mod_remoteip

The REMOTEIPTRUSTEDPROXY directive adds one or more addresses (or address blocks) to trust as presenting a valid RemoteIPHeader value of the useragent IP. Unlike the REMOTEIPINTERNALPROXY directive, any intranet or private IP address reported by such proxies, including the 10/8, 172.16/12, 192.168/16, 169.254/16 and 127/8 blocks (or outside of the IPv6 public 2000::/3 block) are not trusted as the useragent IP, and are left in the REMOTEIPHEADER header's value.

Trusted (Load Balancer) Example

```
RemoteIPHeader X-Forwarded-For
RemoteIPTrustedProxy 10.0.2.16/28
RemoteIPTrustedProxy proxy.example.com
```

RemoteIPTrustedProxyList Directive

Description:	Declare client intranet IP addresses trusted to present the RemoteIPHeader value
Syntax:	`RemoteIPTrustedProxyList filename`
Context:	server config, virtual host
Status:	Base
Module:	mod_remoteip

The REMOTEIPTRUSTEDPROXYLIST directive specifies a file parsed at startup, and builds a list of addresses (or address blocks) to trust as presenting a valid RemoteIPHeader value of the useragent IP.

The '#' hash character designates a comment line, otherwise each whitespace or newline separated entry is processed identically to the REMOTEIPTRUSTEDPROXY directive.

Trusted (Load Balancer) Example

```
RemoteIPHeader X-Forwarded-For
RemoteIPTrustedProxyList conf/trusted-proxies.lst
```

conf/trusted-proxies.lst contents
```
# Identified external proxies;
192.0.2.16/28 #wap phone group of proxies
proxy.isp.example.com #some well known ISP
```

10.92 Apache Module mod_reqtimeout

Description:	Set timeout and minimum data rate for receiving requests
Status:	Extension
ModuleIdentifier:	reqtimeout_module
SourceFile:	mod_reqtimeout.c
Compatibility:	Available in Apache HTTPD 2.2.15 and later

Directives

- RequestReadTimeout

Examples

1. Allow 10 seconds to receive the request including the headers and 30 seconds for receiving the request body:

   ```
   RequestReadTimeout header=10 body=30
   ```

2. Allow at least 10 seconds to receive the request body. If the client sends data, increase the timeout by 1 second for every 1000 bytes received, with no upper limit for the timeout (except for the limit given indirectly by LIMITREQUESTBODY):

   ```
   RequestReadTimeout body=10,MinRate=1000
   ```

3. Allow at least 10 seconds to receive the request including the headers. If the client sends data, increase the timeout by 1 second for every 500 bytes received. But do not allow more than 30 seconds for the request including the headers:

   ```
   RequestReadTimeout header=10-30,MinRate=500
   ```

4. Usually, a server should have both header and body timeouts configured. If a common configuration is used for http and https virtual hosts, the timeouts should not be set too low:

   ```
   RequestReadTimeout header=20-40,MinRate=500 body=20,MinRate=500
   ```

RequestReadTimeout Directive

Description:	Set timeout values for receiving request headers and body from client.
Syntax:	RequestReadTimeout [header=timeout[-maxtimeout][,MinRate=rate] [body=timeout[-maxtimeout][,MinRate=rate]
Default:	header=20-40,MinRate=500 body=20,MinRate=500
Context:	server config, virtual host
Status:	Extension
Module:	mod_reqtimeout
Compatibility:	Available in version 2.2.15 and later; defaulted to disabled in version 2.3.14 and earlier.

This directive can set various timeouts for receiving the request headers and the request body from the client. If the client fails to send headers or body within the configured time, a 408 REQUEST TIME OUT error is sent.

For SSL virtual hosts, the header timeout values include the time needed to do the initial SSL handshake. If the user's browser is configured to query certificate revocation lists and the CRL server is not reachable, the initial SSL handshake may take a significant time until the browser gives up waiting for the CRL. Therefore the header timeout values should not be set to very low values for SSL virtual hosts. The body timeout values include the time needed for SSL renegotiation (if necessary).

When an ACCEPTFILTER is in use (usually the case on Linux and FreeBSD), the socket is not sent to the server process before at least one byte (or the whole request for httpready) is received. The header timeout configured with RequestReadTimeout is only effective after the server process has received the socket.

For each of the two timeout types (header or body), there are three ways to specify the timeout:

- **Fixed timeout value**:

```
type=timeout
```

The time in seconds allowed for reading all of the request headers or body, respectively. A value of 0 means no limit.

- **Disable module for a vhost:**:

```
header=0 body=0
```

This disables MOD_REQTIMEOUT completely.

- **Timeout value that is increased when data is received**:

```
type=timeout,MinRate=data_rate
```

Same as above, but whenever data is received, the timeout value is increased according to the specified minimum data rate (in bytes per second).

- **Timeout value that is increased when data is received, with an upper bound**:

```
type=timeout-maxtimeout,MinRate=data_rate
```

Same as above, but the timeout will not be increased above the second value of the specified timeout range.

10.93 Apache Module mod_request

Description:	Filters to handle and make available HTTP request bodies
Status:	Base
ModuleIdentifier:	request_module
SourceFile:	mod_request.c
Compatibility:	Available in Apache 2.3 and later

Directives

- KeptBodySize

KeptBodySize Directive

Description:	Keep the request body instead of discarding it up to the specified maximum size, for potential use by filters such as mod_include.
Syntax:	KeptBodySize maximum size in bytes
Default:	KeptBodySize 0
Context:	directory
Status:	Base
Module:	mod_request

Under normal circumstances, request handlers such as the default handler for static files will discard the request body when it is not needed by the request handler. As a result, filters such as mod_include are limited to making GET requests only when including other URLs as subrequests, even if the original request was a POST request, as the discarded request body is no longer available once filter processing is taking place.

When this directive has a value greater than zero, request handlers that would otherwise discard request bodies will instead set the request body aside for use by filters up to the maximum size specified. In the case of the mod_include filter, an attempt to POST a request to the static shtml file will cause any subrequests to be POST requests, instead of GET requests as before.

This feature makes it possible to break up complex web pages and web applications into small individual components, and combine the components and the surrounding web page structure together using MOD_INCLUDE. The components can take the form of CGI programs, scripted languages, or URLs reverse proxied into the URL space from another server using MOD_PROXY.

Note: Each request set aside has to be set aside in temporary RAM until the request is complete. As a result, care should be taken to ensure sufficient RAM is available on the server to support the intended load. Use of this directive should be limited to where needed on targeted parts of your URL space, and with the lowest possible value that is still big enough to hold a request body.

If the request size sent by the client exceeds the maximum size allocated by this directive, the server will return 413 Request Entity Too Large.

See also

- mod_include (p. 624) documentation
- mod_auth_form (p. 435) documentation

10.94   Apache Module mod_rewrite

Description:	Provides a rule-based rewriting engine to rewrite requested URLs on the fly
Status:	Extension
ModuleIdentifier:	rewrite_module
SourceFile:	mod_rewrite.c

Summary

The MOD_REWRITE module uses a rule-based rewriting engine, based on a PCRE regular-expression parser, to rewrite requested URLs on the fly. By default, MOD_REWRITE maps a URL to a filesystem path. However, it can also be used to redirect one URL to another URL, or to invoke an internal proxy fetch.

MOD_REWRITE provides a flexible and powerful way to manipulate URLs using an unlimited number of rules. Each rule can have an unlimited number of attached rule conditions, to allow you to rewrite URL based on server variables, environment variables, HTTP headers, or time stamps.

MOD_REWRITE operates on the full URL path, including the path-info section. A rewrite rule can be invoked in httpd.conf or in .htaccess. The path generated by a rewrite rule can include a query string, or can lead to internal sub-processing, external request redirection, or internal proxy throughput.

Further details, discussion, and examples, are provided in the detailed mod_rewrite documentation (p. 136) .

Directives

- RewriteBase
- RewriteCond
- RewriteEngine
- RewriteMap
- RewriteOptions
- RewriteRule

Logging

MOD_REWRITE offers detailed logging of its actions at the trace1 to trace8 log levels. The log level can be set specifically for MOD_REWRITE using the LOGLEVEL directive: Up to level debug, no actions are logged, while trace8 means that practically all actions are logged.

⟹ Using a high trace log level for MOD_REWRITE will slow down your Apache HTTP Server dramatically! Use a log level higher than trace2 only for debugging!

Example

```
LogLevel alert rewrite:trace3
```

⟹ **RewriteLog**

Those familiar with earlier versions of MOD_REWRITE will no doubt be looking for the RewriteLog and RewriteLogLevel directives. This functionality has been completely replaced by the new per-module logging configuration mentioned above.
To get just the MOD_REWRITE-specific log messages, pipe the log file through grep:

```
tail -f error_log|fgrep '[rewrite:'
```

RewriteBase Directive

Description:	Sets the base URL for per-directory rewrites
Syntax:	`RewriteBase URL-path`
Default:	`None`
Context:	directory, .htaccess
Override:	FileInfo
Status:	Extension
Module:	mod_rewrite

The REWRITEBASE directive specifies the URL prefix to be used for per-directory (htaccess) REWRITERULE directives that substitute a relative path.

This directive is *required* when you use a relative path in a substitution in per-directory (htaccess) context unless either of the following conditions are true:

- The original request, and the substitution, are underneath the DOCUMENTROOT (as opposed to reachable by other means, such as ALIAS).

- The *filesystem* path to the directory containing the REWRITERULE, suffixed by the relative substitution is also valid as a URL path on the server (this is rare).

- In Apache HTTP Server 2.4.13 and later, this directive may be omitted when the request is mapped via ALIAS or MOD_USERDIR.

In the example below, REWRITEBASE is necessary to avoid rewriting to http://example.com/opt/myapp-1.2.3/welcome.html since the resource was not relative to the document root. This misconfiguration would normally cause the server to look for an "opt" directory under the document root.

```
DocumentRoot "/var/www/example.com"
AliasMatch "^/myapp" "/opt/myapp-1.2.3"
<Directory "/opt/myapp-1.2.3">
    RewriteEngine On
    RewriteBase /myapp/
    RewriteRule "^index\.html$"  "welcome.html"
</Directory>
```

RewriteCond Directive

Description:	Defines a condition under which rewriting will take place
Syntax:	`RewriteCond TestString CondPattern`
Context:	server config, virtual host, directory, .htaccess
Override:	FileInfo
Status:	Extension
Module:	mod_rewrite

The REWRITECOND directive defines a rule condition. One or more REWRITECOND can precede a REWRITERULE directive. The following rule is then only used if both the current state of the URI matches its pattern, **and** if these conditions are met.

TestString is a string which can contain the following expanded constructs in addition to plain text:

- **RewriteRule backreferences**: These are backreferences of the form **$N** ($0 <= N <= 9$). $1 to $9 provide access to the grouped parts (in parentheses) of the pattern, from the `RewriteRule` which is subject to the current set of `RewriteCond` conditions. $0 provides access to the whole string matched by that pattern.

- **RewriteCond backreferences**: These are backreferences of the form `%N` (0 <= N <= 9). %1 to %9 provide access to the grouped parts (again, in parentheses) of the pattern, from the last matched `RewriteCond` in the current set of conditions. %0 provides access to the whole string matched by that pattern.

- **RewriteMap expansions**: These are expansions of the form `${mapname:key|default}`. See the documentation for RewriteMap for more details.

- **Server-Variables**: These are variables of the form `%{ NAME_OF_VARIABLE }` where *NAME_OF_VARIABLE* can be a string taken from the following list:

HTTP headers:	connection & request:	
HTTP_ACCEPT	AUTH_TYPE	
HTTP_COOKIE	CONN_REMOTE_ADDR	
HTTP_FORWARDED	CONTEXT_PREFIX	
HTTP_HOST	CONTEXT_DOCUMENT_ROOT	
HTTP_PROXY_CONNECTION	IPV6	
HTTP_REFERER	PATH_INFO	
HTTP_USER_AGENT	QUERY_STRING	
	REMOTE_ADDR	
	REMOTE_HOST	
	REMOTE_IDENT	
	REMOTE_PORT	
	REMOTE_USER	
	REQUEST_METHOD	
	SCRIPT_FILENAME	
server internals:	**date and time:**	**specials:**
DOCUMENT_ROOT	TIME_YEAR	API_VERSION
SCRIPT_GROUP	TIME_MON	CONN_REMOTE_ADDR
SCRIPT_USER	TIME_DAY	HTTPS
SERVER_ADDR	TIME_HOUR	IS_SUBREQ
SERVER_ADMIN	TIME_MIN	REMOTE_ADDR
SERVER_NAME	TIME_SEC	REQUEST_FILENAME
SERVER_PORT	TIME_WDAY	REQUEST_SCHEME
SERVER_PROTOCOL	TIME	REQUEST_URI
SERVER_SOFTWARE		THE_REQUEST

These variables all correspond to the similarly named HTTP MIME-headers, C variables of the Apache HTTP Server or `struct tm` fields of the Unix system. Most are documented here (p. 89) or elsewhere in the Manual or in the CGI specification.

SERVER_NAME and SERVER_PORT depend on the values of USECANONICALNAME and USECANONICAL-PHYSICALPORT respectively.

Those that are special to mod_rewrite include those below.

API_VERSION This is the version of the Apache httpd module API (the internal interface between server and module) in the current httpd build, as defined in include/ap_mmn.h. The module API version corresponds to the version of Apache httpd in use (in the release version of Apache httpd 1.3.14, for instance, it is 19990320:10), but is mainly of interest to module authors.

CONN_REMOTE_ADDR Since 2.4.8: The peer IP address of the connection (see the MOD_REMOTEIP module).

HTTPS Will contain the text "on" if the connection is using SSL/TLS, or "off" otherwise. (This variable can be safely used regardless of whether or not MOD_SSL is loaded).

IS_SUBREQ Will contain the text "true" if the request currently being processed is a sub-request, "false" otherwise. Sub-requests may be generated by modules that need to resolve additional files or URIs in order to complete their tasks.

REMOTE_ADDR The IP address of the remote host (see the MOD_REMOTEIP module).

REQUEST_FILENAME The full local filesystem path to the file or script matching the request, if this has already been determined by the server at the time REQUEST_FILENAME is referenced. Otherwise, such as when used in virtual host context, the same value as REQUEST_URI. Depending on the value of ACCEPTPATHINFO, the server may have only used some leading components of the REQUEST_URI to map the request to a file.

REQUEST_SCHEME Will contain the scheme of the request (usually "http" or "https"). This value can be influenced with SERVERNAME.

REQUEST_URI The path component of the requested URI, such as "/index.html". This notably excludes the query string which is available as its own variable named QUERY_STRING.

THE_REQUEST The full HTTP request line sent by the browser to the server (e.g., "GET /index.html HTTP/1.1"). This does not include any additional headers sent by the browser. This value has not been unescaped (decoded), unlike most other variables below.

If the *TestString* has the special value expr, the *CondPattern* will be treated as an ap_expr (p. 89) . HTTP headers referenced in the expression will be added to the Vary header if the novary flag is not given.

Other things you should be aware of:

1. The variables SCRIPT_FILENAME and REQUEST_FILENAME contain the same value - the value of the filename field of the internal request_rec structure of the Apache HTTP Server. The first name is the commonly known CGI variable name while the second is the appropriate counterpart of REQUEST_URI (which contains the value of the uri field of request_rec).

   If a substitution occurred and the rewriting continues, the value of both variables will be updated accordingly.

   If used in per-server context (*i.e.*, before the request is mapped to the filesystem) SCRIPT_FILENAME and REQUEST_FILENAME cannot contain the full local filesystem path since the path is unknown at this stage of processing. Both variables will initially contain the value of REQUEST_URI in that case. In order to obtain the full local filesystem path of the request in per-server context, use an URL-based look-ahead %{LA-U:REQUEST_FILENAME} to determine the final value of REQUEST_FILENAME.

2. %{ENV:variable}, where *variable* can be any environment variable, is also available. This is looked-up via internal Apache httpd structures and (if not found there) via getenv() from the Apache httpd server process.

3. `%{SSL:variable}`, where *variable* is the name of an SSL environment variable (p. 853) , can be used whether or not MOD_SSL is loaded, but will always expand to the empty string if it is not. Example: `%{SSL:SSL_CIPHER_USEKEYSIZE}` may expand to `128`. These variables are available even without setting the `StdEnvVars` option of the SSLOPTIONS directive.

4. `%{HTTP:header}`, where *header* can be any HTTP MIME-header name, can always be used to obtain the value of a header sent in the HTTP request. Example: `%{HTTP:Proxy-Connection}` is the value of the HTTP header "`Proxy-Connection:`". If a HTTP header is used in a condition this header is added to the Vary header of the response in case the condition evaluates to true for the request. It is **not** added if the condition evaluates to false for the request. Adding the HTTP header to the Vary header of the response is needed for proper caching.

   It has to be kept in mind that conditions follow a short circuit logic in the case of the '**ornext|OR**' flag so that certain conditions might not be evaluated at all.

5. `%{LA-U:variable}` can be used for look-aheads which perform an internal (URL-based) sub-request to determine the final value of *variable*. This can be used to access variable for rewriting which is not available at the current stage, but will be set in a later phase. For instance, to rewrite according to the REMOTE_USER variable from within the per-server context (`httpd.conf` file) you must use `%{LA-U:REMOTE_USER}` - this variable is set by the authorization phases, which come *after* the URL translation phase (during which mod_rewrite operates).

   On the other hand, because mod_rewrite implements its per-directory context (`.htaccess` file) via the Fixup phase of the API and because the authorization phases come *before* this phase, you just can use `%{REMOTE_USER}` in that context.

6. `%{LA-F:variable}` can be used to perform an internal (filename-based) sub-request, to determine the final value of *variable*. Most of the time, this is the same as LA-U above.

CondPattern is the condition pattern, a regular expression which is applied to the current instance of the *TestString*. *TestString* is first evaluated, before being matched against *CondPattern*.

CondPattern is usually a *perl compatible regular expression*, but there is additional syntax available to perform other useful tests against the *Teststring*:

1. You can prefix the pattern string with a '!' character (exclamation mark) to negate the result of the condition, no matter what kind of *CondPattern* is used.

2. You can perform lexicographical string comparisons:

   - '<**CondPattern**' (lexicographically precedes)
     Treats the *CondPattern* as a plain string and compares it lexicographically to *TestString*. True if *TestString* lexicographically precedes *CondPattern*.

   - '>**CondPattern**' (lexicographically follows)
     Treats the *CondPattern* as a plain string and compares it lexicographically to *TestString*. True if *TestString* lexicographically follows *CondPattern*.

   - '=**CondPattern**' (lexicographically equal)
     Treats the *CondPattern* as a plain string and compares it lexicographically to *TestString*. True if *TestString* is lexicographically equal to *CondPattern* (the two strings are exactly equal, character for character). If *CondPattern* is "" (two quotation marks) this compares *TestString* to the empty string.

   - '<=**CondPattern**' (lexicographically less than or equal to)
     Treats the *CondPattern* as a plain string and compares it lexicographically to *TestString*. True if *TestString* lexicographically precedes *CondPattern*, or is equal to *CondPattern* (the two strings are equal, character for character).

- '>=**CondPattern**' (lexicographically greater than or equal to)
  Treats the *CondPattern* as a plain string and compares it lexicographically to *TestString*. True if *TestString* lexicographically follows *CondPattern*, or is equal to *CondPattern* (the two strings are equal, character for character).

3. You can perform integer comparisons:

   - '-**eq**' (is numerically **eq**ual to)
     The *TestString* is treated as an integer, and is numerically compared to the *CondPattern*. True if the two are numerically equal.

   - '-**ge**' (is numerically **g**reater than or **e**qual to)
     The *TestString* is treated as an integer, and is numerically compared to the *CondPattern*. True if the *TestString* is numerically greater than or equal to the *CondPattern*.

   - '-**gt**' (is numerically **g**reater **t**han)
     The *TestString* is treated as an integer, and is numerically compared to the *CondPattern*. True if the *TestString* is numerically greater than the *CondPattern*.

   - '-**le**' (is numerically **l**ess than or **e**qual to)
     The *TestString* is treated as an integer, and is numerically compared to the *CondPattern*. True if the *TestString* is numerically less than or equal to the *CondPattern*. Avoid confusion with the **-l** by using the **-L** or **-h** variant.

   - '-**lt**' (is numerically **l**ess **t**han)
     The *TestString* is treated as an integer, and is numerically compared to the *CondPattern*. True if the *TestString* is numerically less than the *CondPattern*. Avoid confusion with the **-l** by using the **-L** or **-h** variant.

4. You can perform various file attribute tests:

   - '-**d**' (is **d**irectory)
     Treats the *TestString* as a pathname and tests whether or not it exists, and is a directory.

   - '-**f**' (is regular **f**ile)
     Treats the *TestString* as a pathname and tests whether or not it exists, and is a regular file.

   - '-**F**' (is existing file, via subrequest)
     Checks whether or not *TestString* is a valid file, accessible via all the server's currently-configured access controls for that path. This uses an internal subrequest to do the check, so use it with care - it can impact your server's performance!

   - '-**H**' (is symbolic link, bash convention)
     See **-l**.

   - '-**l**' (is symbolic **l**ink)
     Treats the *TestString* as a pathname and tests whether or not it exists, and is a symbolic link. May also use the bash convention of **-L** or **-h** if there's a possibility of confusion such as when using the **-lt** or **-le** tests.

   - '-**L**' (is symbolic link, bash convention)
     See **-l**.

   - '-**s**' (is regular file, with **s**ize)
     Treats the *TestString* as a pathname and tests whether or not it exists, and is a regular file with size greater than zero.

   - '-**U**' (is existing URL, via subrequest)
     Checks whether or not *TestString* is a valid URL, accessible via all the server's currently-configured access controls for that path. This uses an internal subrequest to do the check, so use it with care - it can impact your server's performance!

     This flag *only* returns information about things like access control, authentication, and authorization. This flag *does not* return information about the status code the configured handler (static file, CGI, proxy, etc.) would have returned.

- **'-x'** (has **e**xecutable permissions)
  Treats the *TestString* as a pathname and tests whether or not it exists, and has executable permissions. These permissions are determined according to the underlying OS.

5. If the *TestString* has the special value `expr`, the *CondPattern* will be treated as an ap_expr (p. 89) .

   In the below example, `-strmatch` is used to compare the `REFERER` against the site hostname, to block unwanted hotlinking.

   ```
   RewriteCond expr "! %{HTTP_REFERER} -strmatch '*://%{HTTP_HOST}/
   RewriteRule "^/images" "-" [F]
   ```

6. You can also set special flags for *CondPattern* by appending **[*flags*]** as the third argument to the `RewriteCond` directive, where *flags* is a comma-separated list of any of the following flags:

   - **'nocase|NC'** (**no c**ase)
     This makes the test case-insensitive - differences between 'A-Z' and 'a-z' are ignored, both in the expanded *TestString* and the *CondPattern*. This flag is effective only for comparisons between *TestString* and *CondPattern*. It has no effect on filesystem and subrequest checks.

   - **'ornext|OR'** (**or** next condition)
     Use this to combine rule conditions with a local OR instead of the implicit AND. Typical example:

     ```
     RewriteCond "%{REMOTE_HOST}"  "^host1"  [OR]
     RewriteCond "%{REMOTE_HOST}"  "^host2"  [OR]
     RewriteCond "%{REMOTE_HOST}"  "^host3"
     RewriteRule ...some special stuff for any of these hosts...
     ```

     Without this flag you would have to write the condition/rule pair three times.

   - **'novary|NV'** (**no v**ary)
     If a HTTP header is used in the condition, this flag prevents this header from being added to the Vary header of the response.
     Using this flag might break proper caching of the response if the representation of this response varies on the value of this header. So this flag should be only used if the meaning of the Vary header is well understood.

Example:

To rewrite the Homepage of a site according to the "`User-Agent:`" header of the request, you can use the following:

```
RewriteCond   "%{HTTP_USER_AGENT}"   "(iPhone|Blackberry|Android)"
RewriteRule   "^/$"                   "/homepage.mobile.html"  [L]

RewriteRule   "^/$"                   "/homepage.std.html"   [L]
```

Explanation: If you use a browser which identifies itself as a mobile browser (note that the example is incomplete, as there are many other mobile platforms), the mobile version of the homepage is served. Otherwise, the standard page is served.

RewriteEngine Directive

Description:	Enables or disables runtime rewriting engine
Syntax:	`RewriteEngine on|off`
Default:	`RewriteEngine off`
Context:	server config, virtual host, directory, .htaccess
Override:	FileInfo
Status:	Extension
Module:	mod_rewrite

The REWRITEENGINE directive enables or disables the runtime rewriting engine. If it is set to off this module does no runtime processing at all. It does not even update the SCRIPT_URx environment variables.

Use this directive to disable rules in a particular context, rather than commenting out all the REWRITERULE directives.

Note that rewrite configurations are not inherited by virtual hosts. This means that you need to have a RewriteEngine on directive for each virtual host in which you wish to use rewrite rules.

REWRITEMAP directives of the type prg are not started during server initialization if they're defined in a context that does not have REWRITEENGINE set to on

RewriteMap Directive

Description:	Defines a mapping function for key-lookup
Syntax:	RewriteMap MapName MapType:MapSource
Context:	server config, virtual host
Status:	Extension
Module:	mod_rewrite

The REWRITEMAP directive defines a *Rewriting Map* which can be used inside rule substitution strings by the mapping-functions to insert/substitute fields through a key lookup. The source of this lookup can be of various types.

The *MapName* is the name of the map and will be used to specify a mapping-function for the substitution strings of a rewriting rule via one of the following constructs:

${ *MapName* : *LookupKey* }
${ *MapName* : *LookupKey* | *DefaultValue* }

When such a construct occurs, the map *MapName* is consulted and the key *LookupKey* is looked-up. If the key is found, the map-function construct is substituted by *SubstValue*. If the key is not found then it is substituted by *DefaultValue* or by the empty string if no *DefaultValue* was specified. Empty values behave as if the key was absent, therefore it is not possible to distinguish between empty-valued keys and absent keys.

For example, you might define a REWRITEMAP as:

```
RewriteMap "examplemap" "txt:/path/to/file/map.txt"
```

You would then be able to use this map in a REWRITERULE as follows:

```
RewriteRule "^/ex/(.*)" "${examplemap:$1}"
```

The following combinations for *MapType* and *MapSource* can be used:

txt A plain text file containing space-separated key-value pairs, one per line. (Details ... (p. 156))

rnd Randomly selects an entry from a plain text file (Details ... (p. 156))

dbm Looks up an entry in a dbm file containing name, value pairs. Hash is constructed from a plain text file format using the httxt2dbm (p. 315) utility. (Details ... (p. 156))

int One of the four available internal functions provided by RewriteMap: toupper, tolower, escape or unescape. (Details ... (p. 156))

prg Calls an external program or script to process the rewriting. (Details ... (p. 156))

dbd or fastdbd A SQL SELECT statement to be performed to look up the rewrite target. (Details ... (p. 156))

Further details, and numerous examples, may be found in the RewriteMap HowTo (p. 156)

RewriteOptions Directive

Description:	Sets some special options for the rewrite engine
Syntax:	RewriteOptions Options
Context:	server config, virtual host, directory, .htaccess
Override:	FileInfo
Status:	Extension
Module:	mod_rewrite
Compatibility:	MaxRedirects is no longer available in version 2.1 and later

The REWRITEOPTIONS directive sets some special options for the current per-server or per-directory configuration. The *Option* string can currently only be one of the following:

Inherit This forces the current configuration to inherit the configuration of the parent. In per-virtual-server context, this means that the maps, conditions and rules of the main server are inherited. In per-directory context this means that conditions and rules of the parent directory's .htaccess configuration or <DIRECTORY> sections are inherited. The inherited rules are virtually copied to the section where this directive is being used. If used in combination with local rules, the inherited rules are copied behind the local rules. The position of this directive - below or above of local rules - has no influence on this behavior. If local rules forced the rewriting to stop, the inherited rules won't be processed.

> **!** Rules inherited from the parent scope are applied **after** rules specified in the child scope.

InheritBefore Like Inherit above, but the rules from the parent scope are applied **before** rules specified in the child scope.
Available in Apache HTTP Server 2.3.10 and later.

InheritDown If this option is enabled, all child configurations will inherit the configuration of the current configuration. It is equivalent to specifying RewriteOptions Inherit in all child configurations. See the Inherit option for more details on how the parent-child relationships are handled.
Available in Apache HTTP Server 2.4.8 and later.

InheritDownBefore Like InheritDown above, but the rules from the current scope are applied **before** rules specified in any child's scope.
Available in Apache HTTP Server 2.4.8 and later.

IgnoreInherit This option forces the current and child configurations to ignore all rules that would be inherited from a parent specifying InheritDown or InheritDownBefore.
Available in Apache HTTP Server 2.4.8 and later.

AllowNoSlash By default, MOD_REWRITE will ignore URLs that map to a directory on disk but lack a trailing slash, in the expectation that the MOD_DIR module will issue the client with a redirect to the canonical URL with a trailing slash.

When the DIRECTORYSLASH directive is set to off, the AllowNoSlash option can be enabled to ensure that rewrite rules are no longer ignored. This option makes it possible to apply rewrite rules within .htaccess files that match the directory without a trailing slash, if so desired.
Available in Apache HTTP Server 2.4.0 and later.

AllowAnyURI When REWRITERULE is used in VirtualHost or server context with version 2.2.22 or later of httpd, MOD_REWRITE will only process the rewrite rules if the request URI is a URL-path (p. 351) . This avoids some security issues where particular rules could allow "surprising" pattern expansions (see CVE-2011-3368[69] and CVE-2011-4317[70]). To lift the restriction on matching a URL-path, the AllowAnyURI option can be

---

[69]http://cve.mitre.org/cgi-bin/cvename.cgi?name=CVE-2011-3368
[70]http://cve.mitre.org/cgi-bin/cvename.cgi?name=CVE-2011-4317

enabled, and MOD_REWRITE will apply the rule set to any request URI string, regardless of whether that string matches the URL-path grammar required by the HTTP specification.
Available in Apache HTTP Server 2.4.3 and later.

> ### ⚠ Security Warning
>
> Enabling this option will make the server vulnerable to security issues if used with rewrite rules which are not carefully authored. It is **strongly recommended** that this option is not used. In particular, beware of input strings containing the '@' character which could change the interpretation of the transformed URI, as per the above CVE names.

MergeBase With this option, the value of REWRITEBASE is copied from where it's explicitly defined into any sub-directory or sub-location that doesn't define its own REWRITEBASE. This was the default behavior in 2.4.0 through 2.4.3, and the flag to restore it is available Apache HTTP Server 2.4.4 and later.

IgnoreContextInfo In versions 2.4.13 and later, when a relative substitution is made in directory (htaccess) context and REWRITEBASE has not been set, this module uses some extended URL and filesystem context information to change the relative substitution back into a URL. Modules such as MOD_USERDIR and MOD_ALIAS supply this extended context info. This option disables the behavior introduced in 2.4.13 and should only be set if all of the conditions above are present and a substituion has an unexpected result.

RewriteRule Directive

Description:	Defines rules for the rewriting engine
Syntax:	`RewriteRule Pattern Substitution [flags]`
Context:	server config, virtual host, directory, .htaccess
Override:	FileInfo
Status:	Extension
Module:	mod_rewrite

The REWRITERULE directive is the real rewriting workhorse. The directive can occur more than once, with each instance defining a single rewrite rule. The order in which these rules are defined is important - this is the order in which they will be applied at run-time.

Pattern is a perl compatible regular expression. On the first RewriteRule, it is matched against the (%-decoded) URL-path (p. 351) of the request, or, in per-directory context (see below), the URL path relative to that per-directory context. Subsequent patterns are matched against the output of the last matching RewriteRule.

**What is matched?**

In VIRTUALHOST context, The *Pattern* will initially be matched against the part of the URL after the hostname and port, and before the query string (e.g. "/app1/index.html").
In DIRECTORY and htaccess context, the *Pattern* will initially be matched against the *filesystem* path, after removing the prefix that led the server to the current REWRITERULE (e.g. "app1/index.html" or "index.html" depending on where the directives are defined).
If you wish to match against the hostname, port, or query string, use a REWRITECOND with the %{HTTP_HOST}, %{SERVER_PORT}, or %{QUERY_STRING} variables respectively.

Per-directory Rewrites

- The rewrite engine may be used in .htaccess (p. 239) files and in <DIRECTORY> sections, with some additional complexity.

- To enable the rewrite engine in this context, you need to set "RewriteEngine On" **and** "Options FollowSymLinks" must be enabled. If your administrator has disabled override of FollowSymLinks for a user's directory, then you cannot use the rewrite engine. This restriction is required for security reasons.

- When using the rewrite engine in .htaccess files the per-directory prefix (which always is the same for a specific directory) is automatically *removed* for the RewriteRule pattern matching and automatically *added* after any relative (not starting with a slash or protocol name) substitution encounters the end of a rule set. See the REWRITEBASE directive for more information regarding what prefix will be added back to relative substitutions.

- If you wish to match against the full URL-path in a per-directory (htaccess) RewriteRule, use the %{REQUEST_URI} variable in a REWRITECOND.

- The removed prefix always ends with a slash, meaning the matching occurs against a string which *never* has a leading slash. Therefore, a *Pattern* with ^ / never matches in per-directory context.

- Although rewrite rules are syntactically permitted in <LOCATION> and <FILES> sections (including their regular expression counterparts), this should never be necessary and is unsupported. A likely feature to break in these contexts is relative substitutions.

For some hints on regular expressions, see the mod_rewrite Introduction (p. 137) .

In mod_rewrite, the NOT character (' ! ') is also available as a possible pattern prefix. This enables you to negate a pattern; to say, for instance: *"if the current URL does **NOT** match this pattern"*. This can be used for exceptional cases, where it is easier to match the negative pattern, or as a last default rule.

Note
    When using the NOT character to negate a pattern, you cannot include grouped wildcard parts in that pattern. This is because, when the pattern does NOT match (ie, the negation matches), there are no contents for the groups. Thus, if negated patterns are used, you cannot use $N in the substitution string!

The *Substitution* of a rewrite rule is the string that replaces the original URL-path that was matched by *Pattern*. The *Substitution* may be a:

file-system path Designates the location on the file-system of the resource to be delivered to the client. Substitutions are only treated as a file-system path when the rule is configured in server (virtualhost) context and the first component of the path in the substitution exists in the file-system

URL-path A DOCUMENTROOT-relative path to the resource to be served. Note that MOD_REWRITE tries to guess whether you have specified a file-system path or a URL-path by checking to see if the first segment of the path exists at the root of the file-system. For example, if you specify a *Substitution* string of /www/file.html, then this will be treated as a URL-path *unless* a directory named www exists at the root or your file-system (or, in the case of using rewrites in a .htaccess file, relative to your document root), in which case it will be treated as a file-system path. If you wish other URL-mapping directives (such as ALIAS) to be applied to the resulting URL-path, use the [PT] flag as described below.

Absolute URL If an absolute URL is specified, MOD_REWRITE checks to see whether the hostname matches the current host. If it does, the scheme and hostname are stripped out and the resulting path is treated as a URL-path. Otherwise, an external redirect is performed for the given URL. To force an external redirect back to the current host, see the [R] flag below.

– (dash) A dash indicates that no substitution should be performed (the existing path is passed through untouched). This is used when a flag (see below) needs to be applied without changing the path.

In addition to plain text, the *Substitution* string can include

1. back-references (`$N`) to the RewriteRule pattern

2. back-references (`%N`) to the last matched RewriteCond pattern

3. server-variables as in rule condition test-strings (`%{VARNAME}`)

4. mapping-function calls (`${mapname:key|default}`)

Back-references are identifiers of the form **$N** (**N**=0..9), which will be replaced by the contents of the **N**th group of the matched *Pattern*. The server-variables are the same as for the *TestString* of a `RewriteCond` directive. The mapping-functions come from the `RewriteMap` directive and are explained there. These three types of variables are expanded in the order above.

Rewrite rules are applied to the results of previous rewrite rules, in the order in which they are defined in the config file. The URL-path or file-system path (see "What is matched?", above) is **completely replaced** by the *Substitution* and the rewriting process continues until all rules have been applied, or it is explicitly terminated by an **L** flag (p. 168) , or other flag which implies immediate termination, such as **END** or **F**.

$\Longrightarrow$ **Modifying the Query String**

By default, the query string is passed through unchanged. You can, however, create URLs in the substitution string containing a query string part. Simply use a question mark inside the substitution string to indicate that the following text should be re-injected into the query string. When you want to erase an existing query string, end the substitution string with just a question mark. To combine new and old query strings, use the [`QSA`] flag.

Additionally you can set special actions to be performed by appending **[*flags*]** as the third argument to the `RewriteRule` directive. *Flags* is a comma-separated list, surround by square brackets, of any of the flags in the following table. More details, and examples, for each flag, are available in the Rewrite Flags document (p. 168) .

Flag and syntax	Function
B	Escape non-alphanumeric characters *before* applying the transformation. *details ... (p. 168)*
chain—C	Rule is chained to the following rule. If the rule fails, the rule(s) chained to it will be skipped. *details ... (p. 168)*
cookie—CO=*NAME:VAL*	Sets a cookie in the client browser. Full syntax is: CO=*NAME:VAL:domain*[:*lifetime*[:*path*[:*secure*[:*httponly*]]]] *details ... (p. 168)*
discardpath—DPI	Causes the PATH_INFO portion of the rewritten URI to be discarded. *details ... (p. 168)*
END	Stop the rewriting process immediately and don't apply any more rules. Also prevents further execution of rewrite rules in per-directory and .htaccess context. (Available in 2.3.9 and later) *details ... (p. 168)*
env—E=[!]*VAR*[:*VAL*]	Causes an environment variable *VAR* to be set (to the value *VAL* if provided). The form !*VAR* causes the environment variable *VAR* to be unset. *details ... (p. 168)*
forbidden—F	Returns a 403 FORBIDDEN response to the client browser. *details ... (p. 168)*
gone—G	Returns a 410 GONE response to the client browser. *details ... (p. 168)*
Handler—H=*Content-handler*	Causes the resulting URI to be sent to the specified *Content-handler* for processing. *details ... (p. 168)*

last—L	Stop the rewriting process immediately and don't apply any more rules. Especially note caveats for per-directory and .htaccess context (see also the END flag). *details ... (p. 168)*
next—N	Re-run the rewriting process, starting again with the first rule, using the result of the ruleset so far as a starting point. *details ... (p. 168)*
nocase—NC	Makes the pattern comparison case-insensitive. *details ... (p. 168)*
noescape—NE	Prevent mod_rewrite from applying hexcode escaping of special characters in the result of the rewrite. *details ... (p. 168)*
nosubreq—NS	Causes a rule to be skipped if the current request is an internal sub-request. *details ... (p. 168)*
proxy—P	Force the substitution URL to be internally sent as a proxy request. *details ... (p. 168)*
passthrough—PT	Forces the resulting URI to be passed back to the URL mapping engine for processing of other URI-to-filename translators, such as `Alias` or `Redirect`. *details ... (p. 168)*
qsappend—QSA	Appends any query string from the original request URL to any query string created in the rewrite target.*details ... (p. 168)*
qsdiscard—QSD	Discard any query string attached to the incoming URI. *details ... (p. 168)*
redirect—R[=*code*]	Forces an external redirect, optionally with the specified HTTP status code. *details ... (p. 168)*
skip—S=*num*	Tells the rewriting engine to skip the next *num* rules if the current rule matches. *details ... (p. 168)*
type—T=*MIME-type*	Force the MIME-type of the target file to be the specified type. *details ... (p. 168)*

 Home directory expansion

When the substitution string begins with a string resembling "/˜user" (via explicit text or backreferences), mod_rewrite performs home directory expansion independent of the presence or configuration of MOD_USERDIR.

This expansion does not occur when the *PT* flag is used on the REWRITERULE directive.

Here are all possible substitution combinations and their meanings:

**Inside per-server configuration (`httpd.conf`)
for request "GET /somepath/pathinfo":**

Given Rule	Resulting Substitution
^/somepath(.*) otherpath$1	invalid, not supported
^/somepath(.*) otherpath$1 [R]	invalid, not supported
^/somepath(.*) otherpath$1 [P]	invalid, not supported
^/somepath(.*) /otherpath$1	/otherpath/pathinfo
^/somepath(.*) /otherpath$1 [R]	http://thishost/otherpath/pathinfo via external redirection
^/somepath(.*) /otherpath$1 [P]	doesn't make sense, not supported
^/somepath(.*) http://thishost/otherpath$1	/otherpath/pathinfo
^/somepath(.*) http://thishost/otherpath$1 [R]	http://thishost/otherpath/pathinfo via external redirection
^/somepath(.*) http://thishost/otherpath$1 [P]	doesn't make sense, not supported
^/somepath(.*) http://otherhost/otherpath$1	http://otherhost/otherpath/pathinfo via external redirection
^/somepath(.*) http://otherhost/otherpath$1 [R]	http://otherhost/otherpath/pathinfo via external redirection (the [R] flag is redundant)
^/somepath(.*) http://otherhost/otherpath$1 [P]	http://otherhost/otherpath/pathinfo via internal proxy

**Inside per-directory configuration for `/somepath`
(`/physical/path/to/somepath/.htaccess`, with `RewriteBase /somepath`)
for request "GET /somepath/localpath/pathinfo":**

Given Rule	Resulting Substitution
ˆlocalpath(.*) otherpath$1	/somepath/otherpath/pathinfo
ˆlocalpath(.*) otherpath$1 [R]	http://thishost/somepath/otherpath/pathinfo via external redirection
ˆlocalpath(.*) otherpath$1 [P]	doesn't make sense, not supported
ˆlocalpath(.*) /otherpath$1	/otherpath/pathinfo
ˆlocalpath(.*) /otherpath$1 [R]	http://thishost/otherpath/pathinfo via external redirection
ˆlocalpath(.*) /otherpath$1 [P]	doesn't make sense, not supported
ˆlocalpath(.*) http://thishost/otherpath$1	/otherpath/pathinfo
ˆlocalpath(.*) http://thishost/otherpath$1 [R]	http://thishost/otherpath/pathinfo via external redirection
ˆlocalpath(.*) http://thishost/otherpath$1 [P]	doesn't make sense, not supported
ˆlocalpath(.*) http://otherhost/otherpath$1	http://otherhost/otherpath/pathinfo via external redirection
ˆlocalpath(.*) http://otherhost/otherpath$1 [R]	http://otherhost/otherpath/pathinfo via external redirection (the [R] flag is redundant)
ˆlocalpath(.*) http://otherhost/otherpath$1 [P]	http://otherhost/otherpath/pathinfo via internal proxy

10.95   Apache Module mod_sed

Description:	Filter Input (request) and Output (response) content using sed syntax
Status:	Experimental
ModuleIdentifier:	sed_module
SourceFile:	mod_sed.c sed0.c sed1.c regexp.c regexp.h sed.h
Compatibility:	Available in Apache 2.3 and later

Summary

MOD_SED is an in-process content filter. The MOD_SED filter implements the sed editing commands implemented by the Solaris 10 sed program as described in the manual page[71]. However, unlike sed, MOD_SED doesn't take data from standard input. Instead, the filter acts on the entity data sent between client and server. MOD_SED can be used as an input or output filter. MOD_SED is a content filter, which means that it cannot be used to modify client or server http headers.

The MOD_SED output filter accepts a chunk of data, executes the sed scripts on the data, and generates the output which is passed to the next filter in the chain.

The MOD_SED input filter reads the data from the next filter in the chain, executes the sed scripts, and returns the generated data to the caller filter in the filter chain.

Both the input and output filters only process the data if newline characters are seen in the content. At the end of the data, the rest of the data is treated as the last line.

A tutorial article on MOD_SED, and why it is more powerful than simple string or regular expression search and replace, is available on the author's blog[72].

Directives

- InputSed

- OutputSed

Sample Configuration

Adding an output filter

```
# In the following example, the sed filter will change the string
# "monday" to "MON" and the string "sunday" to SUN in html documents
# before sending to the client.
<Directory "/var/www/docs/sed">
    AddOutputFilter Sed html
    OutputSed "s/monday/MON/g"
    OutputSed "s/sunday/SUN/g"
</Directory>
```

---

[71]http://www.gnu.org/software/sed/manual/sed.txt
[72]https://blogs.oracle.com/basant/entry/using_mod_sed_to_filter

Adding an input filter

```
# In the following example, the sed filter will change the string
# "monday" to "MON" and the string "sunday" to SUN in the POST data
# sent to PHP.
<Directory "/var/www/docs/sed">
    AddInputFilter Sed php
    InputSed "s/monday/MON/g"
    InputSed "s/sunday/SUN/g"
</Directory>
```

Sed Commands

Complete details of the `sed` command can be found from the sed manual page[73].

b Branch to the label specified (similar to goto).

h Copy the current line to the hold buffer.

H Append the current line to the hold buffer.

g Copy the hold buffer to the current line.

G Append the hold buffer to the current line.

x Swap the contents of the hold buffer and the current line.

InputSed Directive

Description:	Sed command to filter request data (typically POST data)
Syntax:	`InputSed sed-command`
Context:	directory, .htaccess
Status:	Experimental
Module:	mod_sed

The INPUTSED directive specifies the `sed` command to execute on the request data e.g., POST data.

OutputSed Directive

Description:	Sed command for filtering response content
Syntax:	`OutputSed sed-command`
Context:	directory, .htaccess
Status:	Experimental
Module:	mod_sed

The OUTPUTSED directive specifies the `sed` command to execute on the response.

---

[73]http://www.gnu.org/software/sed/manual/sed.txt

10.96   Apache Module mod_session

Description:	Session support
Status:	Extension
ModuleIdentifier:	session_module
SourceFile:	mod_session.c
Compatibility:	Available in Apache 2.3 and later

Summary

 Warning
The session modules make use of HTTP cookies, and as such can fall victim to Cross Site Scripting attacks, or expose potentially private information to clients. Please ensure that the relevant risks have been taken into account before enabling the session functionality on your server.

This module provides support for a server wide per user session interface. Sessions can be used for keeping track of whether a user has been logged in, or for other per user information that should be kept available across requests.

Sessions may be stored on the server, or may be stored on the browser. Sessions may also be optionally encrypted for added security. These features are divided into several modules in addition to MOD_SESSION; MOD_SESSION_CRYPTO, MOD_SESSION_COOKIE and MOD_SESSION_DBD. Depending on the server requirements, load the appropriate modules into the server (either statically at compile time or dynamically via the LOADMODULE directive).

Sessions may be manipulated from other modules that depend on the session, or the session may be read from and written to using environment variables and HTTP headers, as appropriate.

Directives

- Session
- SessionEnv
- SessionExclude
- SessionHeader
- SessionInclude
- SessionMaxAge

See also

- MOD_SESSION_COOKIE
- MOD_SESSION_CRYPTO
- MOD_SESSION_DBD

What is a session?

At the core of the session interface is a table of key and value pairs that are made accessible across browser requests. These pairs can be set to any valid string, as needed by the application making use of the session.

The "session" is a **application/x-www-form-urlencoded** string containing these key value pairs, as defined by the HTML specification[74].

---

[74]http://www.w3.org/TR/html4/

The session can optionally be encrypted and base64 encoded before being written to the storage mechanism, as defined by the administrator.

Who can use a session?

The session interface is primarily developed for the use by other server modules, such as MOD_AUTH_FORM, however CGI based applications can optionally be granted access to the contents of the session via the HTTP_SESSION environment variable. Sessions have the option to be modified and/or updated by inserting an HTTP response header containing the new session parameters.

Keeping sessions on the server

Apache can be configured to keep track of per user sessions stored on a particular server or group of servers. This functionality is similar to the sessions available in typical application servers.

If configured, sessions are tracked through the use of a session ID that is stored inside a cookie, or extracted from the parameters embedded within the URL query string, as found in a typical GET request.

As the contents of the session are stored exclusively on the server, there is an expectation of privacy of the contents of the session. This does have performance and resource implications should a large number of sessions be present, or where a large number of webservers have to share sessions with one another.

The MOD_SESSION_DBD module allows the storage of user sessions within a SQL database via MOD_DBD.

Keeping sessions on the browser

In high traffic environments where keeping track of a session on a server is too resource intensive or inconvenient, the option exists to store the contents of the session within a cookie on the client browser instead.

This has the advantage that minimal resources are required on the server to keep track of sessions, and multiple servers within a server farm have no need to share session information.

The contents of the session however are exposed to the client, with a corresponding risk of a loss of privacy. The MOD_SESSION_CRYPTO module can be configured to encrypt the contents of the session before writing the session to the client.

The MOD_SESSION_COOKIE allows the storage of user sessions on the browser within an HTTP cookie.

Basic Examples

Creating a session is as simple as turning the session on, and deciding where the session will be stored. In this example, the session will be stored on the browser, in a cookie called session.

Browser based session

```
Session On
SessionCookieName session path=/
```

The session is not useful unless it can be written to or read from. The following example shows how values can be injected into the session through the use of a predetermined HTTP response header called X-Replace-Session.

Writing to a session

```
Session On
SessionCookieName session path=/
SessionHeader X-Replace-Session
```

The header should contain name value pairs expressed in the same format as a query string in a URL, as in the example below. Setting a key to the empty string has the effect of removing that key from the session.

CGI to write to a session

```
#!/bin/bash
echo "Content-Type: text/plain"
echo "X-Replace-Session: key1=foo&key2=&key3=bar"
echo
env
```

If configured, the session can be read back from the HTTP_SESSION environment variable. By default, the session is kept private, so this has to be explicitly turned on with the SESSIONENV directive.

Read from a session

```
Session On
SessionEnv On
SessionCookieName session path=/
SessionHeader X-Replace-Session
```

Once read, the CGI variable HTTP_SESSION should contain the value key1=foo&key3=bar.

Session Privacy

Using the "show cookies" feature of your browser, you would have seen a clear text representation of the session. This could potentially be a problem should the end user need to be kept unaware of the contents of the session, or where a third party could gain unauthorised access to the data within the session.

The contents of the session can be optionally encrypted before being placed on the browser using the MOD_SESSION_CRYPTO module.

Browser based encrypted session

```
Session On
SessionCryptoPassphrase secret
SessionCookieName session path=/
```

The session will be automatically decrypted on load, and encrypted on save by Apache, the underlying application using the session need have no knowledge that encryption is taking place.

Sessions stored on the server rather than on the browser can also be encrypted as needed, offering privacy where potentially sensitive information is being shared between webservers in a server farm using the MOD_SESSION_DBD module.

Cookie Privacy

The HTTP cookie mechanism also offers privacy features, such as the ability to restrict cookie transport to SSL protected pages only, or to prevent browser based javascript from gaining access to the contents of the cookie.

 Warning

Some of the HTTP cookie privacy features are either non-standard, or are not implemented consistently across browsers. The session modules allow you to set cookie parameters, but it makes no guarantee that privacy will be respected by the browser. If security is a concern, use the MOD_SESSION_CRYPTO to encrypt the contents of the session, or store the session on the server using the MOD_SESSION_DBD module.

Standard cookie parameters can be specified after the name of the cookie, as in the example below.

Setting cookie parameters

```
Session On
SessionCryptoPassphrase secret
SessionCookieName session path=/private;domain=example.com;httponly;secure;
```

In cases where the Apache server forms the frontend for backend origin servers, it is possible to have the session cookies removed from the incoming HTTP headers using the SESSIONCOOKIEREMOVE directive. This keeps the contents of the session cookies from becoming accessible from the backend server.

Session Support for Authentication

As is possible within many application servers, authentication modules can use a session for storing the username and password after login. The MOD_AUTH_FORM saves the user's login name and password within the session.

Form based authentication

```
Session On
SessionCryptoPassphrase secret
SessionCookieName session path=/
AuthFormProvider file
AuthUserFile "conf/passwd"
AuthType form
AuthName realm
#...
```

See the MOD_AUTH_FORM module for documentation and complete examples.

Integrating Sessions with External Applications

In order for sessions to be useful, it must be possible to share the contents of a session with external applications, and it must be possible for an external application to write a session of its own.

A typical example might be an application that changes a user's password set by MOD_AUTH_FORM. This application would need to read the current username and password from the session, make the required changes to the user's password, and then write the new password to the session in order to provide a seamless transition to the new password.

A second example might involve an application that registers a new user for the first time. When registration is complete, the username and password is written to the session, providing a seamless transition to being logged in.

Apache modules Modules within the server that need access to the session can use the **mod_session.h** API in order to read from and write to the session. This mechanism is used by modules like MOD_AUTH_FORM.

CGI programs and scripting languages Applications that run within the webserver can optionally retrieve the value of the session from the **HTTP_SESSION** environment variable. The session should be encoded as a **application/x-www-form-urlencoded** string as described by the HTML specification[75]. The environment variable is controlled by the setting of the SESSIONENV directive. The session can be written to by the script by returning a **application/x-www-form-urlencoded** response header with a name set by the SESSIONHEADER directive. In both cases, any encryption or decryption, and the reading the session from or writing the session to the chosen storage mechanism is handled by the MOD_SESSION modules and corresponding configuration.

---

[75]http://www.w3.org/TR/html4/

Applications behind MOD_PROXY If the SESSIONHEADER directive is used to define an HTTP request header, the session, encoded as a **application/x-www-form-urlencoded** string, will be made available to the application. If the same header is provided in the response, the value of this response header will be used to replace the session. As above, any encryption or decryption, and the reading the session from or writing the session to the chosen storage mechanism is handled by the MOD_SESSION modules and corresponding configuration.

Standalone applications Applications might choose to manipulate the session outside the control of the Apache HTTP server. In this case, it is the responsibility of the application to read the session from the chosen storage mechanism, decrypt the session, update the session, encrypt the session and write the session to the chosen storage mechanism, as appropriate.

Session Directive

Description:	Enables a session for the current directory or location
Syntax:	Session On|Off
Default:	Session Off
Context:	server config, virtual host, directory, .htaccess
Override:	AuthConfig
Status:	Extension
Module:	mod_session

The SESSION directive enables a session for the directory or location container. Further directives control where the session will be stored and how privacy is maintained.

SessionEnv Directive

Description:	Control whether the contents of the session are written to the *HTTP_SESSION* environment variable
Syntax:	SessionEnv On|Off
Default:	SessionEnv Off
Context:	server config, virtual host, directory, .htaccess
Override:	AuthConfig
Status:	Extension
Module:	mod_session

If set to *On*, the SESSIONENV directive causes the contents of the session to be written to a CGI environment variable called *HTTP_SESSION*.

The string is written in the URL query format, for example:

```
key1=foo&key3=bar
```

SessionExclude Directive

Description:	Define URL prefixes for which a session is ignored
Syntax:	SessionExclude path
Default:	none
Context:	server config, virtual host, directory, .htaccess
Status:	Extension
Module:	mod_session

The SESSIONEXCLUDE directive allows sessions to be disabled relative to URL prefixes only. This can be used to make a website more efficient, by targeting a more precise URL space for which a session should be maintained. By default, all URLs within the directory or location are included in the session. The SESSIONEXCLUDE directive takes precedence over the SESSIONINCLUDE directive.

 Warning

This directive has a similar purpose to the *path* attribute in HTTP cookies, but should not be confused with this attribute. This directive does not set the *path* attribute, which must be configured separately.

SessionHeader Directive

Description:	Import session updates from a given HTTP response header
Syntax:	`SessionHeader header`
Default:	`none`
Context:	server config, virtual host, directory, .htaccess
Override:	AuthConfig
Status:	Extension
Module:	mod_session

The SESSIONHEADER directive defines the name of an HTTP response header which, if present, will be parsed and written to the current session.

The header value is expected to be in the URL query format, for example:

```
key1=foo&key2=&key3=bar
```

Where a key is set to the empty string, that key will be removed from the session.

SessionInclude Directive

Description:	Define URL prefixes for which a session is valid
Syntax:	`SessionInclude path`
Default:	`all URLs`
Context:	server config, virtual host, directory, .htaccess
Override:	AuthConfig
Status:	Extension
Module:	mod_session

The SESSIONINCLUDE directive allows sessions to be made valid for specific URL prefixes only. This can be used to make a website more efficient, by targeting a more precise URL space for which a session should be maintained. By default, all URLs within the directory or location are included in the session.

 Warning

This directive has a similar purpose to the *path* attribute in HTTP cookies, but should not be confused with this attribute. This directive does not set the *path* attribute, which must be configured separately.

SessionMaxAge Directive

Description:	Define a maximum age in seconds for a session
Syntax:	`SessionMaxAge maxage`
Default:	`SessionMaxAge 0`
Context:	server config, virtual host, directory, .htaccess
Override:	AuthConfig
Status:	Extension
Module:	mod_session

The SESSIONMAXAGE directive defines a time limit for which a session will remain valid. When a session is saved, this time limit is reset and an existing session can be continued. If a session becomes older than this limit without a request to the server to refresh the session, the session will time out and be removed. Where a session is used to stored user login details, this has the effect of logging the user out automatically after the given time.

Setting the maxage to zero disables session expiry.

10.97 Apache Module mod_session_cookie

Description:	Cookie based session support
Status:	Extension
ModuleIdentifier:	session_cookie_module
SourceFile:	mod_session_cookie.c
Compatibility:	Available in Apache 2.3 and later

Summary

 Warning

The session modules make use of HTTP cookies, and as such can fall victim to Cross Site Scripting attacks, or expose potentially private information to clients. Please ensure that the relevant risks have been taken into account before enabling the session functionality on your server.

This submodule of MOD_SESSION provides support for the storage of user sessions on the remote browser within HTTP cookies.

Using cookies to store a session removes the need for the server or a group of servers to store the session locally, or collaborate to share a session, and can be useful for high traffic environments where a server based session might be too resource intensive.

If session privacy is required, the MOD_SESSION_CRYPTO module can be used to encrypt the contents of the session before writing the session to the client.

For more details on the session interface, see the documentation for the MOD_SESSION module.

Directives

- SessionCookieName
- SessionCookieName2
- SessionCookieRemove

See also

- MOD_SESSION
- MOD_SESSION_CRYPTO
- MOD_SESSION_DBD

Basic Examples

To create a simple session and store it in a cookie called *session*, configure the session as follows:

Browser based session

```
Session On
SessionCookieName session path=/
```

For more examples on how the session can be configured to be read from and written to by a CGI application, see the MOD_SESSION examples section.

For documentation on how the session can be used to store username and password details, see the MOD_AUTH_FORM module.

SessionCookieName Directive

Description:	Name and attributes for the RFC2109 cookie storing the session
Syntax:	`SessionCookieName name attributes`
Default:	`none`
Context:	server config, virtual host, directory, .htaccess
Status:	Extension
Module:	mod_session_cookie

The SESSIONCOOKIENAME directive specifies the name and optional attributes of an RFC2109 compliant cookie inside which the session will be stored. RFC2109 cookies are set using the `Set-Cookie` HTTP header.

An optional list of cookie attributes can be specified, as per the example below. These attributes are inserted into the cookie as is, and are not interpreted by Apache. Ensure that your attributes are defined correctly as per the cookie specification.

Cookie with attributes

```
Session On
SessionCookieName session path=/private;domain=example.com;httponly;secure;vers
```

SessionCookieName2 Directive

Description:	Name and attributes for the RFC2965 cookie storing the session
Syntax:	`SessionCookieName2 name attributes`
Default:	`none`
Context:	server config, virtual host, directory, .htaccess
Status:	Extension
Module:	mod_session_cookie

The SESSIONCOOKIENAME2 directive specifies the name and optional attributes of an RFC2965 compliant cookie inside which the session will be stored. RFC2965 cookies are set using the `Set-Cookie2` HTTP header.

An optional list of cookie attributes can be specified, as per the example below. These attributes are inserted into the cookie as is, and are not interpreted by Apache. Ensure that your attributes are defined correctly as per the cookie specification.

Cookie2 with attributes

```
Session On
SessionCookieName2 session path=/private;domain=example.com;httponly;secure;ver
```

SessionCookieRemove Directive

Description:	Control for whether session cookies should be removed from incoming HTTP headers
Syntax:	`SessionCookieRemove On|Off`
Default:	`SessionCookieRemove Off`
Context:	server config, virtual host, directory, .htaccess
Status:	Extension
Module:	mod_session_cookie

The SESSIONCOOKIEREMOVE flag controls whether the cookies containing the session will be removed from the headers during request processing.

In a reverse proxy situation where the Apache server acts as a server frontend for a backend origin server, revealing the contents of the session cookie to the backend could be a potential privacy violation. When set to on, the session cookie will be removed from the incoming HTTP headers.

10.98   Apache Module mod_session_crypto

Description:	Session encryption support
Status:	Experimental
ModuleIdentifier:	session_crypto_module
SourceFile:	mod_session_crypto.c
Compatibility:	Available in Apache 2.3 and later

Summary

 Warning

The session modules make use of HTTP cookies, and as such can fall victim to Cross Site Scripting attacks, or expose potentially private information to clients. Please ensure that the relevant risks have been taken into account before enabling the session functionality on your server.

This submodule of MOD_SESSION provides support for the encryption of user sessions before being written to a local database, or written to a remote browser via an HTTP cookie.

This can help provide privacy to user sessions where the contents of the session should be kept private from the user, or where protection is needed against the effects of cross site scripting attacks.

For more details on the session interface, see the documentation for the MOD_SESSION module.

Directives

- SessionCryptoCipher
- SessionCryptoDriver
- SessionCryptoPassphrase
- SessionCryptoPassphraseFile

See also

- MOD_SESSION
- MOD_SESSION_COOKIE
- MOD_SESSION_DBD

Basic Usage

To create a simple encrypted session and store it in a cookie called *session*, configure the session as follows:

Browser based encrypted session

```
Session On
SessionCookieName session path=/
SessionCryptoPassphrase secret
```

The session will be encrypted with the given key. Different servers can be configured to share sessions by ensuring the same encryption key is used on each server.

If the encryption key is changed, sessions will be invalidated automatically.

For documentation on how the session can be used to store username and password details, see the MOD_AUTH_FORM module.

SessionCryptoCipher Directive

Description:	The crypto cipher to be used to encrypt the session
Syntax:	`SessionCryptoCipher name`
Default:	`aes256`
Context:	server config, virtual host, directory, .htaccess
Status:	Experimental
Module:	mod_session_crypto
Compatibility:	Available in Apache 2.3.0 and later

The SESSIONCRYPTOCIPHER directive allows the cipher to be used during encryption. If not specified, the cipher defaults to `aes256`.

Possible values depend on the crypto driver in use, and could be one of:

- 3des192
- aes128
- aes192
- aes256

SessionCryptoDriver Directive

Description:	The crypto driver to be used to encrypt the session
Syntax:	`SessionCryptoDriver name [param[=value]]`
Default:	`none`
Context:	server config
Status:	Experimental
Module:	mod_session_crypto
Compatibility:	Available in Apache 2.3.0 and later

The SESSIONCRYPTODRIVER directive specifies the name of the crypto driver to be used for encryption. If not specified, the driver defaults to the recommended driver compiled into APR-util.

The *NSS* crypto driver requires some parameters for configuration, which are specified as parameters with optional values after the driver name.

NSS without a certificate database

```
SessionCryptoDriver nss
```

NSS with certificate database

```
SessionCryptoDriver nss dir=certs
```

NSS with certificate database and parameters

```
SessionCryptoDriver nss dir=certs key3=key3.db cert7=cert7.db secmod=secmod
```

NSS with paths containing spaces

```
SessionCryptoDriver nss "dir=My Certs" key3=key3.db cert7=cert7.db secmod=secmo
```

The *NSS* crypto driver might have already been configured by another part of the server, for example from `mod_nss` or MOD_LDAP. If found to have already been configured, a warning will be logged, and the existing configuration will have taken affect. To avoid this warning, use the noinit parameter as follows.

NSS with certificate database

```
SessionCryptoDriver nss noinit
```

To prevent confusion, ensure that all modules requiring NSS are configured with identical parameters.

The *openssl* crypto driver supports an optional parameter to specify the engine to be used for encryption.

OpenSSL with engine support

```
SessionCryptoDriver openssl engine=name
```

SessionCryptoPassphrase Directive

Description:	The key used to encrypt the session
Syntax:	`SessionCryptoPassphrase secret [ secret ... ]`
Default:	`none`
Context:	server config, virtual host, directory, .htaccess
Status:	Experimental
Module:	mod_session_crypto
Compatibility:	Available in Apache 2.3.0 and later

The SESSIONCRYPTOPASSPHRASE directive specifies the keys to be used to enable symmetrical encryption on the contents of the session before writing the session, or decrypting the contents of the session after reading the session.

Keys are more secure when they are long, and consist of truly random characters. Changing the key on a server has the effect of invalidating all existing sessions.

Multiple keys can be specified in order to support key rotation. The first key listed will be used for encryption, while all keys listed will be attempted for decryption. To rotate keys across multiple servers over a period of time, add a new secret to the end of the list, and once rolled out completely to all servers, remove the first key from the start of the list.

As of version 2.4.7 if the value begins with *exec:* the resulting command will be executed and the first line returned to standard output by the program will be used as the key.

```
#key used as-is
SessionCryptoPassphrase secret

#Run /path/to/program to get key
SessionCryptoPassphrase exec:/path/to/program

#Run /path/to/otherProgram and provide arguments
SessionCryptoPassphrase "exec:/path/to/otherProgram argument1"
```

SessionCryptoPassphraseFile Directive

Description:	File containing keys used to encrypt the session
Syntax:	`SessionCryptoPassphraseFile filename`
Default:	`none`
Context:	server config, virtual host, directory
Status:	Experimental
Module:	mod_session_crypto
Compatibility:	Available in Apache 2.3.0 and later

The SESSIONCRYPTOPASSPHRASEFILE directive specifies the name of a configuration file containing the keys to use for encrypting or decrypting the session, specified one per line. The file is read on server start, and a graceful restart will be necessary for httpd to pick up changes to the keys.

Unlike the SESSIONCRYPTOPASSPHRASE directive, the keys are not exposed within the httpd configuration and can be hidden by protecting the file appropriately.

Multiple keys can be specified in order to support key rotation. The first key listed will be used for encryption, while all keys listed will be attempted for decryption. To rotate keys across multiple servers over a period of time, add a new secret to the end of the list, and once rolled out completely to all servers, remove the first key from the start of the list.

10.99   Apache Module mod_session_dbd

Description:	DBD/SQL based session support
Status:	Extension
ModuleIdentifier:	session_dbd_module
SourceFile:	mod_session_dbd.c
Compatibility:	Available in Apache 2.3 and later

Summary

 Warning

The session modules make use of HTTP cookies, and as such can fall victim to Cross Site Scripting attacks, or expose potentially private information to clients. Please ensure that the relevant risks have been taken into account before enabling the session functionality on your server.

This submodule of MOD_SESSION provides support for the storage of user sessions within a SQL database using the MOD_DBD module.

Sessions can either be **anonymous**, where the session is keyed by a unique UUID string stored on the browser in a cookie, or **per user**, where the session is keyed against the userid of the logged in user.

SQL based sessions are hidden from the browser, and so offer a measure of privacy without the need for encryption.

Different webservers within a server farm may choose to share a database, and so share sessions with one another.

For more details on the session interface, see the documentation for the MOD_SESSION module.

Directives

- SessionDBDCookieName
- SessionDBDCookieName2
- SessionDBDCookieRemove
- SessionDBDDeleteLabel
- SessionDBDInsertLabel
- SessionDBDPerUser
- SessionDBDSelectLabel
- SessionDBDUpdateLabel

See also

- MOD_SESSION
- MOD_SESSION_CRYPTO
- MOD_SESSION_COOKIE
- MOD_DBD

DBD Configuration

Before the MOD_SESSION_DBD module can be configured to maintain a session, the MOD_DBD module must be configured to make the various database queries available to the server.

There are four queries required to keep a session maintained, to select an existing session, to update an existing session, to insert a new session, and to delete an expired or empty session. These queries are configured as per the example below.

Sample DBD configuration

```
DBDriver pgsql
DBDParams "dbname=apachesession user=apache password=xxxxx host=localhost"
DBDPrepareSQL "delete from session where key = %s" deletesession
DBDPrepareSQL "update session set value = %s, expiry = %lld, key = %s where key
DBDPrepareSQL "insert into session (value, expiry, key) values (%s, %lld, %s)"
DBDPrepareSQL "select value from session where key = %s and (expiry = 0 or expi
DBDPrepareSQL "delete from session where expiry != 0 and expiry < %lld" cleanse
```

Anonymous Sessions

Anonymous sessions are keyed against a unique UUID, and stored on the browser within an HTTP cookie. This method is similar to that used by most application servers to store session information.

To create a simple anonymous session and store it in a postgres database table called *apachesession*, and save the session ID in a cookie called *session*, configure the session as follows:

SQL based anonymous session

```
Session On
SessionDBDCookieName session path=/
```

For more examples on how the session can be configured to be read from and written to by a CGI application, see the MOD_SESSION examples section.

For documentation on how the session can be used to store username and password details, see the MOD_AUTH_FORM module.

Per User Sessions

Per user sessions are keyed against the username of a successfully authenticated user. It offers the most privacy, as no external handle to the session exists outside of the authenticated realm.

Per user sessions work within a correctly configured authenticated environment, be that using basic authentication, digest authentication or SSL client certificates. Due to the limitations of who came first, the chicken or the egg, per user sessions cannot be used to store authentication credentials from a module like MOD_AUTH_FORM.

To create a simple per user session and store it in a postgres database table called *apachesession*, and with the session keyed to the userid, configure the session as follows:

SQL based per user session

```
Session On
SessionDBDPerUser On
```

Database Housekeeping

Over the course of time, the database can be expected to start accumulating expired sessions. At this point, the MOD_SESSION_DBD module is not yet able to handle session expiry automatically.

 Warning

The administrator will need to set up an external process via cron to clean out expired sessions.

SessionDBDCookieName Directive

Description:	Name and attributes for the RFC2109 cookie storing the session ID
Syntax:	`SessionDBDCookieName name attributes`
Default:	`none`
Context:	server config, virtual host, directory, .htaccess
Status:	Extension
Module:	mod_session_dbd

The SESSIONDBDCOOKIENAME directive specifies the name and optional attributes of an RFC2109 compliant cookie inside which the session ID will be stored. RFC2109 cookies are set using the `Set-Cookie` HTTP header.

An optional list of cookie attributes can be specified, as per the example below. These attributes are inserted into the cookie as is, and are not interpreted by Apache. Ensure that your attributes are defined correctly as per the cookie specification.

Cookie with attributes

```
Session On
SessionDBDCookieName session path=/private;domain=example.com;httponly;secure;v
```

SessionDBDCookieName2 Directive

Description:	Name and attributes for the RFC2965 cookie storing the session ID
Syntax:	`SessionDBDCookieName2 name attributes`
Default:	`none`
Context:	server config, virtual host, directory, .htaccess
Status:	Extension
Module:	mod_session_dbd

The SESSIONDBDCOOKIENAME2 directive specifies the name and optional attributes of an RFC2965 compliant cookie inside which the session ID will be stored. RFC2965 cookies are set using the `Set-Cookie2` HTTP header.

An optional list of cookie attributes can be specified, as per the example below. These attributes are inserted into the cookie as is, and are not interpreted by Apache. Ensure that your attributes are defined correctly as per the cookie specification.

Cookie2 with attributes

```
Session On
SessionDBDCookieName2 session path=/private;domain=example.com;httponly;secure;
```

SessionDBDCookieRemove Directive

Description:	Control for whether session ID cookies should be removed from incoming HTTP headers
Syntax:	`SessionDBDCookieRemove On|Off`
Default:	`SessionDBDCookieRemove On`
Context:	server config, virtual host, directory, .htaccess
Status:	Extension
Module:	mod_session_dbd

The SESSIONDBDCOOKIEREMOVE flag controls whether the cookies containing the session ID will be removed from the headers during request processing.

In a reverse proxy situation where the Apache server acts as a server frontend for a backend origin server, revealing the contents of the session ID cookie to the backend could be a potential privacy violation. When set to on, the session ID cookie will be removed from the incoming HTTP headers.

SessionDBDDeleteLabel Directive

Description:	The SQL query to use to remove sessions from the database
Syntax:	`SessionDBDDeleteLabel label`
Default:	`SessionDBDDeleteLabel deletesession`
Context:	server config, virtual host, directory, .htaccess
Status:	Extension
Module:	mod_session_dbd

The SESSIONDBDDELETELABEL directive sets the default delete query label to be used to delete an expired or empty session. This label must have been previously defined using the DBDPREPARESQL directive.

SessionDBDInsertLabel Directive

Description:	The SQL query to use to insert sessions into the database
Syntax:	`SessionDBDInsertLabel label`
Default:	`SessionDBDInsertLabel insertsession`
Context:	server config, virtual host, directory, .htaccess
Status:	Extension
Module:	mod_session_dbd

The SESSIONDBDINSERTLABEL directive sets the default insert query label to be used to load in a session. This label must have been previously defined using the DBDPREPARESQL directive.

If an attempt to update the session affects no rows, this query will be called to insert the session into the database.

SessionDBDPerUser Directive

Description:	Enable a per user session
Syntax:	`SessionDBDPerUser On|Off`
Default:	`SessionDBDPerUser Off`
Context:	server config, virtual host, directory, .htaccess
Status:	Extension
Module:	mod_session_dbd

The SESSIONDBDPERUSER flag enables a per user session keyed against the user's login name. If the user is not logged in, this directive will be ignored.

SessionDBDSelectLabel Directive

Description:	The SQL query to use to select sessions from the database
Syntax:	`SessionDBDSelectLabel label`
Default:	`SessionDBDSelectLabel selectsession`
Context:	server config, virtual host, directory, .htaccess
Status:	Extension
Module:	mod_session_dbd

The SESSIONDBDSELECTLABEL directive sets the default select query label to be used to load in a session. This label must have been previously defined using the DBDPREPARESQL directive.

SessionDBDUpdateLabel Directive

Description:	The SQL query to use to update existing sessions in the database
Syntax:	`SessionDBDUpdateLabel label`
Default:	`SessionDBDUpdateLabel updatesession`
Context:	server config, virtual host, directory, .htaccess
Status:	Extension
Module:	mod_session_dbd

The SESSIONDBDUPDATELABEL directive sets the default update query label to be used to load in a session. This label must have been previously defined using the DBDPREPARESQL directive.

If an attempt to update the session affects no rows, the insert query will be called to insert the session into the database. If the database supports InsertOrUpdate, override this query to perform the update in one query instead of two.

10.100 Apache Module mod_setenvif

Description:	Allows the setting of environment variables based on characteristics of the request
Status:	Base
ModuleIdentifier:	setenvif_module
SourceFile:	mod_setenvif.c

Summary

The MOD_SETENVIF module allows you to set internal environment variables according to whether different aspects of the request match regular expressions you specify. These environment variables can be used by other parts of the server to make decisions about actions to be taken, as well as becoming available to CGI scripts and SSI pages.

The directives are considered in the order they appear in the configuration files. So more complex sequences can be used, such as this example, which sets netscape if the browser is mozilla but not MSIE.

```
BrowserMatch ^Mozilla netscape
BrowserMatch MSIE !netscape
```

When the server looks up a path via an internal subrequest such as looking for a DIRECTORYINDEX or generating a directory listing with MOD_AUTOINDEX, per-request environment variables are *not* inherited in the subrequest. Additionally, SETENVIF directives are not separately evaluated in the subrequest due to the API phases MOD_SETENVIF takes action in.

Directives

- BrowserMatch
- BrowserMatchNoCase
- SetEnvIf
- SetEnvIfExpr
- SetEnvIfNoCase

See also

- Environment Variables in Apache HTTP Server (p. 82)

BrowserMatch Directive

Description:	Sets environment variables conditional on HTTP User-Agent
Syntax:	BrowserMatch regex [!]env-variable[=value] [[!]env-variable[=value]] ...
Context:	server config, virtual host, directory, .htaccess
Override:	FileInfo
Status:	Base
Module:	mod_setenvif

The BROWSERMATCH is a special cases of the SETENVIF directive that sets environment variables conditional on the User-Agent HTTP request header. The following two lines have the same effect:

```
BrowserMatchNoCase Robot is_a_robot
SetEnvIfNoCase User-Agent Robot is_a_robot
```

Some additional examples:

```
BrowserMatch ^Mozilla forms jpeg=yes browser=netscape
BrowserMatch "^Mozilla/[2-3]" tables agif frames javascript
BrowserMatch MSIE !javascript
```

BrowserMatchNoCase Directive

Description:	Sets environment variables conditional on User-Agent without respect to case
Syntax:	`BrowserMatchNoCase regex [!]env-variable[=value]` `[[!]env-variable[=value]] ...`
Context:	server config, virtual host, directory, .htaccess
Override:	FileInfo
Status:	Base
Module:	mod_setenvif

The BROWSERMATCHNOCASE directive is semantically identical to the BROWSERMATCH directive. However, it provides for case-insensitive matching. For example:

```
BrowserMatchNoCase mac platform=macintosh
BrowserMatchNoCase win platform=windows
```

The BROWSERMATCH and BROWSERMATCHNOCASE directives are special cases of the SETENVIF and SETENV-IFNOCASE directives. The following two lines have the same effect:

```
BrowserMatchNoCase Robot is_a_robot
SetEnvIfNoCase User-Agent Robot is_a_robot
```

SetEnvIf Directive

Description:	Sets environment variables based on attributes of the request
Syntax:	`SetEnvIf attribute regex [!]env-variable[=value]` `[[!]env-variable[=value]] ...`
Context:	server config, virtual host, directory, .htaccess
Override:	FileInfo
Status:	Base
Module:	mod_setenvif

The SETENVIF directive defines environment variables based on attributes of the request. The *attribute* specified in the first argument can be one of four things:

1. An HTTP request header field (see RFC2616[76] for more information about these); for example: `Host`, `User-Agent`, `Referer`, and `Accept-Language`. A regular expression may be used to specify a set of request headers.

2. One of the following aspects of the request:

   - `Remote_Host` - the hostname (if available) of the client making the request
   - `Remote_Addr` - the IP address of the client making the request
   - `Server_Addr` - the IP address of the server on which the request was received (only with versions later than 2.0.43)

---

[76]http://www.rfc-editor.org/rfc/rfc2616.txt

- `Request_Method` - the name of the method being used (`GET`, `POST`, *et cetera*)

- `Request_Protocol` - the name and version of the protocol with which the request was made (*e.g.*, "HTTP/0.9", "HTTP/1.1", *etc.*)

- `Request_URI` - the resource requested on the HTTP request line – generally the portion of the URL following the scheme and host portion without the query string. See the REWRITECOND directive of MOD_REWRITE for extra information on how to match your query string.

3. The name of an environment variable in the list of those associated with the request. This allows SETEN-VIF directives to test against the result of prior matches. Only those environment variables defined by earlier `SetEnvIf[NoCase]` directives are available for testing in this manner. 'Earlier' means that they were defined at a broader scope (such as server-wide) or previously in the current directive's scope. Environment variables will be considered only if there was no match among request characteristics and a regular expression was not used for the *attribute*.

The second argument (*regex*) is a regular expression. If the *regex* matches against the *attribute*, then the remainder of the arguments are evaluated.

The rest of the arguments give the names of variables to set, and optionally values to which they should be set. These take the form of

1. *varname*, or

2. `!`*varname*, or

3. *varname=value*

In the first form, the value will be set to "1". The second will remove the given variable if already defined, and the third will set the variable to the literal value given by *value*. Since version 2.0.51, Apache httpd will recognize occurrences of $1..$9 within *value* and replace them by parenthesized subexpressions of *regex*.

```
SetEnvIf Request_URI "\.gif$" object_is_image=gif
SetEnvIf Request_URI "\.jpg$" object_is_image=jpg
SetEnvIf Request_URI "\.xbm$" object_is_image=xbm

SetEnvIf Referer www\.mydomain\.example\.com intra_site_referral

SetEnvIf object_is_image xbm XBIT_PROCESSING=1

SetEnvIf ^TS  ^[a-z]  HAVE_TS
```

The first three will set the environment variable `object_is_image` if the request was for an image file, and the fourth sets `intra_site_referral` if the referring page was somewhere on the `www.mydomain.example.com` Web site.

The last example will set environment variable `HAVE_TS` if the request contains any headers that begin with "TS" whose values begins with any character in the set [a-z].

See also

- Environment Variables in Apache HTTP Server (p. 82) , for additional examples.

SetEnvIfExpr Directive

Description:	Sets environment variables based on an ap_expr expression
Syntax:	`SetEnvIfExpr expr [!]env-variable[=value]` `[[!]env-variable[=value]] ...`
Context:	server config, virtual host, directory, .htaccess
Override:	FileInfo
Status:	Base
Module:	mod_setenvif

The SETENVIFEXPR directive defines environment variables based on an <IF> ap_expr. These expressions will be evaluated at runtime, and applied *env-variable* in the same fashion as SETENVIF.

```
SetEnvIfExpr "tolower(req('X-Sendfile')) == 'd:\images\very_big.iso')" iso_deli
```

This would set the environment variable `iso_delivered` every time our application attempts to send it via `X-Sendfile`

A more useful example would be to set the variable rfc1918 if the remote IP address is a private address according to RFC 1918:

```
SetEnvIfExpr "-R '10.0.0.0/8' || -R '172.16.0.0/12' || -R '192.168.0.0/16'" rfc
```

See also

- Expressions in Apache HTTP Server (p. 89) , for a complete reference and more examples.
- <IF> can be used to achieve similar results.
- MOD_FILTER

SetEnvIfNoCase Directive

Description:	Sets environment variables based on attributes of the request without respect to case
Syntax:	`SetEnvIfNoCase attribute regex [!]env-variable[=value]` `[[!]env-variable[=value]] ...`
Context:	server config, virtual host, directory, .htaccess
Override:	FileInfo
Status:	Base
Module:	mod_setenvif

The SETENVIFNOCASE is semantically identical to the SETENVIF directive, and differs only in that the regular expression matching is performed in a case-insensitive manner. For example:

```
SetEnvIfNoCase Host Example\.Org site=example
```

This will cause the `site` environment variable to be set to `"example"` if the HTTP request header field `Host:` was included and contained `Example.Org`, `example.org`, or any other combination.

10.101 Apache Module mod_slotmem_plain

Description:	Slot-based shared memory provider.
Status:	Extension
ModuleIdentifier:	slotmem_plain_module
SourceFile:	mod_slotmem_plain.c

Summary

mod_slotmem_plain is a memory provider which provides for creation and access to a plain memory segment in which the datasets are organized in "slots."

If the memory needs to be shared between threads and processes, a better provider would be MOD_SLOTMEM_SHM.

mod_slotmem_plain provides the following API functions:

apr_status_t doall(ap_slotmem_instance_t *s, ap_slotmem_callback_fn_t *func, void *data, apr_pool_t *pool)
call the callback on all worker slots

apr_status_t create(ap_slotmem_instance_t **new, const char *name, apr_size_t item_size, unsigned int item_num
create a new slotmem with each item size is item_size.

apr_status_t attach(ap_slotmem_instance_t **new, const char *name, apr_size_t *item_size, unsigned int *item_n
attach to an existing slotmem.

apr_status_t dptr(ap_slotmem_instance_t *s, unsigned int item_id, voidmem)** get the direct pointer to the memory associated with this worker slot.

apr_status_t get(ap_slotmem_instance_t *s, unsigned int item_id, unsigned char *dest, apr_size_t dest_len)
get/read the memory from this slot to dest

apr_status_t put(ap_slotmem_instance_t *slot, unsigned int item_id, unsigned char *src, apr_size_t src_len)
put/write the data from src to this slot

unsigned int num_slots(ap_slotmem_instance_t *s) return the total number of slots in the segment

apr_size_t slot_size(ap_slotmem_instance_t *s) return the total data size, in bytes, of a slot in the segment

apr_status_t grab(ap_slotmem_instance_t *s, unsigned int *item_id); grab or allocate the first free slot and mark as in-use (does not do any data copying)

apr_status_t fgrab(ap_slotmem_instance_t *s, unsigned int item_id); forced grab or allocate the specified slot and mark as in-use (does not do any data copying)

apr_status_t release(ap_slotmem_instance_t *s, unsigned int item_id); release or free a slot and mark as not in-use (does not do any data copying)

Directives This module provides no directives.

10.102   Apache Module mod_slotmem_shm

Description:	Slot-based shared memory provider.
Status:	Extension
ModuleIdentifier:	slotmem_shm_module
SourceFile:	mod_slotmem_shm.c

Summary

mod_slotmem_shm is a memory provider which provides for creation and access to a shared memory segment in which the datasets are organized in "slots."

All shared memory is cleared and cleaned with each restart, whether graceful or not. The data itself is stored and restored within a file noted by the name parameter in the create and attach calls. If not specified with an absolute path, the file will be created relative to the path specified by the DEFAULTRUNTIMEDIR directive.

mod_slotmem_shm provides the following API functions:

apr_status_t doall(ap_slotmem_instance_t *s, ap_slotmem_callback_fn_t *func, void *data, apr_pool_t *pool)
   call the callback on all worker slots

apr_status_t create(ap_slotmem_instance_t **new, const char *name, apr_size_t item_size, unsigned int item_num
   create a new slotmem with each item size is item_size. name is used to generate a filename for the persistent store of the shared memory if configured. Values are:

   "none" Anonymous shared memory and no persistent store

   "file-name" [DefaultRuntimeDir]/file-name

   "/absolute-file-name" Absolute file name

apr_status_t attach(ap_slotmem_instance_t **new, const char *name, apr_size_t *item_size, unsigned int *item_nu
   attach to an existing slotmem. See create for description of name parameter.

apr_status_t dptr(ap_slotmem_instance_t *s, unsigned int item_id, voidmem)** get the direct pointer to the memory associated with this worker slot.

apr_status_t get(ap_slotmem_instance_t *s, unsigned int item_id, unsigned char *dest, apr_size_t dest_len)
   get/read the memory from this slot to dest

apr_status_t put(ap_slotmem_instance_t *slot, unsigned int item_id, unsigned char *src, apr_size_t src_len)
   put/write the data from src to this slot

unsigned int num_slots(ap_slotmem_instance_t *s) return the total number of slots in the segment

apr_size_t slot_size(ap_slotmem_instance_t *s) return the total data size, in bytes, of a slot in the segment

apr_status_t grab(ap_slotmem_instance_t *s, unsigned int *item_id); grab or allocate the first free slot and mark as in-use (does not do any data copying)

apr_status_t fgrab(ap_slotmem_instance_t *s, unsigned int item_id); forced grab or allocate the specified slot and mark as in-use (does not do any data copying)

apr_status_t release(ap_slotmem_instance_t *s, unsigned int item_id); release or free a slot and mark as not in-use (does not do any data copying)

Directives This module provides no directives.

10.103 Apache Module mod_so

Description:	Loading of executable code and modules into the server at start-up or restart time
Status:	Extension
ModuleIdentifier:	so_module
SourceFile:	mod_so.c
Compatibility:	This is a Base module (always included) on Windows

Summary

On selected operating systems this module can be used to load modules into Apache HTTP Server at runtime via the Dynamic Shared Object (p. 65) (DSO) mechanism, rather than requiring a recompilation.

On Unix, the loaded code typically comes from shared object files (usually with .so extension), on Windows this may either the .so or .dll extension.

Warning

Modules built for one major version of the Apache HTTP Server will generally not work on another. (e.g. 1.3 vs. 2.0, or 2.0 vs. 2.2) There are usually API changes between one major version and another that require that modules be modified to work with the new version.

Directives

- LoadFile
- LoadModule

Creating Loadable Modules for Windows

Note

On Windows, where loadable files typically have a file extension of .dll, Apache httpd modules are called mod_whatever.so, just as they are on other platforms. However, you may encounter third-party modules, such as PHP for example, that continue to use the .dll convention.

While mod_so still loads modules with ApacheModuleFoo.dll names, the new naming convention is preferred; if you are converting your loadable module for 2.0, please fix the name to this 2.0 convention.

The Apache httpd module API is unchanged between the Unix and Windows versions. Many modules will run on Windows with no or little change from Unix, although others rely on aspects of the Unix architecture which are not present in Windows, and will not work.

When a module does work, it can be added to the server in one of two ways. As with Unix, it can be compiled into the server. Because Apache httpd for Windows does not have the Configure program of Apache httpd for Unix, the module's source file must be added to the ApacheCore project file, and its symbols must be added to the os\win32\modules.c file.

The second way is to compile the module as a DLL, a shared library that can be loaded into the server at runtime, using the LoadModule directive. These module DLLs can be distributed and run on any Apache httpd for Windows installation, without recompilation of the server.

To create a module DLL, a small change is necessary to the module's source file: The module record must be exported from the DLL (which will be created later; see below). To do this, add the AP_MODULE_DECLARE_DATA (defined in the Apache httpd header files) to your module's module record definition. For example, if your module has:

```
module foo_module;
```

Replace the above with:

```
module AP_MODULE_DECLARE_DATA foo_module;
```

Note that this will only be activated on Windows, so the module can continue to be used, unchanged, with Unix if needed. Also, if you are familiar with .DEF files, you can export the module record with that method instead.

Now, create a DLL containing your module. You will need to link this against the libhttpd.lib export library that is created when the libhttpd.dll shared library is compiled. You may also have to change the compiler settings to ensure that the Apache httpd header files are correctly located. You can find this library in your server root's modules directory. It is best to grab an existing module .dsp file from the tree to assure the build environment is configured correctly, or alternately compare the compiler and link options to your .dsp.

This should create a DLL version of your module. Now simply place it in the `modules` directory of your server root, and use the LOADMODULE directive to load it.

LoadFile Directive

Description:	Link in the named object file or library
Syntax:	`LoadFile filename [filename] ...`
Context:	server config, virtual host
Status:	Extension
Module:	mod_so

The LoadFile directive links in the named object files or libraries when the server is started or restarted; this is used to load additional code which may be required for some module to work. *Filename* is either an absolute path or relative to ServerRoot (p. 354).

For example:

```
LoadFile libexec/libxmlparse.so
```

LoadModule Directive

Description:	Links in the object file or library, and adds to the list of active modules
Syntax:	`LoadModule module filename`
Context:	server config, virtual host
Status:	Extension
Module:	mod_so

The LoadModule directive links in the object file or library *filename* and adds the module structure named *module* to the list of active modules. *Module* is the name of the external variable of type `module` in the file, and is listed as the Module Identifier (p. 350) in the module documentation. Example:

```
LoadModule status_module modules/mod_status.so
```

loads the named module from the modules subdirectory of the ServerRoot.

10.104 Apache Module mod_socache_dbm

Description:	DBM based shared object cache provider.
Status:	Extension
ModuleIdentifier:	socache_dbm_module
SourceFile:	mod_socache_dbm.c

Summary

mod_socache_dbm is a shared object cache provider which provides for creation and access to a cache backed by a DBM database.

```
dbm:/path/to/datafile
```

Details of other shared object cache providers can be found here (p. 104) .

Directives This module provides no directives.

10.105   Apache Module mod_socache_dc

Description:	Distcache based shared object cache provider.
Status:	Extension
ModuleIdentifier:	socache_dc_module
SourceFile:	mod_socache_dc.c

Summary

mod_socache_dc is a shared object cache provider which provides for creation and access to a cache backed by the distcache[77] distributed session caching libraries.

Details of other shared object cache providers can be found here (p. 104) .

Directives This module provides no directives.

---

[77]http://www.distcache.org/

10.106   Apache Module mod_socache_memcache

Description:	Memcache based shared object cache provider.
Status:	Extension
ModuleIdentifier:	socache_memcache_module
SourceFile:	mod_socache_memcache.c

Summary

mod_socache_memcache is a shared object cache provider which provides for creation and access to a cache backed by the memcached[78] high-performance, distributed memory object caching system.

This shared object cache provider's "create" method requires a comma separated list of memcached host/port specifications. If using this provider via another modules configuration (such as SSLSESSIONCACHE), provide the list of servers as the optional "arg" parameter.

```
SSLSessionCache memcache:memcache.example.com:12345,memcache2.example.com:12345
```

Details of other shared object cache providers can be found here (p. 104).

Directives

- MemcacheConnTTL

MemcacheConnTTL Directive

Description:	Keepalive time for idle connections
Syntax:	MemcacheConnTTL num[units]
Default:	MemcacheConnTTL 15s
Context:	server config, virtual host
Status:	Extension
Module:	mod_socache_memcache
Compatibility:	Available in Apache 2.4.17 and later

Set the time to keep idle connections with the memcache server(s) alive (threaded platforms only).

Valid values for MEMCACHECONNTTL are times up to one hour. 0 means no timeout.

⟹ This timeout defaults to units of seconds, but accepts suffixes for milliseconds (ms), seconds (s), minutes (min), and hours (h).

Before Apache 2.4.17, this timeout was hardcoded and its value was 600 usec. So, the closest configuration to match the legacy behaviour is to set MEMCACHECONNTTL to 1ms.

```
# Set a timeout of 10 minutes
MemcacheConnTTL 10min
# Set a timeout of 60 seconds
MemcacheConnTTL 60
```

---

[78]http://memcached.org/

10.107   Apache Module mod_socache_shmcb

Description:	shmcb based shared object cache provider.
Status:	Extension
ModuleIdentifier:	socache_shmcb_module
SourceFile:	mod_socache_shmcb.c

Summary

mod_socache_shmcb is a shared object cache provider which provides for creation and access to a cache backed by a high-performance cyclic buffer inside a shared memory segment.

```
shmcb:/path/to/datafile(512000)
```

Details of other shared object cache providers can be found here (p. 104) .

Directives This module provides no directives.

10.108 Apache Module mod_speling

Description:	Attempts to correct mistaken URLs by ignoring capitalization, or attempting to correct various minor misspellings.
Status:	Extension
ModuleIdentifier:	speling_module
SourceFile:	mod_speling.c

Summary

Requests to documents sometimes cannot be served by the core apache server because the request was misspelled or miscapitalized. This module addresses this problem by trying to find a matching document, even after all other modules gave up. It does its work by comparing each document name in the requested directory against the requested document name **without regard to case**, and allowing **up to one misspelling** (character insertion / omission / transposition or wrong character). A list is built with all document names which were matched using this strategy.

If, after scanning the directory,

- no matching document was found, Apache will proceed as usual and return a "document not found" error.

- only one document is found that "almost" matches the request, then it is returned in the form of a redirection response.

- more than one document with a close match was found, then the list of the matches is returned to the client, and the client can select the correct candidate.

Directives

- CheckCaseOnly
- CheckSpelling

CheckCaseOnly Directive

Description:	Limits the action of the speling module to case corrections
Syntax:	`CheckCaseOnly on|off`
Default:	`CheckCaseOnly Off`
Context:	server config, virtual host, directory, .htaccess
Override:	Options
Status:	Extension
Module:	mod_speling

When set, this directive limits the action of the spelling correction to lower/upper case changes. Other potential corrections are not performed.

CheckSpelling Directive

Description:	Enables the spelling module
Syntax:	`CheckSpelling on|off`
Default:	`CheckSpelling Off`
Context:	server config, virtual host, directory, .htaccess
Override:	Options
Status:	Extension
Module:	mod_speling

This directive enables or disables the spelling module. When enabled, keep in mind that

- the directory scan which is necessary for the spelling correction will have an impact on the server's performance when many spelling corrections have to be performed at the same time.

- the document trees should not contain sensitive files which could be matched inadvertently by a spelling "correction".

- the module is unable to correct misspelled user names (as in `http://my.host/~apahce/`), just file names or directory names.

- spelling corrections apply strictly to existing files, so a request for the `<Location "/status">` may get incorrectly treated as the negotiated file `"/stats.html"`.

mod_speling should not be enabled in DAV (p. 558) enabled directories, because it will try to "spell fix" newly created resource names against existing filenames, e.g., when trying to upload a new document `doc43.html` it might redirect to an existing document `doc34.html`, which is not what was intended.

10.109   Apache Module mod_ssl

Description:	Strong cryptography using the Secure Sockets Layer (SSL) and Transport Layer Security (TLS) protocols
Status:	Extension
ModuleIdentifier:	ssl_module
SourceFile:	mod_ssl.c

Summary

This module provides SSL v3 and TLS v1.x support for the Apache HTTP Server. SSL v2 is no longer supported.

This module relies on OpenSSL[79] to provide the cryptography engine.

Further details, discussion, and examples are provided in the SSL documentation (p. 182) .

Directives

- SSLCACertificateFile
- SSLCACertificatePath
- SSLCADNRequestFile
- SSLCADNRequestPath
- SSLCARevocationCheck
- SSLCARevocationFile
- SSLCARevocationPath
- SSLCertificateChainFile
- SSLCertificateFile
- SSLCertificateKeyFile
- SSLCipherSuite
- SSLCompression
- SSLCryptoDevice
- SSLEngine
- SSLFIPS
- SSLHonorCipherOrder
- SSLInsecureRenegotiation
- SSLOCSPDefaultResponder
- SSLOCSPEnable
- SSLOCSPOverrideResponder
- SSLOCSPResponderTimeout
- SSLOCSPResponseMaxAge
- SSLOCSPResponseTimeSkew
- SSLOCSPUseRequestNonce
- SSLOpenSSLConfCmd
- SSLOptions

---

[79]http://www.openssl.org/

- SSLPassPhraseDialog
- SSLProtocol
- SSLProxyCACertificateFile
- SSLProxyCACertificatePath
- SSLProxyCARevocationCheck
- SSLProxyCARevocationFile
- SSLProxyCARevocationPath
- SSLProxyCheckPeerCN
- SSLProxyCheckPeerExpire
- SSLProxyCheckPeerName
- SSLProxyCipherSuite
- SSLProxyEngine
- SSLProxyMachineCertificateChainFile
- SSLProxyMachineCertificateFile
- SSLProxyMachineCertificatePath
- SSLProxyProtocol
- SSLProxyVerify
- SSLProxyVerifyDepth
- SSLRandomSeed
- SSLRenegBufferSize
- SSLRequire
- SSLRequireSSL
- SSLSessionCache
- SSLSessionCacheTimeout
- SSLSessionTicketKeyFile
- SSLSessionTickets
- SSLSRPUnknownUserSeed
- SSLSRPVerifierFile
- SSLStaplingCache
- SSLStaplingErrorCacheTimeout
- SSLStaplingFakeTryLater
- SSLStaplingForceURL
- SSLStaplingResponderTimeout
- SSLStaplingResponseMaxAge
- SSLStaplingResponseTimeSkew
- SSLStaplingReturnResponderErrors
- SSLStaplingStandardCacheTimeout
- SSLStrictSNIVHostCheck
- SSLUserName
- SSLUseStapling
- SSLVerifyClient
- SSLVerifyDepth

Environment Variables

This module can be configured to provide several items of SSL information as additional environment variables to the SSI and CGI namespace. This information is not provided by default for performance reasons. (See SSLOPTIONS StdEnvVars, below.) The generated variables are listed in the table below. For backward compatibility the information can be made available under different names, too. Look in the Compatibility (p. 192) chapter for details on the compatibility variables.

Variable Name:	Value Type:	Description:
HTTPS	flag	HTTPS is being used.
SSL_PROTOCOL	string	The SSL protocol version (SSLv3, TLSv1, TLSv1.1, TLS
SSL_SESSION_ID	string	The hex-encoded SSL session id
SSL_SESSION_RESUMED	string	Initial or Resumed SSL Session. Note: multiple requests served over the same (Initial or Resumed) SSL session if KeepAlive is in use
SSL_SECURE_RENEG	string	true if secure renegotiation is supported, else false
SSL_CIPHER	string	The cipher specification name
SSL_CIPHER_EXPORT	string	true if cipher is an export cipher
SSL_CIPHER_USEKEYSIZE	number	Number of cipher bits (actually used)
SSL_CIPHER_ALGKEYSIZE	number	Number of cipher bits (possible)
SSL_COMPRESS_METHOD	string	SSL compression method negotiated
SSL_VERSION_INTERFACE	string	The mod_ssl program version
SSL_VERSION_LIBRARY	string	The OpenSSL program version
SSL_CLIENT_M_VERSION	string	The version of the client certificate
SSL_CLIENT_M_SERIAL	string	The serial of the client certificate
SSL_CLIENT_S_DN	string	Subject DN in client's certificate
SSL_CLIENT_S_DN_*x509*	string	Component of client's Subject DN
SSL_CLIENT_SAN_Email_*n*	string	Client certificate's subjectAltName extension entries rfc822Name
SSL_CLIENT_SAN_DNS_*n*	string	Client certificate's subjectAltName extension entries dNSName
SSL_CLIENT_SAN_OTHER_msUPN_*n*	string	Client certificate's subjectAltName extension entries otherName, Microsoft User Principal Name form 1.3.6.1.4.1.311.20.2.3)
SSL_CLIENT_I_DN	string	Issuer DN of client's certificate
SSL_CLIENT_I_DN_*x509*	string	Component of client's Issuer DN
SSL_CLIENT_V_START	string	Validity of client's certificate (start time)
SSL_CLIENT_V_END	string	Validity of client's certificate (end time)
SSL_CLIENT_V_REMAIN	string	Number of days until client's certificate expires
SSL_CLIENT_A_SIG	string	Algorithm used for the signature of client's certificate
SSL_CLIENT_A_KEY	string	Algorithm used for the public key of client's certificate
SSL_CLIENT_CERT	string	PEM-encoded client certificate
SSL_CLIENT_CERT_CHAIN_*n*	string	PEM-encoded certificates in client certificate chain
SSL_CLIENT_CERT_RFC4523_CEA	string	Serial number and issuer of the certificate. The format that of the CertificateExactAssertion in RFC4523
SSL_CLIENT_VERIFY	string	NONE, SUCCESS, GENEROUS or FAILED:*reason*
SSL_SERVER_M_VERSION	string	The version of the server certificate
SSL_SERVER_M_SERIAL	string	The serial of the server certificate
SSL_SERVER_S_DN	string	Subject DN in server's certificate
SSL_SERVER_SAN_Email_*n*	string	Server certificate's subjectAltName extension entries rfc822Name
SSL_SERVER_SAN_DNS_*n*	string	Server certificate's subjectAltName extension entries dNSName
SSL_SERVER_SAN_OTHER_dnsSRV_*n*	string	Server certificate's subjectAltName extension entries of ty erName, SRVName form (OID 1.3.6.1.5.5.7.8.7, RFC 498

`SSL_SERVER_S_DN_x509`	string	Component of server's Subject DN
`SSL_SERVER_I_DN`	string	Issuer DN of server's certificate
`SSL_SERVER_I_DN_x509`	string	Component of server's Issuer DN
`SSL_SERVER_V_START`	string	Validity of server's certificate (start time)
`SSL_SERVER_V_END`	string	Validity of server's certificate (end time)
`SSL_SERVER_A_SIG`	string	Algorithm used for the signature of server's certificate
`SSL_SERVER_A_KEY`	string	Algorithm used for the public key of server's certificate
`SSL_SERVER_CERT`	string	PEM-encoded server certificate
`SSL_SRP_USER`	string	SRP username
`SSL_SRP_USERINFO`	string	SRP user info
`SSL_TLS_SNI`	string	Contents of the SNI TLS extension (if supplied with Clien

x509 specifies a component of an X.509 DN; one of `C`, `ST`, `L`, `O`, `OU`, `CN`, `T`, `I`, `G`, `S`, `D`, `UID`, `Email`. In Apache 2.1 and later, *x509* may also include a numeric *_n* suffix. If the DN in question contains multiple attributes of the same name, this suffix is used as a zero-based index to select a particular attribute. For example, where the server certificate subject DN included two OU attributes, `SSL_SERVER_S_DN_OU_0` and `SSL_SERVER_S_DN_OU_1` could be used to reference each. A variable name without a *_n* suffix is equivalent to that name with a *_0* suffix; the first (or only) attribute. When the environment table is populated using the `StdEnvVars` option of the SSLOPTIONS directive, the first (or only) attribute of any DN is added only under a non-suffixed name; i.e. no *_0* suffixed entries are added.

The format of the *_DN* variables has changed in Apache HTTPD 2.3.11. See the `LegacyDNStringFormat` option for SSLOPTIONS for details.

`SSL_CLIENT_V_REMAIN` is only available in version 2.1 and later.

A number of additional environment variables can also be used in SSLREQUIRE expressions, or in custom log formats:

`HTTP_USER_AGENT`	`PATH_INFO`	`AUTH_TYPE`
`HTTP_REFERER`	`QUERY_STRING`	`SERVER_SOFTWARE`
`HTTP_COOKIE`	`REMOTE_HOST`	`API_VERSION`
`HTTP_FORWARDED`	`REMOTE_IDENT`	`TIME_YEAR`
`HTTP_HOST`	`IS_SUBREQ`	`TIME_MON`
`HTTP_PROXY_CONNECTION`	`DOCUMENT_ROOT`	`TIME_DAY`
`HTTP_ACCEPT`	`SERVER_ADMIN`	`TIME_HOUR`
`THE_REQUEST`	`SERVER_NAME`	`TIME_MIN`
`REQUEST_FILENAME`	`SERVER_PORT`	`TIME_SEC`
`REQUEST_METHOD`	`SERVER_PROTOCOL`	`TIME_WDAY`
`REQUEST_SCHEME`	`REMOTE_ADDR`	`TIME`
`REQUEST_URI`	`REMOTE_USER`	

In these contexts, two special formats can also be used:

ENV:*variablename* This will expand to the standard environment variable *variablename*.

HTTP:*headername* This will expand to the value of the request header with name *headername*.

Custom Log Formats

When MOD_SSL is built into Apache or at least loaded (under DSO situation) additional functions exist for the Custom Log Format (p. 661) of MOD_LOG_CONFIG. First there is an additional "`%{`*varname*`}x`" eXtension format function which can be used to expand any variables provided by any module, especially those provided by mod_ssl which can you find in the above table.

For backward compatibility there is additionally a special "%{*name*}c" cryptography format function provided. Information about this function is provided in the Compatibility (p. 192) chapter.

Example

```
CustomLog "logs/ssl_request_log" "%t %h %{SSL_PROTOCOL}x %{SSL_CIPHER}x \"%r\"
```

These formats even work without setting the StdEnvVars option of the SSLOPTIONS directive.

Request Notes

MOD_SSL sets "notes" for the request which can be used in logging with the %{*name*}n format string in MOD_LOG_CONFIG.

The notes supported are as follows:

ssl-access-forbidden This note is set to the value 1 if access was denied due to an SSLREQUIRE or SSLRE-QUIRESSL directive.

ssl-secure-reneg If MOD_SSL is built against a version of OpenSSL which supports the secure renegotiation extension, this note is set to the value 1 if SSL is in used for the current connection, and the client also supports the secure renegotiation extension. If the client does not support the secure renegotiation extension, the note is set to the value 0. If MOD_SSL is not built against a version of OpenSSL which supports secure renegotiation, or if SSL is not in use for the current connection, the note is not set.

Authorization providers for use with Require

MOD_SSL provides a few authentication providers for use with MOD_AUTHZ_CORE's REQUIRE directive.

Require ssl

The ssl provider denies access if a connection is not encrypted with SSL. This is similar to the SSLREQUIRESSL directive.

```
Require ssl
```

Require ssl-verify-client

The ssl provider allows access if the user is authenticated with a valid client certificate. This is only useful if SSLVerifyClient optional is in effect.

The following example grants access if the user is authenticated either with a client certificate or by username and password.

```
        Require ssl-verify-client
        Require valid-user
```

SSLCACertificateFile Directive

Description:	File of concatenated PEM-encoded CA Certificates for Client Auth
Syntax:	SSLCACertificateFile file-path
Context:	server config, virtual host
Status:	Extension
Module:	mod_ssl

This directive sets the *all-in-one* file where you can assemble the Certificates of Certification Authorities (CA) whose *clients* you deal with. These are used for Client Authentication. Such a file is simply the concatenation of the various PEM-encoded Certificate files, in order of preference. This can be used alternatively and/or additionally to SSLCAC-ERTIFICATEPATH.

Example

```
SSLCACertificateFile "/usr/local/apache2/conf/ssl.crt/ca-bundle-client.crt"
```

SSLCACertificatePath Directive

Description:	Directory of PEM-encoded CA Certificates for Client Auth
Syntax:	SSLCACertificatePath directory-path
Context:	server config, virtual host
Status:	Extension
Module:	mod_ssl

This directive sets the directory where you keep the Certificates of Certification Authorities (CAs) whose clients you deal with. These are used to verify the client certificate on Client Authentication.

The files in this directory have to be PEM-encoded and are accessed through hash filenames. So usually you can't just place the Certificate files there: you also have to create symbolic links named *hash-value*.N. And you should always make sure this directory contains the appropriate symbolic links.

Example

```
SSLCACertificatePath "/usr/local/apache2/conf/ssl.crt/"
```

SSLCADNRequestFile Directive

Description:	File of concatenated PEM-encoded CA Certificates for defining acceptable CA names
Syntax:	SSLCADNRequestFile file-path
Context:	server config, virtual host
Status:	Extension
Module:	mod_ssl

When a client certificate is requested by mod_ssl, a list of *acceptable Certificate Authority names* is sent to the client in the SSL handshake. These CA names can be used by the client to select an appropriate client certificate out of those it has available.

If neither of the directives SSLCADNREQUESTPATH or SSLCADNREQUESTFILE are given, then the set of acceptable CA names sent to the client is the names of all the CA certificates given by the SSLCACERTIFICATEFILE and SSLCACERTIFICATEPATH directives; in other words, the names of the CAs which will actually be used to verify the client certificate.

In some circumstances, it is useful to be able to send a set of acceptable CA names which differs from the actual CAs used to verify the client certificate - for example, if the client certificates are signed by intermediate CAs. In such cases, SSLCADNREQUESTPATH and/or SSLCADNREQUESTFILE can be used; the acceptable CA names are then taken from the complete set of certificates in the directory and/or file specified by this pair of directives.

SSLCADNREQUESTFILE must specify an *all-in-one* file containing a concatenation of PEM-encoded CA certificates.

Example

```
SSLCADNRequestFile "/usr/local/apache2/conf/ca-names.crt"
```

SSLCADNRequestPath Directive

Description:	Directory of PEM-encoded CA Certificates for defining acceptable CA names
Syntax:	SSLCADNRequestPath directory-path
Context:	server config, virtual host
Status:	Extension
Module:	mod_ssl

This optional directive can be used to specify the set of *acceptable CA names* which will be sent to the client when a client certificate is requested. See the SSLCADNREQUESTFILE directive for more details.

The files in this directory have to be PEM-encoded and are accessed through hash filenames. So usually you can't just place the Certificate files there: you also have to create symbolic links named *hash-value*.N. And you should always make sure this directory contains the appropriate symbolic links.

Example

```
SSLCADNRequestPath "/usr/local/apache2/conf/ca-names.crt/"
```

SSLCARevocationCheck Directive

Description:	Enable CRL-based revocation checking
Syntax:	SSLCARevocationCheck chain|leaf|none
Default:	SSLCARevocationCheck none
Context:	server config, virtual host
Status:	Extension
Module:	mod_ssl

Enables certificate revocation list (CRL) checking. At least one of SSLCAREVOCATIONFILE or SSLCAREVOCATIONPATH must be configured. When set to chain (recommended setting), CRL checks are applied to all certificates in the chain, while setting it to leaf limits the checks to the end-entity cert.

 **When set to chain or leaf, CRLs *must* be available for successful validation**

Prior to version 2.3.15, CRL checking in mod_ssl also succeeded when no CRL(s) were found in any of the locations configured with SSLCAREVOCATIONFILE or SSLCAREVOCATIONPATH. With the introduction of this directive, the behavior has been changed: when checking is enabled, CRLs *must* be present for the validation to succeed - otherwise it will fail with an "unable to get certificate CRL" error.

Example

```
SSLCARevocationCheck chain
```

SSLCARevocationFile Directive

Description:	File of concatenated PEM-encoded CA CRLs for Client Auth
Syntax:	`SSLCARevocationFile file-path`
Context:	server config, virtual host
Status:	Extension
Module:	mod_ssl

This directive sets the *all-in-one* file where you can assemble the Certificate Revocation Lists (CRL) of Certification Authorities (CA) whose *clients* you deal with. These are used for Client Authentication. Such a file is simply the concatenation of the various PEM-encoded CRL files, in order of preference. This can be used alternatively and/or additionally to SSLCAREVOCATIONPATH.

Example

```
SSLCARevocationFile "/usr/local/apache2/conf/ssl.crl/ca-bundle-client.crl"
```

SSLCARevocationPath Directive

Description:	Directory of PEM-encoded CA CRLs for Client Auth
Syntax:	`SSLCARevocationPath directory-path`
Context:	server config, virtual host
Status:	Extension
Module:	mod_ssl

This directive sets the directory where you keep the Certificate Revocation Lists (CRL) of Certification Authorities (CAs) whose clients you deal with. These are used to revoke the client certificate on Client Authentication.

The files in this directory have to be PEM-encoded and are accessed through hash filenames. So usually you have not only to place the CRL files there. Additionally you have to create symbolic links named *hash-value*.rN. And you should always make sure this directory contains the appropriate symbolic links.

Example

```
SSLCARevocationPath "/usr/local/apache2/conf/ssl.crl/"
```

SSLCertificateChainFile Directive

Description:	File of PEM-encoded Server CA Certificates
Syntax:	`SSLCertificateChainFile file-path`
Context:	server config, virtual host
Status:	Extension
Module:	mod_ssl

⟹ **SSLCertificateChainFile is deprecated**

`SSLCertificateChainFile` became obsolete with version 2.4.8, when SSLCERTIFI-CATEFILE was extended to also load intermediate CA certificates from the server certificate file.

This directive sets the optional *all-in-one* file where you can assemble the certificates of Certification Authorities (CA) which form the certificate chain of the server certificate. This starts with the issuing CA certificate of the server certificate and can range up to the root CA certificate. Such a file is simply the concatenation of the various PEM-encoded CA Certificate files, usually in certificate chain order.

This should be used alternatively and/or additionally to SSLCACERTIFICATEPATH for explicitly constructing the server certificate chain which is sent to the browser in addition to the server certificate. It is especially useful to avoid conflicts with CA certificates when using client authentication. Because although placing a CA certificate of the server certificate chain into SSLCACERTIFICATEPATH has the same effect for the certificate chain construction, it has the side-effect that client certificates issued by this same CA certificate are also accepted on client authentication.

But be careful: Providing the certificate chain works only if you are using a *single* RSA *or* DSA based server certificate. If you are using a coupled RSA+DSA certificate pair, this will work only if actually both certificates use the *same* certificate chain. Else the browsers will be confused in this situation.

Example

```
SSLCertificateChainFile "/usr/local/apache2/conf/ssl.crt/ca.crt"
```

SSLCertificateFile Directive

Description:	Server PEM-encoded X.509 certificate data file
Syntax:	`SSLCertificateFile file-path`
Context:	server config, virtual host
Status:	Extension
Module:	mod_ssl

This directive points to a file with certificate data in PEM format. At a minimum, the file must include an end-entity (leaf) certificate. The directive can be used multiple times (referencing different filenames) to support multiple algorithms for server authentication - typically RSA, DSA, and ECC. The number of supported algorithms depends on the OpenSSL version being used for mod_ssl: with version 1.0.0 or later, `openssl list-public-key-algorithms` will output a list of supported algorithms.

The files may also include intermediate CA certificates, sorted from leaf to root. This is supported with version 2.4.8 and later, and obsoletes SSLCERTIFICATECHAINFILE. When running with OpenSSL 1.0.2 or later, this allows to configure the intermediate CA chain on a per-certificate basis.

Custom DH parameters and an EC curve name for ephemeral keys, can also be added to end of the first file configured using SSLCERTIFICATEFILE. This is supported in version 2.4.7 or later. Such parameters can be generated using the commands `openssl dhparam` and `openssl ecparam`. The parameters can be added as-is to the end of the first certificate file. Only the first file can be used for custom parameters, as they are applied independently of the authentication algorithm type.

Finally the end-entity certificate's private key can also be added to the certificate file instead of using a separate SSLCERTIFICATEKEYFILE directive. This practice is highly discouraged. If it is used, the certificate files using such an embedded key must be configured after the certificates using a separate key file. If the private key is encrypted, the pass phrase dialog is forced at startup time.

⟹ DH parameter interoperability with primes > 1024 bit

Beginning with version 2.4.7, mod_ssl makes use of standardized DH parameters with prime lengths of 2048, 3072 and 4096 bits and with additional prime lengths of 6144 and 8192 bits beginning with version 2.4.10 (from RFC 3526[a]), and hands them out to clients based on the length of the certificate's RSA/DSA key. With Java-based clients in particular (Java 7 or earlier), this may lead to handshake failures - see this FAQ answer (p. 202) for working around such issues.

[a]http://www.ietf.org/rfc/rfc3526.txt

Example

```
SSLCertificateFile "/usr/local/apache2/conf/ssl.crt/server.crt"
```

SSLCertificateKeyFile Directive

Description:	Server PEM-encoded private key file
Syntax:	`SSLCertificateKeyFile file-path`
Context:	server config, virtual host
Status:	Extension
Module:	mod_ssl

This directive points to the PEM-encoded private key file for the server. If the contained private key is encrypted, the pass phrase dialog is forced at startup time.

The directive can be used multiple times (referencing different filenames) to support multiple algorithms for server authentication. For each SSLCERTIFICATEKEYFILE directive, there must be a matching SSLCERTIFICATEFILE directive.

The private key may also be combined with the certificate in the file given by SSLCERTIFICATEFILE, but this practice is highly discouraged. If it is used, the certificate files using such an embedded key must be configured after the certificates using a separate key file.

Example

```
SSLCertificateKeyFile "/usr/local/apache2/conf/ssl.key/server.key"
```

SSLCipherSuite Directive

Description:	Cipher Suite available for negotiation in SSL handshake
Syntax:	`SSLCipherSuite cipher-spec`
Default:	`SSLCipherSuite DEFAULT (depends on OpenSSL version)`
Context:	server config, virtual host, directory, .htaccess
Override:	AuthConfig
Status:	Extension
Module:	mod_ssl

This complex directive uses a colon-separated *cipher-spec* string consisting of OpenSSL cipher specifications to configure the Cipher Suite the client is permitted to negotiate in the SSL handshake phase. Notice that this directive can be used both in per-server and per-directory context. In per-server context it applies to the standard SSL handshake when a connection is established. In per-directory context it forces a SSL renegotiation with the reconfigured Cipher Suite after the HTTP request was read but before the HTTP response is sent.

An SSL cipher specification in *cipher-spec* is composed of 4 major attributes plus a few extra minor ones:

- *Key Exchange Algorithm*:
  RSA, Diffie-Hellman, Elliptic Curve Diffie-Hellman, Secure Remote Password
- *Authentication Algorithm*:
  RSA, Diffie-Hellman, DSS, ECDSA, or none.
- *Cipher/Encryption Algorithm*:
  AES, DES, Triple-DES, RC4, RC2, IDEA, etc.
- *MAC Digest Algorithm*:
  MD5, SHA or SHA1, SHA256, SHA384.

An SSL cipher can also be an export cipher. SSLv2 ciphers are no longer supported. To specify which ciphers to use, one can either specify all the Ciphers, one at a time, or use aliases to specify the preference and order for the ciphers (see Table 1). The actually available ciphers and aliases depends on the used openssl version. Newer openssl versions may include additional ciphers.

Tag	Description
Key Exchange Algorithm:	
kRSA	RSA key exchange
kDHr	Diffie-Hellman key exchange with RSA key
kDHd	Diffie-Hellman key exchange with DSA key
kEDH	Ephemeral (temp.key) Diffie-Hellman key exchange (no cert)
kSRP	Secure Remote Password (SRP) key exchange
Authentication Algorithm:	
aNULL	No authentication
aRSA	RSA authentication
aDSS	DSS authentication
aDH	Diffie-Hellman authentication
Cipher Encoding Algorithm:	
eNULL	No encryption
NULL	alias for eNULL
AES	AES encryption
DES	DES encryption
3DES	Triple-DES encryption
RC4	RC4 encryption
RC2	RC2 encryption
IDEA	IDEA encryption
MAC Digest Algorithm:	
MD5	MD5 hash function
SHA1	SHA1 hash function
SHA	alias for SHA1
SHA256	SHA256 hash function
SHA384	SHA384 hash function
Aliases:	
SSLv3	all SSL version 3.0 ciphers
TLSv1	all TLS version 1.0 ciphers
EXP	all export ciphers
EXPORT40	all 40-bit export ciphers only
EXPORT56	all 56-bit export ciphers only
LOW	all low strength ciphers (no export, single DES)
MEDIUM	all ciphers with 128 bit encryption
HIGH	all ciphers using Triple-DES
RSA	all ciphers using RSA key exchange
DH	all ciphers using Diffie-Hellman key exchange
EDH	all ciphers using Ephemeral Diffie-Hellman key exchange
ECDH	Elliptic Curve Diffie-Hellman key exchange
ADH	all ciphers using Anonymous Diffie-Hellman key exchange
AECDH	all ciphers using Anonymous Elliptic Curve Diffie-Hellman exchange
SRP	all ciphers using Secure Remote Password (SRP) key exchang
DSS	all ciphers using DSS authentication
ECDSA	all ciphers using ECDSA authentication
aNULL	all ciphers using no authentication

Now where this becomes interesting is that these can be put together to specify the order and ciphers you wish to use. To speed this up there are also aliases (SSLv3, TLSv1, EXP, LOW, MEDIUM, HIGH) for certain groups of ciphers. These tags can be joined together with prefixes to form the *cipher-spec*. Available prefixes are:

- none: add cipher to list
- +: move matching ciphers to the current location in list
- −: remove cipher from list (can be added later again)
- !: kill cipher from list completely (can **not** be added later again)

⟹ **aNULL, eNULL and EXP ciphers are always disabled**

Beginning with version 2.4.7, null and export-grade ciphers are always disabled, as mod_ssl unconditionally adds !aNULL:!eNULL:!EXP to any cipher string at initialization.

A simpler way to look at all of this is to use the "openssl ciphers -v" command which provides a nice way to successively create the correct *cipher-spec* string. The default *cipher-spec* string depends on the version of the OpenSSL libraries used. Let's suppose it is "RC4-SHA:AES128-SHA:HIGH:MEDIUM:!aNULL:!MD5" which means the following: Put RC4-SHA and AES128-SHA at the beginning. We do this, because these ciphers offer a good compromise between speed and security. Next, include high and medium security ciphers. Finally, remove all ciphers which do not authenticate, i.e. for SSL the Anonymous Diffie-Hellman ciphers, as well as all ciphers which use MD5 as hash algorithm, because it has been proven insufficient.

```
$ openssl ciphers -v 'RC4-SHA:AES128-SHA:HIGH:MEDIUM:!aNULL:!MD5'
RC4-SHA              SSLv3 Kx=RSA    Au=RSA   Enc=RC4(128)   Mac=SHA1
AES128-SHA           SSLv3 Kx=RSA    Au=RSA   Enc=AES(128)   Mac=SHA1
DHE-RSA-AES256-SHA   SSLv3 Kx=DH     Au=RSA   Enc=AES(256)   Mac=SHA1
...                  ...             ...      ...            ...
SEED-SHA             SSLv3 Kx=RSA    Au=RSA   Enc=SEED(128)  Mac=SHA1
PSK-RC4-SHA          SSLv3 Kx=PSK    Au=PSK   Enc=RC4(128)   Mac=SHA1
KRB5-RC4-SHA         SSLv3 Kx=KRB5   Au=KRB5  Enc=RC4(128)   Mac=SHA1
```

The complete list of particular RSA & DH ciphers for SSL is given in Table 2.

Example

```
SSLCipherSuite RSA:!EXP:!NULL:+HIGH:+MEDIUM:-LOW
```

Cipher-Tag	Protocol	Key Ex.	Auth.	Enc.	MAC
RSA Ciphers:					
DES-CBC3-SHA	SSLv3	RSA	RSA	3DES(168)	SHA1
IDEA-CBC-SHA	SSLv3	RSA	RSA	IDEA(128)	SHA1
RC4-SHA	SSLv3	RSA	RSA	RC4(128)	SHA1
RC4-MD5	SSLv3	RSA	RSA	RC4(128)	MD5
DES-CBC-SHA	SSLv3	RSA	RSA	DES(56)	SHA1
EXP-DES-CBC-SHA	SSLv3	RSA(512)	RSA	DES(40)	SHA1
EXP-RC2-CBC-MD5	SSLv3	RSA(512)	RSA	RC2(40)	MD5
EXP-RC4-MD5	SSLv3	RSA(512)	RSA	RC4(40)	MD5
NULL-SHA	SSLv3	RSA	RSA	None	SHA1
NULL-MD5	SSLv3	RSA	RSA	None	MD5
Diffie-Hellman Ciphers:					
ADH-DES-CBC3-SHA	SSLv3	DH	None	3DES(168)	SHA1
ADH-DES-CBC-SHA	SSLv3	DH	None	DES(56)	SHA1
ADH-RC4-MD5	SSLv3	DH	None	RC4(128)	MD5
EDH-RSA-DES-CBC3-SHA	SSLv3	DH	RSA	3DES(168)	SHA1

EDH-DSS-DES-CBC3-SHA	SSLv3	DH	DSS	3DES(168)	SHA1
EDH-RSA-DES-CBC-SHA	SSLv3	DH	RSA	DES(56)	SHA1
EDH-DSS-DES-CBC-SHA	SSLv3	DH	DSS	DES(56)	SHA1
EXP-EDH-RSA-DES-CBC-SHA	SSLv3	DH(512)	RSA	DES(40)	SHA1
EXP-EDH-DSS-DES-CBC-SHA	SSLv3	DH(512)	DSS	DES(40)	SHA1
EXP-ADH-DES-CBC-SHA	SSLv3	DH(512)	None	DES(40)	SHA1
EXP-ADH-RC4-MD5	SSLv3	DH(512)	None	RC4(40)	MD5

SSLCompression Directive

Description:	Enable compression on the SSL level
Syntax:	SSLCompression on|off
Default:	SSLCompression off
Context:	server config, virtual host
Status:	Extension
Module:	mod_ssl
Compatibility:	Available in httpd 2.4.3 and later, if using OpenSSL 0.9.8 or later; virtual host scope available if using OpenSSL 1.0.0 or later. The default used to be on in version 2.4.3.

This directive allows to enable compression on the SSL level.

! Enabling compression causes security issues in most setups (the so called CRIME attack).

SSLCryptoDevice Directive

Description:	Enable use of a cryptographic hardware accelerator
Syntax:	SSLCryptoDevice engine
Default:	SSLCryptoDevice builtin
Context:	server config
Status:	Extension
Module:	mod_ssl

This directive enables use of a cryptographic hardware accelerator board to offload some of the SSL processing overhead. This directive can only be used if the SSL toolkit is built with "engine" support; OpenSSL 0.9.7 and later releases have "engine" support by default, the separate "-engine" releases of OpenSSL 0.9.6 must be used.

To discover which engine names are supported, run the command "openssl engine".

Example

```
# For a Broadcom accelerator:
SSLCryptoDevice ubsec
```

SSLEngine Directive

Description:	SSL Engine Operation Switch
Syntax:	SSLEngine on|off|optional
Default:	SSLEngine off
Context:	server config, virtual host
Status:	Extension
Module:	mod_ssl

This directive toggles the usage of the SSL/TLS Protocol Engine. This is should be used inside a <VIRTUALHOST> section to enable SSL/TLS for a that virtual host. By default the SSL/TLS Protocol Engine is disabled for both the main server and all configured virtual hosts.

Example

```
<VirtualHost _default_:443>
SSLEngine on
#...
</VirtualHost>
```

In Apache 2.1 and later, SSLENGINE can be set to optional. This enables support for RFC 2817[80], Upgrading to TLS Within HTTP/1.1. At this time no web browsers support RFC 2817.

SSLFIPS Directive

Description:	SSL FIPS mode Switch
Syntax:	SSLFIPS on|off
Default:	SSLFIPS off
Context:	server config
Status:	Extension
Module:	mod_ssl

This directive toggles the usage of the SSL library FIPS_mode flag. It must be set in the global server context and cannot be configured with conflicting settings (SSLFIPS on followed by SSLFIPS off or similar). The mode applies to all SSL library operations.

If httpd was compiled against an SSL library which did not support the FIPS_mode flag, SSLFIPS on will fail. Refer to the FIPS 140-2 Security Policy document of the SSL provider library for specific requirements to use mod_ssl in a FIPS 140-2 approved mode of operation; note that mod_ssl itself is not validated, but may be described as using FIPS 140-2 validated cryptographic module, when all components are assembled and operated under the guidelines imposed by the applicable Security Policy.

SSLHonorCipherOrder Directive

Description:	Option to prefer the server's cipher preference order
Syntax:	SSLHonorCipherOrder on|off
Default:	SSLHonorCipherOrder off
Context:	server config, virtual host
Status:	Extension
Module:	mod_ssl

When choosing a cipher during an SSLv3 or TLSv1 handshake, normally the client's preference is used. If this directive is enabled, the server's preference will be used instead.

Example

```
SSLHonorCipherOrder on
```

---

[80]http://www.ietf.org/rfc/rfc2817.txt

SSLInsecureRenegotiation Directive

Description:	Option to enable support for insecure renegotiation
Syntax:	`SSLInsecureRenegotiation on|off`
Default:	`SSLInsecureRenegotiation off`
Context:	server config, virtual host
Status:	Extension
Module:	mod_ssl
Compatibility:	Available in httpd 2.2.15 and later, if using OpenSSL 0.9.8m or later

As originally specified, all versions of the SSL and TLS protocols (up to and including TLS/1.2) were vulnerable to a Man-in-the-Middle attack (CVE-2009-3555[81]) during a renegotiation. This vulnerability allowed an attacker to "prefix" a chosen plaintext to the HTTP request as seen by the web server. A protocol extension was developed which fixed this vulnerability if supported by both client and server.

If MOD_SSL is linked against OpenSSL version 0.9.8m or later, by default renegotiation is only supported with clients supporting the new protocol extension. If this directive is enabled, renegotiation will be allowed with old (unpatched) clients, albeit insecurely.

 Security warning

If this directive is enabled, SSL connections will be vulnerable to the Man-in-the-Middle prefix attack as described in CVE-2009-3555[a].

[a]http://cve.mitre.org/cgi-bin/cvename.cgi?name=CAN-2009-3555

Example

```
SSLInsecureRenegotiation on
```

The SSL_SECURE_RENEG environment variable can be used from an SSI or CGI script to determine whether secure renegotiation is supported for a given SSL connection.

SSLOCSPDefaultResponder Directive

Description:	Set the default responder URI for OCSP validation
Syntax:	`SSLOCSDefaultResponder uri`
Context:	server config, virtual host
Status:	Extension
Module:	mod_ssl

This option sets the default OCSP responder to use. If SSLOCSPOVERRIDERESPONDER is not enabled, the URI given will be used only if no responder URI is specified in the certificate being verified.

SSLOCSPEnable Directive

Description:	Enable OCSP validation of the client certificate chain
Syntax:	`SSLOCSPEnable on|off`
Default:	`SSLOCSPEnable off`
Context:	server config, virtual host
Status:	Extension
Module:	mod_ssl

---

[81]http://cve.mitre.org/cgi-bin/cvename.cgi?name=CAN-2009-3555

This option enables OCSP validation of the client certificate chain. If this option is enabled, certificates in the client's certificate chain will be validated against an OCSP responder after normal verification (including CRL checks) have taken place.

The OCSP responder used is either extracted from the certificate itself, or derived by configuration; see the SSLOC-SPDEFAULTRESPONDER and SSLOCSPOVERRIDERESPONDER directives.

Example

```
SSLVerifyClient on
SSLOCSPEnable on
SSLOCSPDefaultResponder "http://responder.example.com:8888/responder"
SSLOCSPOverrideResponder on
```

SSLOCSPOverrideResponder Directive

Description:	Force use of the default responder URI for OCSP validation
Syntax:	SSLOCSPOverrideResponder on|off
Default:	SSLOCSPOverrideResponder off
Context:	server config, virtual host
Status:	Extension
Module:	mod_ssl

This option forces the configured default OCSP responder to be used during OCSP certificate validation, regardless of whether the certificate being validated references an OCSP responder.

SSLOCSPResponderTimeout Directive

Description:	Timeout for OCSP queries
Syntax:	SSLOCSPResponderTimeout seconds
Default:	SSLOCSPResponderTimeout 10
Context:	server config, virtual host
Status:	Extension
Module:	mod_ssl

This option sets the timeout for queries to OCSP responders, when SSLOCSPENABLE is turned on.

SSLOCSPResponseMaxAge Directive

Description:	Maximum allowable age for OCSP responses
Syntax:	SSLOCSPResponseMaxAge seconds
Default:	SSLOCSPResponseMaxAge -1
Context:	server config, virtual host
Status:	Extension
Module:	mod_ssl

This option sets the maximum allowable age ("freshness") for OCSP responses. The default value (-1) does not enforce a maximum age, which means that OCSP responses are considered valid as long as their nextUpdate field is in the future.

SSLOCSPResponseTimeSkew Directive

Description:	Maximum allowable time skew for OCSP response validation
Syntax:	`SSLOCSPResponseTimeSkew seconds`
Default:	`SSLOCSPResponseTimeSkew 300`
Context:	server config, virtual host
Status:	Extension
Module:	mod_ssl

This option sets the maximum allowable time skew for OCSP responses (when checking their `thisUpdate` and `nextUpdate` fields).

SSLOCSPUseRequestNonce Directive

Description:	Use a nonce within OCSP queries
Syntax:	`SSLOCSPUseRequestNonce on|off`
Default:	`SSLOCSPUseRequestNonce on`
Context:	server config, virtual host
Status:	Extension
Module:	mod_ssl
Compatibility:	Available in httpd 2.4.10 and later

This option determines whether queries to OCSP responders should contain a nonce or not. By default, a query nonce is always used and checked against the response's one. When the responder does not use nonces (e.g. Microsoft OCSP Responder), this option should be turned `off`.

SSLOpenSSLConfCmd Directive

Description:	Configure OpenSSL parameters through its *SSL_CONF* API
Syntax:	`SSLOpenSSLConfCmd command-name command-value`
Context:	server config, virtual host
Status:	Extension
Module:	mod_ssl
Compatibility:	Available in httpd 2.4.8 and later, if using OpenSSL 1.0.2 or later

This directive exposes OpenSSL's *SSL_CONF* API to mod_ssl, allowing a flexible configuration of OpenSSL parameters without the need of implementing additional MOD_SSL directives when new features are added to OpenSSL.

The set of available SSLOPENSSLCONFCMD commands depends on the OpenSSL version being used for MOD_SSL (at least version 1.0.2 is required). For a list of supported command names, see the section *Supported configuration file commands* in the SSL_CONF_cmd(3)[82] manual page for OpenSSL.

Some of the SSLOPENSSLCONFCMD commands can be used as an alternative to existing directives (such as SSL-CIPHERSUITE or SSLPROTOCOL), though it should be noted that the syntax / allowable values for the parameters may sometimes differ.

Examples

```
SSLOpenSSLConfCmd Options -SessionTicket,ServerPreference
SSLOpenSSLConfCmd ECDHParameters brainpoolP256r1
SSLOpenSSLConfCmd ServerInfoFile "/usr/local/apache2/conf/server-info.pem"
SSLOpenSSLConfCmd Protocol "-ALL, TLSv1.2"
SSLOpenSSLConfCmd SignatureAlgorithms RSA+SHA384:ECDSA+SHA256
```

---

[82]http://www.openssl.org/docs/man1.0.2/ssl/SSL_CONF_cmd.html#SUPPORTED-CONFIGURATION-FILE-COMMANDS

SSLOptions Directive

Description:	Configure various SSL engine run-time options
Syntax:	SSLOptions [+|-]option ...
Context:	server config, virtual host, directory, .htaccess
Override:	Options
Status:	Extension
Module:	mod_ssl

This directive can be used to control various run-time options on a per-directory basis. Normally, if multiple SSLOptions could apply to a directory, then the most specific one is taken completely; the options are not merged. However if *all* the options on the SSLOptions directive are preceded by a plus (+) or minus (−) symbol, the options are merged. Any options preceded by a + are added to the options currently in force, and any options preceded by a − are removed from the options currently in force.

The available *option*s are:

- StdEnvVars

  When this option is enabled, the standard set of SSL related CGI/SSI environment variables are created. This per default is disabled for performance reasons, because the information extraction step is a rather expensive operation. So one usually enables this option for CGI and SSI requests only.

- ExportCertData

  When this option is enabled, additional CGI/SSI environment variables are created: SSL_SERVER_CERT, SSL_CLIENT_CERT and SSL_CLIENT_CERT_CHAIN_n (with $n = 0,1,2,..$). These contain the PEM-encoded X.509 Certificates of server and client for the current HTTPS connection and can be used by CGI scripts for deeper Certificate checking. Additionally all other certificates of the client certificate chain are provided, too. This bloats up the environment a little bit which is why you have to use this option to enable it on demand.

- FakeBasicAuth

  When this option is enabled, the Subject Distinguished Name (DN) of the Client X509 Certificate is translated into a HTTP Basic Authorization username. This means that the standard Apache authentication methods can be used for access control. The user name is just the Subject of the Client's X509 Certificate (can be determined by running OpenSSL's openssl x509 command: openssl x509 -noout -subject -in *certificate*.crt). Note that no password is obtained from the user. Every entry in the user file needs this password: "xxj31ZMTZzkVA", which is the DES-encrypted version of the word 'password'. Those who live under MD5-based encryption (for instance under FreeBSD or BSD/OS, etc.) should use the following MD5 hash of the same word: "1OXLyS...$Owx8s2/m9/gfkcRVXzgoE/".

  Note that the AUTHBASICFAKE directive within MOD_AUTH_BASIC can be used as a more general mechanism for faking basic authentication, giving control over the structure of both the username and password.

- StrictRequire

  This *forces* forbidden access when SSLRequireSSL or SSLRequire successfully decided that access should be forbidden. Usually the default is that in the case where a "Satisfy any" directive is used, and other access restrictions are passed, denial of access due to SSLRequireSSL or SSLRequire is overridden (because that's how the Apache Satisfy mechanism should work.) But for strict access restriction you can use SSLRequireSSL and/or SSLRequire in combination with an "SSLOptions +StrictRequire". Then an additional "Satisfy Any" has no chance once mod_ssl has decided to deny access.

- OptRenegotiate

  This enables optimized SSL connection renegotiation handling when SSL directives are used in per-directory context. By default a strict scheme is enabled where *every* per-directory reconfiguration of SSL parameters causes a *full* SSL renegotiation handshake. When this option is used mod_ssl tries to avoid unnecessary handshakes by doing more granular (but still safe) parameter checks. Nevertheless these granular checks sometimes may not be what the user expects, so enable this on a per-directory basis only, please.

- `LegacyDNStringFormat`

  This option influences how values of the `SSL_{CLIENT,SERVER}_{I,S}_DN` variables are formatted. Since version 2.3.11, Apache HTTPD uses a RFC 2253 compatible format by default. This uses commas as delimiters between the attributes, allows the use of non-ASCII characters (which are converted to UTF8), escapes various special characters with backslashes, and sorts the attributes with the "C" attribute last.

  If `LegacyDNStringFormat` is set, the old format will be used which sorts the "C" attribute first, uses slashes as separators, and does not handle non-ASCII and special characters in any consistent way.

Example

```
SSLOptions +FakeBasicAuth -StrictRequire
<Files ~ "\.(cgi|shtml)$">
    SSLOptions +StdEnvVars -ExportCertData
<Files>
```

SSLPassPhraseDialog Directive

Description:	Type of pass phrase dialog for encrypted private keys
Syntax:	`SSLPassPhraseDialog type`
Default:	`SSLPassPhraseDialog builtin`
Context:	server config
Status:	Extension
Module:	mod_ssl

When Apache starts up it has to read the various Certificate (see SSLCERTIFICATEFILE) and Private Key (see SSLCERTIFICATEKEYFILE) files of the SSL-enabled virtual servers. Because for security reasons the Private Key files are usually encrypted, mod_ssl needs to query the administrator for a Pass Phrase in order to decrypt those files. This query can be done in two ways which can be configured by *type*:

- `builtin`

  This is the default where an interactive terminal dialog occurs at startup time just before Apache detaches from the terminal. Here the administrator has to manually enter the Pass Phrase for each encrypted Private Key file. Because a lot of SSL-enabled virtual hosts can be configured, the following reuse-scheme is used to minimize the dialog: When a Private Key file is encrypted, all known Pass Phrases (at the beginning there are none, of course) are tried. If one of those known Pass Phrases succeeds no dialog pops up for this particular Private Key file. If none succeeded, another Pass Phrase is queried on the terminal and remembered for the next round (where it perhaps can be reused).

  This scheme allows mod_ssl to be maximally flexible (because for N encrypted Private Key files you *can* use N different Pass Phrases - but then you have to enter all of them, of course) while minimizing the terminal dialog (i.e. when you use a single Pass Phrase for all N Private Key files this Pass Phrase is queried only once).

- `|/path/to/program [args...]`

  This mode allows an external program to be used which acts as a pipe to a particular input device; the program is sent the standard prompt text used for the `builtin` mode on `stdin`, and is expected to write password strings on `stdout`. If several passwords are needed (or an incorrect password is entered), additional prompt text will be written subsequent to the first password being returned, and more passwords must then be written back.

- `exec:/path/to/program`

  Here an external program is configured which is called at startup for each encrypted Private Key file. It is called with two arguments (the first is of the form "`servername:portnumber`", the second is either "RSA", "DSA", "ECC" or an integer index starting at 3 if more than three keys are configured), which indicate for which server and algorithm it has to print the corresponding Pass Phrase to stdout. In versions 2.4.8 (unreleased) and 2.4.9, it is called with one argument, a string of the form "servername:portnumber:index" (with index being a zero-based integer number), which indicate the server, TCP port and certificate number. The intent is that this external program first runs security checks to make sure that the system is not compromised by an attacker, and only when these checks were passed successfully it provides the Pass Phrase.

Both these security checks, and the way the Pass Phrase is determined, can be as complex as you like. Mod_ssl just defines the interface: an executable program which provides the Pass Phrase on stdout. Nothing more or less! So, if you're really paranoid about security, here is your interface. Anything else has to be left as an exercise to the administrator, because local security requirements are so different.

The reuse-algorithm above is used here, too. In other words: The external program is called only once per unique Pass Phrase.

Example

```
SSLPassPhraseDialog "exec:/usr/local/apache/sbin/pp-filter"
```

SSLProtocol Directive

Description:	Configure usable SSL/TLS protocol versions
Syntax:	SSLProtocol [+|-]protocol ...
Default:	SSLProtocol all -SSLv3 (up to 2.4.16: all)
Context:	server config, virtual host
Status:	Extension
Module:	mod_ssl

This directive can be used to control which versions of the SSL/TLS protocol will be accepted in new connections.

The available (case-insensitive) *protocol*s are:

- SSLv3

  This is the Secure Sockets Layer (SSL) protocol, version 3.0, from the Netscape Corporation. It is the successor to SSLv2 and the predecessor to TLSv1, but is deprecated in RFC 7568[83].

- TLSv1

  This is the Transport Layer Security (TLS) protocol, version 1.0. It is the successor to SSLv3 and is defined in RFC 2246[84]. It is supported by nearly every client.

- TLSv1.1 (when using OpenSSL 1.0.1 and later)

  A revision of the TLS 1.0 protocol, as defined in RFC 4346[85].

- TLSv1.2 (when using OpenSSL 1.0.1 and later)

  A revision of the TLS 1.1 protocol, as defined in RFC 5246[86].

- all

  This is a shortcut for "+SSLv3 +TLSv1" or - when using OpenSSL 1.0.1 and later - "+SSLv3 +TLSv1 +TLSv1.1 +TLSv1.2", respectively (except for OpenSSL versions compiled with the "no-ssl3" configuration option, where all does not include +SSLv3).

Example

```
SSLProtocol TLSv1
```

---

[83]http://www.ietf.org/rfc/rfc7568.txt
[84]http://www.ietf.org/rfc/rfc2246.txt
[85]http://www.ietf.org/rfc/rfc4346.txt
[86]http://www.ietf.org/rfc/rfc5246.txt

SSLProxyCACertificateFile Directive

Description:	File of concatenated PEM-encoded CA Certificates for Remote Server Auth
Syntax:	`SSLProxyCACertificateFile file-path`
Context:	server config, virtual host
Status:	Extension
Module:	mod_ssl

This directive sets the *all-in-one* file where you can assemble the Certificates of Certification Authorities (CA) whose *remote servers* you deal with. These are used for Remote Server Authentication. Such a file is simply the concatenation of the various PEM-encoded Certificate files, in order of preference. This can be used alternatively and/or additionally to SSLPROXYCACERTIFICATEPATH.

Example

```
SSLProxyCACertificateFile "/usr/local/apache2/conf/ssl.crt/ca-bundle-remote-ser
```

SSLProxyCACertificatePath Directive

Description:	Directory of PEM-encoded CA Certificates for Remote Server Auth
Syntax:	`SSLProxyCACertificatePath directory-path`
Context:	server config, virtual host
Status:	Extension
Module:	mod_ssl

This directive sets the directory where you keep the Certificates of Certification Authorities (CAs) whose remote servers you deal with. These are used to verify the remote server certificate on Remote Server Authentication.

The files in this directory have to be PEM-encoded and are accessed through hash filenames. So usually you can't just place the Certificate files there: you also have to create symbolic links named *hash-value*.N. And you should always make sure this directory contains the appropriate symbolic links.

Example

```
SSLProxyCACertificatePath "/usr/local/apache2/conf/ssl.crt/"
```

SSLProxyCARevocationCheck Directive

Description:	Enable CRL-based revocation checking for Remote Server Auth
Syntax:	`SSLProxyCARevocationCheck chain|leaf|none`
Default:	`SSLProxyCARevocationCheck none`
Context:	server config, virtual host
Status:	Extension
Module:	mod_ssl

Enables certificate revocation list (CRL) checking for the *remote servers* you deal with. At least one of SSLPROXYCAREVOCATIONFILE or SSLPROXYCAREVOCATIONPATH must be configured. When set to `chain` (recommended setting), CRL checks are applied to all certificates in the chain, while setting it to `leaf` limits the checks to the end-entity cert.

> **When set to `chain` or `leaf`, CRLs *must* be available for successful validation**

Prior to version 2.3.15, CRL checking in mod_ssl also succeeded when no CRL(s) were found in any of the locations configured with SSLPROXYCAREVOCATIONFILE or SSLPROXY-CAREVOCATIONPATH. With the introduction of this directive, the behavior has been changed: when checking is enabled, CRLs *must* be present for the validation to succeed - otherwise it will fail with an `"unable to get certificate CRL"` error.

Example

```
SSLProxyCARevocationCheck chain
```

SSLProxyCARevocationFile Directive

Description:	File of concatenated PEM-encoded CA CRLs for Remote Server Auth
Syntax:	`SSLProxyCARevocationFile file-path`
Context:	server config, virtual host
Status:	Extension
Module:	mod_ssl

This directive sets the *all-in-one* file where you can assemble the Certificate Revocation Lists (CRL) of Certification Authorities (CA) whose *remote servers* you deal with. These are used for Remote Server Authentication. Such a file is simply the concatenation of the various PEM-encoded CRL files, in order of preference. This can be used alternatively and/or additionally to SSLPROXYCAREVOCATIONPATH.

Example

```
SSLProxyCARevocationFile "/usr/local/apache2/conf/ssl.crl/ca-bundle-remote-serv
```

SSLProxyCARevocationPath Directive

Description:	Directory of PEM-encoded CA CRLs for Remote Server Auth
Syntax:	`SSLProxyCARevocationPath directory-path`
Context:	server config, virtual host
Status:	Extension
Module:	mod_ssl

This directive sets the directory where you keep the Certificate Revocation Lists (CRL) of Certification Authorities (CAs) whose remote servers you deal with. These are used to revoke the remote server certificate on Remote Server Authentication.

The files in this directory have to be PEM-encoded and are accessed through hash filenames. So usually you have not only to place the CRL files there. Additionally you have to create symbolic links named *hash-value*.`rN`. And you should always make sure this directory contains the appropriate symbolic links.

Example

```
SSLProxyCARevocationPath "/usr/local/apache2/conf/ssl.crl/"
```

SSLProxyCheckPeerCN Directive

Description:	Whether to check the remote server certificate's CN field
Syntax:	SSLProxyCheckPeerCN on|off
Default:	SSLProxyCheckPeerCN on
Context:	server config, virtual host
Status:	Extension
Module:	mod_ssl

This directive sets whether the remote server certificate's CN field is compared against the hostname of the request URL. If both are not equal a 502 status code (Bad Gateway) is sent.

In 2.4.5 and later, SSLProxyCheckPeerCN has been superseded by SSLPROXYCHECKPEERNAME, and its setting is only taken into account when SSLProxyCheckPeerName off is specified at the same time.

Example

```
SSLProxyCheckPeerCN on
```

SSLProxyCheckPeerExpire Directive

Description:	Whether to check if remote server certificate is expired
Syntax:	SSLProxyCheckPeerExpire on|off
Default:	SSLProxyCheckPeerExpire on
Context:	server config, virtual host
Status:	Extension
Module:	mod_ssl

This directive sets whether it is checked if the remote server certificate is expired or not. If the check fails a 502 status code (Bad Gateway) is sent.

Example

```
SSLProxyCheckPeerExpire on
```

SSLProxyCheckPeerName Directive

Description:	Configure host name checking for remote server certificates
Syntax:	SSLProxyCheckPeerName on|off
Default:	SSLProxyCheckPeerName on
Context:	server config, virtual host
Status:	Extension
Module:	mod_ssl
Compatibility:	Apache HTTP Server 2.4.5 and later

This directive configures host name checking for server certificates when mod_ssl is acting as an SSL client. The check will succeed if the host name from the request URI is found in either the subjectAltName extension or (one of) the CN attribute(s) in the certificate's subject. If the check fails, the SSL request is aborted and a 502 status code (Bad Gateway) is returned. The directive supersedes SSLPROXYCHECKPEERCN, which only checks for the expected host name in the first CN attribute.

Wildcard matching is supported in one specific flavor: subjectAltName entries of type dNSName or CN attributes starting with *. will match for any DNS name with the same number of labels and the same suffix (i.e., *.example.org matches for foo.example.org, but not for foo.bar.example.org).

SSLProxyCipherSuite Directive

Description:	Cipher Suite available for negotiation in SSL proxy handshake
Syntax:	SSLProxyCipherSuite cipher-spec
Default:	SSLProxyCipherSuite ALL:!ADH:RC4+RSA:+HIGH:+MEDIUM:+LOW:+EXP
Context:	server config, virtual host, directory, .htaccess
Override:	AuthConfig
Status:	Extension
Module:	mod_ssl

Equivalent to SSLCipherSuite, but for the proxy connection. Please refer to SSLCIPHERSUITE for additional information.

SSLProxyEngine Directive

Description:	SSL Proxy Engine Operation Switch
Syntax:	SSLProxyEngine on|off
Default:	SSLProxyEngine off
Context:	server config, virtual host
Status:	Extension
Module:	mod_ssl

This directive toggles the usage of the SSL/TLS Protocol Engine for proxy. This is usually used inside a <VIRTUALHOST> section to enable SSL/TLS for proxy usage in a particular virtual host. By default the SSL/TLS Protocol Engine is disabled for proxy both for the main server and all configured virtual hosts.

Note that the SSLProxyEngine directive should not, in general, be included in a virtual host that will be acting as a forward proxy (using <Proxy> or <ProxyRequest> directives. SSLProxyEngine is not required to enable a forward proxy server to proxy SSL/TLS requests.

Example

```
<VirtualHost _default_:443>
    SSLProxyEngine on
    #...
</VirtualHost>
```

SSLProxyMachineCertificateChainFile Directive

Description:	File of concatenated PEM-encoded CA certificates to be used by the proxy for choosing a certificate
Syntax:	SSLProxyMachineCertificateChainFile filename
Context:	server config
Override:	Not applicable
Status:	Extension
Module:	mod_ssl

This directive sets the all-in-one file where you keep the certificate chain for all of the client certs in use. This directive will be needed if the remote server presents a list of CA certificates that are not direct signers of one of the configured client certificates.

This referenced file is simply the concatenation of the various PEM-encoded certificate files. Upon startup, each client certificate configured will be examined and a chain of trust will be constructed.

Security warning

If this directive is enabled, all of the certificates in the file will be trusted as if they were also in SSLPROXYCACERTIFICATEFILE.

Example

```
SSLProxyMachineCertificateChainFile "/usr/local/apache2/conf/ssl.crt/proxyCA.pe
```

SSLProxyMachineCertificateFile Directive

Description:	File of concatenated PEM-encoded client certificates and keys to be used by the proxy
Syntax:	SSLProxyMachineCertificateFile filename
Context:	server config
Override:	Not applicable
Status:	Extension
Module:	mod_ssl

This directive sets the all-in-one file where you keep the certificates and keys used for authentication of the proxy server to remote servers.

This referenced file is simply the concatenation of the various PEM-encoded certificate files, in order of preference. Use this directive alternatively or additionally to SSLProxyMachineCertificatePath.

 Currently there is no support for encrypted private keys

Example

```
SSLProxyMachineCertificateFile "/usr/local/apache2/conf/ssl.crt/proxy.pem"
```

SSLProxyMachineCertificatePath Directive

Description:	Directory of PEM-encoded client certificates and keys to be used by the proxy
Syntax:	SSLProxyMachineCertificatePath directory
Context:	server config
Override:	Not applicable
Status:	Extension
Module:	mod_ssl

This directive sets the directory where you keep the certificates and keys used for authentication of the proxy server to remote servers.

The files in this directory must be PEM-encoded and are accessed through hash filenames. Additionally, you must create symbolic links named *hash-value*.N. And you should always make sure this directory contains the appropriate symbolic links.

 Currently there is no support for encrypted private keys

Example

```
SSLProxyMachineCertificatePath "/usr/local/apache2/conf/proxy.crt/"
```

SSLProxyProtocol Directive

Description:	Configure usable SSL protocol flavors for proxy usage
Syntax:	`SSLProxyProtocol [+|-]protocol ...`
Default:	`SSLProxyProtocol all -SSLv3 (up to 2.4.16: all)`
Context:	server config, virtual host
Override:	Options
Status:	Extension
Module:	mod_ssl

This directive can be used to control the SSL protocol flavors mod_ssl should use when establishing its server environment for proxy . It will only connect to servers using one of the provided protocols.

Please refer to SSLPROTOCOL for additional information.

SSLProxyVerify Directive

Description:	Type of remote server Certificate verification
Syntax:	`SSLProxyVerify level`
Default:	`SSLProxyVerify none`
Context:	server config, virtual host
Status:	Extension
Module:	mod_ssl

When a proxy is configured to forward requests to a remote SSL server, this directive can be used to configure certificate verification of the remote server.

The following levels are available for *level*:

- **none**: no remote server Certificate is required at all
- **optional**: the remote server *may* present a valid Certificate
- **require**: the remote server *has to* present a valid Certificate
- **optional_no_ca**: the remote server may present a valid Certificate but it need not to be (successfully) verifiable.

In practice only levels **none** and **require** are really interesting, because level **optional** doesn't work with all servers and level **optional_no_ca** is actually against the idea of authentication (but can be used to establish SSL test pages, etc.)

Example

```
SSLProxyVerify require
```

SSLProxyVerifyDepth Directive

Description:	Maximum depth of CA Certificates in Remote Server Certificate verification
Syntax:	`SSLProxyVerifyDepth number`
Default:	`SSLProxyVerifyDepth 1`
Context:	server config, virtual host
Status:	Extension
Module:	mod_ssl

This directive sets how deeply mod_ssl should verify before deciding that the remote server does not have a valid certificate.

The depth actually is the maximum number of intermediate certificate issuers, i.e. the number of CA certificates which are max allowed to be followed while verifying the remote server certificate. A depth of 0 means that self-signed remote server certificates are accepted only, the default depth of 1 means the remote server certificate can be self-signed or has to be signed by a CA which is directly known to the server (i.e. the CA's certificate is under SSLPROXYCACERTIFICATEPATH), etc.

Example

```
SSLProxyVerifyDepth 10
```

SSLRandomSeed Directive

Description:	Pseudo Random Number Generator (PRNG) seeding source
Syntax:	SSLRandomSeed context source [bytes]
Context:	server config
Status:	Extension
Module:	mod_ssl

This configures one or more sources for seeding the Pseudo Random Number Generator (PRNG) in OpenSSL at startup time (*context* is startup) and/or just before a new SSL connection is established (*context* is connect). This directive can only be used in the global server context because the PRNG is a global facility.

The following *source* variants are available:

- builtin This is the always available builtin seeding source. Its usage consumes minimum CPU cycles under runtime and hence can be always used without drawbacks. The source used for seeding the PRNG contains of the current time, the current process id and (when applicable) a randomly chosen 1KB extract of the inter-process scoreboard structure of Apache. The drawback is that this is not really a strong source and at startup time (where the scoreboard is still not available) this source just produces a few bytes of entropy. So you should always, at least for the startup, use an additional seeding source.

- file:/path/to/source

  This variant uses an external file /path/to/source as the source for seeding the PRNG. When *bytes* is specified, only the first *bytes* number of bytes of the file form the entropy (and *bytes* is given to /path/to/source as the first argument). When *bytes* is not specified the whole file forms the entropy (and 0 is given to /path/to/source as the first argument). Use this especially at startup time, for instance with an available /dev/random and/or /dev/urandom devices (which usually exist on modern Unix derivatives like FreeBSD and Linux).

  But be careful: Usually /dev/random provides only as much entropy data as it actually has, i.e. when you request 512 bytes of entropy, but the device currently has only 100 bytes available two things can happen: On some platforms you receive only the 100 bytes while on other platforms the read blocks until enough bytes are available (which can take a long time). Here using an existing /dev/urandom is better, because it never blocks and actually gives the amount of requested data. The drawback is just that the quality of the received data may not be the best.

- exec:/path/to/program

  This variant uses an external executable /path/to/program as the source for seeding the PRNG. When *bytes* is specified, only the first *bytes* number of bytes of its stdout contents form the entropy. When *bytes* is not specified, the entirety of the data produced on stdout form the entropy. Use this only at startup time when you need a very strong seeding with the help of an external program (for instance as in the example above with the truerand utility you can find in the mod_ssl distribution which is based on the AT&T *truerand* library).

Using this in the connection context slows down the server too dramatically, of course. So usually you should avoid using external programs in that context.

- `egd:/path/to/egd-socket` (Unix only)

This variant uses the Unix domain socket of the external Entropy Gathering Daemon (EGD) (see http://www.lothar.com/tech /crypto/[87]) to seed the PRNG. Use this if no random device exists on your platform.

Example

```
SSLRandomSeed startup builtin
SSLRandomSeed startup "file:/dev/random"
SSLRandomSeed startup "file:/dev/urandom" 1024
SSLRandomSeed startup "exec:/usr/local/bin/truerand" 16
SSLRandomSeed connect builtin
SSLRandomSeed connect "file:/dev/random"
SSLRandomSeed connect "file:/dev/urandom" 1024
```

SSLRenegBufferSize Directive

Description:	Set the size for the SSL renegotiation buffer
Syntax:	`SSLRenegBufferSize bytes`
Default:	`SSLRenegBufferSize 131072`
Context:	directory, .htaccess
Override:	AuthConfig
Status:	Extension
Module:	mod_ssl

If an SSL renegotiation is required in per-location context, for example, any use of SSLVERIFYCLIENT in a Directory or Location block, then MOD_SSL must buffer any HTTP request body into memory until the new SSL handshake can be performed. This directive can be used to set the amount of memory that will be used for this buffer.

> **!** Note that in many configurations, the client sending the request body will be untrusted so a denial of service attack by consumption of memory must be considered when changing this configuration setting.

Example

```
SSLRenegBufferSize 262144
```

SSLRequire Directive

Description:	Allow access only when an arbitrarily complex boolean expression is true
Syntax:	`SSLRequire expression`
Context:	directory, .htaccess
Override:	AuthConfig
Status:	Extension
Module:	mod_ssl

---

[87] http://www.lothar.com/tech/crypto/

⟹ **SSLRequire is deprecated**

> SSLRequire is deprecated and should in general be replaced by Require expr (p. 488)
> . The so called ap_expr (p. 89) syntax of Require expr is a superset of the syntax of
> SSLRequire, with the following exception:
>
> In SSLRequire, the comparison operators <, <=, ... are completely equivalent to the oper-
> ators lt, le, ... and work in a somewhat peculiar way that first compares the length of two
> strings and then the lexical order. On the other hand, ap_expr (p. 89) has two sets of compari-
> son operators: The operators <, <=, ... do lexical string comparison, while the operators -lt,
> -le, ... do integer comparison. For the latter, there are also aliases without the leading dashes:
> lt, le, ...

This directive specifies a general access requirement which has to be fulfilled in order to allow access. It is a very
powerful directive because the requirement specification is an arbitrarily complex boolean expression containing any
number of access checks.

The *expression* must match the following syntax (given as a BNF grammar notation):

```
expr     ::= "true" | "false"
         | "!" expr
         | expr "&&" expr
         | expr "||" expr
         | "(" expr ")"
         | comp

comp     ::= word "==" word | word "eq" word
         | word "!=" word | word "ne" word
         | word "<"  word | word "lt" word
         | word "<=" word | word "le" word
         | word ">"  word | word "gt" word
         | word ">=" word | word "ge" word
         | word "in" "{" wordlist "}"
         | word "in" "PeerExtList(" word ")"
         | word "=~" regex
         | word "!~" regex

wordlist ::= word
         | wordlist "," word

word     ::= digit
         | cstring
         | variable
         | function

digit    ::= [0-9]+
cstring  ::= "..."
variable ::= "%{" varname "}"
function ::= funcname "(" funcargs ")"
```

For varname any of the variables described in Environment Variables can be used. For funcname the available
functions are listed in the ap_expr documentation (p. 89) .

The *expression* is parsed into an internal machine representation when the configuration is loaded, and then evaluated
during request processing. In .htaccess context, the *expression* is both parsed and executed each time the .htaccess file
is encountered during request processing.

Example

```
SSLRequire (    %{SSL_CIPHER} !~ m/^(EXP|NULL)-/                       \
           and %{SSL_CLIENT_S_DN_O} eq "Snake Oil, Ltd."              \
           and %{SSL_CLIENT_S_DN_OU} in {"Staff", "CA", "Dev"}        \
           and %{TIME_WDAY} -ge 1 and %{TIME_WDAY} -le 5              \
           and %{TIME_HOUR} -ge 8 and %{TIME_HOUR} -le 20        ) \
           or %{REMOTE_ADDR} =~ m/^192\.76\.162\.[0-9]+$/
```

The `PeerExtList(object-ID)` function expects to find zero or more instances of the X.509 certificate extension identified by the given *object ID* (OID) in the client certificate. The expression evaluates to true if the left-hand side string matches exactly against the value of an extension identified with this OID. (If multiple extensions with the same OID are present, at least one extension must match).

Example

```
SSLRequire "foobar" in PeerExtList("1.2.3.4.5.6")
```

⟹ Notes on the PeerExtList function

- The object ID can be specified either as a descriptive name recognized by the SSL library, such as `"nsComment"`, or as a numeric OID, such as `"1.2.3.4.5.6"`.

- Expressions with types known to the SSL library are rendered to a string before comparison. For an extension with a type not recognized by the SSL library, mod_ssl will parse the value if it is one of the primitive ASN.1 types UTF8String, IA5String, VisibleString, or BMPString. For an extension of one of these types, the string value will be converted to UTF-8 if necessary, then compared against the left-hand-side expression.

See also

- Environment Variables in Apache HTTP Server (p. 82) , for additional examples.
- Require expr (p. 488)
- Generic expression syntax in Apache HTTP Server (p. 89)

SSLRequireSSL Directive

Description:	Deny access when SSL is not used for the HTTP request
Syntax:	SSLRequireSSL
Context:	directory, .htaccess
Override:	AuthConfig
Status:	Extension
Module:	mod_ssl

This directive forbids access unless HTTP over SSL (i.e. HTTPS) is enabled for the current connection. This is very handy inside the SSL-enabled virtual host or directories for defending against configuration errors that expose stuff that should be protected. When this directive is present all requests are denied which are not using SSL.

Example

```
SSLRequireSSL
```

SSLSessionCache Directive

Description:	Type of the global/inter-process SSL Session Cache
Syntax:	`SSLSessionCache type`
Default:	`SSLSessionCache none`
Context:	server config
Status:	Extension
Module:	mod_ssl

This configures the storage type of the global/inter-process SSL Session Cache. This cache is an optional facility which speeds up parallel request processing. For requests to the same server process (via HTTP keep-alive), OpenSSL already caches the SSL session information locally. But because modern clients request inlined images and other data via parallel requests (usually up to four parallel requests are common) those requests are served by *different* pre-forked server processes. Here an inter-process cache helps to avoid unnecessary session handshakes.

The following five storage *types* are currently supported:

- `none`

  This disables the global/inter-process Session Cache. This will incur a noticeable speed penalty and may cause problems if using certain browsers, particularly if client certificates are enabled. This setting is not recommended.

- `nonenotnull`

  This disables any global/inter-process Session Cache. However it does force OpenSSL to send a non-null session ID to accommodate buggy clients that require one.

- `dbm:/path/to/datafile`

  This makes use of a DBM hashfile on the local disk to synchronize the local OpenSSL memory caches of the server processes. This session cache may suffer reliability issues under high load. To use this, ensure that MOD_SOCACHE_DBM is loaded.

- `shmcb:/path/to/datafile[`(*size*)`]`

  This makes use of a high-performance cyclic buffer (approx. *size* bytes in size) inside a shared memory segment in RAM (established via `/path/to/datafile`) to synchronize the local OpenSSL memory caches of the server processes. This is the recommended session cache. To use this, ensure that MOD_SOCACHE_SHMCB is loaded.

- `dc:UNIX:/path/to/socket`

  This makes use of the distcache[88] distributed session caching libraries. The argument should specify the location of the server or proxy to be used using the distcache address syntax; for example, `UNIX:/path/to/socket` specifies a UNIX domain socket (typically a local dc_client proxy); `IP:server.example.com:9001` specifies an IP address. To use this, ensure that MOD_SOCACHE_DC is loaded.

Examples

```
SSLSessionCache "dbm:/usr/local/apache/logs/ssl_gcache_data"
SSLSessionCache "shmcb:/usr/local/apache/logs/ssl_gcache_data(512000)"
```

The `ssl-cache` mutex is used to serialize access to the session cache to prevent corruption. This mutex can be configured using the MUTEX directive.

---

[88]http://www.distcache.org/

SSLSessionCacheTimeout Directive

Description:	Number of seconds before an SSL session expires in the Session Cache
Syntax:	`SSLSessionCacheTimeout seconds`
Default:	`SSLSessionCacheTimeout 300`
Context:	server config, virtual host
Status:	Extension
Module:	mod_ssl
Compatibility:	Applies also to RFC 5077 TLS session resumption in Apache 2.4.10 and later

This directive sets the timeout in seconds for the information stored in the global/inter-process SSL Session Cache, the OpenSSL internal memory cache and for sessions resumed by TLS session resumption (RFC 5077). It can be set as low as 15 for testing, but should be set to higher values like 300 in real life.

Example

```
SSLSessionCacheTimeout 600
```

SSLSessionTicketKeyFile Directive

Description:	Persistent encryption/decryption key for TLS session tickets
Syntax:	`SSLSessionTicketKeyFile file-path`
Context:	server config, virtual host
Status:	Extension
Module:	mod_ssl
Compatibility:	Available in httpd 2.4.0 and later, if using OpenSSL 0.9.8h or later

Optionally configures a secret key for encrypting and decrypting TLS session tickets, as defined in RFC 5077[89]. Primarily suitable for clustered environments where TLS sessions information should be shared between multiple nodes. For single-instance httpd setups, it is recommended to *not* configure a ticket key file, but to rely on (random) keys generated by mod_ssl at startup, instead.

The ticket key file must contain 48 bytes of random data, preferrably created from a high-entropy source. On a Unix-based system, a ticket key file can be created as follows:

```
dd if=/dev/random of=/path/to/file.tkey bs=1 count=48
```

Ticket keys should be rotated (replaced) on a frequent basis, as this is the only way to invalidate an existing session ticket - OpenSSL currently doesn't allow to specify a limit for ticket lifetimes. A new ticket key only gets used after restarting the web server. All existing session tickets become invalid after a restart.

⚠ The ticket key file contains sensitive keying material and should be protected with file permissions similar to those used for SSLCERTIFICATEKEYFILE.

---

[89]http://www.ietf.org/rfc/rfc5077.txt

SSLSessionTickets Directive

Description:	Enable or disable use of TLS session tickets
Syntax:	`SSLSessionTickets on|off`
Default:	`SSLSessionTickets on`
Context:	server config, virtual host
Status:	Extension
Module:	mod_ssl
Compatibility:	Available in httpd 2.4.11 and later, if using OpenSSL 0.9.8f or later.

This directive allows to enable or disable the use of TLS session tickets (RFC 5077).

> **!** TLS session tickets are enabled by default. Using them without restarting the web server with an appropriate frequency (e.g. daily) compromises perfect forward secrecy.

SSLSRPUnknownUserSeed Directive

Description:	SRP unknown user seed
Syntax:	`SSLSRPUnknownUserSeed secret-string`
Context:	server config, virtual host
Status:	Extension
Module:	mod_ssl
Compatibility:	Available in httpd 2.4.4 and later, if using OpenSSL 1.0.1 or later

This directive sets the seed used to fake SRP user parameters for unknown users, to avoid leaking whether a given user exists. Specify a secret string. If this directive is not used, then Apache will return the UNKNOWN_PSK_IDENTITY alert to clients who specify an unknown username.

> **Example**
> ```
> SSLSRPUnknownUserSeed "secret"
> ```

SSLSRPVerifierFile Directive

Description:	Path to SRP verifier file
Syntax:	`SSLSRPVerifierFile file-path`
Context:	server config, virtual host
Status:	Extension
Module:	mod_ssl
Compatibility:	Available in httpd 2.4.4 and later, if using OpenSSL 1.0.1 or later

This directive enables TLS-SRP and sets the path to the OpenSSL SRP (Secure Remote Password) verifier file containing TLS-SRP usernames, verifiers, salts, and group parameters.

> **Example**
> ```
> SSLSRPVerifierFile "/path/to/file.srpv"
> ```

The verifier file can be created with the `openssl` command line utility:

> **Creating the SRP verifier file**
> ```
> openssl srp -srpvfile passwd.srpv -userinfo "some info" -add username
> ```

The value given with the optional `-userinfo` parameter is avalable in the `SSL_SRP_USERINFO` request environment variable.

SSLStaplingCache Directive

Description:	Configures the OCSP stapling cache
Syntax:	SSLStaplingCache type
Context:	server config
Status:	Extension
Module:	mod_ssl
Compatibility:	Available if using OpenSSL 0.9.8h or later

Configures the cache used to store OCSP responses which get included in the TLS handshake if SSLUSESTAPLING is enabled. Configuration of a cache is mandatory for OCSP stapling. With the exception of none and nonenotnull, the same storage types are supported as with SSLSESSIONCACHE.

SSLStaplingErrorCacheTimeout Directive

Description:	Number of seconds before expiring invalid responses in the OCSP stapling cache
Syntax:	SSLStaplingErrorCacheTimeout seconds
Default:	SSLStaplingErrorCacheTimeout 600
Context:	server config, virtual host
Status:	Extension
Module:	mod_ssl
Compatibility:	Available if using OpenSSL 0.9.8h or later

Sets the timeout in seconds before *invalid* responses in the OCSP stapling cache (configured through SSLSTAPLING-CACHE) will expire. To set the cache timeout for valid responses, see SSLSTAPLINGSTANDARDCACHETIMEOUT.

SSLStaplingFakeTryLater Directive

Description:	Synthesize "tryLater" responses for failed OCSP stapling queries
Syntax:	SSLStaplingFakeTryLater on|off
Default:	SSLStaplingFakeTryLater on
Context:	server config, virtual host
Status:	Extension
Module:	mod_ssl
Compatibility:	Available if using OpenSSL 0.9.8h or later

When enabled and a query to an OCSP responder for stapling purposes fails, mod_ssl will synthesize a "tryLater" response for the client. Only effective if SSLSTAPLINGRETURNRESPONDERERRORS is also enabled.

SSLStaplingForceURL Directive

Description:	Override the OCSP responder URI specified in the certificate's AIA extension
Syntax:	SSLStaplingForceURL uri
Context:	server config, virtual host
Status:	Extension
Module:	mod_ssl
Compatibility:	Available if using OpenSSL 0.9.8h or later

This directive overrides the URI of an OCSP responder as obtained from the authorityInfoAccess (AIA) extension of the certificate. One potential use is when a proxy is used for retrieving OCSP queries.

SSLStaplingResponderTimeout Directive

Description:	Timeout for OCSP stapling queries
Syntax:	`SSLStaplingResponderTimeout seconds`
Default:	`SSLStaplingResponderTimeout 10`
Context:	server config, virtual host
Status:	Extension
Module:	mod_ssl
Compatibility:	Available if using OpenSSL 0.9.8h or later

This option sets the timeout for queries to OCSP responders when SSLUSESTAPLING is enabled and mod_ssl is querying a responder for OCSP stapling purposes.

SSLStaplingResponseMaxAge Directive

Description:	Maximum allowable age for OCSP stapling responses
Syntax:	`SSLStaplingResponseMaxAge seconds`
Default:	`SSLStaplingResponseMaxAge -1`
Context:	server config, virtual host
Status:	Extension
Module:	mod_ssl
Compatibility:	Available if using OpenSSL 0.9.8h or later

This option sets the maximum allowable age ("freshness") when considering OCSP responses for stapling purposes, i.e. when SSLUSESTAPLING is turned on. The default value (-1) does not enforce a maximum age, which means that OCSP responses are considered valid as long as their `nextUpdate` field is in the future.

SSLStaplingResponseTimeSkew Directive

Description:	Maximum allowable time skew for OCSP stapling response validation
Syntax:	`SSLStaplingResponseTimeSkew seconds`
Default:	`SSLStaplingResponseTimeSkew 300`
Context:	server config, virtual host
Status:	Extension
Module:	mod_ssl
Compatibility:	Available if using OpenSSL 0.9.8h or later

This option sets the maximum allowable time skew when mod_ssl checks the `thisUpdate` and `nextUpdate` fields of OCSP responses which get included in the TLS handshake (OCSP stapling). Only applicable if SSLUSESTAPLING is turned on.

SSLStaplingReturnResponderErrors Directive

Description:	Pass stapling related OCSP errors on to client
Syntax:	`SSLStaplingReturnResponderErrors on|off`
Default:	`SSLStaplingReturnResponderErrors on`
Context:	server config, virtual host
Status:	Extension
Module:	mod_ssl
Compatibility:	Available if using OpenSSL 0.9.8h or later

When enabled, mod_ssl will pass responses from unsuccessful stapling related OCSP queries (such as status errors, expired responses etc.) on to the client. If set to `off`, no stapled responses for failed queries will be included in the

TLS handshake.

SSLStaplingStandardCacheTimeout Directive

Description:	Number of seconds before expiring responses in the OCSP stapling cache
Syntax:	SSLStaplingStandardCacheTimeout seconds
Default:	SSLStaplingStandardCacheTimeout 3600
Context:	server config, virtual host
Status:	Extension
Module:	mod_ssl
Compatibility:	Available if using OpenSSL 0.9.8h or later

Sets the timeout in seconds before responses in the OCSP stapling cache (configured through SSLSTAPLINGCACHE) will expire. This directive applies to *valid* responses, while SSLSTAPLINGERRORCACHETIMEOUT is used for controlling the timeout for invalid/unavailable responses.

SSLStrictSNIVHostCheck Directive

Description:	Whether to allow non-SNI clients to access a name-based virtual host.
Syntax:	SSLStrictSNIVHostCheck on|off
Default:	SSLStrictSNIVHostCheck off
Context:	server config, virtual host
Status:	Extension
Module:	mod_ssl
Compatibility:	Available in Apache 2.2.12 and later

This directive sets whether a non-SNI client is allowed to access a name-based virtual host. If set to on in the default name-based virtual host, clients that are SNI unaware will not be allowed to access *any* virtual host, belonging to this particular IP / port combination. If set to on in any other virtual host, SNI unaware clients are not allowed to access this particular virtual host.

 This option is only available if httpd was compiled against an SNI capable version of OpenSSL.

Example

```
SSLStrictSNIVHostCheck on
```

SSLUserName Directive

Description:	Variable name to determine user name
Syntax:	SSLUserName varname
Context:	server config, directory, .htaccess
Override:	AuthConfig
Status:	Extension
Module:	mod_ssl

This directive sets the "user" field in the Apache request object. This is used by lower modules to identify the user with a character string. In particular, this may cause the environment variable REMOTE_USER to be set. The *varname* can be any of the SSL environment variables.

Note that this directive has no effect if the FakeBasicAuth option is used (see SSLOptions).

Example

```
SSLUserName SSL_CLIENT_S_DN_CN
```

SSLUseStapling Directive

Description:	Enable stapling of OCSP responses in the TLS handshake
Syntax:	SSLUseStapling on|off
Default:	SSLUseStapling off
Context:	server config, virtual host
Status:	Extension
Module:	mod_ssl
Compatibility:	Available if using OpenSSL 0.9.8h or later

This option enables OCSP stapling, as defined by the "Certificate Status Request" TLS extension specified in RFC 6066. If enabled (and requested by the client), mod_ssl will include an OCSP response for its own certificate in the TLS handshake. Configuring an SSLSTAPLINGCACHE is a prerequisite for enabling OCSP stapling.

OCSP stapling relieves the client of querying the OCSP responder on its own, but it should be noted that with the RFC 6066 specification, the server's CertificateStatus reply may only include an OCSP response for a single cert. For server certificates with intermediate CA certificates in their chain (the typical case nowadays), stapling in its current implementation therefore only partially achieves the stated goal of "saving roundtrips and resources" - see also RFC 6961[90] (TLS Multiple Certificate Status Extension).

When OCSP stapling is enabled, the ssl-stapling mutex is used to control access to the OCSP stapling cache in order to prevent corruption, and the sss-stapling-refresh mutex is used to control refreshes of OCSP responses. These mutexes can be configured using the MUTEX directive.

SSLVerifyClient Directive

Description:	Type of Client Certificate verification
Syntax:	SSLVerifyClient level
Default:	SSLVerifyClient none
Context:	server config, virtual host, directory, .htaccess
Override:	AuthConfig
Status:	Extension
Module:	mod_ssl

This directive sets the Certificate verification level for the Client Authentication. Notice that this directive can be used both in per-server and per-directory context. In per-server context it applies to the client authentication process used in the standard SSL handshake when a connection is established. In per-directory context it forces a SSL renegotiation with the reconfigured client verification level after the HTTP request was read but before the HTTP response is sent.

The following levels are available for *level*:

- **none**: no client Certificate is required at all
- **optional**: the client *may* present a valid Certificate
- **require**: the client *has to* present a valid Certificate
- **optional_no_ca**: the client may present a valid Certificate but it need not to be (successfully) verifiable.

---

[90]http://www.ietf.org/rfc/rfc6961.txt

In practice only levels **none** and **require** are really interesting, because level **optional** doesn't work with all browsers and level **optional_no_ca** is actually against the idea of authentication (but can be used to establish SSL test pages, etc.)

Example

```
SSLVerifyClient require
```

SSLVerifyDepth Directive

Description:	Maximum depth of CA Certificates in Client Certificate verification
Syntax:	SSLVerifyDepth number
Default:	SSLVerifyDepth 1
Context:	server config, virtual host, directory, .htaccess
Override:	AuthConfig
Status:	Extension
Module:	mod_ssl

This directive sets how deeply mod_ssl should verify before deciding that the clients don't have a valid certificate. Notice that this directive can be used both in per-server and per-directory context. In per-server context it applies to the client authentication process used in the standard SSL handshake when a connection is established. In per-directory context it forces a SSL renegotiation with the reconfigured client verification depth after the HTTP request was read but before the HTTP response is sent.

The depth actually is the maximum number of intermediate certificate issuers, i.e. the number of CA certificates which are max allowed to be followed while verifying the client certificate. A depth of 0 means that self-signed client certificates are accepted only, the default depth of 1 means the client certificate can be self-signed or has to be signed by a CA which is directly known to the server (i.e. the CA's certificate is under SSLCACERTIFICATEPATH), etc.

Example

```
SSLVerifyDepth 10
```

10.110 Apache Module mod_status

Description:	Provides information on server activity and performance
Status:	Base
ModuleIdentifier:	status_module
SourceFile:	mod_status.c

Summary

The Status module allows a server administrator to find out how well their server is performing. A HTML page is presented that gives the current server statistics in an easily readable form. If required this page can be made to automatically refresh (given a compatible browser). Another page gives a simple machine-readable list of the current server state.

The details given are:

- The number of worker serving requests

- The number of idle worker

- The status of each worker, the number of requests that worker has performed and the total number of bytes served by the worker (*)

- A total number of accesses and byte count served (*)

- The time the server was started/restarted and the time it has been running for

- Averages giving the number of requests per second, the number of bytes served per second and the average number of bytes per request (*)

- The current percentage CPU used by each worker and in total by all workers combined (*)

- The current hosts and requests being processed (*)

The lines marked "(*)" are only available if EXTENDEDSTATUS is On. In version 2.3.6, loading mod_status will toggle EXTENDEDSTATUS On by default.

Directives This module provides no directives.

Enabling Status Support

To enable status reports only for browsers from the example.com domain add this code to your `httpd.conf` configuration file

```
<Location "/server-status">
    SetHandler server-status
    Require host example.com
</Location>
```

You can now access server statistics by using a Web browser to access the page `http://your.server.name/server-status`

Automatic Updates

You can get the status page to update itself automatically if you have a browser that supports "refresh". Access the page `http://your.server.name/server-status?refresh=N` to refresh the page every N seconds.

Machine Readable Status File

A machine-readable version of the status file is available by accessing the page `http://your.server.name/server-status?auto`. This is useful when automatically run, see the Perl program `log_server_status`, which you will find in the `/support` directory of your Apache HTTP Server installation.

> It should be noted that if MOD_STATUS is loaded into the server, its handler capability is available in *all* configuration files, including *per*-directory files (*e.g.*, `.htaccess`). This may have security-related ramifications for your site.

Using server-status to troubleshoot

The `server-status` page may be used as a starting place for troubleshooting a situation where your server is consuming all available resources (CPU or memory), and you wish to identify which requests or clients are causing the problem.

First, ensure that you have EXTENDEDSTATUS set on, so that you can see the full request and client information for each child or thread.

Now look in your process list (using `top`, or similar process viewing utility) to identify the specific processes that are the main culprits. Order the output of `top` by CPU usage, or memory usage, depending on what problem you're trying to address.

Reload the `server-status` page, and look for those process ids, and you'll be able to see what request is being served by that process, for what client. Requests are transient, so you may need to try several times before you catch it in the act, so to speak.

This process *should* give you some idea what client, or what type of requests, are primarily responsible for your load problems. Often you will identify a particular web application that is misbehaving, or a particular client that is attacking your site.

10.111 Apache Module mod_substitute

Description:	Perform search and replace operations on response bodies
Status:	Extension
ModuleIdentifier:	substitute_module
SourceFile:	mod_substitute.c
Compatibility:	Available in Apache HTTP Server 2.2.7 and later

Summary

MOD_SUBSTITUTE provides a mechanism to perform both regular expression and fixed string substitutions on response bodies.

Directives

- Substitute
- SubstituteInheritBefore
- SubstituteMaxLineLength

Substitute Directive

Description:	Pattern to filter the response content
Syntax:	Substitute s/pattern/substitution/[infq]
Context:	directory, .htaccess
Override:	FileInfo
Status:	Extension
Module:	mod_substitute

The SUBSTITUTE directive specifies a search and replace pattern to apply to the response body.

The meaning of the pattern can be modified by using any combination of these flags:

i Perform a case-insensitive match.

n By default the pattern is treated as a regular expression. Using the n flag forces the pattern to be treated as a fixed string.

f The f flag causes mod_substitute to flatten the result of a substitution allowing for later substitutions to take place on the boundary of this one. This is the default.

q The q flag causes mod_substitute to not flatten the buckets after each substitution. This can result in much faster response and a decrease in memory utilization, but should only be used if there is no possibility that the result of one substitution will ever match a pattern or regex of a subsequent one.

Example

```
<Location "/">
    AddOutputFilterByType SUBSTITUTE text/html
    Substitute "s/foo/bar/ni"
</Location>
```

If either the pattern or the substitution contain a slash character then an alternative delimiter should be used:

Example of using an alternate delimiter

```
<Location "/">
    AddOutputFilterByType SUBSTITUTE text/html
    Substitute "s|<BR */?>|<br />|i"
</Location>
```

Backreferences can be used in the comparison and in the substitution, when regular expressions are used, as illustrated in the following example:

Example of using backreferences and captures

```
<Location "/">
    AddOutputFilterByType SUBSTITUTE text/html
    # "foo=k,bar=k" -> "foo/bar=k"
    Substitute "s|foo=(\w+),bar=\1|foo/bar=$1"
</Location>
```

A common use scenario for `mod_substitute` is the situation in which a front-end server proxies requests to a back-end server which returns HTML with hard-coded embedded URLs that refer to the back-end server. These URLs don't work for the end-user, since the back-end server is unreachable.

In this case, `mod_substutite` can be used to rewrite those URLs into something that will work from the front end:

Rewriting URLs embedded in proxied content

```
ProxyPass "/blog/" "http://internal.blog.example.com"
ProxyPassReverse "/blog/" "http://internal.blog.example.com/"

Substitute "s|http://internal.blog.example.com/|http://www.example.com/blog/|i"
```

PROXYPASSREVERSE modifies any `Location` (redirect) headers that are sent by the back-end server, and, in this example, `Substitute` takes care of the rest of the problem by fixing up the HTML response as well.

SubstituteInheritBefore Directive

Description:	Change the merge order of inherited patterns
Syntax:	`SubstituteInheritBefore on|off`
Default:	`SubstituteInheritBefore off`
Context:	directory, .htaccess
Override:	FileInfo
Status:	Extension
Module:	mod_substitute
Compatibility:	Available in httpd 2.4.17 and later

Whether to apply the inherited SUBSTITUTE patterns first (`on`), or after the ones of the current context (`off`). SUBSTITUTEINHERITBEFORE is itself inherited, hence contexts that inherit it (those that don't specify their own SUBSTITUTEINHERITBEFORE value) will apply the closest defined merge order.

SubstituteMaxLineLength Directive

Description:	Set the maximum line size
Syntax:	SubstituteMaxLineLength bytes(b|B|k|K|m|M|g|G)
Default:	SubstituteMaxLineLength 1m
Context:	directory, .htaccess
Override:	FileInfo
Status:	Extension
Module:	mod_substitute
Compatibility:	Available in httpd 2.4.11 and later

The maximum line size handled by MOD_SUBSTITUTE is limited to restrict memory use. The limit can be configured using SUBSTITUTEMAXLINELENGTH. The value can be given as the number of bytes and can be suffixed with a single letter b, B, k, K, m, M, g, G to provide the size in bytes, kilobytes, megabytes or gigabytes respectively.

Example

```
<Location "/">
    AddOutputFilterByType SUBSTITUTE text/html
    SubstituteMaxLineLength 10m
    Substitute "s/foo/bar/ni"
</Location>
```

10.112   Apache Module mod_suexec

Description:	Allows CGI scripts to run as a specified user and Group
Status:	Extension
ModuleIdentifier:	suexec_module
SourceFile:	mod_suexec.c

Summary

This module, in combination with the suexec support program allows CGI scripts to run as a specified user and Group.

Directives

- SuexecUserGroup

See also

- SuEXEC support (p. 105)

SuexecUserGroup Directive

Description:	User and group for CGI programs to run as
Syntax:	SuexecUserGroup User Group
Context:	server config, virtual host
Status:	Extension
Module:	mod_suexec

The SUEXECUSERGROUP directive allows you to specify a user and group for CGI programs to run as. Non-CGI requests are still processed with the user specified in the USER directive.

Example

```
SuexecUserGroup nobody nogroup
```

Startup will fail if this directive is specified but the suEXEC feature is disabled.

See also

- SUEXEC

10.113   Apache Module mod_unique_id

Description:	Provides an environment variable with a unique identifier for each request
Status:	Extension
ModuleIdentifier:	unique_id_module
SourceFile:	mod_unique_id.c

Summary

This module provides a magic token for each request which is guaranteed to be unique across "all" requests under very specific conditions. The unique identifier is even unique across multiple machines in a properly configured cluster of machines. The environment variable UNIQUE_ID is set to the identifier for each request. Unique identifiers are useful for various reasons which are beyond the scope of this document.

Directives This module provides no directives.

Theory

First a brief recap of how the Apache server works on Unix machines. This feature currently isn't supported on Windows NT. On Unix machines, Apache creates several children, the children process requests one at a time. Each child can serve multiple requests in its lifetime. For the purpose of this discussion, the children don't share any data with each other. We'll refer to the children as *httpd processes*.

Your website has one or more machines under your administrative control, together we'll call them a cluster of machines. Each machine can possibly run multiple instances of Apache. All of these collectively are considered "the universe", and with certain assumptions we'll show that in this universe we can generate unique identifiers for each request, without extensive communication between machines in the cluster.

The machines in your cluster should satisfy these requirements. (Even if you have only one machine you should synchronize its clock with NTP.)

- The machines' times are synchronized via NTP or other network time protocol.
- The machines' hostnames all differ, such that the module can do a hostname lookup on the hostname and receive a different IP address for each machine in the cluster.

As far as operating system assumptions go, we assume that pids (process ids) fit in 32-bits. If the operating system uses more than 32-bits for a pid, the fix is trivial but must be performed in the code.

Given those assumptions, at a single point in time we can identify any httpd process on any machine in the cluster from all other httpd processes. The machine's IP address and the pid of the httpd process are sufficient to do this. A httpd process can handle multiple requests simultaneously if you use a multi-threaded MPM. In order to identify threads, we use a thread index Apache httpd uses internally. So in order to generate unique identifiers for requests we need only distinguish between different points in time.

To distinguish time we will use a Unix timestamp (seconds since January 1, 1970 UTC), and a 16-bit counter. The timestamp has only one second granularity, so the counter is used to represent up to 65536 values during a single second. The quadruple (*ip_addr, pid, time_stamp, counter*) is sufficient to enumerate 65536 requests per second per httpd process. There are issues however with pid reuse over time, and the counter is used to alleviate this issue.

When an httpd child is created, the counter is initialized with (current microseconds divided by 10) modulo 65536 (this formula was chosen to eliminate some variance problems with the low order bits of the microsecond timers on some systems). When a unique identifier is generated, the time stamp used is the time the request arrived at the web server. The counter is incremented every time an identifier is generated (and allowed to roll over).

The kernel generates a pid for each process as it forks the process, and pids are allowed to roll over (they're 16-bits on many Unixes, but newer systems have expanded to 32-bits). So over time the same pid will be reused. However unless it is reused within the same second, it does not destroy the uniqueness of our quadruple. That is, we assume the system does not spawn 65536 processes in a one second interval (it may even be 32768 processes on some Unixes, but even this isn't likely to happen).

Suppose that time repeats itself for some reason. That is, suppose that the system's clock is screwed up and it revisits a past time (or it is too far forward, is reset correctly, and then revisits the future time). In this case we can easily show that we can get pid and time stamp reuse. The choice of initializer for the counter is intended to help defeat this. Note that we really want a random number to initialize the counter, but there aren't any readily available numbers on most systems (*i.e.*, you can't use rand() because you need to seed the generator, and can't seed it with the time because time, at least at one second resolution, has repeated itself). This is not a perfect defense.

How good a defense is it? Suppose that one of your machines serves at most 500 requests per second (which is a very reasonable upper bound at this writing, because systems generally do more than just shovel out static files). To do that it will require a number of children which depends on how many concurrent clients you have. But we'll be pessimistic and suppose that a single child is able to serve 500 requests per second. There are 1000 possible starting counter values such that two sequences of 500 requests overlap. So there is a 1.5% chance that if time (at one second resolution) repeats itself this child will repeat a counter value, and uniqueness will be broken. This was a very pessimistic example, and with real world values it's even less likely to occur. If your system is such that it's still likely to occur, then perhaps you should make the counter 32 bits (by editing the code).

You may be concerned about the clock being "set back" during summer daylight savings. However this isn't an issue because the times used here are UTC, which "always" go forward. Note that x86 based Unixes may need proper configuration for this to be true – they should be configured to assume that the motherboard clock is on UTC and compensate appropriately. But even still, if you're running NTP then your UTC time will be correct very shortly after reboot.

The UNIQUE_ID environment variable is constructed by encoding the 144-bit (32-bit IP address, 32 bit pid, 32 bit time stamp, 16 bit counter, 32 bit thread index) quadruple using the alphabet [A-Za-z0-9@-] in a manner similar to MIME base64 encoding, producing 24 characters. The MIME base64 alphabet is actually [A-Za-z0-9+/] however + and / need to be specially encoded in URLs, which makes them less desirable. All values are encoded in network byte ordering so that the encoding is comparable across architectures of different byte ordering. The actual ordering of the encoding is: time stamp, IP address, pid, counter. This ordering has a purpose, but it should be emphasized that applications should not dissect the encoding. Applications should treat the entire encoded UNIQUE_ID as an opaque token, which can be compared against other UNIQUE_IDs for equality only.

The ordering was chosen such that it's possible to change the encoding in the future without worrying about collision with an existing database of UNIQUE_IDs. The new encodings should also keep the time stamp as the first element, and can otherwise use the same alphabet and bit length. Since the time stamps are essentially an increasing sequence, it's sufficient to have a *flag second* in which all machines in the cluster stop serving any request, and stop using the old encoding format. Afterwards they can resume requests and begin issuing the new encodings.

This we believe is a relatively portable solution to this problem. The identifiers generated have essentially an infinite life-time because future identifiers can be made longer as required. Essentially no communication is required between machines in the cluster (only NTP synchronization is required, which is low overhead), and no communication between httpd processes is required (the communication is implicit in the pid value assigned by the kernel). In very specific situations the identifier can be shortened, but more information needs to be assumed (for example the 32-bit IP address is overkill for any site, but there is no portable shorter replacement for it).

10.114 Apache Module mod_unixd

Description:	Basic (required) security for Unix-family platforms.
Status:	Base
ModuleIdentifier:	unixd_module
SourceFile:	mod_unixd.c

Directives

- ChrootDir
- Group
- Suexec
- User

See also

- suEXEC support (p. 105)

ChrootDir Directive

Description:	Directory for apache to run chroot(8) after startup.
Syntax:	`ChrootDir /path/to/directory`
Default:	`none`
Context:	server config
Status:	Base
Module:	MOD_UNIXD
Compatibility:	Available in Apache 2.2.10 and later

This directive tells the server to *chroot(8)* to the specified directory after startup, but before accepting requests over the 'net.

Note that running the server under chroot is not simple, and requires additional setup, particularly if you are running scripts such as CGI or PHP. Please make sure you are properly familiar with the operation of chroot before attempting to use this feature.

Group Directive

Description:	Group under which the server will answer requests
Syntax:	`Group unix-group`
Default:	`Group #-1`
Context:	server config
Status:	Base
Module:	mod_unixd

The GROUP directive sets the group under which the server will answer requests. In order to use this directive, the server must be run initially as `root`. If you start the server as a non-root user, it will fail to change to the specified group, and will instead continue to run as the group of the original user. *Unix-group* is one of:

A group name Refers to the given group by name.

 # followed by a group number. Refers to a group by its number.

Example

```
Group www-group
```

It is recommended that you set up a new group specifically for running the server. Some admins use user `nobody`, but this is not always possible or desirable.

 Security

Don't set GROUP (or USER) to `root` unless you know exactly what you are doing, and what the dangers are.

See also

- VHostGroup
- SuexecUserGroup

Suexec Directive

Description:	Enable or disable the suEXEC feature
Syntax:	`Suexec On|Off`
Default:	`On if suexec binary exists with proper owner and mode, Off otherwise`
Context:	server config
Status:	Base
Module:	mod_unixd

When On, startup will fail if the suexec binary doesn't exist or has an invalid owner or file mode.

When Off, suEXEC will be disabled even if the suexec binary exists and has a valid owner and file mode.

User Directive

Description:	The userid under which the server will answer requests
Syntax:	`User unix-userid`
Default:	`User #-1`
Context:	server config
Status:	Base
Module:	mod_unixd

The USER directive sets the user ID as which the server will answer requests. In order to use this directive, the server must be run initially as `root`. If you start the server as a non-root user, it will fail to change to the lesser privileged user, and will instead continue to run as that original user. If you do start the server as `root`, then it is normal for the parent process to remain running as root. *Unix-userid* is one of:

A username Refers to the given user by name.

 # followed by a user number. Refers to a user by its number.

The user should have no privileges that result in it being able to access files that are not intended to be visible to the outside world, and similarly, the user should not be able to execute code that is not meant for HTTP requests. It is recommended that you set up a new user and group specifically for running the server. Some admins use user `nobody`, but this is not always desirable, since the `nobody` user can have other uses on the system.

Security
Don't set USER (or GROUP) to `root` unless you know exactly what you are doing, and what the dangers are.

See also

- VHostUser
- SuexecUserGroup

10.115   Apache Module mod_userdir

Description:	User-specific directories
Status:	Base
ModuleIdentifier:	userdir_module
SourceFile:	mod_userdir.c

Summary

This module allows user-specific directories to be accessed using the `http://example.com/~user/` syntax.

Directives

- UserDir

See also

- Mapping URLs to the Filesystem (p. 61)
- public_html tutorial (p. 245)

UserDir Directive

Description:	Location of the user-specific directories
Syntax:	`UserDir directory-filename [directory-filename]` ...
Context:	server config, virtual host
Status:	Base
Module:	mod_userdir

The USERDIR directive sets the real directory in a user's home directory to use when a request for a document for a user is received. *Directory-filename* is one of the following:

- The name of a directory or a pattern such as those shown below.

- The keyword `disabled`. This turns off *all* username-to-directory translations except those explicitly named with the `enabled` keyword (see below).

- The keyword `disabled` followed by a space-delimited list of usernames. Usernames that appear in such a list will *never* have directory translation performed, even if they appear in an `enabled` clause.

- The keyword `enabled` followed by a space-delimited list of usernames. These usernames will have directory translation performed even if a global disable is in effect, but not if they also appear in a `disabled` clause.

If neither the `enabled` nor the `disabled` keywords appear in the `Userdir` directive, the argument is treated as a filename pattern, and is used to turn the name into a directory specification. A request for `http://www.example.com/~bob/one/two.html` will be translated to:

UserDir directive used	Translated path
UserDir public_html	~bob/public_html/one/two.html
UserDir /usr/web	/usr/web/bob/one/two.html
UserDir /home/*/www	/home/bob/www/one/two.html

The following directives will send redirects to the client:

UserDir directive used	Translated path
UserDir http://www.example.com/users	http://www.example.com/users/bob/one/two.html
UserDir http://www.example.com/*/usr	http://www.example.com/bob/usr/one/two.html
UserDir http://www.example.com/~*/	http://www.example.com/~bob/one/two.html

Be careful when using this directive; for instance, "UserDir ./" would map "/~root" to "/" - which is probably undesirable. It is strongly recommended that your configuration include a "UserDir disabled root" declaration. See also the DIRECTORY directive and the Security Tips (p. 338) page for more information.

Additional examples:

To allow a few users to have UserDir directories, but not anyone else, use the following:

```
UserDir disabled
UserDir enabled user1 user2 user3
```

To allow most users to have UserDir directories, but deny this to a few, use the following:

```
UserDir disabled user4 user5 user6
```

It is also possible to specify alternative user directories. If you use a command like:

```
UserDir public_html /usr/web http://www.example.com/
```

With a request for http://www.example.com/~bob/one/two.html, will try to find the page at ~bob/public_html/one/two.html first, then /usr/web/bob/one/two.html, and finally it will send a redirect to http://www.example.com/bob/one/two.html.

If you add a redirect, it must be the last alternative in the list. Apache httpd cannot determine if the redirect succeeded or not, so if you have the redirect earlier in the list, that will always be the alternative that is used.

User directory substitution is not active by default in versions 2.1.4 and later. In earlier versions, UserDir public_html was assumed if no USERDIR directive was present.

 **Merging details**

Lists of specific enabled and disabled users are replaced, not merged, from global to virtual host scope

See also

- Per-user web directories tutorial (p. 245)

10.116   Apache Module mod_usertrack

Description:	*Clickstream* logging of user activity on a site
Status:	Extension
ModuleIdentifier:	usertrack_module
SourceFile:	mod_usertrack.c

Summary

Provides tracking of a user through your website via browser cookies.

Directives

- CookieDomain
- CookieExpires
- CookieName
- CookieStyle
- CookieTracking

Logging

MOD_USERTRACK sets a cookie which can be logged via MOD_LOG_CONFIG configurable logging formats:

```
LogFormat "%{Apache}n %r %t" usertrack
CustomLog logs/clickstream.log usertrack
```

CookieDomain Directive

Description:	The domain to which the tracking cookie applies
Syntax:	CookieDomain domain
Context:	server config, virtual host, directory, .htaccess
Override:	FileInfo
Status:	Extension
Module:	mod_usertrack

This directive controls the setting of the domain to which the tracking cookie applies. If not present, no domain is included in the cookie header field.

The domain string **must** begin with a dot, and **must** include at least one embedded dot. That is, .example.com is legal, but www.example.com and .com are not.

$\Longrightarrow$ Most browsers in use today will not allow cookies to be set for a two-part top level domain, such as .co.uk, although such a domain ostensibly fulfills the requirements above.

These domains are equivalent to top level domains such as .com, and allowing such cookies may be a security risk. Thus, if you are under a two-part top level domain, you should still use your actual domain, as you would with any other top level domain (for example .example.co.uk).

```
CookieDomain .example.com
```

CookieExpires Directive

Description:	Expiry time for the tracking cookie
Syntax:	`CookieExpires expiry-period`
Context:	server config, virtual host, directory, .htaccess
Override:	FileInfo
Status:	Extension
Module:	mod_usertrack

When used, this directive sets an expiry time on the cookie generated by the usertrack module. The *expiry-period* can be given either as a number of seconds, or in the format such as "2 weeks 3 days 7 hours". Valid denominations are: years, months, weeks, days, hours, minutes and seconds. If the expiry time is in any format other than one number indicating the number of seconds, it must be enclosed by double quotes.

If this directive is not used, cookies last only for the current browser session.

```
CookieExpires "3 weeks"
```

CookieName Directive

Description:	Name of the tracking cookie
Syntax:	`CookieName token`
Default:	`CookieName Apache`
Context:	server config, virtual host, directory, .htaccess
Override:	FileInfo
Status:	Extension
Module:	mod_usertrack

This directive allows you to change the name of the cookie this module uses for its tracking purposes. By default the cookie is named `"Apache"`.

You must specify a valid cookie name; results are unpredictable if you use a name containing unusual characters. Valid characters include A-Z, a-z, 0-9, `"_"`, and `"-"`.

```
CookieName clicktrack
```

CookieStyle Directive

Description:	Format of the cookie header field
Syntax:	`CookieStyle Netscape|Cookie|Cookie2|RFC2109|RFC2965`
Default:	`CookieStyle Netscape`
Context:	server config, virtual host, directory, .htaccess
Override:	FileInfo
Status:	Extension
Module:	mod_usertrack

This directive controls the format of the cookie header field. The three formats allowed are:

- **Netscape**, which is the original but now deprecated syntax. This is the default, and the syntax Apache has historically used.
- **Cookie** or **RFC2109**, which is the syntax that superseded the Netscape syntax.
- **Cookie2** or **RFC2965**, which is the most current cookie syntax.

Not all clients can understand all of these formats, but you should use the newest one that is generally acceptable to your users' browsers. At the time of writing, most browsers support all three of these formats, with `Cookie2` being the preferred format.

```
CookieStyle Cookie2
```

CookieTracking Directive

Description:	Enables tracking cookie
Syntax:	`CookieTracking on|off`
Default:	`CookieTracking off`
Context:	server config, virtual host, directory, .htaccess
Override:	FileInfo
Status:	Extension
Module:	mod_usertrack

When MOD_USERTRACK is loaded, and `CookieTracking on` is set, Apache will send a user-tracking cookie for all new requests. This directive can be used to turn this behavior on or off on a per-server or per-directory basis. By default, enabling MOD_USERTRACK will **not** activate cookies.

```
CookieTracking on
```

10.117 Apache Module mod_version

Description:	Version dependent configuration
Status:	Extension
ModuleIdentifier:	version_module
SourceFile:	mod_version.c

Summary

This module is designed for the use in test suites and large networks which have to deal with different httpd versions and different configurations. It provides a new container – <IFVERSION>, which allows a flexible version checking including numeric comparisons and regular expressions.

Examples

```
<IfVersion 2.4.2>
    # current httpd version is exactly 2.4.2
</IfVersion>

<IfVersion >= 2.5>
    # use really new features :-)
</IfVersion>
```

See below for further possibilities.

Directives

- <IfVersion>

IfVersion Directive

Description:	contains version dependent configuration
Syntax:	<IfVersion [[!]operator] version> ... </IfVersion>
Context:	server config, virtual host, directory, .htaccess
Override:	All
Status:	Extension
Module:	mod_version

The <IFVERSION> section encloses configuration directives which are executed only if the `httpd` version matches the desired criteria. For normal (numeric) comparisons the *version* argument has the format `major[.minor[.patch]]`, e.g. `2.1.0` or `2.2`. *minor* and *patch* are optional. If these numbers are omitted, they are assumed to be zero. The following numerical *operator*s are possible:

operator	description
= or ==	httpd version is equal
>	httpd version is greater than
>=	httpd version is greater or equal
<	httpd version is less than
<=	httpd version is less or equal

Example

```
<IfVersion >= 2.3>
    # this happens only in versions greater or
    # equal 2.3.0.
</IfVersion>
```

Besides the numerical comparison it is possible to match a regular expression against the httpd version. There are two ways to write it:

operator	description
= or ==	*version* has the form / `regex` /
~	*version* has the form `regex`

Example

```
<IfVersion = /^2.4.[01234]$/>
    # e.g. workaround for buggy versions
</IfVersion>
```

In order to reverse the meaning, all operators can be preceded by an exclamation mark (!):

```
<IfVersion !~ ^2.4.[01234]$>
    # not for those versions
</IfVersion>
```

If the *operator* is omitted, it is assumed to be =.

10.118   Apache Module mod_vhost_alias

Description:	Provides for dynamically configured mass virtual hosting
Status:	Extension
ModuleIdentifier:	vhost_alias_module
SourceFile:	mod_vhost_alias.c

Summary

This module creates dynamically configured virtual hosts, by allowing the IP address and/or the `Host:` header of the HTTP request to be used as part of the pathname to determine what files to serve. This allows for easy use of a huge number of virtual hosts with similar configurations.

Note

> If MOD_ALIAS or MOD_USERDIR are used for translating URIs to filenames, they will override the directives of MOD_VHOST_ALIAS described below. For example, the following configuration will map `/cgi-bin/script.pl` to `/usr/local/apache2/cgi-bin/script.pl` in all cases:
>
> ```
> ScriptAlias "/cgi-bin/" "/usr/local/apache2/cgi-bin/"
> VirtualScriptAlias "/never/found/%0/cgi-bin/"
> ```

Directives

- VirtualDocumentRoot
- VirtualDocumentRootIP
- VirtualScriptAlias
- VirtualScriptAliasIP

See also

- USECANONICALNAME
- Dynamically configured mass virtual hosting (p. 120)

Directory Name Interpolation

All the directives in this module interpolate a string into a pathname. The interpolated string (henceforth called the "name") may be either the server name (see the USECANONICALNAME directive for details on how this is determined) or the IP address of the virtual host on the server in dotted-quad format. The interpolation is controlled by specifiers inspired by `printf` which have a number of formats:

`%%`	insert a `%`
`%p`	insert the port number of the virtual host
`%N.M`	insert (part of) the name

`N` and `M` are used to specify substrings of the name. `N` selects from the dot-separated components of the name, and `M` selects characters within whatever `N` has selected. `M` is optional and defaults to zero if it isn't present; the dot must be present if and only if `M` is present. The interpretation is as follows:

0	the whole name
1	the first part
2	the second part
-1	the last part
-2	the penultimate part
2+	the second and all subsequent parts
-2+	the penultimate and all preceding parts
1+ and -1+	the same as 0

If N or M is greater than the number of parts available a single underscore is interpolated.

Examples

For simple name-based virtual hosts you might use the following directives in your server configuration file:

```
UseCanonicalName    Off
VirtualDocumentRoot "/usr/local/apache/vhosts/%0"
```

A request for `http://www.example.com/directory/file.html` will be satisfied by the file `/usr/local/apache/vhosts/www.example.com/directory/file.html`.

For a very large number of virtual hosts it is a good idea to arrange the files to reduce the size of the vhosts directory. To do this you might use the following in your configuration file:

```
UseCanonicalName    Off
VirtualDocumentRoot "/usr/local/apache/vhosts/%3+/%2.1/%2.2/%2.3/%2"
```

A request for `http://www.domain.example.com/directory/file.html` will be satisfied by the file `/usr/local/apache/vhosts/example.com/d/o/m/domain/directory/file.html`.

A more even spread of files can be achieved by hashing from the end of the name, for example:

```
VirtualDocumentRoot "/usr/local/apache/vhosts/%3+/%2.-1/%2.-2/%2.-3/%2"
```

The example request would come from `/usr/local/apache/vhosts/example.com/n/i/a/domain/dir`

Alternatively you might use:

```
VirtualDocumentRoot "/usr/local/apache/vhosts/%3+/%2.1/%2.2/%2.3/%2.4+"
```

The example request would come from `/usr/local/apache/vhosts/example.com/d/o/m/ain/direct`

A very common request by users is the ability to point multiple domains to multiple document roots without having to worry about the length or number of parts of the hostname being requested. If the requested hostname is `sub.www.domain.example.com` instead of simply `www.domain.example.com`, then using %3+ will result in the document root being `/usr/local/apache/vhosts/domain.example.com/...` instead of the intended `example.com` directory. In such cases, it can be beneficial to use the combination %-2.0.%-1.0, which will always yield the domain name and the tld, for example `example.com` regardless of the number of subdomains appended to the hostname. As such, one can make a configuration that will direct all first, second or third level subdomains to the same directory:

```
VirtualDocumentRoot "/usr/local/apache/vhosts/%-2.0.%-1.0"
```

In the example above, both `www.example.com` as well as `www.sub.example.com` or `example.com` will all point to `/usr/local/apache/vhosts/example.com`.

For IP-based virtual hosting you might use the following in your configuration file:

```
UseCanonicalName DNS
VirtualDocumentRootIP "/usr/local/apache/vhosts/%1/%2/%3/%4/docs"
VirtualScriptAliasIP  "/usr/local/apache/vhosts/%1/%2/%3/%4/cgi-bin"
```

A request for `http://www.domain.example.com/directory/file.html` would be satisfied by the file `/usr/local/apache/vhosts/10/20/30/40/docs/directory/file.html` if the IP address of www.domain.example.com were 10.20.30.40. A request for `http://www.domain.example.com/cgi-bin/script.pl` would be satisfied by executing the program `/usr/local/apache/vhosts/10/20/30/40/cgi-bin/script.pl`.

If you want to include the . character in a `VirtualDocumentRoot` directive, but it clashes with a % directive, you can work around the problem in the following way:

```
VirtualDocumentRoot "/usr/local/apache/vhosts/%2.0.%3.0"
```

A request for `http://www.domain.example.com/directory/file.html` will be satisfied by the file `/usr/local/apache/vhosts/domain.example/directory/file.html`.

The LOGFORMAT directives %V and %A are useful in conjunction with this module.

VirtualDocumentRoot Directive

Description:	Dynamically configure the location of the document root for a given virtual host
Syntax:	VirtualDocumentRoot interpolated-directory|none
Default:	VirtualDocumentRoot none
Context:	server config, virtual host
Status:	Extension
Module:	mod_vhost_alias

The VIRTUALDOCUMENTROOT directive allows you to determine where Apache HTTP Server will find your documents based on the value of the server name. The result of expanding *interpolated-directory* is used as the root of the document tree in a similar manner to the DOCUMENTROOT directive's argument. If *interpolated-directory* is none then VIRTUALDOCUMENTROOT is turned off. This directive cannot be used in the same context as VIRTUALDOCUMENTROOTIP.

 Note

VIRTUALDOCUMENTROOT will override any DOCUMENTROOT directives you may have put in the same context or child contexts. Putting a VIRTUALDOCUMENTROOT in the global server scope will effectively override DOCUMENTROOT directives in any virtual hosts defined later on, unless you set VIRTUALDOCUMENTROOT to None in each virtual host.

VirtualDocumentRootIP Directive

Description:	Dynamically configure the location of the document root for a given virtual host
Syntax:	VirtualDocumentRootIP interpolated-directory|none
Default:	VirtualDocumentRootIP none
Context:	server config, virtual host
Status:	Extension
Module:	mod_vhost_alias

The VIRTUALDOCUMENTROOTIP directive is like the VIRTUALDOCUMENTROOT directive, except that it uses the IP address of the server end of the connection for directory interpolation instead of the server name.

VirtualScriptAlias Directive

Description:	Dynamically configure the location of the CGI directory for a given virtual host
Syntax:	`VirtualScriptAlias interpolated-directory|none`
Default:	`VirtualScriptAlias none`
Context:	server config, virtual host
Status:	Extension
Module:	mod_vhost_alias

The VIRTUALSCRIPTALIAS directive allows you to determine where Apache httpd will find CGI scripts in a similar manner to VIRTUALDOCUMENTROOT does for other documents. It matches requests for URIs starting `/cgi-bin/`, much like SCRIPTALIAS `/cgi-bin/` would.

VirtualScriptAliasIP Directive

Description:	Dynamically configure the location of the CGI directory for a given virtual host
Syntax:	`VirtualScriptAliasIP interpolated-directory|none`
Default:	`VirtualScriptAliasIP none`
Context:	server config, virtual host
Status:	Extension
Module:	mod_vhost_alias

The VIRTUALSCRIPTALIASIP directive is like the VIRTUALSCRIPTALIAS directive, except that it uses the IP address of the server end of the connection for directory interpolation instead of the server name.

10.119   Apache Module mod_watchdog

Description:	provides infrastructure for other modules to periodically run tasks
Status:	Base
ModuleIdentifier:	watchdog_module
SourceFile:	mod_watchdog.c
Compatibility:	Available in Apache 2.3 and later

Summary

MOD_WATCHDOG defines programmatic hooks for other modules to periodically run tasks. These modules can register handlers for MOD_WATCHDOG hooks. Currently, the following modules in the Apache distribution use this functionality:

- MOD_HEARTBEAT
- MOD_HEARTMONITOR

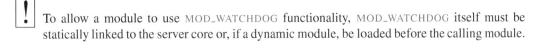 To allow a module to use MOD_WATCHDOG functionality, MOD_WATCHDOG itself must be statically linked to the server core or, if a dynamic module, be loaded before the calling module.

Directives

- WatchdogInterval

WatchdogInterval Directive

Description:	Watchdog interval in seconds
Syntax:	`WatchdogInterval number-of-seconds`
Default:	`WatchdogInterval 1`
Context:	server config
Status:	Base
Module:	mod_watchdog

Sets the interval at which the watchdog_step hook runs. Default is to run every second.

10.120   Apache Module mod_xml2enc

Description:	Enhanced charset/internationalisation support for libxml2-based filter modules
Status:	Base
ModuleIdentifier:	xml2enc_module
SourceFile:	mod_xml2enc.c
Compatibility:	Version 2.4 and later. Available as a third-party module for 2.2.x versions

Summary

This module provides enhanced internationalisation support for markup-aware filter modules such as MOD_PROXY_HTML. It can automatically detect the encoding of input data and ensure they are correctly processed by the libxml2[91] parser, including converting to Unicode (UTF-8) where necessary. It can also convert data to an encoding of choice after markup processing, and will ensure the correct *charset* value is set in the HTTP *Content-Type* header.

Directives

- xml2EncAlias
- xml2EncDefault
- xml2StartParse

Usage

There are two usage scenarios: with modules programmed to work with mod_xml2enc, and with those that are not aware of it:

Filter modules enabled for mod_xml2enc Modules such as MOD_PROXY_HTML version 3.1 and up use the xml2enc_charset optional function to retrieve the charset argument to pass to the libxml2 parser, and may use the xml2enc_filter optional function to postprocess to another encoding. Using mod_xml2enc with an enabled module, no configuration is necessary: the other module will configure mod_xml2enc for you (though you may still want to customise it using the configuration directives below).

Non-enabled modules To use it with a libxml2-based module that isn't explicitly enabled for mod_xml2enc, you will have to configure the filter chain yourself. So to use it with a filter **foo** provided by a module **mod_foo** to improve the latter's i18n support with HTML and XML, you could use

```
FilterProvider iconv     xml2enc Content-Type $text/html
FilterProvider iconv     xml2enc Content-Type $xml
FilterProvider markup    foo Content-Type $text/html
FilterProvider markup    foo Content-Type $xml
FilterChain      iconv markup
```

mod_foo will now support any character set supported by either (or both) of libxml2 or apr_xlate/iconv.

Programming API

Programmers writing libxml2-based filter modules are encouraged to enable them for mod_xml2enc, to provide strong i18n support for your users without reinventing the wheel. The programming API is exposed in *mod_xml2enc.h*, and a usage example is MOD_PROXY_HTML.

---

[91]http://xmlsoft.org/

Detecting an Encoding

Unlike MOD_CHARSET_LITE, mod_xml2enc is designed to work with data whose encoding cannot be known in advance and thus configured. It therefore uses 'sniffing' techniques to detect the encoding of HTTP data as follows:

1. If the HTTP *Content-Type* header includes a *charset* parameter, that is used.

2. If the data start with an XML Byte Order Mark (BOM) or an XML encoding declaration, that is used.

3. If an encoding is declared in an HTML <META> element, that is used.

4. If none of the above match, the default value set by XML2ENCDEFAULT is used.

The rules are applied in order. As soon as a match is found, it is used and detection is stopped.

Output Encoding

libxml2[92] always uses UTF-8 (Unicode) internally, and libxml2-based filter modules will output that by default. mod_xml2enc can change the output encoding through the API, but there is currently no way to configure that directly.

Changing the output encoding should (in theory, at least) never be necessary, and is not recommended due to the extra processing load on the server of an unnecessary conversion.

Unsupported Encodings

If you are working with encodings that are not supported by any of the conversion methods available on your platform, you can still alias them to a supported encoding using XML2ENCALIAS.

xml2EncAlias Directive

Description:	Recognise Aliases for encoding values
Syntax:	xml2EncAlias charset alias [alias ...]
Context:	server config
Status:	Base
Module:	mod_xml2enc

This server-wide directive aliases one or more encoding to another encoding. This enables encodings not recognised by libxml2 to be handled internally by libxml2's encoding support using the translation table for a recognised encoding. This serves two purposes: to support character sets (or names) not recognised either by libxml2 or iconv, and to skip conversion for an encoding where it is known to be unnecessary.

xml2EncDefault Directive

Description:	Sets a default encoding to assume when absolutely no information can be automatically detected
Syntax:	xml2EncDefault name
Context:	server config, virtual host, directory, .htaccess
Status:	Base
Module:	mod_xml2enc
Compatibility:	Version 2.4.0 and later; available as a third-party module for earlier versions.

---

[92]http://xmlsoft.org/

If you are processing data with known encoding but no encoding information, you can set this default to help mod_xml2enc process the data correctly. For example, to work with the default value of Latin1 (*iso-8859-1* speci-fied in HTTP/1.0, use

```
xml2EncDefault iso-8859-1
```

xml2StartParse Directive

Description:	Advise the parser to skip leading junk.
Syntax:	`xml2StartParse element [element ...]`
Context:	server config, virtual host, directory, .htaccess
Status:	Base
Module:	mod_xml2enc

Specify that the markup parser should start at the first instance of any of the elements specified. This can be used as a workaround where a broken backend inserts leading junk that messes up the parser (example here[93]).

It should never be used for XML, nor well-formed HTML.

---

[93] http://bahumbug.wordpress.com/2006/10/12/mod_proxy_html-revisited/

10.121 Apache Module mpm_common

Description:	A collection of directives that are implemented by more than one multi-processing module (MPM)
Status:	MPM

Directives

- CoreDumpDirectory
- EnableExceptionHook
- GracefulShutdownTimeout
- Listen
- ListenBackLog
- ListenCoresBucketsRatio
- MaxConnectionsPerChild
- MaxMemFree
- MaxRequestWorkers
- MaxSpareThreads
- MinSpareThreads
- PidFile
- ReceiveBufferSize
- ScoreBoardFile
- SendBufferSize
- ServerLimit
- StartServers
- StartThreads
- ThreadLimit
- ThreadsPerChild
- ThreadStackSize

CoreDumpDirectory Directive

Description:	Directory where Apache HTTP Server attempts to switch before dumping core
Syntax:	`CoreDumpDirectory directory`
Default:	`See usage for the default setting`
Context:	server config
Status:	MPM
Module:	EVENT, WORKER, PREFORK

This controls the directory to which Apache httpd attempts to switch before dumping core. If your operating system is configured to create core files in the working directory of the crashing process, CoreDumpDirectory is necessary to change working directory from the default ServerRoot directory, which should not be writable by the user the server runs as.

If you want a core dump for debugging, you can use this directive to place it in a different location. This directive has no effect if your operating system is not configured to write core files to the working directory of the crashing processes.

**Core Dumps on Linux**

If Apache httpd starts as root and switches to another user, the Linux kernel *disables* core dumps even if the directory is writable for the process. Apache httpd (2.0.46 and later) reenables core dumps on Linux 2.4 and beyond, but only if you explicitly configure a CORE-DUMPDIRECTORY.

Core Dumps on BSD

To enable core-dumping of suid-executables on BSD-systems (such as FreeBSD), set `kern.sugid_coredump` to 1.

Specific signals

COREDUMPDIRECTORY processing only occurs for a select set of fatal signals: SIGFPE, SIGILL, SIGABORT, SIGSEGV, and SIGBUS.

On some operating systems, SIGQUIT also results in a core dump but does not go through COREDUMPDIRECTORY or ENABLEEXCEPTIONHOOK processing, so the core location is dictated entirely by the operating system.

EnableExceptionHook Directive

Description:	Enables a hook that runs exception handlers after a crash
Syntax:	`EnableExceptionHook On|Off`
Default:	`EnableExceptionHook Off`
Context:	server config
Status:	MPM
Module:	EVENT, WORKER, PREFORK

For safety reasons this directive is only available if the server was configured with the `--enable-exception-hook` option. It enables a hook that allows external modules to plug in and do something after a child crashed.

There are already two modules, `mod_whatkilledus` and `mod_backtrace` that make use of this hook. Please have a look at Jeff Trawick's EnableExceptionHook site[94] for more information about these.

GracefulShutdownTimeout Directive

Description:	Specify a timeout after which a gracefully shutdown server will exit.
Syntax:	`GracefulShutdownTimeout seconds`
Default:	`GracefulShutdownTimeout 0`
Context:	server config
Status:	MPM
Module:	EVENT, WORKER, PREFORK
Compatibility:	Available in version 2.2 and later

The GRACEFULSHUTDOWNTIMEOUT specifies how many seconds after receiving a "graceful-stop" signal, a server should continue to run, handling the existing connections.

Setting this value to zero means that the server will wait indefinitely until all remaining requests have been fully served.

---

[94]http://people.apache.org/~trawick/exception_hook.html

Listen Directive

Description:	IP addresses and ports that the server listens to
Syntax:	`Listen [IP-address:]portnumber [protocol]`
Context:	server config
Status:	MPM
Module:	EVENT, WORKER, PREFORK, MPM_WINNT, MPM_NETWARE, MPMT_OS2
Compatibility:	The *protocol* argument was added in 2.1.5

The LISTEN directive instructs Apache httpd to listen to only specific IP addresses or ports; by default it responds to requests on all IP interfaces. LISTEN is now a required directive. If it is not in the config file, the server will fail to start. This is a change from previous versions of Apache httpd.

The LISTEN directive tells the server to accept incoming requests on the specified port or address-and-port combination. If only a port number is specified, the server listens to the given port on all interfaces. If an IP address is given as well as a port, the server will listen on the given port and interface.

Multiple LISTEN directives may be used to specify a number of addresses and ports to listen to. The server will respond to requests from any of the listed addresses and ports.

For example, to make the server accept connections on both port 80 and port 8000, use:

```
Listen 80
Listen 8000
```

To make the server accept connections on two specified interfaces and port numbers, use

```
Listen 192.170.2.1:80
Listen 192.170.2.5:8000
```

IPv6 addresses must be surrounded in square brackets, as in the following example:

```
Listen [2001:db8::a00:20ff:fea7:ccea]:80
```

The optional *protocol* argument is not required for most configurations. If not specified, `https` is the default for port 443 and `http` the default for all other ports. The protocol is used to determine which module should handle a request, and to apply protocol specific optimizations with the ACCEPTFILTER directive.

You only need to set the protocol if you are running on non-standard ports. For example, running an `https` site on port 8443:

```
Listen 192.170.2.1:8443 https
```

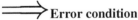**Error condition**

Multiple LISTEN directives for the same ip address and port will result in an `Address already in use` error message.

See also

- DNS Issues (p. 111)

- Setting which addresses and ports Apache HTTP Server uses (p. 78)

- Further discussion of the `Address already in use` error message, including other causes.[95]

---

[95]http://wiki.apache.org/httpd/CouldNotBindToAddress

ListenBackLog Directive

Description:	Maximum length of the queue of pending connections
Syntax:	`ListenBacklog backlog`
Default:	`ListenBacklog 511`
Context:	server config
Status:	MPM
Module:	EVENT, WORKER, PREFORK, MPM_WINNT, MPM_NETWARE, MPMT_OS2

The maximum length of the queue of pending connections. Generally no tuning is needed or desired, however on some systems it is desirable to increase this when under a TCP SYN flood attack. See the backlog parameter to the `listen(2)` system call.

This will often be limited to a smaller number by the operating system. This varies from OS to OS. Also note that many OSes do not use exactly what is specified as the backlog, but use a number based on (but normally larger than) what is set.

ListenCoresBucketsRatio Directive

Description:	Ratio between the number of CPU cores (online) and the number of listeners' buckets
Syntax:	`ListenCoresBucketsRatio ratio`
Default:	`ListenCoresBucketsRatio 0 (disabled)`
Context:	server config
Status:	MPM
Module:	EVENT, WORKER, PREFORK
Compatibility:	Available in Apache HTTP Server 2.4.17, with a kernel supporting the socket option SO_REUSEPORT and distributing new connections evenly accross listening processes' (or threads') sockets using it (eg. Linux 3.9 and later, but not the current implementations of SO_REUSEPORT in *BSDs.

A *ratio* between the number of (online) CPU cores and the number of listeners' buckets can be used to make Apache HTTP Server create `num_cpu_cores / ratio` listening buckets, each containing its own LISTEN-ing socket(s) on the same port(s), and then make each child handle a single bucket (with round-robin distribution of the buckets at children creation time).

LISTENCORESBUCKETSRATIO can improve the scalability when accepting new connections is/becomes the bottleneck. On systems with a large number of CPU cores, enabling this feature has been tested to show significant performances improvement and shorter responses time.

There must be at least twice the number of CPU cores than the configured *ratio* for this to be active. The recommended *ratio* is 8, hence at least 16 cores should be available at runtime when this value is used.

MaxConnectionsPerChild Directive

Description:	Limit on the number of connections that an individual child server will handle during its life
Syntax:	`MaxConnectionsPerChild number`
Default:	`MaxConnectionsPerChild 0`
Context:	server config
Status:	MPM
Module:	EVENT, WORKER, PREFORK, MPM_WINNT, MPM_NETWARE, MPMT_OS2
Compatibility:	Available Apache HTTP Server 2.3.9 and later. The old name `MaxRequestsPerChild` is still supported.

The MAXCONNECTIONSPERCHILD directive sets the limit on the number of connections that an individual child server process will handle. After MAXCONNECTIONSPERCHILD connections, the child process will die. If MAXCONNECTIONSPERCHILD is 0, then the process will never expire.

Setting MAXCONNECTIONSPERCHILD to a non-zero value limits the amount of memory that process can consume by (accidental) memory leakage.

MaxMemFree Directive

Description:	Maximum amount of memory that the main allocator is allowed to hold without calling `free()`
Syntax:	`MaxMemFree KBytes`
Default:	`MaxMemFree 2048`
Context:	server config
Status:	MPM
Module:	EVENT, WORKER, PREFORK, MPM_WINNT, MPM_NETWARE

The MAXMEMFREE directive sets the maximum number of free Kbytes that every allocator is allowed to hold without calling `free()`. In threaded MPMs, every thread has its own allocator. When set to zero, the threshold will be set to unlimited.

MaxRequestWorkers Directive

Description:	Maximum number of connections that will be processed simultaneously
Syntax:	`MaxRequestWorkers number`
Default:	`See usage for details`
Context:	server config
Status:	MPM
Module:	EVENT, WORKER, PREFORK

The MAXREQUESTWORKERS directive sets the limit on the number of simultaneous requests that will be served. Any connection attempts over the MAXREQUESTWORKERS limit will normally be queued, up to a number based on the LISTENBACKLOG directive. Once a child process is freed at the end of a different request, the connection will then be serviced.

For non-threaded servers (*i.e.*, PREFORK), MAXREQUESTWORKERS translates into the maximum number of child processes that will be launched to serve requests. The default value is 256; to increase it, you must also raise SERVER-LIMIT.

For threaded and hybrid servers (*e.g.* EVENT or WORKER) MAXREQUESTWORKERS restricts the total number of threads that will be available to serve clients. For hybrid MPMs the default value is 16 (SERVERLIMIT) multiplied by the value of 25 (THREADSPERCHILD). Therefore, to increase MAXREQUESTWORKERS to a value that requires more than 16 processes, you must also raise SERVERLIMIT.

MAXREQUESTWORKERS was called MAXCLIENTS before version 2.3.13. The old name is still supported.

MaxSpareThreads Directive

Description:	Maximum number of idle threads
Syntax:	`MaxSpareThreads number`
Default:	`See usage for details`
Context:	server config
Status:	MPM
Module:	EVENT, WORKER, MPM_NETWARE, MPMT_OS2

Maximum number of idle threads. Different MPMs deal with this directive differently.

For WORKER and EVENT, the default is `MaxSpareThreads 250`. These MPMs deal with idle threads on a server-wide basis. If there are too many idle threads in the server then child processes are killed until the number of idle threads is less than this number.

For MPM_NETWARE the default is `MaxSpareThreads 100`. Since this MPM runs a single-process, the spare thread count is also server-wide.

MPMT_OS2 works similar to MPM_NETWARE. For MPMT_OS2 the default value is `10`.

**Restrictions**

The range of the MAXSPARETHREADS value is restricted. Apache httpd will correct the given value automatically according to the following rules:

- MPM_NETWARE wants the value to be greater than MINSPARETHREADS.
- For WORKER and EVENT, the value must be greater or equal to the sum of MINS-PARETHREADS and THREADSPERCHILD.

See also

- MINSPARETHREADS
- STARTSERVERS
- MAXSPARESERVERS

MinSpareThreads Directive

Description:	Minimum number of idle threads available to handle request spikes
Syntax:	`MinSpareThreads number`
Default:	`See usage for details`
Context:	server config
Status:	MPM
Module:	EVENT, WORKER, MPM_NETWARE, MPMT_OS2

Minimum number of idle threads to handle request spikes. Different MPMs deal with this directive differently.

WORKER and EVENT use a default of `MinSpareThreads 75` and deal with idle threads on a server-wide basis. If there aren't enough idle threads in the server then child processes are created until the number of idle threads is greater than *number*.

MPM_NETWARE uses a default of `MinSpareThreads 10` and, since it is a single-process MPM, tracks this on a server-wide bases.

MPMT_OS2 works similar to MPM_NETWARE. For MPMT_OS2 the default value is `5`.

See also

- MAXSPARETHREADS
- STARTSERVERS
- MINSPARESERVERS

PidFile Directive

Description:	File where the server records the process ID of the daemon
Syntax:	`PidFile filename`
Default:	`PidFile logs/httpd.pid`
Context:	server config
Status:	MPM
Module:	EVENT, WORKER, PREFORK, MPM_WINNT, MPMT_OS2

The PIDFILE directive sets the file to which the server records the process id of the daemon. If the filename is not absolute then it is assumed to be relative to the SERVERROOT.

Example

```
PidFile /var/run/apache.pid
```

It is often useful to be able to send the server a signal, so that it closes and then re-opens its ERRORLOG and TRANS-FERLOG, and re-reads its configuration files. This is done by sending a SIGHUP (kill -1) signal to the process id listed in the PIDFILE.

The PIDFILE is subject to the same warnings about log file placement and security (p. 338).

Note

> As of Apache HTTP Server 2, we recommended that you only use the `apachectl` script, or the init script that your OS provides, for (re-)starting or stopping the server.

ReceiveBufferSize Directive

Description:	TCP receive buffer size
Syntax:	`ReceiveBufferSize bytes`
Default:	`ReceiveBufferSize 0`
Context:	server config
Status:	MPM
Module:	EVENT, WORKER, PREFORK, MPM_WINNT, MPM_NETWARE, MPMT_OS2

The server will set the TCP receive buffer size to the number of bytes specified.

If set to the value of 0, the server will use the OS default.

ScoreBoardFile Directive

Description:	Location of the file used to store coordination data for the child processes
Syntax:	`ScoreBoardFile file-path`
Default:	`ScoreBoardFile logs/apache_runtime_status`
Context:	server config
Status:	MPM
Module:	EVENT, WORKER, PREFORK, MPM_WINNT

Apache HTTP Server uses a scoreboard to communicate between its parent and child processes. Some architectures require a file to facilitate this communication. If the file is left unspecified, Apache httpd first attempts to create the scoreboard entirely in memory (using anonymous shared memory) and, failing that, will attempt to create the file on disk (using file-based shared memory). Specifying this directive causes Apache httpd to always create the file on the disk.

Example

```
ScoreBoardFile /var/run/apache_runtime_status
```

File-based shared memory is useful for third-party applications that require direct access to the scoreboard.

If you use a SCOREBOARDFILE then you may see improved speed by placing it on a RAM disk. But be careful that you heed the same warnings about log file placement and security (p. 338).

See also

- Stopping and Restarting Apache HTTP Server (p. 27)

SendBufferSize Directive

Description:	TCP buffer size
Syntax:	SendBufferSize bytes
Default:	SendBufferSize 0
Context:	server config
Status:	MPM
Module:	EVENT, WORKER, PREFORK, MPM_WINNT, MPM_NETWARE, MPMT_OS2

Sets the server's TCP send buffer size to the number of bytes specified. It is often useful to set this past the OS's standard default value on high speed, high latency connections (*i.e.*, 100ms or so, such as transcontinental fast pipes).

If set to the value of 0, the server will use the default value provided by your OS.

Further configuration of your operating system may be required to elicit better performance on high speed, high latency connections.

> On some operating systems, changes in TCP behavior resulting from a larger SENDBUFFER-SIZE may not be seen unless ENABLESENDFILE is set to OFF. This interaction applies only to static files.

ServerLimit Directive

Description:	Upper limit on configurable number of processes
Syntax:	ServerLimit number
Default:	See usage for details
Context:	server config
Status:	MPM
Module:	EVENT, WORKER, PREFORK

For the PREFORK MPM, this directive sets the maximum configured value for MAXREQUESTWORKERS for the lifetime of the Apache httpd process. For the WORKER and EVENT MPMs, this directive in combination with THREAD-LIMIT sets the maximum configured value for MAXREQUESTWORKERS for the lifetime of the Apache httpd process. Any attempts to change this directive during a restart will be ignored, but MAXREQUESTWORKERS can be modified during a restart.

Special care must be taken when using this directive. If SERVERLIMIT is set to a value much higher than necessary, extra, unused shared memory will be allocated. If both SERVERLIMIT and MAXREQUESTWORKERS are set to values higher than the system can handle, Apache httpd may not start or the system may become unstable.

With the PREFORK MPM, use this directive only if you need to set MAXREQUESTWORKERS higher than 256 (default). Do not set the value of this directive any higher than what you might want to set MAXREQUESTWORKERS to.

With WORKER and EVENT, use this directive only if your MAXREQUESTWORKERS and THREADSPERCHILD settings require more than 16 server processes (default). Do not set the value of this directive any higher than the number of server processes required by what you may want for MAXREQUESTWORKERS and THREADSPERCHILD.

> Note
>
> There is a hard limit of ServerLimit 20000 compiled into the server (for the PREFORK MPM 200000). This is intended to avoid nasty effects caused by typos. To increase it even further past this limit, you will need to modify the value of MAX_SERVER_LIMIT in the mpm source file and rebuild the server.

See also

- Stopping and Restarting Apache HTTP Server (p. 27)

StartServers Directive

Description:	Number of child server processes created at startup
Syntax:	`StartServers number`
Default:	`See usage for details`
Context:	server config
Status:	MPM
Module:	EVENT, WORKER, PREFORK, MPMT_OS2

The STARTSERVERS directive sets the number of child server processes created on startup. As the number of processes is dynamically controlled depending on the load, (see MINSPARETHREADS, MAXSPARETHREADS, MINSPARESERVERS, MAXSPARESERVERS) there is usually little reason to adjust this parameter.

The default value differs from MPM to MPM. WORKER and EVENT default to `StartServers 3`; PREFORK defaults to 5; MPMT_OS2 defaults to 2.

StartThreads Directive

Description:	Number of threads created on startup
Syntax:	`StartThreads number`
Default:	`See usage for details`
Context:	server config
Status:	MPM
Module:	MPM_NETWARE

Number of threads created on startup. As the number of threads is dynamically controlled depending on the load, (see MINSPARETHREADS, MAXSPARETHREADS, MINSPARESERVERS, MAXSPARESERVERS) there is usually little reason to adjust this parameter.

For MPM_NETWARE the default is `StartThreads 50` and, since there is only a single process, this is the total number of threads created at startup to serve requests.

ThreadLimit Directive

Description:	Sets the upper limit on the configurable number of threads per child process
Syntax:	`ThreadLimit number`
Default:	`See usage for details`
Context:	server config
Status:	MPM
Module:	EVENT, WORKER, MPM_WINNT

This directive sets the maximum configured value for THREADSPERCHILD for the lifetime of the Apache httpd process. Any attempts to change this directive during a restart will be ignored, but THREADSPERCHILD can be modified during a restart up to the value of this directive.

Special care must be taken when using this directive. If THREADLIMIT is set to a value much higher than THREADSPERCHILD, extra unused shared memory will be allocated. If both THREADLIMIT and THREADSPERCHILD are set to values higher than the system can handle, Apache httpd may not start or the system may become unstable. Do not set the value of this directive any higher than your greatest predicted setting of THREADSPERCHILD for the current run of Apache httpd.

The default value for THREADLIMIT is `1920` when used with MPM_WINNT and `64` when used with the others.

Note

There is a hard limit of `ThreadLimit 20000` (or `ThreadLimit 100000` with EVENT, `ThreadLimit 15000` with MPM_WINNT) compiled into the server. This is intended to avoid nasty effects caused by typos. To increase it even further past this limit, you will need to modify the value of MAX_THREAD_LIMIT in the mpm source file and rebuild the server.

ThreadsPerChild Directive

Description:	Number of threads created by each child process
Syntax:	`ThreadsPerChild number`
Default:	`See usage for details`
Context:	server config
Status:	MPM
Module:	EVENT, WORKER, MPM_WINNT

This directive sets the number of threads created by each child process. The child creates these threads at startup and never creates more. If using an MPM like MPM_WINNT, where there is only one child process, this number should be high enough to handle the entire load of the server. If using an MPM like WORKER, where there are multiple child processes, the *total* number of threads should be high enough to handle the common load on the server.

The default value for THREADSPERCHILD is 64 when used with MPM_WINNT and 25 when used with the others.

ThreadStackSize Directive

Description:	The size in bytes of the stack used by threads handling client connections
Syntax:	`ThreadStackSize size`
Default:	`65536 on NetWare; varies on other operating systems`
Context:	server config
Status:	MPM
Module:	EVENT, WORKER, MPM_WINNT, MPM_NETWARE, MPMT_OS2
Compatibility:	Available in Apache HTTP Server 2.1 and later

The THREADSTACKSIZE directive sets the size of the stack (for autodata) of threads which handle client connections and call modules to help process those connections. In most cases the operating system default for stack size is reasonable, but there are some conditions where it may need to be adjusted:

- On platforms with a relatively small default thread stack size (e.g., HP-UX), Apache httpd may crash when using some third-party modules which use a relatively large amount of autodata storage. Those same modules may have worked fine on other platforms where the default thread stack size is larger. This type of crash is resolved by setting THREADSTACKSIZE to a value higher than the operating system default. This type of adjustment is necessary only if the provider of the third-party module specifies that it is required, or if diagnosis of an Apache httpd crash indicates that the thread stack size was too small.

- On platforms where the default thread stack size is significantly larger than necessary for the web server configuration, a higher number of threads per child process will be achievable if THREADSTACKSIZE is set to a value lower than the operating system default. This type of adjustment should only be made in a test environment which allows the full set of web server processing can be exercised, as there may be infrequent requests which require more stack to process. The minimum required stack size strongly depends on the modules used, but any change in the web server configuration can invalidate the current THREADSTACKSIZE setting.

- On Linux, this directive can only be used to increase the default stack size, as the underlying system call uses the value as a *minimum* stack size. The (often large) soft limit for `ulimit -s` (8MB if unlimited) is used as the default stack size.

It is recommended to not reduce THREADSTACKSIZE unless a high number of threads per child process is needed. On some platforms (including Linux), a setting of 128000 is already too low and causes crashes with some common modules.

10.122   Apache Module event

Description:	A variant of the WORKER MPM with the goal of consuming threads only for connections with active processing
Status:	MPM
ModuleIdentifier:	mpm_event_module
SourceFile:	event.c

Summary

The EVENT Multi-Processing Module (MPM) is designed to allow more requests to be served simultaneously by passing off some processing work to supporting threads, freeing up the main threads to work on new requests. It is based on the WORKER MPM, which implements a hybrid multi-process multi-threaded server. Run-time configuration directives are identical to those provided by WORKER.

To use the EVENT MPM, add --with-mpm=event to the configure script's arguments when building the httpd.

Directives

- AsyncRequestWorkerFactor
- CoreDumpDirectory (p. 917)
- EnableExceptionHook (p. 918)
- Group (p. 899)
- Listen (p. 919)
- ListenBacklog (p. 920)
- MaxConnectionsPerChild (p. 920)
- MaxMemFree (p. 921)
- MaxRequestWorkers (p. 921)
- MaxSpareThreads (p. 921)
- MinSpareThreads (p. 922)
- PidFile (p. 922)
- ScoreBoardFile (p. 923)
- SendBufferSize (p. 924)
- ServerLimit (p. 924)
- StartServers (p. 925)
- ThreadLimit (p. 925)
- ThreadsPerChild (p. 926)
- ThreadStackSize (p. 926)
- User (p. 900)

See also

- The worker MPM (p. 939)

How it Works

This MPM tries to fix the 'keep alive problem' in HTTP. After a client completes the first request, the client can keep the connection open, and send further requests using the same socket. This can save significant overhead in creating TCP connections. However, Apache HTTP Server traditionally keeps an entire child process/thread waiting for data from the client, which brings its own disadvantages. To solve this problem, this MPM uses a dedicated thread to handle both the Listening sockets, all sockets that are in a Keep Alive state, and sockets where the handler and protocol filters have done their work and the only remaining thing to do is send the data to the client. The status page of MOD_STATUS shows how many connections are in the mentioned states.

The improved connection handling may not work for certain connection filters that have declared themselves as incompatible with event. In these cases, this MPM will fall back to the behaviour of the WORKER MPM and reserve one worker thread per connection. All modules shipped with the server are compatible with the event MPM.

A similar restriction is currently present for requests involving an output filter that needs to read and/or modify the whole response body, like for example mod_ssl, mod_deflate, or mod_include. If the connection to the client blocks while the filter is processing the data, and the amount of data produced by the filter is too big to be buffered in memory, the thread used for the request is not freed while httpd waits until the pending data is sent to the client.

The MPM assumes that the underlying `apr_pollset` implementation is reasonably threadsafe. This enables the MPM to avoid excessive high level locking, or having to wake up the listener thread in order to send it a keep-alive socket. This is currently only compatible with KQueue and EPoll.

Requirements

This MPM depends on APR's atomic compare-and-swap operations for thread synchronization. If you are compiling for an x86 target and you don't need to support 386s, or you are compiling for a SPARC and you don't need to run on pre-UltraSPARC chips, add `--enable-nonportable-atomics=yes` to the `configure` script's arguments. This will cause APR to implement atomic operations using efficient opcodes not available in older CPUs.

This MPM does not perform well on older platforms which lack good threading, but the requirement for EPoll or KQueue makes this moot.

- To use this MPM on FreeBSD, FreeBSD 5.3 or higher is recommended. However, it is possible to run this MPM on FreeBSD 5.2.1, if you use `libkse` (see `man libmap.conf`).

- For NetBSD, at least version 2.0 is recommended.

- For Linux, a 2.6 kernel is recommended. It is also necessary to ensure that your version of `glibc` has been compiled with support for EPoll.

AsyncRequestWorkerFactor Directive

Description:	Limit concurrent connections per process
Syntax:	`AsyncRequestWorkerFactor factor`
Default:	2
Context:	server config
Status:	MPM
Module:	event
Compatibility:	Available in version 2.3.13 and later

The event MPM handles some connections in an asynchronous way, where request worker threads are only allocated for short periods of time as needed, and other connections with one request worker thread reserved per connection. This can lead to situations where all workers are tied up and no worker thread is available to handle new work on established async connections.

To mitigate this problem, the event MPM does two things: Firstly, it limits the number of connections accepted per process, depending on the number of idle request workers. Secondly, if all workers are busy, it will close connections in keep-alive state even if the keep-alive timeout has not expired. This allows the respective clients to reconnect to a different process which may still have worker threads available.

This directive can be used to fine-tune the per-process connection limit. A process will only accept new connections if the current number of connections (not counting connections in the "closing" state) is lower than:

THREADSPERCHILD + (ASYNCREQUESTWORKERFACTOR * *number of idle workers*)

This means the absolute maximum numbers of concurrent connections is:

(ASYNCREQUESTWORKERFACTOR + 1) * MAXREQUESTWORKERS

MAXREQUESTWORKERS was called MAXCLIENTS prior to version 2.3.13. The above value shows that the old name did not accurately describe its meaning for the event MPM.

ASYNCREQUESTWORKERFACTOR can take non-integer arguments, e.g "1.5".

10.123 Apache Module mpm_netware

Description:	Multi-Processing Module implementing an exclusively threaded web server optimized for Novell NetWare
Status:	MPM
ModuleIdentifier:	mpm_netware_module
SourceFile:	mpm_netware.c

Summary

This Multi-Processing Module (MPM) implements an exclusively threaded web server that has been optimized for Novell NetWare.

The main thread is responsible for launching child worker threads which listen for connections and serve them when they arrive. Apache HTTP Server always tries to maintain several *spare* or idle worker threads, which stand ready to serve incoming requests. In this way, clients do not need to wait for a new child threads to be spawned before their requests can be served.

The STARTTHREADS, MINSPARETHREADS, MAXSPARETHREADS, and MAXTHREADS regulate how the main thread creates worker threads to serve requests. In general, Apache httpd is very self-regulating, so most sites do not need to adjust these directives from their default values. Sites with limited memory may need to decrease MAX-THREADS to keep the server from thrashing (spawning and terminating idle threads). More information about tuning process creation is provided in the performance hints (p. 327) documentation.

MAXCONNECTIONSPERCHILD controls how frequently the server recycles processes by killing old ones and launching new ones. On the NetWare OS it is highly recommended that this directive remain set to 0. This allows worker threads to continue servicing requests indefinitely.

Directives

- Listen (p. 919)

- ListenBacklog (p. 920)

- MaxConnectionsPerChild (p. 920)

- MaxMemFree (p. 921)

- MaxSpareThreads (p. 921)

- MaxThreads

- MinSpareThreads (p. 922)

- ReceiveBufferSize (p. 923)

- SendBufferSize (p. 924)

- StartThreads (p. 925)

- ThreadStackSize (p. 926)

See also

- Setting which addresses and ports Apache httpd uses (p. 78)

MaxThreads Directive

Description:	Set the maximum number of worker threads
Syntax:	`MaxThreads number`
Default:	`MaxThreads 2048`
Context:	server config
Status:	MPM
Module:	mpm_netware

The MAXTHREADS directive sets the desired maximum number worker threads allowable. The default value is also the compiled in hard limit. Therefore it can only be lowered, for example:

```
MaxThreads 512
```

10.124 Apache Module mpmt_os2

Description:	Hybrid multi-process, multi-threaded MPM for OS/2
Status:	MPM
ModuleIdentifier:	mpm_mpmt_os2_module
SourceFile:	mpmt_os2.c

Summary

The Server consists of a main, parent process and a small, static number of child processes.

The parent process' job is to manage the child processes. This involves spawning children as required to ensure there are always STARTSERVERS processes accepting connections.

Each child process consists of a pool of worker threads and a main thread that accepts connections and passes them to the workers via a work queue. The worker thread pool is dynamic, managed by a maintenance thread so that the number of idle threads is kept between MINSPARETHREADS and MAXSPARETHREADS.

Directives

- Group (p. 899)
- Listen (p. 919)
- ListenBacklog (p. 920)
- MaxConnectionsPerChild (p. 920)
- MaxSpareThreads (p. 921)
- MinSpareThreads (p. 922)
- PidFile (p. 922)
- ReceiveBufferSize (p. 923)
- SendBufferSize (p. 924)
- StartServers (p. 925)
- User (p. 900)

See also

- Setting which addresses and ports Apache uses (p. 78)

10.125   Apache Module prefork

Description:	Implements a non-threaded, pre-forking web server
Status:	MPM
ModuleIdentifier:	mpm_prefork_module
SourceFile:	prefork.c

Summary

This Multi-Processing Module (MPM) implements a non-threaded, pre-forking web server. Each server process may answer incoming requests, and a parent process manages the size of the server pool. It is appropriate for sites that need to avoid threading for compatibility with non-thread-safe libraries. It is also the best MPM for isolating each request, so that a problem with a single request will not affect any other.

This MPM is very self-regulating, so it is rarely necessary to adjust its configuration directives. Most important is that MAXREQUESTWORKERS be big enough to handle as many simultaneous requests as you expect to receive, but small enough to assure that there is enough physical RAM for all processes.

Directives

- CoreDumpDirectory (p. 917)
- EnableExceptionHook (p. 918)
- Group (p. 899)
- Listen (p. 919)
- ListenBacklog (p. 920)
- MaxConnectionsPerChild (p. 920)
- MaxMemFree (p. 921)
- MaxRequestWorkers (p. 921)
- MaxSpareServers
- MinSpareServers
- PidFile (p. 922)
- ReceiveBufferSize (p. 923)
- ScoreBoardFile (p. 923)
- SendBufferSize (p. 924)
- ServerLimit (p. 924)
- StartServers (p. 925)
- User (p. 900)

See also

- Setting which addresses and ports Apache HTTP Server uses (p. 78)

How it Works

A single control process is responsible for launching child processes which listen for connections and serve them when they arrive. Apache httpd always tries to maintain several *spare* or idle server processes, which stand ready to serve incoming requests. In this way, clients do not need to wait for a new child processes to be forked before their requests can be served.

The STARTSERVERS, MINSPARESERVERS, MAXSPARESERVERS, and MAXREQUESTWORKERS regulate how the parent process creates children to serve requests. In general, Apache httpd is very self-regulating, so most sites do not need to adjust these directives from their default values. Sites which need to serve more than 256 simultaneous requests may need to increase MAXREQUESTWORKERS, while sites with limited memory may need to decrease MAXREQUESTWORKERS to keep the server from thrashing (swapping memory to disk and back). More information about tuning process creation is provided in the performance hints (p. 327) documentation.

While the parent process is usually started as `root` under Unix in order to bind to port 80, the child processes are launched by Apache httpd as a less-privileged user. The USER and GROUP directives are used to set the privileges of the Apache httpd child processes. The child processes must be able to read all the content that will be served, but should have as few privileges beyond that as possible.

MAXCONNECTIONSPERCHILD controls how frequently the server recycles processes by killing old ones and launching new ones.

This MPM uses the `mpm-accept` mutex to serialize access to incoming connections when subject to the thundering herd problem (generally, when there are multiple listening sockets). The implementation aspects of this mutex can be configured with the MUTEX directive. The performance hints (p. 327) documentation has additional information about this mutex.

MaxSpareServers Directive

Description:	Maximum number of idle child server processes
Syntax:	`MaxSpareServers number`
Default:	`MaxSpareServers 10`
Context:	server config
Status:	MPM
Module:	prefork

The MAXSPARESERVERS directive sets the desired maximum number of *idle* child server processes. An idle process is one which is not handling a request. If there are more than MAXSPARESERVERS idle, then the parent process will kill off the excess processes.

Tuning of this parameter should only be necessary on very busy sites. Setting this parameter to a large number is almost always a bad idea. If you are trying to set the value equal to or lower than MINSPARESERVERS, Apache HTTP Server will automatically adjust it to MINSPARESERVERS + 1.

See also

- MINSPARESERVERS
- STARTSERVERS
- MAXSPARETHREADS

MinSpareServers Directive

Description:	Minimum number of idle child server processes
Syntax:	`MinSpareServers number`
Default:	`MinSpareServers 5`
Context:	server config
Status:	MPM
Module:	prefork

The MINSPARESERVERS directive sets the desired minimum number of *idle* child server processes. An idle process is one which is not handling a request. If there are fewer than MINSPARESERVERS idle, then the parent process creates new children: It will spawn one, wait a second, then spawn two, wait a second, then spawn four, and it will continue exponentially until it is spawning 32 children per second. It will stop whenever it satisfies the MINSPARESERVERS setting.

Tuning of this parameter should only be necessary on very busy sites. Setting this parameter to a large number is almost always a bad idea.

See also

- MAXSPARESERVERS
- STARTSERVERS
- MINSPARETHREADS

10.126 Apache Module mpm_winnt

Description:	Multi-Processing Module optimized for Windows NT.
Status:	MPM
ModuleIdentifier:	mpm_winnt_module
SourceFile:	mpm_winnt.c

Summary

This Multi-Processing Module (MPM) is the default for the Windows NT operating systems. It uses a single control process which launches a single child process which in turn creates threads to handle requests

Capacity is configured using the THREADSPERCHILD directive, which sets the maximum number of concurrent client connections.

By default, this MPM uses advanced Windows APIs for accepting new client connections. In some configurations, third-party products may interfere with this implementation, with the following messages written to the web server log:

```
Child:  Encountered too many AcceptEx faults accepting client
connections.
winnt_mpm:  falling back to 'AcceptFilter none'.
```

The MPM falls back to a safer implementation, but some client requests were not processed correctly. In order to avoid this error, use ACCEPTFILTER with accept filter none.

```
AcceptFilter http none
AcceptFilter https none
```

In Apache httpd 2.0 and 2.2, WIN32DISABLEACCEPTEX *was used for this purpose.*

The WinNT MPM differs from the Unix MPMs such as worker and event in several areas:

- When a child process is exiting due to shutdown, restart, or MAXCONNECTIONSPERCHILD, active requests in the exiting process have TIMEOUT seconds to finish before processing is aborted. Alternate types of restart and shutdown are not implemented.

- New child processes read the configuration files instead of inheriting the configuration from the parent. The behavior will be the same as on Unix if the child process is created at startup or restart, but if a child process is created because the prior one crashed or reached MAXCONNECTIONSPERCHILD, any pending changes to the configuration will become active in the child at that point, and the parent and child will be using a different configuration. If planned configuration changes have been partially implemented and the current configuration cannot be parsed, the replacement child process cannot start up and the server will halt. Because of this behavior, configuration files should not be changed until the time of a server restart.

- The `monitor` and `fatal_exception` hooks are not currently implemented.

- ACCEPTFILTER is implemented in the MPM and has a different type of control over handling of new connections. (Refer to the ACCEPTFILTER documentation for details.)

Directives

- AcceptFilter (p. 356)
- CoreDumpDirectory (p. 917)

- Listen (p. 919)
- ListenBacklog (p. 920)
- MaxConnectionsPerChild (p. 920)
- MaxMemFree (p. 921)
- PidFile (p. 922)
- ReceiveBufferSize (p. 923)
- ScoreBoardFile (p. 923)
- SendBufferSize (p. 924)
- ThreadLimit (p. 925)
- ThreadsPerChild (p. 926)
- ThreadStackSize (p. 926)

See also

- Using Apache HTTP Server on Microsoft Windows (p. 251)

10.127 Apache Module worker

Description:	Multi-Processing Module implementing a hybrid multi-threaded multi-process web server
Status:	MPM
ModuleIdentifier:	mpm_worker_module
SourceFile:	worker.c

Summary

This Multi-Processing Module (MPM) implements a hybrid multi-process multi-threaded server. By using threads to serve requests, it is able to serve a large number of requests with fewer system resources than a process-based server. However, it retains much of the stability of a process-based server by keeping multiple processes available, each with many threads.

The most important directives used to control this MPM are THREADSPERCHILD, which controls the number of threads deployed by each child process and MAXREQUESTWORKERS, which controls the maximum total number of threads that may be launched.

Directives

- CoreDumpDirectory (p. 917)
- EnableExceptionHook (p. 918)
- Group (p. 899)
- Listen (p. 919)
- ListenBacklog (p. 920)
- MaxConnectionsPerChild (p. 920)
- MaxMemFree (p. 921)
- MaxRequestWorkers (p. 921)
- MaxSpareThreads (p. 921)
- MinSpareThreads (p. 922)
- PidFile (p. 922)
- ReceiveBufferSize (p. 923)
- ScoreBoardFile (p. 923)
- SendBufferSize (p. 924)
- ServerLimit (p. 924)
- StartServers (p. 925)
- ThreadLimit (p. 925)
- ThreadsPerChild (p. 926)
- ThreadStackSize (p. 926)
- User (p. 900)

See also

- Setting which addresses and ports Apache HTTP Server uses (p. 78)

How it Works

A single control process (the parent) is responsible for launching child processes. Each child process creates a fixed number of server threads as specified in the THREADSPERCHILD directive, as well as a listener thread which listens for connections and passes them to a server thread for processing when they arrive.

Apache HTTP Server always tries to maintain a pool of *spare* or idle server threads, which stand ready to serve incoming requests. In this way, clients do not need to wait for a new threads or processes to be created before their requests can be served. The number of processes that will initially launch is set by the STARTSERVERS directive. During operation, the server assesses the total number of idle threads in all processes, and forks or kills processes to keep this number within the boundaries specified by MINSPARETHREADS and MAXSPARETHREADS. Since this process is very self-regulating, it is rarely necessary to modify these directives from their default values. The maximum number of clients that may be served simultaneously (i.e., the maximum total number of threads in all processes) is determined by the MAXREQUESTWORKERS directive. The maximum number of active child processes is determined by the MAXREQUESTWORKERS directive divided by the THREADSPERCHILD directive.

Two directives set hard limits on the number of active child processes and the number of server threads in a child process, and can only be changed by fully stopping the server and then starting it again. SERVERLIMIT is a hard limit on the number of active child processes, and must be greater than or equal to the MAXREQUESTWORKERS directive divided by the THREADSPERCHILD directive. THREADLIMIT is a hard limit of the number of server threads, and must be greater than or equal to the THREADSPERCHILD directive.

In addition to the set of active child processes, there may be additional child processes which are terminating, but where at least one server thread is still handling an existing client connection. Up to MAXREQUESTWORKERS terminating processes may be present, though the actual number can be expected to be much smaller. This behavior can be avoided by disabling the termination of individual child processes, which is achieved using the following:

- set the value of MAXCONNECTIONSPERCHILD to zero
- set the value of MAXSPARETHREADS to the same value as MAXREQUESTWORKERS

A typical configuration of the process-thread controls in the WORKER MPM could look as follows:

```
ServerLimit         16
StartServers         2
MaxRequestWorkers  150
MinSpareThreads     25
MaxSpareThreads     75
ThreadsPerChild     25
```

While the parent process is usually started as `root` under Unix in order to bind to port 80, the child processes and threads are launched by the server as a less-privileged user. The USER and GROUP directives are used to set the privileges of the Apache HTTP Server child processes. The child processes must be able to read all the content that will be served, but should have as few privileges beyond that as possible. In addition, unless `suexec` is used, these directives also set the privileges which will be inherited by CGI scripts.

MAXCONNECTIONSPERCHILD controls how frequently the server recycles processes by killing old ones and launching new ones.

This MPM uses the `mpm-accept` mutex to serialize access to incoming connections when subject to the thundering herd problem (generally, when there are multiple listening sockets). The implementation aspects of this mutex can be configured with the MUTEX directive. The performance hints (p. 327) documentation has additional information about this mutex.

Chapter 11

Developer Documentation

11.1　Developer Documentation for the Apache HTTP Server 2.4

 Warning
Many of the documents listed here are in need of update. They are in different stages of
progress. Please be patient, and point out any discrepancies or errors on the developer/ pages
directly to the dev@httpd.apache.org[a] mailing list.

---

[a]http://httpd.apache.org/lists.html#http-dev

2.4 development documents

- Developing modules for the Apache HTTP Server 2.4 (p. 966)
- Hook Functions in 2.4 (p. 995)
- Request Processing in 2.4 (p. 1002)
- How filters work in 2.4 (p. 1005)
- Guidelines for output filters in 2.4 (p. 1008)
- Documenting code in 2.4 (p. 994)
- Thread Safety Issues in 2.4 (p. 1015)

Upgrading to 2.4

- API changes in 2.3/2.4 (p. 959)
- Converting Modules from 1.3 to 2.x (p. 998)

External Resources

- Autogenerated Apache HTTP Server (trunk) code documentation[1]
- Developer articles at apachetutor[2] include:

  - Request Processing[3]
  - Configuration for Modules[4]
  - Resource Management[5]
  - Connection Pooling[6]
  - Introduction to Buckets and Brigades[7]

---

[1]http://ci.apache.org/projects/httpd/trunk/doxygen/
[2]http://www.apachetutor.org/
[3]http://www.apachetutor.org/dev/request
[4]http://www.apachetutor.org/dev/config
[5]http://www.apachetutor.org/dev/pools
[6]http://www.apachetutor.org/dev/reslist
[7]http://www.apachetutor.org/dev/brigades

11.2 Apache 1.3 API notes

 Warning

This document has not been updated to take into account changes made in the 2.0 version of the Apache HTTP Server. Some of the information may still be relevant, but please use it with care.

These are some notes on the Apache API and the data structures you have to deal with, *etc.* They are not yet nearly complete, but hopefully, they will help you get your bearings. Keep in mind that the API is still subject to change as we gain experience with it. (See the TODO file for what *might* be coming). However, it will be easy to adapt modules to any changes that are made. (We have more modules to adapt than you do).

A few notes on general pedagogical style here. In the interest of conciseness, all structure declarations here are incomplete – the real ones have more slots that I'm not telling you about. For the most part, these are reserved to one component of the server core or another, and should be altered by modules with caution. However, in some cases, they really are things I just haven't gotten around to yet. Welcome to the bleeding edge.

Finally, here's an outline, to give you some bare idea of what's coming up, and in what order:

- Basic concepts.

  - Handlers, Modules, and Requests
  - A brief tour of a module

- How handlers work

  - A brief tour of the `request_rec`
  - Where request_rec structures come from
  - Handling requests, declining, and returning error codes
  - Special considerations for response handlers
  - Special considerations for authentication handlers
  - Special considerations for logging handlers

- Resource allocation and resource pools
- Configuration, commands and the like

  - Per-directory configuration structures
  - Command handling
  - Side notes — per-server configuration, virtual servers, *etc.*

Basic concepts

We begin with an overview of the basic concepts behind the API, and how they are manifested in the code.

Handlers, Modules, and Requests

Apache breaks down request handling into a series of steps, more or less the same way the Netscape server API does (although this API has a few more stages than NetSite does, as hooks for stuff I thought might be useful in the future). These are:

- URI -> Filename translation

- Auth ID checking [is the user who they say they are?]

- Auth access checking [is the user authorized *here*?]

- Access checking other than auth

- Determining MIME type of the object requested

- 'Fixups' – there aren't any of these yet, but the phase is intended as a hook for possible extensions like SETENV, which don't really fit well elsewhere.

- Actually sending a response back to the client.

- Logging the request

These phases are handled by looking at each of a succession of *modules*, looking to see if each of them has a handler for the phase, and attempting invoking it if so. The handler can typically do one of three things:

- *Handle* the request, and indicate that it has done so by returning the magic constant OK.

- *Decline* to handle the request, by returning the magic integer constant DECLINED. In this case, the server behaves in all respects as if the handler simply hadn't been there.

- Signal an error, by returning one of the HTTP error codes. This terminates normal handling of the request, although an ErrorDocument may be invoked to try to mop up, and it will be logged in any case.

Most phases are terminated by the first module that handles them; however, for logging, 'fixups', and non-access authentication checking, all handlers always run (barring an error). Also, the response phase is unique in that modules may declare multiple handlers for it, via a dispatch table keyed on the MIME type of the requested object. Modules may declare a response-phase handler which can handle *any* request, by giving it the key */* (*i.e.*, a wildcard MIME type specification). However, wildcard handlers are only invoked if the server has already tried and failed to find a more specific response handler for the MIME type of the requested object (either none existed, or they all declined).

The handlers themselves are functions of one argument (a request_rec structure. vide infra), which returns an integer, as above.

A brief tour of a module

At this point, we need to explain the structure of a module. Our candidate will be one of the messier ones, the CGI module – this handles both CGI scripts and the SCRIPTALIAS config file command. It's actually a great deal more complicated than most modules, but if we're going to have only one example, it might as well be the one with its fingers in every place.

Let's begin with handlers. In order to handle the CGI scripts, the module declares a response handler for them. Because of SCRIPTALIAS, it also has handlers for the name translation phase (to recognize SCRIPTALIASed URIs), the type-checking phase (any SCRIPTALIASed request is typed as a CGI script).

The module needs to maintain some per (virtual) server information, namely, the SCRIPTALIASes in effect; the module structure therefore contains pointers to a functions which builds these structures, and to another which combines two of them (in case the main server and a virtual server both have SCRIPTALIASes declared).

Finally, this module contains code to handle the SCRIPTALIAS command itself. This particular module only declares one command, but there could be more, so modules have *command tables* which declare their commands, and describe where they are permitted, and how they are to be invoked.

A final note on the declared types of the arguments of some of these commands: a pool is a pointer to a *resource pool* structure; these are used by the server to keep track of the memory which has been allocated, files opened, *etc.*, either to service a particular request, or to handle the process of configuring itself. That way, when the request is over (or, for the configuration pool, when the server is restarting), the memory can be freed, and the files closed, *en masse*, without anyone having to write explicit code to track them all down and dispose of them. Also, a cmd_parms structure contains various information about the config file being read, and other status information, which is sometimes of use to the function which processes a config-file command (such as SCRIPTALIAS). With no further ado, the module itself:

```
/* Declarations of handlers.  */
int translate_scriptalias (request_rec *);
int type_scriptalias (request_rec *);
int cgi_handler (request_rec *);
/* Subsidiary dispatch table for response-phase
 * handlers, by MIME type */
handler_rec cgi_handlers[] = {
    { "application/x-httpd-cgi", cgi_handler },
    { NULL }
};
/* Declarations of routines to manipulate the
 * module's configuration info.  Note that these are
 * returned, and passed in, as void *'s; the server
 * core keeps track of them, but it doesn't, and can't,
 * know their internal structure.
 */
void *make_cgi_server_config (pool *);
void *merge_cgi_server_config (pool *, void *, void *);
/* Declarations of routines to handle config-file commands */
extern char *script_alias(cmd_parms *, void *per_dir_config, char
*fake, char *real);
command_rec cgi_cmds[] = {
    { "ScriptAlias", script_alias, NULL, RSRC_CONF, TAKE2,
        "a fakename and a realname"},
    { NULL }
};
module cgi_module = {
  STANDARD_MODULE_STUFF,
  NULL,                     /* initializer */
  NULL,                     /* dir config creator */
  NULL,                     /* dir merger */
  make_cgi_server_config,   /* server config */
  merge_cgi_server_config,  /* merge server config */
  cgi_cmds,                 /* command table */
  cgi_handlers,             /* handlers */
  translate_scriptalias,    /* filename translation */
  NULL,                     /* check_user_id */
  NULL,                     /* check auth */
  NULL,                     /* check access */
  type_scriptalias,         /* type_checker */
  NULL,                     /* fixups */
  NULL,                     /* logger */
  NULL                      /* header parser */
};
```

How handlers work

The sole argument to handlers is a `request_rec` structure. This structure describes a particular request which has been made to the server, on behalf of a client. In most cases, each connection to the client generates only one `request_rec` structure.

A brief tour of the request_rec

The `request_rec` contains pointers to a resource pool which will be cleared when the server is finished handling the request; to structures containing per-server and per-connection information, and most importantly, information on the request itself.

The most important such information is a small set of character strings describing attributes of the object being requested, including its URI, filename, content-type and content-encoding (these being filled in by the translation and type-check handlers which handle the request, respectively).

Other commonly used data items are tables giving the MIME headers on the client's original request, MIME headers to be sent back with the response (which modules can add to at will), and environment variables for any subprocesses which are spawned off in the course of servicing the request. These tables are manipulated using the `ap_table_get` and `ap_table_set` routines.

> Note that the `Content-type` header value *cannot* be set by module content-handlers using the `ap_table_*()` routines. Rather, it is set by pointing the `content_type` field in the `request_rec` structure to an appropriate string. *e.g.*,

```
r->content_type = "text/html";
```

Finally, there are pointers to two data structures which, in turn, point to per-module configuration structures. Specifically, these hold pointers to the data structures which the module has built to describe the way it has been configured to operate in a given directory (via `.htaccess` files or <DIRECTORY> sections), for private data it has built in the course of servicing the request (so modules' handlers for one phase can pass 'notes' to their handlers for other phases). There is another such configuration vector in the `server_rec` data structure pointed to by the `request_rec`, which contains per (virtual) server configuration data.

Here is an abridged declaration, giving the fields most commonly used:

```
struct request_rec {

pool *pool;

conn_rec *connection;

server_rec *server;

/* What object is being requested */

char *uri;

char *filename;

char *path_info;

char *args;            /* QUERY_ARGS, if any */
struct stat finfo;     /* Set by server core;
                        * st_mode set to zero if no such file */

char *content_type;

char *content_encoding;

/* MIME header environments, in and out.  Also,
 * an array containing environment variables to
 * be passed to subprocesses, so people can write
 * modules to add to that environment.
 *
 * The difference between headers_out and
 * err_headers_out is that the latter are printed
 * even on error, and persist across internal
 * redirects (so the headers printed for
 * ERRORDOCUMENT handlers will have them).
 */

table *headers_in;

table *headers_out;

table *err_headers_out;

table *subprocess_env;

/* Info about the request itself...  */


int header_only;      /* HEAD request, as opposed to GET */
char *protocol;       /* Protocol, as given to us, or HTTP/0.9 */
char *method;         /* GET, HEAD, POST, etc. */
int method_number;    /* M_GET, M_POST, etc. */

/* Info for logging */

char *the_request;

int bytes_sent;

/* A flag which modules can set, to indicate that
 * the data being returned is volatile, and clients
 * should be told not to cache it.
 */

int no_cache;

/* Various other config info which may change
 * with .htaccess files
 * These are config vectors, with one void*
 * pointer for each module (the thing pointed
 * to being the module's business).
 */


void *per_dir_config;   /* Options set in config files, etc. */
void *request_config;   /* Notes on *this* request */

};
```

Where request_rec structures come from

Most `request_rec` structures are built by reading an HTTP request from a client, and filling in the fields. However, there are a few exceptions:

- If the request is to an imagemap, a type map (*i.e.*, a `*.var` file), or a CGI script which returned a local 'Location:', then the resource which the user requested is going to be ultimately located by some URI other than what the client originally supplied. In this case, the server does an *internal redirect*, constructing a new `request_rec` for the new URI, and processing it almost exactly as if the client had requested the new URI directly.

- If some handler signaled an error, and an `ErrorDocument` is in scope, the same internal redirect machinery comes into play.

- Finally, a handler occasionally needs to investigate 'what would happen if' some other request were run. For instance, the directory indexing module needs to know what MIME type would be assigned to a request for each directory entry, in order to figure out what icon to use.

  Such handlers can construct a *sub-request*, using the functions `ap_sub_req_lookup_file`, `ap_sub_req_lookup_uri`, and `ap_sub_req_method_uri`; these construct a new `request_rec` structure and processes it as you would expect, up to but not including the point of actually sending a response. (These functions skip over the access checks if the sub-request is for a file in the same directory as the original request).

  (Server-side includes work by building sub-requests and then actually invoking the response handler for them, via the function `ap_run_sub_req`).

Handling requests, declining, and returning error codes

As discussed above, each handler, when invoked to handle a particular `request_rec`, has to return an `int` to indicate what happened. That can either be

- `OK` – the request was handled successfully. This may or may not terminate the phase.

- `DECLINED` – no erroneous condition exists, but the module declines to handle the phase; the server tries to find another.

- an HTTP error code, which aborts handling of the request.

Note that if the error code returned is `REDIRECT`, then the module should put a `Location` in the request's `headers_out`, to indicate where the client should be redirected *to*.

Special considerations for response handlers

Handlers for most phases do their work by simply setting a few fields in the `request_rec` structure (or, in the case of access checkers, simply by returning the correct error code). However, response handlers have to actually send a request back to the client.

They should begin by sending an HTTP response header, using the function `ap_send_http_header`. (You don't have to do anything special to skip sending the header for HTTP/0.9 requests; the function figures out on its own that it shouldn't do anything). If the request is marked `header_only`, that's all they should do; they should return after that, without attempting any further output.

Otherwise, they should produce a request body which responds to the client as appropriate. The primitives for this are `ap_rputc` and `ap_rprintf`, for internally generated output, and `ap_send_fd`, to copy the contents of some `FILE *` straight to the client.

At this point, you should more or less understand the following piece of code, which is the handler which handles GET requests which have no more specific handler; it also shows how conditional GETs can be handled, if it's desirable to do so in a particular response handler – ap_set_last_modified checks against the If-modified-since value supplied by the client, if any, and returns an appropriate code (which will, if nonzero, be USE_LOCAL_COPY). No similar considerations apply for ap_set_content_length, but it returns an error code for symmetry.

```
int default_handler (request_rec *r)
{
    int errstatus;
    FILE *f;

    if (r->method_number != M_GET) return DECLINED;
    if (r->finfo.st_mode == 0) return NOT_FOUND;

    if ((errstatus = ap_set_content_length (r, r->finfo.st_size))
        || (errstatus = ap_set_last_modified (r, r->finfo.st_mtime)))
    return errstatus;

    f = fopen (r->filename, "r");

    if (f == NULL) {
        log_reason("file permissions deny server access", r->filename,
        r);
        return FORBIDDEN;
    }

    register_timeout ("send", r);
    ap_send_http_header (r);

    if (!r->header_only) send_fd (f, r);
    ap_pfclose (r->pool, f);
    return OK;
}
```

Finally, if all of this is too much of a challenge, there are a few ways out of it. First off, as shown above, a response handler which has not yet produced any output can simply return an error code, in which case the server will automatically produce an error response. Secondly, it can punt to some other handler by invoking ap_internal_redirect, which is how the internal redirection machinery discussed above is invoked. A response handler which has internally redirected should always return OK.

(Invoking ap_internal_redirect from handlers which are *not* response handlers will lead to serious confusion).

Special considerations for authentication handlers

Stuff that should be discussed here in detail:

- Authentication-phase handlers not invoked unless auth is configured for the directory.
- Common auth configuration stored in the core per-dir configuration; it has accessors ap_auth_type, ap_auth_name, and ap_requires.
- Common routines, to handle the protocol end of things, at least for HTTP basic authentication (ap_get_basic_auth_pw, which sets the connection->user structure field automatically, and ap_note_basic_auth_failure, which arranges for the proper WWW-Authenticate: header to be sent back).

Special considerations for logging handlers

When a request has internally redirected, there is the question of what to log. Apache handles this by bundling the entire chain of redirects into a list of request_rec structures which are threaded through the r->prev and r->next pointers. The request_rec which is passed to the logging handlers in such cases is the one which was originally built for the initial request from the client; note that the bytes_sent field will only be correct in the last request in the chain (the one for which a response was actually sent).

Resource allocation and resource pools

One of the problems of writing and designing a server-pool server is that of preventing leakage, that is, allocating resources (memory, open files, *etc.*), without subsequently releasing them. The resource pool machinery is designed to make it easy to prevent this from happening, by allowing resource to be allocated in such a way that they are *automatically* released when the server is done with them.

The way this works is as follows: the memory which is allocated, file opened, *etc.*, to deal with a particular request are tied to a *resource pool* which is allocated for the request. The pool is a data structure which itself tracks the resources in question.

When the request has been processed, the pool is *cleared*. At that point, all the memory associated with it is released for reuse, all files associated with it are closed, and any other clean-up functions which are associated with the pool are run. When this is over, we can be confident that all the resource tied to the pool have been released, and that none of them have leaked.

Server restarts, and allocation of memory and resources for per-server configuration, are handled in a similar way. There is a *configuration pool*, which keeps track of resources which were allocated while reading the server configuration files, and handling the commands therein (for instance, the memory that was allocated for per-server module configuration, log files and other files that were opened, and so forth). When the server restarts, and has to reread the configuration files, the configuration pool is cleared, and so the memory and file descriptors which were taken up by reading them the last time are made available for reuse.

It should be noted that use of the pool machinery isn't generally obligatory, except for situations like logging handlers, where you really need to register cleanups to make sure that the log file gets closed when the server restarts (this is most easily done by using the function ap_pfopen, which also arranges for the underlying file descriptor to be closed before any child processes, such as for CGI scripts, are execed), or in case you are using the timeout machinery (which isn't yet even documented here). However, there are two benefits to using it: resources allocated to a pool never leak (even if you allocate a scratch string, and just forget about it); also, for memory allocation, ap_palloc is generally faster than malloc.

We begin here by describing how memory is allocated to pools, and then discuss how other resources are tracked by the resource pool machinery.

Allocation of memory in pools

Memory is allocated to pools by calling the function ap_palloc, which takes two arguments, one being a pointer to a resource pool structure, and the other being the amount of memory to allocate (in chars). Within handlers for handling requests, the most common way of getting a resource pool structure is by looking at the pool slot of the relevant request_rec; hence the repeated appearance of the following idiom in module code:

```
int my_handler(request_rec *r)
{
    struct my_structure *foo;
    ...
    foo = (foo *)ap_palloc (r->pool, sizeof(my_structure));
}
```

Note that *there is no ap_pfree* – ap_palloced memory is freed only when the associated resource pool is cleared. This means that ap_palloc does not have to do as much accounting as malloc(); all it does in the typical case is to round up the size, bump a pointer, and do a range check.

(It also raises the possibility that heavy use of ap_palloc could cause a server process to grow excessively large. There are two ways to deal with this, which are dealt with below; briefly, you can use malloc, and try to be sure that all of the memory gets explicitly freed, or you can allocate a sub-pool of the main pool, allocate your memory in the sub-pool, and clear it out periodically. The latter technique is discussed in the section on sub-pools below, and is used in the directory-indexing code, in order to avoid excessive storage allocation when listing directories with thousands of files).

Allocating initialized memory

There are functions which allocate initialized memory, and are frequently useful. The function ap_pcalloc has the same interface as ap_palloc, but clears out the memory it allocates before it returns it. The function ap_pstrdup takes a resource pool and a char * as arguments, and allocates memory for a copy of the string the pointer points to, returning a pointer to the copy. Finally ap_pstrcat is a varargs-style function, which takes a pointer to a resource pool, and at least two char * arguments, the last of which must be NULL. It allocates enough memory to fit copies of each of the strings, as a unit; for instance:

```
ap_pstrcat (r->pool, "foo", "/", "bar", NULL);
```

returns a pointer to 8 bytes worth of memory, initialized to "foo/bar".

Commonly-used pools in the Apache Web server

A pool is really defined by its lifetime more than anything else. There are some static pools in http_main which are passed to various non-http_main functions as arguments at opportune times. Here they are:

permanent_pool never passed to anything else, this is the ancestor of all pools

pconf
- subpool of permanent_pool
- created at the beginning of a config "cycle"; exists until the server is terminated or restarts; passed to all config-time routines, either via cmd->pool, or as the "pool *p" argument on those which don't take pools
- passed to the module init() functions

ptemp
- sorry I lie, this pool isn't called this currently in 1.3, I renamed it this in my pthreads development. I'm referring to the use of ptrans in the parent... contrast this with the later definition of ptrans in the child.
- subpool of permanent_pool
- created at the beginning of a config "cycle"; exists until the end of config parsing; passed to config-time routines *via* cmd->temp_pool. Somewhat of a "bastard child" because it isn't available everywhere. Used for temporary scratch space which may be needed by some config routines but which is deleted at the end of config.

pchild   • subpool of permanent_pool

>   • created when a child is spawned (or a thread is created); lives until that child (thread) is destroyed
>   • passed to the module child_init functions
>   • destruction happens right after the child_exit functions are called... (which may explain why I think child_exit is redundant and unneeded)

ptrans   • should be a subpool of pchild, but currently is a subpool of permanent_pool, see above

>   • cleared by the child before going into the accept() loop to receive a connection
>   • used as connection->pool

r->pool   • for the main request this is a subpool of connection->pool; for subrequests it is a subpool of the parent request's pool.

>   • exists until the end of the request (*i.e.*, ap_destroy_sub_req, or in child_main after process_request has finished)
>   • note that r itself is allocated from r->pool; *i.e.*, r->pool is first created and then r is the first thing palloc()d from it

For almost everything folks do, `r->pool` is the pool to use. But you can see how other lifetimes, such as pchild, are useful to some modules... such as modules that need to open a database connection once per child, and wish to clean it up when the child dies.

You can also see how some bugs have manifested themself, such as setting `connection->user` to a value from `r->pool` – in this case connection exists for the lifetime of `ptrans`, which is longer than `r->pool` (especially if `r->pool` is a subrequest!). So the correct thing to do is to allocate from `connection->pool`.

And there was another interesting bug in MOD_INCLUDE / MOD_CGI. You'll see in those that they do this test to decide if they should use `r->pool` or `r->main->pool`. In this case the resource that they are registering for cleanup is a child process. If it were registered in `r->pool`, then the code would `wait()` for the child when the subrequest finishes. With MOD_INCLUDE this could be any old `#include`, and the delay can be up to 3 seconds... and happened quite frequently. Instead the subprocess is registered in `r->main->pool` which causes it to be cleaned up when the entire request is done – *i.e.*, after the output has been sent to the client and logging has happened.

Tracking open files, etc.

As indicated above, resource pools are also used to track other sorts of resources besides memory. The most common are open files. The routine which is typically used for this is `ap_pfopen`, which takes a resource pool and two strings as arguments; the strings are the same as the typical arguments to `fopen`, *e.g.*,

```
...
FILE *f = ap_pfopen (r->pool, r->filename, "r");
if (f == NULL) { ... } else { ... }
```

There is also a `ap_popenf` routine, which parallels the lower-level `open` system call. Both of these routines arrange for the file to be closed when the resource pool in question is cleared.

Unlike the case for memory, there *are* functions to close files allocated with `ap_pfopen`, and `ap_popenf`, namely `ap_pfclose` and `ap_pclosef`. (This is because, on many systems, the number of files which a single process can have open is quite limited). It is important to use these functions to close files allocated with `ap_pfopen` and `ap_popenf`, since to do otherwise could cause fatal errors on systems such as Linux, which react badly if the same `FILE*` is closed more than once.

(Using the `close` functions is not mandatory, since the file will eventually be closed regardless, but you should consider it in cases where your module is opening, or could open, a lot of files).

Other sorts of resources – cleanup functions

More text goes here. Describe the cleanup primitives in terms of which the file stuff is implemented; also, `spawn_process`.

Pool cleanups live until `clear_pool()` is called: `clear_pool(a)` recursively calls `destroy_pool()` on all subpools of a; then calls all the cleanups for a; then releases all the memory for a. `destroy_pool(a)` calls `clear_pool(a)` and then releases the pool structure itself. *i.e.*, `clear_pool(a)` doesn't delete a, it just frees up all the resources and you can start using it again immediately.

Fine control – creating and dealing with sub-pools, with a note on sub-requests

On rare occasions, too-free use of `ap_palloc()` and the associated primitives may result in undesirably profligate resource allocation. You can deal with such a case by creating a *sub-pool*, allocating within the sub-pool rather than the main pool, and clearing or destroying the sub-pool, which releases the resources which were associated with it. (This really *is* a rare situation; the only case in which it comes up in the standard module set is in case of listing directories, and then only with *very* large directories. Unnecessary use of the primitives discussed here can hair up your code quite a bit, with very little gain).

The primitive for creating a sub-pool is `ap_make_sub_pool`, which takes another pool (the parent pool) as an argument. When the main pool is cleared, the sub-pool will be destroyed. The sub-pool may also be cleared or destroyed at any time, by calling the functions `ap_clear_pool` and `ap_destroy_pool`, respectively. (The difference is that `ap_clear_pool` frees resources associated with the pool, while `ap_destroy_pool` also deallocates the pool itself. In the former case, you can allocate new resources within the pool, and clear it again, and so forth; in the latter case, it is simply gone).

One final note – sub-requests have their own resource pools, which are sub-pools of the resource pool for the main request. The polite way to reclaim the resources associated with a sub request which you have allocated (using the `ap_sub_req_...` functions) is `ap_destroy_sub_req`, which frees the resource pool. Before calling this function, be sure to copy anything that you care about which might be allocated in the sub-request's resource pool into someplace a little less volatile (for instance, the filename in its `request_rec` structure).

(Again, under most circumstances, you shouldn't feel obliged to call this function; only 2K of memory or so are allocated for a typical sub request, and it will be freed anyway when the main request pool is cleared. It is only when you are allocating many, many sub-requests for a single main request that you should seriously consider the `ap_destroy_...` functions).

Configuration, commands and the like

One of the design goals for this server was to maintain external compatibility with the NCSA 1.3 server — that is, to read the same configuration files, to process all the directives therein correctly, and in general to be a drop-in replacement for NCSA. On the other hand, another design goal was to move as much of the server's functionality into modules which have as little as possible to do with the monolithic server core. The only way to reconcile these goals is to move the handling of most commands from the central server into the modules.

However, just giving the modules command tables is not enough to divorce them completely from the server core. The server has to remember the commands in order to act on them later. That involves maintaining data which is private to the modules, and which can be either per-server, or per-directory. Most things are per-directory, including in particular access control and authorization information, but also information on how to determine file types from suffixes, which can be modified by ADDTYPE and FORCETYPE directives, and so forth. In general, the governing philosophy is that anything which *can* be made configurable by directory should be; per-server information is generally used in the standard set of modules for information like ALIASes and REDIRECTs which come into play before the request is tied to a particular place in the underlying file system.

Another requirement for emulating the NCSA server is being able to handle the per-directory configuration files, generally called .htaccess files, though even in the NCSA server they can contain directives which have nothing at all to do with access control. Accordingly, after URI -> filename translation, but before performing any other phase, the server walks down the directory hierarchy of the underlying filesystem, following the translated pathname, to read any .htaccess files which might be present. The information which is read in then has to be *merged* with the applicable information from the server's own config files (either from the <DIRECTORY> sections in access.conf, or from defaults in srm.conf, which actually behaves for most purposes almost exactly like <Directory />).

Finally, after having served a request which involved reading .htaccess files, we need to discard the storage allocated for handling them. That is solved the same way it is solved wherever else similar problems come up, by tying those structures to the per-transaction resource pool.

Per-directory configuration structures

Let's look out how all of this plays out in mod_mime.c, which defines the file typing handler which emulates the NCSA server's behavior of determining file types from suffixes. What we'll be looking at, here, is the code which implements the ADDTYPE and ADDENCODING commands. These commands can appear in .htaccess files, so they must be handled in the module's private per-directory data, which in fact, consists of two separate tables for MIME types and encoding information, and is declared as follows:

```
typedef struct {
    table *forced_types;      /* Additional AddTyped stuff */
    table *encoding_types;    /* Added with AddEncoding... */
} mime_dir_config;
```

When the server is reading a configuration file, or <DIRECTORY> section, which includes one of the MIME module's commands, it needs to create a mime_dir_config structure, so those commands have something to act on. It does this by invoking the function it finds in the module's 'create per-dir config slot', with two arguments: the name of the directory to which this configuration information applies (or NULL for srm.conf), and a pointer to a resource pool in which the allocation should happen.

(If we are reading a .htaccess file, that resource pool is the per-request resource pool for the request; otherwise it is a resource pool which is used for configuration data, and cleared on restarts. Either way, it is important for the structure being created to vanish when the pool is cleared, by registering a cleanup on the pool if necessary).

For the MIME module, the per-dir config creation function just ap_pallocs the structure above, and a creates a couple of tables to fill it. That looks like this:

```
void *create_mime_dir_config (pool *p, char *dummy)
{
    mime_dir_config *new =
        (mime_dir_config *) ap_palloc (p, sizeof(mime_dir_config));

    new->forced_types = ap_make_table (p, 4);
    new->encoding_types = ap_make_table (p, 4);

    return new;
}
```

Now, suppose we've just read in a .htaccess file. We already have the per-directory configuration structure for the next directory up in the hierarchy. If the .htaccess file we just read in didn't have any ADDTYPE or ADDENCODING commands, its per-directory config structure for the MIME module is still valid, and we can just use it. Otherwise, we need to merge the two structures somehow.

To do that, the server invokes the module's per-directory config merge function, if one is present. That function takes three arguments: the two structures being merged, and a resource pool in which to allocate the result. For the MIME module, all that needs to be done is overlay the tables from the new per-directory config structure with those from the parent:

```
void *merge_mime_dir_configs (pool *p, void *parent_dirv, void
*subdirv)
{
    mime_dir_config *parent_dir - (mime_dir_config *)parent_dirv;
    mime_dir_config *subdir = (mime_dir_config *)subdirv;
    mime_dir_config *new =
        (mime_dir_config *)ap_palloc (p, sizeof(mime_dir_config));

    new->forced_types = ap_overlay_tables (p, subdir->forced_types,
        parent_dir->forced_types);

    new->encoding_types = ap_overlay_tables (p, subdir->encoding_types,
        parent_dir->encoding_types);

    return new;
}
```

As a note – if there is no per-directory merge function present, the server will just use the subdirectory's configuration info, and ignore the parent's. For some modules, that works just fine (*e.g.*, for the includes module, whose per-directory configuration information consists solely of the state of the XBITHACK), and for those modules, you can just not declare one, and leave the corresponding structure slot in the module itself NULL.

Command handling

Now that we have these structures, we need to be able to figure out how to fill them. That involves processing the actual ADDTYPE and ADDENCODING commands. To find commands, the server looks in the module's command table. That table contains information on how many arguments the commands take, and in what formats, where it is permitted, and so forth. That information is sufficient to allow the server to invoke most command-handling functions with pre-parsed arguments. Without further ado, let's look at the ADDTYPE command handler, which looks like this (the ADDENCODING command looks basically the same, and won't be shown here):

```
char *add_type(cmd_parms *cmd, mime_dir_config *m, char *ct, char *ext)
{
    if (*ext == '.')  ++ext;
    ap_table_set (m->forced_types, ext, ct);
    return NULL;
}
```

This command handler is unusually simple. As you can see, it takes four arguments, two of which are pre-parsed arguments, the third being the per-directory configuration structure for the module in question, and the fourth being a pointer to a cmd_parms structure. That structure contains a bunch of arguments which are frequently of use to some, but not all, commands, including a resource pool (from which memory can be allocated, and to which cleanups should be tied), and the (virtual) server being configured, from which the module's per-server configuration data can be obtained if required.

Another way in which this particular command handler is unusually simple is that there are no error conditions which it can encounter. If there were, it could return an error message instead of NULL; this causes an error to be printed out on the server's `stderr`, followed by a quick exit, if it is in the main config files; for a `.htaccess` file, the syntax error is logged in the server error log (along with an indication of where it came from), and the request is bounced with a server error response (HTTP error status, code 500).

The MIME module's command table has entries for these commands, which look like this:

```
command_rec mime_cmds[] = {
    { "AddType", add_type, NULL, OR_FILEINFO, TAKE2,
        "a mime type followed by a file extension" },
    { "AddEncoding", add_encoding, NULL, OR_FILEINFO, TAKE2,
        "an encoding (e.g., gzip), followed by a file extension" },
    { NULL }
};
```

The entries in these tables are:

- The name of the command

- The function which handles it

- a (`void *`) pointer, which is passed in the `cmd_parms` structure to the command handler — this is useful in case many similar commands are handled by the same function.

- A bit mask indicating where the command may appear. There are mask bits corresponding to each `AllowOverride` option, and an additional mask bit, `RSRC_CONF`, indicating that the command may appear in the server's own config files, but *not* in any `.htaccess` file.

- A flag indicating how many arguments the command handler wants pre-parsed, and how they should be passed in. `TAKE2` indicates two pre-parsed arguments. Other options are `TAKE1`, which indicates one pre-parsed argument, `FLAG`, which indicates that the argument should be `On` or `Off`, and is passed in as a boolean flag, `RAW_ARGS`, which causes the server to give the command the raw, unparsed arguments (everything but the command name itself). There is also `ITERATE`, which means that the handler looks the same as `TAKE1`, but that if multiple arguments are present, it should be called multiple times, and finally `ITERATE2`, which indicates that the command handler looks like a `TAKE2`, but if more arguments are present, then it should be called multiple times, holding the first argument constant.

- Finally, we have a string which describes the arguments that should be present. If the arguments in the actual config file are not as required, this string will be used to help give a more specific error message. (You can safely leave this `NULL`).

Finally, having set this all up, we have to use it. This is ultimately done in the module's handlers, specifically for its file-typing handler, which looks more or less like this; note that the per-directory configuration structure is extracted from the `request_rec`'s per-directory configuration vector by using the `ap_get_module_config` function.

```
int find_ct(request_rec *r)
{
    int i;
    char *fn = ap_pstrdup (r->pool, r->filename);
    mime_dir_config *conf = (mime_dir_config *)
        ap_get_module_config(r->per_dir_config, &mime_module);

    char *type;
    if (S_ISDIR(r->finfo.st_mode)) {
        r->content_type = DIR_MAGIC_TYPE;
        return OK;
    }
    if((i=ap_rind(fn,'.'))  < 0) return DECLINED;
    ++i;
    if ((type = ap_table_get (conf->encoding_types, &fn[i])))
    {
        r->content_encoding = type;
        /* go back to previous extension to try to use it as a type */
        fn[i-1] = '\0';
        if((i=ap_rind(fn,'.'))  < 0) return OK;
        ++i;
    }
    if ((type = ap_table_get (conf->forced_types, &fn[i])))
    {
        r->content_type = type;
    }
    return OK;
}
```

Side notes – per-server configuration, virtual servers, *etc*.

The basic ideas behind per-server module configuration are basically the same as those for per-directory configuration; there is a creation function and a merge function, the latter being invoked where a virtual server has partially overridden the base server configuration, and a combined structure must be computed. (As with per-directory configuration, the default if no merge function is specified, and a module is configured in some virtual server, is that the base configuration is simply ignored).

The only substantial difference is that when a command needs to configure the per-server private module data, it needs to go to the cmd_parms data to get at it. Here's an example, from the alias module, which also indicates how a syntax error can be returned (note that the per-directory configuration argument to the command handler is declared as a dummy, since the module doesn't actually have per-directory config data):

```
char *add_redirect(cmd_parms *cmd, void *dummy, char *f, char *url)
{
    server_rec *s = cmd->server;
    alias_server_conf *conf = (alias_server_conf *)
        ap_get_module_config(s->module_config,&alias_module);
    alias_entry *new = ap_push_array (conf->redirects);
    if (!ap_is_url (url)) return "Redirect to non-URL";
    new->fake = f; new->real = url;
    return NULL;
}
```

11.3 API Changes in Apache HTTP Server 2.4 since 2.2

This document describes changes to the Apache HTTPD API from version 2.2 to 2.4, that may be of interest to module/application developers and core hacks. As of the first GA release of the 2.4 branch API compatibility is preserved for the life of the 2.4 branch. (The VERSIONING[8] description for the 2.4 release provides more information about API compatibility.)

API changes fall into two categories: APIs that are altogether new, and existing APIs that are expanded or changed. The latter are further divided into those where all changes are backwards-compatible (so existing modules can ignore them), and those that might require attention by maintainers. As with the transition from HTTPD 2.0 to 2.2, existing modules and applications will require recompiling and may call for some attention, but most should not require any substantial updating (although some may be able to take advantage of API changes to offer significant improvements).

For the purpose of this document, the API is split according to the public header files. These headers are themselves the reference documentation, and can be used to generate a browsable HTML reference with `make docs`.

Changed APIs

ap_expr (NEW!)

Introduces a new API to parse and evaluate boolean and algebraic expressions, including provision for a standard syntax and customised variants.

ap_listen (changed; backwards-compatible)

Introduces a new API to enable httpd child processes to serve different purposes.

ap_mpm (changed)

`ap_mpm_run` is replaced by a new `mpm` hook. Also `ap_graceful_stop_signalled` is lost, and `ap_mpm_register_timed_callback` is new.

ap_regex (changed)

In addition to the existing regexp wrapper, a new higher-level API `ap_rxplus` is now provided. This provides the capability to compile Perl-style expressions like `s/regexp/replacement/flags` and to execute them against arbitrary strings. Support for regexp backreferences is also added.

ap_slotmem (NEW!)

Introduces an API for modules to allocate and manage memory slots, most commonly for shared memory.

ap_socache (NEW!)

API to manage a shared object cache.

heartbeat (NEW!)

common structures for heartbeat modules

---

[8]http://svn.apache.org/repos/asf/httpd/httpd/branches/2.4.x/VERSIONING

ap_parse_htaccess (changed)

The function signature for `ap_parse_htaccess` has been changed. A `apr_table_t` of individual directives allowed for override must now be passed (override remains).

http_config (changed)

- Introduces per-module, per-directory loglevels, including macro wrappers.
- New `AP_DECLARE_MODULE` macro to declare all modules.
- New `APLOG_USE_MODULE` macro necessary for per-module loglevels in multi-file modules.
- New API to retain data across module unload/load
- New `check_config` hook
- New `ap_process_fnmatch_configs()` function to process wildcards
- Change `ap_configfile_t`, `ap_cfg_getline()`, `ap_cfg_getc()` to return error codes, and add `ap_pcfg_strerror()` for retrieving an error description.
- Any config directive permitted in ACCESS_CONF context must now correctly handle being called from an .htaccess file via the new ALLOWOVERRIDELIST directive. ap_check_cmd_context() accepts a new flag NOT_IN_HTACCESS to detect this case.

http_core (changed)

- REMOVED `ap_default_type`, `ap_requires`, all 2.2 authnz API
- Introduces Optional Functions for logio and authnz
- New function `ap_get_server_name_for_url` to support IPv6 literals.
- New function `ap_register_errorlog_handler` to register error log format string handlers.
- Arguments of `error_log` hook have changed. Declaration has moved to `http_core.h`.
- New function `ap_state_query` to determine if the server is in the initial configuration preflight phase or not. This is both easier to use and more correct than the old method of creating a pool userdata entry in the process pool.
- New function `ap_get_conn_socket` to get the socket descriptor for a connection. This should be used instead of accessing the core connection config directly.

httpd (changed)

- Introduce per-directory, per-module loglevel
- New loglevels `APLOG_TRACEn`
- Introduce errorlog ids for requests and connections
- Support for mod_request kept_body
- Support buffering filter data for async requests
- New `CONN_STATE` values
- Function changes: `ap_escape_html` updated; `ap_unescape_all`, `ap_escape_path_segment_buffer`
- Modules that load other modules later than the EXEC_ON_READ config reading stage need to call `ap_reserve_module_slots()` or `ap_reserve_module_slots_directive()` in their `pre_config` hook.

- The useragent IP address per request can now be tracked independently of the client IP address of the connection, for support of deployments with load balancers.

http_log (changed)

- Introduce per-directory, per-module loglevel
- New loglevels `APLOG_TRACEn`
- `ap_log_*error` become macro wrappers (backwards-compatible if `APLOG_MARK` macro is used, except that is no longer possible to use `#ifdef` inside the argument list)
- piped logging revamped
- `module_index` added to error_log hook
- new function: `ap_log_command_line`

http_request (changed)

- New auth_internal API and auth_provider API
- New `EOR` bucket type
- New function `ap_process_async_request`
- New flags `AP_AUTH_INTERNAL_PER_CONF` and `AP_AUTH_INTERNAL_PER_URI`
- New `access_checker_ex` hook to apply additional access control and/or bypass authentication.
- New functions `ap_hook_check_access_ex`, `ap_hook_check_access`, `ap_hook_check_authn`, `ap_hook_check_authz` which accept `AP_AUTH_INTERNAL_PER_*` flags
- DEPRECATED   direct   use   of   `ap_hook_access_checker`,   `access_checker_ex`, `ap_hook_check_user_id`, `ap_hook_auth_checker`

When possible, registering all access control hooks (including authentication and authorization hooks) using `AP_AUTH_INTERNAL_PER_CONF` is recommended. If all modules' access control hooks are registered with this flag, then whenever the server handles an internal sub-request that matches the same set of access control configuration directives as the initial request (which is the common case), it can avoid invoking the access control hooks another time.

If your module requires the old behavior and must perform access control checks on every sub-request with a different URI from the initial request, even if that URI matches the same set of access control configuration directives, then use `AP_AUTH_INTERNAL_PER_URI`.

mod_auth (NEW!)

Introduces the new provider framework for authn and authz

mod_cache (changed)

Introduces a `commit_entity()` function to the cache provider interface, allowing atomic writes to cache. Add a `cache_status()` hook to report the cache decision. All private structures and functions were removed.

mod_core (NEW!)

This introduces low-level APIs to send arbitrary headers, and exposes functions to handle HTTP OPTIONS and TRACE.

mod_cache_disk (changed)

Changes the disk format of the disk cache to support atomic cache updates without locking. The device/inode pair of the body file is embedded in the header file, allowing confirmation that the header and body belong to one another.

mod_disk_cache (renamed)

The mod_disk_cache module has been renamed to mod_cache_disk in order to be consistent with the naming of other modules within the server.

mod_request (NEW!)

The API for MOD_REQUEST, to make input data available to multiple application/handler modules where required, and to parse HTML form data.

mpm_common (changed)

- REMOVES: `accept`, `lockfile`, `lock_mech`, `set_scoreboard` (locking uses the new ap_mutex API)
- NEW API to drop privileges (delegates this platform-dependent function to modules)
- NEW Hooks: `mpm_query`, `timed_callback`, and `get_name`
- CHANGED interfaces: `monitor` hook, `ap_reclaim_child_processes`, `ap_relieve_child_processes`

scoreboard (changed)

`ap_get_scoreboard_worker` is made non-backwards-compatible as an alternative version is introduced. Additional proxy_balancer support. Child status stuff revamped.

util_cookies (NEW!)

Introduces a new API for managing HTTP Cookies.

util_ldap (changed)

no description available

util_mutex (NEW!)

A wrapper for APR proc and global mutexes in httpd, providing common configuration for the underlying mechanism and location of lock files.

util_script (changed)

NEW: `ap_args_to_table`

util_time (changed)

NEW: `ap_recent_ctime_ex`

Specific information on upgrading modules from 2.2

Logging

In order to take advantage of per-module loglevel configuration, any source file that calls the `ap_log_*` functions should declare which module it belongs to. If the module's module_struct is called `foo_module`, the following code can be used to remain backward compatible with HTTPD 2.0 and 2.2:

```
#include <http_log.h>
#ifdef APLOG_USE_MODULE
APLOG_USE_MODULE(foo);
#endif
```

Note: This is absolutely required for C++-language modules. It can be skipped for C-language modules, though that breaks module-specific log level support for files without it.

The number of parameters of the `ap_log_*` functions and the definition of `APLOG_MARK` has changed. Normally, the change is completely transparent. However, changes are required if a module uses `APLOG_MARK` as a parameter to its own functions or if a module calls `ap_log_*` without passing `APLOG_MARK`. A module which uses wrappers around `ap_log_*` typically uses both of these constructs.

The easiest way to change code which passes `APLOG_MARK` to its own functions is to define and use a different macro that expands to the parameters required by those functions, as `APLOG_MARK` should only be used when calling `ap_log_*` directly. In this way, the code will remain compatible with HTTPD 2.0 and 2.2.

Code which calls `ap_log_*` without passing `APLOG_MARK` will necessarily differ between 2.4 and earlier releases, as 2.4 requires a new third argument, `APLOG_MODULE_INDEX`.

```
/* code for httpd 2.0/2.2 */
ap_log_perror(file, line, APLOG_ERR, 0, p, "Failed to allocate dynamic
lock structure");
/* code for httpd 2.4 */
ap_log_perror(file, line, APLOG_MODULE_INDEX, APLOG_ERR, 0, p, "Failed
to allocate dynamic lock structure");
```

`ap_log_*error` are now implemented as macros. This means that it is no longer possible to use `#ifdef` inside the argument list of `ap_log_*error`, as this would cause undefined behavior according to C99.

A `server_rec` pointer must be passed to `ap_log_error()` when called after startup. This was always appropriate, but there are even more limitations with a NULL `server_rec` in 2.4 than in previous releases. Beginning with 2.3.12, the global variable `ap_server_conf` can always be used as the `server_rec` parameter, as it will be NULL only when it is valid to pass NULL to `ap_log_error()`. `ap_server_conf` should be used only when a more appropriate `server_rec` is not available.

Consider the following changes to take advantage of the new `APLOG_TRACE1..8` log levels:

- Check current use of `APLOG_DEBUG` and consider if one of the `APLOG_TRACEn` levels is more appropriate.

- If your module currently has a mechanism for configuring the amount of debug logging which is performed, consider eliminating that mechanism and relying on the use of different APLOG_TRACEn levels. If expensive trace processing needs to be bypassed depending on the configured log level, use the APLOGtrace*n* and APLOGrtrace*n* macros to first check if tracing is enabled.

Modules sometimes add process id and/or thread id to their log messages. These ids are now logged by default, so it may not be necessary for the module to log them explicitly. (Users may remove them from the error log format, but they can be instructed to add it back if necessary for problem diagnosis.)

If your module uses these existing APIs...

ap_default_type() This is no longer available; Content-Type must be configured explicitly or added by the application.

ap_get_server_name() If the returned server name is used in a URL, use ap_get_server_name_for_url() instead. This new function handles the odd case where the server name is an IPv6 literal address.

ap_get_server_version() For logging purposes, where detailed information is appropriate, use ap_get_server_description(). When generating output, where the amount of information should be configurable by ServerTokens, use ap_get_server_banner().

ap_graceful_stop_signalled() Replace with a call to ap_mpm_query(AP_MPMQ_MPM_STATE) and checking for state AP_MPMQ_STOPPING.

ap_max_daemons_limit, ap_my_generation, and ap_threads_per_child Use ap_mpm_query() query codes AP_MPMQ_MAX_DAEMON_USED, AP_MPMQ_GENERATION, and AP_MPMQ_MAX_THREADS, respectively.

ap_mpm_query() Ensure that it is not used until after the register-hooks hook has completed. Otherwise, an MPM built as a DSO would not have had a chance to enable support for this function.

ap_requires() The core server now provides better infrastructure for handling REQUIRE configuration. Register an auth provider function for each supported entity using ap_register_auth_provider(). The function will be called as necessary during REQUIRE processing. (Consult bundled modules for detailed examples.)

ap_server_conf->process->pool userdata Optional:

- If your module uses this to determine which pass of the startup hooks is being run, use ap_state_query(AP_SQ_MAIN_STATE).
- If your module uses this to maintain data across the unloading and reloading of your module, use ap_retained_data_create() and ap_retained_data_get().

apr_global_mutex_create(), apr_proc_mutex_create() Optional: See ap_mutex_register(), ap_global_mutex_create(), and ap_proc_mutex_create(); these allow your mutexes to be configurable with the MUTEX directive; you can also remove any configuration mechanisms in your module for such mutexes

CORE_PRIVATE This is now unnecessary and ignored.

dav_new_error() and dav_new_error_tag() Previously, these assumed that errno contained information describing the failure. Now, an apr_status_t parameter must be provided. Pass 0/APR_SUCCESS if there is no such error information, or a valid apr_status_t value otherwise.

mpm_default.h, DEFAULT_LOCKFILE, DEFAULT_THREAD_LIMIT, DEFAULT_PIDLOG, etc. The header file and most of the default configuration values set in it are no longer visible to modules. (Most can still be overridden at build time.) DEFAULT_PIDLOG and DEFAULT_REL_RUNTIMEDIR are now universally available via ap_config.h.

`unixd_config` This has been renamed to ap_unixd_config.

`unixd_setup_child()` This has been renamed to ap_unixd_setup_child(), but most callers should call the added ap_run_drop_privileges() hook.

`conn_rec->remote_ip and conn_rec->remote_addr` These fields have been renamed in order to distinguish between the client IP address of the connection and the useragent IP address of the request (potentially overridden by a load balancer or proxy). References to either of these fields must be updated with one of the following options, as appropriate for the module:

- When you require the IP address of the user agent, which might be connected directly to the server, or might optionally be separated from the server by a transparent load balancer or proxy, use `request_rec->useragent_ip` and `request_rec->useragent_addr`.
- When you require the IP address of the client that is connected directly to the server, which might be the useragent or might be the load balancer or proxy itself, use `conn_rec->client_ip` and `conn_rec->client_addr`.

If your module interfaces with this feature...

suEXEC Optional: If your module logs an error when `ap_unixd_config.suexec_enabled` is 0, also log the value of the new field `suexec_disabled_reason`, which contains an explanation of why it is not available.

Extended status data in the scoreboard In previous releases, `ExtendedStatus` had to be set to `On`, which in turn required that mod_status was loaded. In 2.4, just set `ap_extended_status` to 1 in a pre-config hook and the extended status data will be available.

Does your module...

Parse query args Consider if `ap_args_to_table()` would be helpful.

Parse form data... Use `ap_parse_form_data()`.

Check for request header fields `Content-Length` and `Transfer-Encoding` to see if a body was specified Use `ap_request_has_body()`.

Implement cleanups which clear pointer variables Use `ap_pool_cleanup_set_null()`.

Create run-time files such as shared memory files, pid files, etc. Use `ap_runtime_dir_relative()` so that the global configuration for the location of such files, either by the DEFAULT_REL_RUNTIMEDIR compile setting or the DEFAULTRUNTIMEDIR directive, will be respected. *Apache httpd 2.4.2 and above.*

11.4   Developing modules for the Apache HTTP Server 2.4

This document explains how you can develop modules for the Apache HTTP Server 2.4

See also

- Request Processing in Apache 2.4 (p. 1002)

- Apache 2.x Hook Functions (p. 995)

Introduction

What we will be discussing in this document

This document will discuss how you can create modules for the Apache HTTP Server 2.4, by exploring an example module called `mod_example`. In the first part of this document, the purpose of this module will be to calculate and print out various digest values for existing files on your web server, whenever we access the URL `http://hostname/filename.sum`. For instance, if we want to know the MD5 digest value of the file located at `http://www.example.com/index.html`, we would visit `http://www.example.com/index.html.sum`.

In the second part of this document, which deals with configuration directive and context awareness, we will be looking at a module that simply writes out its own configuration to the client.

Prerequisites

First and foremost, you are expected to have a basic knowledge of how the C programming language works. In most cases, we will try to be as pedagogical as possible and link to documents describing the functions used in the examples, but there are also many cases where it is necessary to either just assume that "it works" or do some digging yourself into what the hows and whys of various function calls.

Lastly, you will need to have a basic understanding of how modules are loaded and configured in the Apache HTTP Server, as well as how to get the headers for Apache if you do not have them already, as these are needed for compiling new modules.

Compiling your module

To compile the source code we are building in this document, we will be using APXS (p. 291) . Assuming your source file is called mod_example.c, compiling, installing and activating the module is as simple as:

```
apxs -i -a -c mod_example.c
```

Defining a module

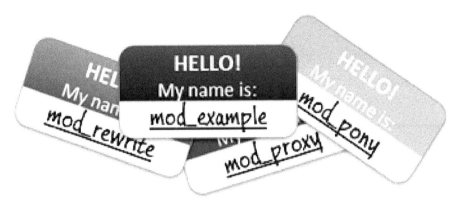

Every module starts with the same declaration, or name tag if you will, that defines a module as *a separate entity within Apache*:

```
module AP_MODULE_DECLARE_DATA    example_module =
{
    STANDARD20_MODULE_STUFF,
    create_dir_conf, /* Per-directory configuration handler */
    merge_dir_conf,  /* Merge handler for per-directory configurations */
    create_svr_conf, /* Per-server configuration handler */
    merge_svr_conf,  /* Merge handler for per-server configurations */
    directives,      /* Any directives we may have for httpd */
    register_hooks   /* Our hook registering function */
};
```

This bit of code lets the server know that we have now registered a new module in the system, and that its name is example_module. The name of the module is used primarily for two things:

- Letting the server know how to load the module using the LoadModule
- Setting up a namespace for the module to use in configurations

For now, we're only concerned with the first purpose of the module name, which comes into play when we need to load the module:

```
LoadModule example_module modules/mod_example.so
```

In essence, this tells the server to open up mod_example.so and look for a module called example_module.

Within this name tag of ours is also a bunch of references to how we would like to handle things: Which directives do we respond to in a configuration file or .htaccess, how do we operate within specific contexts, and what handlers are we interested in registering with the Apache HTTP service. We'll return to all these elements later in this document.

Getting started: Hooking into the server

An introduction to hooks

When handling requests in Apache HTTP Server 2.4, the first thing you will need to do is create a hook into the request handling process. A hook is essentially a message telling the server that you are willing to either serve or at least take a glance at certain requests given by clients. All handlers, whether it's mod_rewrite, mod_authn_*, mod_proxy and so on, are hooked into specific parts of the request process. As you are probably aware, modules serve different purposes; Some are authentication/authorization handlers, others are file or script handlers while some third modules rewrite URIs or proxies content. Furthermore, in the end, it is up to the user of the server how and when each module will come into place. Thus, the server itself does not presume to know which module is responsible for handling a specific request, and will ask each module whether they have an interest in a given request or not. It is then up to each module to either gently decline serving a request, accept serving it or flat out deny the request from being served, as authentication/authorization modules do:

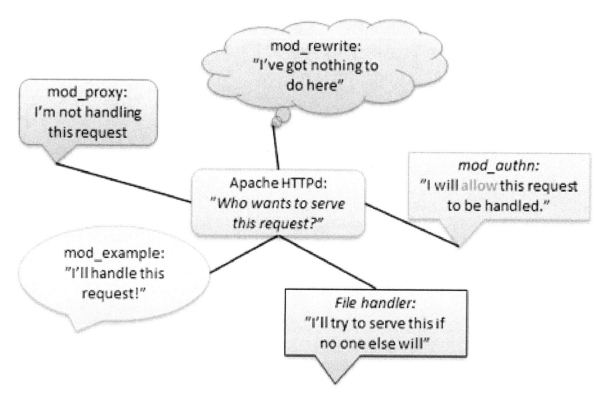

To make it a bit easier for handlers such as our mod_example to know whether the client is requesting content we should handle or not, the server has directives for hinting to modules whether their assistance is needed or not. Two of these are ADDHANDLER and SETHANDLER. Let's take a look at an example using ADDHANDLER. In our example case, we want every request ending with .sum to be served by mod_example, so we'll add a configuration directive that tells the server to do just that:

```
AddHandler example-handler .sum
```

What this tells the server is the following: *Whenever we receive a request for a URI ending in .sum, we are to let all modules know that we are looking for whoever goes by the name of "example-handler"* . Thus, when a request is being served that ends in .sum, the server will let all modules know, that this request should be served by "example-handler ". As you will see later, when we start building mod_example, we will check for this handler tag relayed by AddHandler and reply to the server based on the value of this tag.

Hooking into httpd

To begin with, we only want to create a simple handler, that replies to the client browser when a specific URL is requested, so we won't bother setting up configuration handlers and directives just yet. Our initial module definition will look like this:

```
module AP_MODULE_DECLARE_DATA   example_module =
```

```
{
    STANDARD20_MODULE_STUFF,
    NULL,
    NULL,
    NULL,
    NULL,
    NULL,
    register_hooks   /* Our hook registering function */
};
```

This lets the server know that we are not interested in anything fancy, we just want to hook onto the requests and possibly handle some of them.

The reference in our example declaration, `register_hooks` is the name of a function we will create to manage how we hook onto the request process. In this example module, the function has just one purpose; To create a simple hook that gets called after all the rewrites, access control etc has been handled. Thus, we will let the server know, that we want to hook into its process as one of the last modules:

```
static void register_hooks(apr_pool_t *pool)
{
    /* Create a hook in the request handler, so we get called when a request ar
    ap_hook_handler(example_handler, NULL, NULL, APR_HOOK_LAST);
}
```

The `example_handler` reference is the function that will handle the request. We will discuss how to create a handler in the next chapter.

Other useful hooks

Hooking into the request handling phase is but one of many hooks that you can create. Some other ways of hooking are:

- `ap_hook_child_init`: Place a hook that executes when a child process is spawned (commonly used for initializing modules after the server has forked)

- `ap_hook_pre_config`: Place a hook that executes before any configuration data has been read (very early hook)

- `ap_hook_post_config`: Place a hook that executes after configuration has been parsed, but before the server has forked

- `ap_hook_translate_name`: Place a hook that executes when a URI needs to be translated into a filename on the server (think `mod_rewrite`)

- `ap_hook_quick_handler`: Similar to `ap_hook_handler`, except it is run before any other request hooks (translation, auth, fixups etc)

- `ap_hook_log_transaction`: Place a hook that executes when the server is about to add a log entry of the current request

Building a handler

A handler is essentially a function that receives a callback when a request to the server is made. It is passed a record of the current request (how it was made, which headers and requests were passed along, who's giving the request and so on), and is put in charge of either telling the server that it's not interested in the request or handle the request with the tools provided.

A simple "Hello, world!" handler

Let's start off by making a very simple request handler that does the following:

1. Check that this is a request that should be served by "example-handler"

2. Set the content type of our output to text/html

3. Write "Hello, world!" back to the client browser

4. Let the server know that we took care of this request and everything went fine

In C code, our example handler will now look like this:

```
static int example_handler(request_rec *r)
{
    /* First off, we need to check if this is a call for the "example-handler"
     * If it is, we accept it and do our things, if not, we simply return DECLI
     * and the server will try somewhere else.
     */
    if (!r->handler || strcmp(r->handler, "example-handler")) return (DECLINED)

    /* Now that we are handling this request, we'll write out "Hello, world!" t
     * To do so, we must first set the appropriate content type, followed by ou
     */
    ap_set_content_type(r, "text/html");
    ap_rprintf(r, "Hello, world!");

    /* Lastly, we must tell the server that we took care of this request and ev
     * We do so by simply returning the value OK to the server.
     */
    return OK;
}
```

Now, we put all we have learned together and end up with a program that looks like mod_example_1.c[9] . The functions used in this example will be explained later in the section "Some useful functions you should know".

The request_rec structure

The most essential part of any request is the *request record* . In a call to a handler function, this is represented by the request_rec* structure passed along with every call that is made. This struct, typically just referred to as r in modules, contains all the information you need for your module to fully process any HTTP request and respond accordingly.

Some key elements of the request_rec structure are:

- r->handler (char*) : Contains the name of the handler the server is currently asking to do the handling of this request

- r->method (char*) : Contains the HTTP method being used, f.x. GET or POST

- r->filename (char*) : Contains the translated filename the client is requesting

- r->args (char*) : Contains the query string of the request, if any

---

[9]http://people.apache.org/~humbedooh/mods/examples/mod_example_1.c

- r->headers_in (apr_table_t*): Contains all the headers sent by the client

- r->connection (conn_rec*): A record containing information about the current connection

- r->user (char*): If the URI requires authentication, this is set to the username provided

- r->useragent_ip (char*): The IP address of the client connecting to us

- r->pool (apr_pool_t*): The memory pool of this request. We'll discuss this in the "Memory management" chapter.

A complete list of all the values contained within the request_rec structure can be found in the httpd.h[10] header file or at http://ci.apache.org/projects/httpd/trunk/doxygen/structrequest_rec.html.

Let's try out some of these variables in another example handler:

```
static int example_handler(request_rec *r)
{
    /* Set the appropriate content type */
    ap_set_content_type(r, "text/html");

    /* Print out the IP address of the client connecting to us: */
    ap_rprintf(r, "<h2>Hello, %s!</h2>", r->useragent_ip);

    /* If we were reached through a GET or a POST request, be happy, else sad.
    if ( !strcmp(r->method, "POST") || !strcmp(r->method, "GET") ) {
        ap_rputs("You used a GET or a POST method, that makes us happy!<br/>",
    }
    else {
        ap_rputs("You did not use POST or GET, that makes us sad :(<br/>", r);
    }

    /* Lastly, if there was a query string, let's print that too! */
    if (r->args) {
        ap_rprintf(r, "Your query string was: %s", r->args);
    }
    return OK;
}
```

Return values

Apache relies on return values from handlers to signify whether a request was handled or not, and if so, whether the request went well or not. If a module is not interested in handling a specific request, it should always return the value DECLINED. If it is handling a request, it should either return the generic value OK, or a specific HTTP status code, for example:

```
static int example_handler(request_rec *r)
{
    /* Return 404: Not found */
    return HTTP_NOT_FOUND;
}
```

Returning OK or a HTTP status code does not necessarily mean that the request will end. The server may still have other handlers that are interested in this request, for instance the logging modules which, upon a successful request,

---

[10]http://svn.apache.org/repos/asf/httpd/httpd/trunk/include/httpd.h

will write down a summary of what was requested and how it went. To do a full stop and prevent any further processing after your module is done, you can return the value DONE to let the server know that it should cease all activity on this request and carry on with the next, without informing other handlers.

General response codes:

- DECLINED: We are not handling this request

- OK: We handled this request and it went well

- DONE: We handled this request and the server should just close this thread without further processing

HTTP specific return codes (excerpt):

- HTTP_OK (200): Request was okay

- HTTP_MOVED_PERMANENTLY (301): The resource has moved to a new URL

- HTTP_UNAUTHORIZED (401): Client is not authorized to visit this page

- HTTP_FORBIDDEN (403): Permission denied

- HTTP_NOT_FOUND (404): File not found

- HTTP_INTERNAL_SERVER_ERROR (500): Internal server error (self explanatory)

Some useful functions you should know

- ap_rputs(const char *string, request_rec *r):
  Sends a string of text to the client. This is a shorthand version of ap_rwrite[11].

  ```
  ap_rputs("Hello, world!", r);
  ```

- ap_rprintf[12]:
  This function works just like printf, except it sends the result to the client.

  ```
  ap_rprintf(r, "Hello, %s!", r->useragent_ip);
  ```

- ap_set_content_type[13](request_rec *r, const char *type):
  Sets the content type of the output you are sending.

  ```
  ap_set_content_type(r, "text/plain"); /* force a raw text output */
  ```

Memory management

Managing your resources in Apache HTTP Server 2.4 is quite easy, thanks to the memory pool system. In essence, each server, connection and request have their own memory pool that gets cleaned up when its scope ends, e.g. when a request is done or when a server process shuts down. All your module needs to do is latch onto this memory pool, and you won't have to worry about having to clean up after yourself - pretty neat, huh?

In our module, we will primarily be allocating memory for each request, so it's appropriate to use the r->pool reference when creating new objects. A few of the functions for allocating memory within a pool are:

---

[11]http://ci.apache.org/projects/httpd/trunk/doxygen/group__APACHE__CORE__PROTO.html#gac827cd0537d2b6213a7c06d7c26cc36e

[12]http://ci.apache.org/projects/httpd/trunk/doxygen/group__APACHE__CORE__PROTO.html#ga5e91eb6ca777c9a427b2e82bf1eeb81d

[13]http://ci.apache.org/projects/httpd/trunk/doxygen/group__APACHE__CORE__PROTO.html#gaa2f8412c400197338ec509f4a45e4579

- `void* apr_palloc`[14]`( apr_pool_t *p, apr_size_t size)`: Allocates `size` number of bytes in the pool for you

- `void* apr_pcalloc`[15]`( apr_pool_t *p, apr_size_t size)`: Allocates `size` number of bytes in the pool for you and sets all bytes to 0

- `char* apr_pstrdup`[16]`( apr_pool_t *p, const char *s)`: Creates a duplicate of the string `s`. This is useful for copying constant values so you can edit them

- `char* apr_psprintf`[17]`( apr_pool_t *p, const char *fmt, ...)`: Similar to `sprintf`, except the server supplies you with an appropriately allocated target variable

Let's put these functions into an example handler:

```
static int example_handler(request_rec *r)
{
    const char *original = "You can't edit this!";
    char *copy;
    int *integers;

    /* Allocate space for 10 integer values and set them all to zero. */
    integers = apr_pcalloc(r->pool, sizeof(int)*10);

    /* Create a copy of the 'original' variable that we can edit. */
    copy = apr_pstrdup(r->pool, original);
    return OK;
}
```

This is all well and good for our module, which won't need any pre-initialized variables or structures. However, if we wanted to initialize something early on, before the requests come rolling in, we could simply add a call to a function in our `register_hooks` function to sort it out:

```
static void register_hooks(apr_pool_t *pool)
{
    /* Call a function that initializes some stuff */
    example_init_function(pool);
    /* Create a hook in the request handler, so we get called when a request ar
    ap_hook_handler(example_handler, NULL, NULL, APR_HOOK_LAST);
}
```

In this pre-request initialization function we would not be using the same pool as we did when allocating resources for request-based functions. Instead, we would use the pool given to us by the server for allocating memory on a per-process based level.

Parsing request data

In our example module, we would like to add a feature, that checks which type of digest, MD5 or SHA1 the client would like to see. This could be solved by adding a query string to the request. A query string is typically comprised of several keys and values put together in a string, for instance `valueA=yes&valueB=no&valueC=maybe`. It is

---

[14]http://apr.apache.org/docs/apr/1.4/group__apr__pools.html#ga85f1e193c31d109affda72f9a92c6915
[15]http://apr.apache.org/docs/apr/1.4/group__apr__pools.html#gaf61c098ad258069d64cdf8c0a9369f9e
[16]http://apr.apache.org/docs/apr/1.4/group__apr__strings.html#gabc79e99ff19abbd7cfd18308c5f85d47
[17]http://apr.apache.org/docs/apr/1.4/group__apr__strings.html#ga3eca76b8d293c5c3f8021e45eda813d8

up to the module itself to parse these and get the data it requires. In our example, we'll be looking for a key called `digest`, and if set to `md5`, we'll produce an MD5 digest, otherwise we'll produce a SHA1 digest.

Since the introduction of Apache HTTP Server 2.4, parsing request data from GET and POST requests have never been easier. All we require to parse both GET and POST data is four simple lines:

```
apr_table_t *GET;
apr_array_header_t *POST;



ap_args_to_table(r, &GET);

ap_parse_form_data(r, NULL, &POST, -1, 8192);
```

In our specific example module, we're looking for the `digest` value from the query string, which now resides inside a table called `GET`. To extract this value, we need only perform a simple operation:

```
/* Get the "digest" key from the query string, if any. */
const char *digestType = apr_table_get(GET, "digest");

/* If no key was returned, we will set a default value instead. */
if (!digestType) digestType = "sha1";
```

The structures used for the POST and GET data are not exactly the same, so if we were to fetch a value from POST data instead of the query string, we would have to resort to a few more lines, as outlined in this example in the last chapter of this document.

Making an advanced handler

Now that we have learned how to parse form data and manage our resources, we can move on to creating an advanced version of our module, that spits out the MD5 or SHA1 digest of files:

```
static int example_handler(request_rec *r)
{
    int rc, exists;
    apr_finfo_t finfo;
    apr_file_t *file;
    char *filename;
    char buffer[256];
    apr_size_t readBytes;
    int n;
    apr_table_t *GET;
    apr_array_header_t *POST;
    const char *digestType;


    /* Check that the "example-handler" handler is being called. */
    if (!r->handler || strcmp(r->handler, "example-handler")) return (DECLINED)

    /* Figure out which file is being requested by removing the .sum from it */
    filename = apr_pstrdup(r->pool, r->filename);
```

```
filename[strlen(filename)-4] = 0; /* Cut off the last 4 characters. */

/* Figure out if the file we request a sum on exists and isn't a directory
rc = apr_stat(&finfo, filename, APR_FINFO_MIN, r->pool);
if (rc == APR_SUCCESS) {
    exists =
    (
        (finfo.filetype != APR_NOFILE)
    &&  !(finfo.filetype & APR_DIR)
    );
    if (!exists) return HTTP_NOT_FOUND; /* Return a 404 if not found. */
}
/* If apr_stat failed, we're probably not allowed to check this file. */
else return HTTP_FORBIDDEN;

/* Parse the GET and, optionally, the POST data sent to us */

ap_args_to_table(r, &GET);
ap_parse_form_data(r, NULL, &POST, -1, 8192);

/* Set the appropriate content type */
ap_set_content_type(r, "text/html");

/* Print a title and some general information */
ap_rprintf(r, "<h2>Information on %s:</h2>", filename);
ap_rprintf(r, "<b>Size:</b> %u bytes<br/>", finfo.size);

/* Get the digest type the client wants to see */
digestType = apr_table_get(GET, "digest");
if (!digestType) digestType = "MD5";


rc = apr_file_open(&file, filename, APR_READ, APR_OS_DEFAULT, r->pool);
if (rc == APR_SUCCESS) {

    /* Are we trying to calculate the MD5 or the SHA1 digest? */
    if (!strcasecmp(digestType, "md5")) {
        /* Calculate the MD5 sum of the file */
        union {
            char      chr[16];
            uint32_t  num[4];
        } digest;
        apr_md5_ctx_t md5;
        apr_md5_init(&md5);
        readBytes = 256;
        while ( apr_file_read(file, buffer, &readBytes) == APR_SUCCESS ) {
            apr_md5_update(&md5, buffer, readBytes);
        }
        apr_md5_final(digest.chr, &md5);

        /* Print out the MD5 digest */
        ap_rputs("<b>MD5: </b><code>", r);
        for (n = 0; n < APR_MD5_DIGESTSIZE/4; n++) {
```

```
                ap_rprintf(r, "%08x", digest.num[n]);
            }
            ap_rputs("</code>", r);
            /* Print a link to the SHA1 version */
            ap_rputs("<br/><a href='?digest=sha1'>View the SHA1 hash instead</a
        }
        else {
            /* Calculate the SHA1 sum of the file */
            union {
                char      chr[20];
                uint32_t  num[5];
            } digest;
            apr_sha1_ctx_t sha1;
            apr_sha1_init(&sha1);
            readBytes = 256;
            while ( apr_file_read(file, buffer, &readBytes) == APR_SUCCESS ) {
                apr_sha1_update(&sha1, buffer, readBytes);
            }
            apr_sha1_final(digest.chr, &sha1);

            /* Print out the SHA1 digest */
            ap_rputs("<b>SHA1: </b><code>", r);
            for (n = 0; n < APR_SHA1_DIGESTSIZE/4; n++) {
                ap_rprintf(r, "%08x", digest.num[n]);
            }
            ap_rputs("</code>", r);

            /* Print a link to the MD5 version */
            ap_rputs("<br/><a href='?digest=md5'>View the MD5 hash instead</a>"
        }
        apr_file_close(file);

    }
    /* Let the server know that we responded to this request. */
    return OK;
}
```

This version in its entirety can be found here: mod_example_2.c[18].

Adding configuration options

In this next segment of this document, we will turn our eyes away from the digest module and create a new example module, whose only function is to write out its own configuration. The purpose of this is to examine how the server works with configuration, and what happens when you start writing advanced configurations for your modules.

An introduction to configuration directives

If you are reading this, then you probably already know what a configuration directive is. Simply put, a directive is a way of telling an individual module (or a set of modules) how to behave, such as these directives control how mod_rewrite works:

---

[18]http://people.apache.org/~humbedooh/mods/examples/mod_example_2.c

```
RewriteEngine On
RewriteCond "%{REQUEST_URI}" "^/foo/bar"
RewriteRule "^/foo/bar/(.*)$" "/foobar?page=$1"
```

Each of these configuration directives are handled by a separate function, that parses the parameters given and sets up a configuration accordingly.

Making an example configuration

To begin with, we'll create a basic configuration in C-space:

```
typedef struct {
    int         enabled;     /* Enable or disable our module */
    const char *path;        /* Some path to...something */
    int         typeOfAction; /* 1 means action A, 2 means action B and so on *
} example_config;
```

Now, let's put this into perspective by creating a very small module that just prints out a hard-coded configuration. You'll notice that we use the `register_hooks` function for initializing the configuration values to their defaults:

```
typedef struct {
    int         enabled;     /* Enable or disable our module */
    const char *path;        /* Some path to...something */
    int         typeOfAction; /* 1 means action A, 2 means action B and so on *
} example_config;

static example_config config;

static int example_handler(request_rec *r)
{
    if (!r->handler || strcmp(r->handler, "example-handler")) return(DECLINED);
    ap_set_content_type(r, "text/plain");
    ap_rprintf(r, "Enabled: %u\n", config.enabled);
    ap_rprintf(r, "Path: %s\n", config.path);
    ap_rprintf(r, "TypeOfAction: %x\n", config.typeOfAction);
    return OK;
}

static void register_hooks(apr_pool_t *pool)
{
    config.enabled = 1;
    config.path = "/foo/bar";
    config.typeOfAction = 0x00;
    ap_hook_handler(example_handler, NULL, NULL, APR_HOOK_LAST);
}

/* Define our module as an entity and assign a function for registering hooks

module AP_MODULE_DECLARE_DATA   example_module =
{
    STANDARD20_MODULE_STUFF,
    NULL,              /* Per-directory configuration handler */
```

```
    NULL,                   /* Merge handler for per-directory configurations */
    NULL,                   /* Per-server configuration handler */
    NULL,                   /* Merge handler for per-server configurations */
    NULL,                   /* Any directives we may have for httpd */
    register_hooks    /* Our hook registering function */
};
```

So far so good. To access our new handler, we could add the following to our configuration:

```
<Location "/example">
    SetHandler example-handler
</Location>
```

When we visit, we'll see our current configuration being spit out by our module.

Registering directives with the server

What if we want to change our configuration, not by hard-coding new values into the module, but by using either the httpd.conf file or possibly a .htaccess file? It's time to let the server know that we want this to be possible. To do so, we must first change our *name tag* to include a reference to the configuration directives we want to register with the server:

```
module AP_MODULE_DECLARE_DATA    example_module =
{
    STANDARD20_MODULE_STUFF,
    NULL,                   /* Per-directory configuration handler */
    NULL,                   /* Merge handler for per-directory configurations */
    NULL,                   /* Per-server configuration handler */
    NULL,                   /* Merge handler for per-server configurations */
    example_directives, /* Any directives we may have for httpd */
    register_hooks    /* Our hook registering function */
};
```

This will tell the server that we are now accepting directives from the configuration files, and that the structure called example_directives holds information on what our directives are and how they work. Since we have three different variables in our module configuration, we will add a structure with three directives and a NULL at the end:

```
static const command_rec        example_directives[] =
{
    AP_INIT_TAKE1("exampleEnabled", example_set_enabled, NULL, RSRC_CONF, "Enab
    AP_INIT_TAKE1("examplePath", example_set_path, NULL, RSRC_CONF, "The path t
    AP_INIT_TAKE2("exampleAction", example_set_action, NULL, RSRC_CONF, "Specia
    { NULL }
};
```

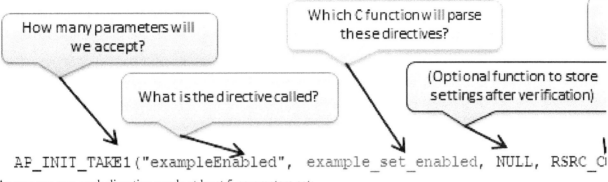

As you can see, each directive needs at least 5 parameters set:

1. AP_INIT_TAKE1[19]: This is a macro that tells the server that this directive takes one and only one argument. If we required two arguments, we could use the macro AP_INIT_TAKE2[20] and so on (refer to httpd_conf.h for more macros).

2. exampleEnabled: This is the name of our directive. More precisely, it is what the user must put in his/her configuration in order to invoke a configuration change in our module.

3. example_set_enabled: This is a reference to a C function that parses the directive and sets the configuration accordingly. We will discuss how to make this in the following paragraph.

4. RSRC_CONF: This tells the server where the directive is permitted. We'll go into details on this value in the later chapters, but for now, RSRC_CONF means that the server will only accept these directives in a server context.

5. "Enable or disable....": This is simply a brief description of what the directive does.

(The "missing" parameter in our definition, which is usually set to NULL, is an optional function that can be run after the initial function to parse the arguments have been run. This is usually omitted, as the function for verifying arguments might as well be used to set them.)

The directive handler function

Now that we have told the server to expect some directives for our module, it's time to make a few functions for handling these. What the server reads in the configuration file(s) is text, and so naturally, what it passes along to our directive handler is one or more strings, that we ourselves need to recognize and act upon. You'll notice, that since we set our exampleAction directive to accept two arguments, its C function also has an additional parameter defined:

```
/* Handler for the "exampleEnabled" directive */
const char *example_set_enabled(cmd_parms *cmd, void *cfg, const char *arg)
{
    if(!strcasecmp(arg, "on")) config.enabled = 1;
    else config.enabled = 0;
    return NULL;
}

/* Handler for the "examplePath" directive */
const char *example_set_path(cmd_parms *cmd, void *cfg, const char *arg)
{
```

---

[19]http://ci.apache.org/projects/httpd/trunk/doxygen/group__APACHE__CORE__CONFIG.html#ga07c7d22ae17805e61204463326cf9c34
[20]http://ci.apache.org/projects/httpd/trunk/doxygen/group__APACHE__CORE__CONFIG.html#gafaec43534fcf200f37d9fecbf9247c21

```
        config.path = arg;
        return NULL;
}


/* Handler for the "exampleAction" directive */
/* Let's pretend this one takes one argument (file or db), and a second (deny o
/* and we store it in a bit-wise manner. */
const char *example_set_action(cmd_parms *cmd, void *cfg, const char *arg1, con
{
        if(!strcasecmp(arg1, "file")) config.typeOfAction = 0x01;
        else config.typeOfAction = 0x02;

        if(!strcasecmp(arg2, "deny")) config.typeOfAction += 0x10;
        else config.typeOfAction += 0x20;
        return NULL;
}
```

Putting it all together

Now that we have our directives set up, and handlers configured for them, we can assemble our module into one big file:

```
/* mod_example_config_simple.c: */
#include <stdio.h>
#include "apr_hash.h"
#include "ap_config.h"
#include "ap_provider.h"
#include "httpd.h"
#include "http_core.h"
#include "http_config.h"
#include "http_log.h"
#include "http_protocol.h"
#include "http_request.h"

/*
 ==========================================================================
 Our configuration prototype and declaration:
 ==========================================================================
 */
typedef struct {
    int         enabled;      /* Enable or disable our module */
    const char *path;         /* Some path to...something */
    int         typeOfAction; /* 1 means action A, 2 means action B and so on *
} example_config;

static example_config config;

/*
 ==========================================================================
 Our directive handlers:
 ==========================================================================
 */
/* Handler for the "exampleEnabled" directive */
```

```
const char *example_set_enabled(cmd_parms *cmd, void *cfg, const char *arg)
{
    if(!strcasecmp(arg, "on")) config.enabled = 1;
    else config.enabled = 0;
    return NULL;
}


/* Handler for the "examplePath" directive */
const char *example_set_path(cmd_parms *cmd, void *cfg, const char *arg)
{
    config.path = arg;
    return NULL;
}


/* Handler for the "exampleAction" directive */
/* Let's pretend this one takes one argument (file or db), and a second (deny o
/* and we store it in a bit-wise manner. */
const char *example_set_action(cmd_parms *cmd, void *cfg, const char *arg1, con
{
    if(!strcasecmp(arg1, "file")) config.typeOfAction = 0x01;
    else config.typeOfAction = 0x02;

    if(!strcasecmp(arg2, "deny")) config.typeOfAction += 0x10;
    else config.typeOfAction += 0x20;
    return NULL;
}


/*
 ===============================================================================
 The directive structure for our name tag:
 ===============================================================================
 */
static const command_rec        example_directives[] =
{
    AP_INIT_TAKE1("exampleEnabled", example_set_enabled, NULL, RSRC_CONF, "Enab
    AP_INIT_TAKE1("examplePath", example_set_path, NULL, RSRC_CONF, "The path t
    AP_INIT_TAKE2("exampleAction", example_set_action, NULL, RSRC_CONF, "Specia
    { NULL }
};
/*
 ===============================================================================
 Our module handler:
 ===============================================================================
 */
static int example_handler(request_rec *r)
{
    if(!r->handler || strcmp(r->handler, "example-handler")) return(DECLINED);
    ap_set_content_type(r, "text/plain");
    ap_rprintf(r, "Enabled: %u\n", config.enabled);
    ap_rprintf(r, "Path: %s\n", config.path);
    ap_rprintf(r, "TypeOfAction: %x\n", config.typeOfAction);
    return OK;
}
```

```
/*
  ==============================================================================
  The hook registration function (also initializes the default config values):
  ==============================================================================
 */
static void register_hooks(apr_pool_t *pool)
{
    config.enabled = 1;
    config.path = "/foo/bar";
    config.typeOfAction = 3;
    ap_hook_handler(example_handler, NULL, NULL, APR_HOOK_LAST);
}
/*
  ==============================================================================
  Our module name tag:
  ==============================================================================
 */
module AP_MODULE_DECLARE_DATA   example_module =
{
    STANDARD20_MODULE_STUFF,
    NULL,                /* Per-directory configuration handler */
    NULL,                /* Merge handler for per-directory configurations */
    NULL,                /* Per-server configuration handler */
    NULL,                /* Merge handler for per-server configurations */
    example_directives, /* Any directives we may have for httpd */
    register_hooks       /* Our hook registering function */
};
```

In our httpd.conf file, we can now change the hard-coded configuration by adding a few lines:

```
ExampleEnabled On
ExamplePath "/usr/bin/foo"
ExampleAction file allow
```

And thus we apply the configuration, visit /example on our web site, and we see the configuration has adapted to what we wrote in our configuration file.

Context aware configurations

Introduction to context aware configurations

In Apache HTTP Server 2.4, different URLs, virtual hosts, directories etc can have very different meanings to the user of the server, and thus different contexts within which modules must operate. For example, let's assume you have this configuration set up for mod_rewrite:

```
<Directory "/var/www">
    RewriteCond "%{HTTP_HOST}" "^example.com$"
    RewriteRule "(.*)" "http://www.example.com/$1"
</Directory>
<Directory "/var/www/sub">
    RewriteRule "^foobar$" "index.php?foobar=true"
</Directory>
```

In this example, you will have set up two different contexts for mod_rewrite:

1. Inside `/var/www`, all requests for `http://example.com` must go to `http://www.example.com`

2. Inside `/var/www/sub`, all requests for `foobar` must go to `index.php?foobar=true`

If mod_rewrite (or the entire server for that matter) wasn't context aware, then these rewrite rules would just apply to every and any request made, regardless of where and how they were made, but since the module can pull the context specific configuration straight from the server, it does not need to know itself, which of the directives are valid in this context, since the server takes care of this.

So how does a module get the specific configuration for the server, directory or location in question? It does so by making one simple call:

```
example_config *config = (example_config*) ap_get_module_config(r->per_dir_conf
```

That's it! Of course, a whole lot goes on behind the scenes, which we will discuss in this chapter, starting with how the server came to know what our configuration looks like, and how it came to be set up as it is in the specific context.

Our basic configuration setup

In this chapter, we will be working with a slightly modified version of our previous context structure. We will set a `context` variable that we can use to track which context configuration is being used by the server in various places:

```
typedef struct {
    char        context[256];
    char        path[256];
    int         typeOfAction;
    int         enabled;
} example_config;
```

Our handler for requests will also be modified, yet still very simple:

```
static int example_handler(request_rec *r)
{
    if(!r->handler || strcmp(r->handler, "example-handler")) return(DECLINED);
    example_config *config = (example_config*) ap_get_module_config(r->per_dir_
    ap_set_content_type(r, "text/plain");
    ap_rprintf("Enabled: %u\n", config->enabled);
    ap_rprintf("Path: %s\n", config->path);
    ap_rprintf("TypeOfAction: %x\n", config->typeOfAction);
    ap_rprintf("Context: %s\n", config->context);
    return OK;
}
```

Choosing a context

Before we can start making our module context aware, we must first define, which contexts we will accept. As we saw in the previous chapter, defining a directive required five elements be set:

```
AP_INIT_TAKE1("exampleEnabled", example_set_enabled, NULL, RSRC_CONF, "Enable o
```

The RSRC_CONF definition told the server that we would only allow this directive in a global server context, but since we are now trying out a context aware version of our module, we should set this to something more lenient, namely the value ACCESS_CONF, which lets us use the directive inside <Directory> and <Location> blocks. For more control over the placement of your directives, you can combine the following restrictions together to form a specific rule:

- RSRC_CONF: Allow in .conf files (not .htaccess) outside <Directory> or <Location>
- ACCESS_CONF: Allow in .conf files (not .htaccess) inside <Directory> or <Location>
- OR_OPTIONS: Allow in .conf files and .htaccess when AllowOverride Options is set
- OR_FILEINFO: Allow in .conf files and .htaccess when AllowOverride FileInfo is set
- OR_AUTHCFG: Allow in .conf files and .htaccess when AllowOverride AuthConfig is set
- OR_INDEXES: Allow in .conf files and .htaccess when AllowOverride Indexes is set
- OR_ALL: Allow anywhere in .conf files and .htaccess

Using the server to allocate configuration slots

A much smarter way to manage your configurations is by letting the server help you create them. To do so, we must first start off by changing our *name tag* to let the server know, that it should assist us in creating and managing our configurations. Since we have chosen the per-directory (or per-location) context for our module configurations, we'll add a per-directory creator and merger function reference in our tag:

```
module AP_MODULE_DECLARE_DATA    example_module =
{
    STANDARD20_MODULE_STUFF,
    create_dir_conf, /* Per-directory configuration handler */
    merge_dir_conf,  /* Merge handler for per-directory configurations */
    NULL,            /* Per-server configuration handler */
    NULL,            /* Merge handler for per-server configurations */
    directives,      /* Any directives we may have for httpd */
    register_hooks   /* Our hook registering function */
};
```

Creating new context configurations

Now that we have told the server to help us create and manage configurations, our first step is to make a function for creating new, blank configurations. We do so by creating the function we just referenced in our name tag as the Per-directory configuration handler:

```
void *create_dir_conf(apr_pool_t *pool, char *context) {
    context = context ? context : "(undefined context)";
    example_config *cfg = apr_pcalloc(pool, sizeof(example_config));
    if(cfg) {
        /* Set some default values */
        strcpy(cfg->context, context);
        cfg->enabled = 0;
        cfg->path = "/foo/bar";
        cfg->typeOfAction = 0x11;
    }
    return cfg;
}
```

Merging configurations

Our next step in creating a context aware configuration is merging configurations. This part of the process particularly applies to scenarios where you have a parent configuration and a child, such as the following:

```
<Directory "/var/www">
    ExampleEnabled On
    ExamplePath "/foo/bar"
    ExampleAction file allow
</Directory>
<Directory "/var/www/subdir">
    ExampleAction file deny
</Directory>
```

In this example, it is natural to assume that the directory /var/www/subdir should inherit the values set for the /var/www directory, as we did not specify an ExampleEnabled nor an ExamplePath for this directory. The server does not presume to know if this is true, but cleverly does the following:

1. Creates a new configuration for /var/www

2. Sets the configuration values according to the directives given for /var/www

3. Creates a new configuration for /var/www/subdir

4. Sets the configuration values according to the directives given for /var/www/subdir

5. **Proposes a merge** of the two configurations into a new configuration for /var/www/subdir

This proposal is handled by the merge_dir_conf function we referenced in our name tag. The purpose of this function is to assess the two configurations and decide how they are to be merged:

```
void *merge_dir_conf(apr_pool_t *pool, void *BASE, void *ADD) {
    example_config *base = (example_config *) BASE ; /* This is what was set in
    example_config *add = (example_config *) ADD ;   /* This is what is set in
    example_config *conf = (example_config *) create_dir_conf(pool, "Merged con

    /* Merge configurations */
    conf->enabled = ( add->enabled == 0 ) ? base->enabled : add->enabled ;
    conf->typeOfAction = add->typeOfAction ? add->typeOfAction : base->typeOfAc
    strcpy(conf->path, strlen(add->path) ? add->path : base->path);

    return conf ;
}
```

Trying out our new context aware configurations

Now, let's try putting it all together to create a new module that is context aware. First off, we'll create a configuration that lets us test how the module works:

```
<Location "/a">
    SetHandler example-handler
    ExampleEnabled on
    ExamplePath "/foo/bar"
```

```
        ExampleAction file allow
</Location>

<Location "/a/b">
        ExampleAction file deny
        ExampleEnabled off
</Location>

<Location "/a/b/c">
        ExampleAction db deny
        ExamplePath "/foo/bar/baz"
        ExampleEnabled on
</Location>
```

Then we'll assemble our module code. Note, that since we are now using our name tag as reference when fetching configurations in our handler, I have added some prototypes to keep the compiler happy:

```
/*$6
 +++++++++++++++++++++++++++++++++++++++++++++++++++++++++++++++++++++++++++++++
 * mod_example_config.c
 +++++++++++++++++++++++++++++++++++++++++++++++++++++++++++++++++++++++++++++++
 */


#include <stdio.h>
#include "apr_hash.h"
#include "ap_config.h"
#include "ap_provider.h"
#include "httpd.h"
#include "http_core.h"
#include "http_config.h"
#include "http_log.h"
#include "http_protocol.h"
#include "http_request.h"

/*$1
 ~~~~~~~~~~~~~~~~~~~~~~~~~~~~~~~~~~~~~~~~~~~~~~~~~~~~~~~~~~~~~~~~~~~~~~~~~~~~~~~~~
    Configuration structure
 ~~~~~~~~~~~~~~~~~~~~~~~~~~~~~~~~~~~~~~~~~~~~~~~~~~~~~~~~~~~~~~~~~~~~~~~~~~~~~~~~~
 */

typedef struct
{
    char    context[256];
    char    path[256];
    int     typeOfAction;
    int     enabled;
} example_config;

/*$1
 ~~~~~~~~~~~~~~~~~~~~~~~~~~~~~~~~~~~~~~~~~~~~~~~~~~~~~~~~~~~~~~~~~~~~~~~~~~~~~~~~~
    Prototypes
 ~~~~~~~~~~~~~~~~~~~~~~~~~~~~~~~~~~~~~~~~~~~~~~~~~~~~~~~~~~~~~~~~~~~~~~~~~~~~~~~~~
```

```
 */

static int     example_handler(request_rec *r);
const char     *example_set_enabled(cmd_parms *cmd, void *cfg, const char *arg);
const char     *example_set_path(cmd_parms *cmd, void *cfg, const char *arg);
const char     *example_set_action(cmd_parms *cmd, void *cfg, const char *arg1,
void           *create_dir_conf(apr_pool_t *pool, char *context);
void           *merge_dir_conf(apr_pool_t *pool, void *BASE, void *ADD);
static void    register_hooks(apr_pool_t *pool);

/*$1
  ~~~~~~~~~~~~~~~~~~~~~~~~~~~~~~~~~~~~~~~~~~~~~~~~~~~~~~~~~~~~~~~~~~~~~~~~~~~~~~~~~~
    Configuration directives
  ~~~~~~~~~~~~~~~~~~~~~~~~~~~~~~~~~~~~~~~~~~~~~~~~~~~~~~~~~~~~~~~~~~~~~~~~~~~~~~~~~~
 */

static const command_rec    directives[] =
{
    AP_INIT_TAKE1("exampleEnabled", example_set_enabled, NULL, ACCESS_CONF, "En
    AP_INIT_TAKE1("examplePath", example_set_path, NULL, ACCESS_CONF, "The path
    AP_INIT_TAKE2("exampleAction", example_set_action, NULL, ACCESS_CONF, "Spec
    { NULL }
};

/*$1
  ~~~~~~~~~~~~~~~~~~~~~~~~~~~~~~~~~~~~~~~~~~~~~~~~~~~~~~~~~~~~~~~~~~~~~~~~~~~~~~~~~~
    Our name tag
  ~~~~~~~~~~~~~~~~~~~~~~~~~~~~~~~~~~~~~~~~~~~~~~~~~~~~~~~~~~~~~~~~~~~~~~~~~~~~~~~~~~
 */

module AP_MODULE_DECLARE_DATA    example_module =
{
    STANDARD20_MODULE_STUFF,
    create_dir_conf,    /* Per-directory configuration handler */
    merge_dir_conf,     /* Merge handler for per-directory configurations */
    NULL,               /* Per-server configuration handler */
    NULL,               /* Merge handler for per-server configurations */
    directives,         /* Any directives we may have for httpd */
    register_hooks      /* Our hook registering function */
};

/*
  ==============================================================================
    Hook registration function
  ==============================================================================
 */
static void register_hooks(apr_pool_t *pool)
{
    ap_hook_handler(example_handler, NULL, NULL, APR_HOOK_LAST);
}

/*
  ==============================================================================
```

```
    Our example web service handler
    ============================================================================
 */
static int example_handler(request_rec *r)
{
    if(!r->handler || strcmp(r->handler, "example-handler")) return(DECLINED);

    /*~~~~~~~~~~~~~~~~~~~~~~~~~~~~~~~~~~~~~~~~~~~~~~~~~~~~~~~~~~~~~~~~~~~~~~~~~~~
    example_config    *config = (example_config *) ap_get_module_config(r->per_
    /*~~~~~~~~~~~~~~~~~~~~~~~~~~~~~~~~~~~~~~~~~~~~~~~~~~~~~~~~~~~~~~~~~~~~~~~~~~~

    ap_set_content_type(r, "text/plain");
    ap_rprintf(r, "Enabled: %u\n", config->enabled);
    ap_rprintf(r, "Path: %s\n", config->path);
    ap_rprintf(r, "TypeOfAction: %x\n", config->typeOfAction);
    ap_rprintf(r, "Context: %s\n", config->context);
    return OK;
}


/*
    ============================================================================
    Handler for the "exampleEnabled" directive
    ============================================================================
 */
const char *example_set_enabled(cmd_parms *cmd, void *cfg, const char *arg)
{
    /*~~~~~~~~~~~~~~~~~~~~~~~~~~~~~~~~~~~~~~~~~~~~~~~*/
    example_config    *conf = (example_config *) cfg;
    /*~~~~~~~~~~~~~~~~~~~~~~~~~~~~~~~~~~~~~~~~~~~~~~~*/

    if(conf)
    {
        if(!strcasecmp(arg, "on"))
            conf->enabled = 1;
        else
            conf->enabled = 0;
    }

    return NULL;
}


/*
    ============================================================================
    Handler for the "examplePath" directive
    ============================================================================
 */
const char *example_set_path(cmd_parms *cmd, void *cfg, const char *arg)
{
    /*~~~~~~~~~~~~~~~~~~~~~~~~~~~~~~~~~~~~~~~~~~~~~~~*/
    example_config    *conf = (example_config *) cfg;
    /*~~~~~~~~~~~~~~~~~~~~~~~~~~~~~~~~~~~~~~~~~~~~~~~*/

    if(conf)
```

```
        {
            strcpy(conf->path, arg);
        }

        return NULL;
}


/*
  ===============================================================================
    Handler for the "exampleAction" directive ;
    Let's pretend this one takes one argument (file or db), and a second (deny
    and we store it in a bit-wise manner.
  ===============================================================================
 */
const char *example_set_action(cmd_parms *cmd, void *cfg, const char *arg1, con
{
    /*~~~~~~~~~~~~~~~~~~~~~~~~~~~~~~~~~~~~~~~~~~~~~~*/
    example_config   *conf = (example_config *) cfg;
    /*~~~~~~~~~~~~~~~~~~~~~~~~~~~~~~~~~~~~~~~~~~~~~~*/

    if(conf)
    {
        {
            if(!strcasecmp(arg1, "file"))
                conf->typeOfAction = 0x01;
            else
                conf->typeOfAction = 0x02;
            if(!strcasecmp(arg2, "deny"))
                conf->typeOfAction += 0x10;
            else
                conf->typeOfAction += 0x20;
        }
    }

    return NULL;
}


/*
  ===============================================================================
    Function for creating new configurations for per-directory contexts
  ===============================================================================
 */
void *create_dir_conf(apr_pool_t *pool, char *context)
{
    context = context ? context : "Newly created configuration";

    /*~~~~~~~~~~~~~~~~~~~~~~~~~~~~~~~~~~~~~~~~~~~~~~~~~~~~~~~~~~~~~~~~~~~~~~*/
    example_config   *cfg = apr_pcalloc(pool, sizeof(example_config));
    /*~~~~~~~~~~~~~~~~~~~~~~~~~~~~~~~~~~~~~~~~~~~~~~~~~~~~~~~~~~~~~~~~~~~~~~*/

    if(cfg)
    {
        {
```

```
        /* Set some default values */
        strcpy(cfg->context, context);
        cfg->enabled = 0;
        memset(cfg->path, 0, 256);
        cfg->typeOfAction = 0x00;
    }
}

return cfg;
}

/*
 ==============================================================================
    Merging function for configurations
 ==============================================================================
 */
void *merge_dir_conf(apr_pool_t *pool, void *BASE, void *ADD)
{
    /*~~~~~~~~~~~~~~~~~~~~~~~~~~~~~~~~~~~~~~~~~~~~~~~~~~~~~~~~~~~~~~~~~~~~~~~~*/
    example_config    *base = (example_config *) BASE;
    example_config    *add = (example_config *) ADD;
    example_config    *conf = (example_config *) create_dir_conf(pool, "Merged
    /*~~~~~~~~~~~~~~~~~~~~~~~~~~~~~~~~~~~~~~~~~~~~~~~~~~~~~~~~~~~~~~~~~~~~~~~~*/

    conf->enabled = (add->enabled == 0) ? base->enabled : add->enabled;
    conf->typeOfAction = add->typeOfAction ? add->typeOfAction : base->typeOfAc
    strcpy(conf->path, strlen(add->path) ? add->path : base->path);
    return conf;
}
```

Summing up

We have now looked at how to create simple modules for Apache HTTP Server 2.4 and configuring them. What you do next is entirely up to you, but it is my hope that something valuable has come out of reading this documentation. If you have questions on how to further develop modules, you are welcome to join our mailing lists[21] or check out the rest of our documentation for further tips.

Some useful snippets of code

Retrieve variables from POST form data

```
typedef struct {
    const char *key;
    const char *value;
} keyValuePair;

keyValuePair *readPost(request_rec *r) {
    apr_array_header_t *pairs = NULL;
    apr_off_t len;
    apr_size_t size;
```

---

[21]http://httpd.apache.org/lists.html

```
    int res;
    int i = 0;
    char *buffer;
    keyValuePair *kvp;

    res = ap_parse_form_data(r, NULL, &pairs, -1, HUGE_STRING_LEN);
    if (res != OK || !pairs) return NULL; /* Return NULL if we failed or if the
    kvp = apr_pcalloc(r->pool, sizeof(keyValuePair) * (pairs->nelts + 1));
    while (pairs && !apr_is_empty_array(pairs)) {
        ap_form_pair_t *pair = (ap_form_pair_t *) apr_array_pop(pairs);
        apr_brigade_length(pair->value, 1, &len);
        size = (apr_size_t) len;
        buffer = apr_palloc(r->pool, size + 1);
        apr_brigade_flatten(pair->value, buffer, &size);
        buffer[len] = 0;
        kvp[i].key = apr_pstrdup(r->pool, pair->name);
        kvp[i].value = buffer;
        i++;
    }
    return kvp;
}


static int example_handler(request_rec *r)
{
    /*~~~~~~~~~~~~~~~~~~~~~~~~*/
    keyValuePair *formData;
    /*~~~~~~~~~~~~~~~~~~~~~~~~*/

    formData = readPost(r);
    if (formData) {
        int i;
        for (i = 0; &formData[i]; i++) {
            if (formData[i].key && formData[i].value) {
                ap_rprintf(r, "%s = %s\n", formData[i].key, formData[i].value);
            } else if (formData[i].key) {
                ap_rprintf(r, "%s\n", formData[i].key);
            } else if (formData[i].value) {
                ap_rprintf(r, "= %s\n", formData[i].value);
            } else {
                break;
            }
        }
    }
    return OK;
}
```

Printing out every HTTP header received

```
static int example_handler(request_rec *r)
{
    /*~~~~~~~~~~~~~~~~~~~~~~~~~~~~~~~~~~~~~~~~~~~~~*/
    const apr_array_header_t    *fields;
    int                         i;
```

```
    apr_table_entry_t               *e = 0;
    /*~~~~~~~~~~~~~~~~~~~~~~~~~~~~~~~~~~~~~~~*/

    fields = apr_table_elts(r->headers_in);
    e = (apr_table_entry_t *) fields->elts;
    for(i = 0; i < fields->nelts; i++) {
        ap_rprintf(r, "%s: %s\n", e[i].key, e[i].val);
    }
    return OK;
}
```

Reading the request body into memory

```
static int util_read(request_rec *r, const char **rbuf, apr_off_t *size)
{
    /*~~~~~~~~~*/
    int rc = OK;
    /*~~~~~~~~~*/

    if((rc = ap_setup_client_block(r, REQUEST_CHUNKED_ERROR))) {
        return(rc);
    }

    if(ap_should_client_block(r)) {

        /*~~~~~~~~~~~~~~~~~~~~~~~~~~~~~~~~~~~~~~~*/
        char            argsbuffer[HUGE_STRING_LEN];
        apr_off_t    rsize, len_read, rpos = 0;
        apr_off_t length = r->remaining;
        /*~~~~~~~~~~~~~~~~~~~~~~~~~~~~~~~~~~~~~~~*/

        *rbuf = (const char *) apr_pcalloc(r->pool, (apr_size_t) (length + 1));
        *size = length;
        while((len_read = ap_get_client_block(r, argsbuffer, sizeof(argsbuffer)
            if((rpos + len_read) > length) {
                rsize = length - rpos;
            }
            else {
                rsize = len_read;
            }

            memcpy((char *) *rbuf + rpos, argsbuffer, (size_t) rsize);
            rpos += rsize;
        }
    }
    return(rc);
}

static int example_handler(request_rec *r)
{
    /*~~~~~~~~~~~~~~~~~~*/
    apr_off_t    size;
    const char  *buffer;
```

```
/*~~~~~~~~~~~~~~~~~*/

if(util_read(r, &buffer, &size) == OK) {
    ap_rprintf(r, "We read a request body that was %" APR_OFF_T_FMT " bytes
}
return OK;
}
```

11.5   Documenting code in Apache 2.4

Apache 2.4 uses Doxygen[22] to document the APIs and global variables in the code. This will explain the basics of how to document using Doxygen.

Brief Description

To start a documentation block, use /**
To end a documentation block, use */

In the middle of the block, there are multiple tags we can use:

```
Description of this functions purpose
@param parameter_name description
@return description
@deffunc signature of the function
```

The `deffunc` is not always necessary. DoxyGen does not have a full parser in it, so any prototype that use a macro in the return type declaration is too complex for scandoc. Those functions require a `deffunc`. An example (using > rather than >):

```
/**
 * return the final element of the pathname
 * @param pathname The path to get the final element of
 * @return the final element of the path
 * @tip Examples:
 * <pre>
 * "/foo/bar/gum" -&gt; "gum"
 * "/foo/bar/gum/" -&gt; ""
 * "gum" -&gt; "gum"
 * "wi\\n32\\stuff" -&gt; "stuff"
 * </pre>
 * @deffunc const char * ap_filename_of_pathname(const char *pathname)
 */
```

At the top of the header file, always include:

```
/**
 * @package Name of library header
 */
```

Doxygen uses a new HTML file for each package. The HTML files are named {Name_of_library_header}.html, so try to be concise with your names.

For a further discussion of the possibilities please refer to the Doxygen site[23].

---

[22]http://www.doxygen.org/
[23]http://www.doxygen.org/

11.6 Hook Functions in the Apache HTTP Server 2.x

 Warning

This document is still in development and may be partially out of date.

In general, a hook function is one that the Apache HTTP Server will call at some point during the processing of a request. Modules can provide functions that are called, and specify when they get called in comparison to other modules.

Creating a hook function

In order to create a new hook, four things need to be done:

Declare the hook function

Use the AP_DECLARE_HOOK macro, which needs to be given the return type of the hook function, the name of the hook, and the arguments. For example, if the hook returns an int and takes a request_rec * and an int and is called do_something, then declare it like this:

```
AP_DECLARE_HOOK(int, do_something, (request_rec *r, int n))
```

This should go in a header which modules will include if they want to use the hook.

Create the hook structure

Each source file that exports a hook has a private structure which is used to record the module functions that use the hook. This is declared as follows:

```
APR_HOOK_STRUCT(
  APR_HOOK_LINK(do_something)
  ...
)
```

Implement the hook caller

The source file that exports the hook has to implement a function that will call the hook. There are currently three possible ways to do this. In all cases, the calling function is called ap_run_hookname().

Void hooks

If the return value of a hook is void, then all the hooks are called, and the caller is implemented like this:

```
AP_IMPLEMENT_HOOK_VOID(do_something, (request_rec *r, int n), (r, n))
```

The second and third arguments are the dummy argument declaration and the dummy arguments as they will be used when calling the hook. In other words, this macro expands to something like this:

```
void ap_run_do_something(request_rec *r, int n)
{
    ...
    do_something(r, n);
}
```

Hooks that return a value

If the hook returns a value, then it can either be run until the first hook that does something interesting, like so:

```
AP_IMPLEMENT_HOOK_RUN_FIRST(int, do_something, (request_rec *r, int n), (r, n),
```

The first hook that does *not* return DECLINED stops the loop and its return value is returned from the hook caller. Note that DECLINED is the traditional hook return value meaning "I didn't do anything", but it can be whatever suits you.

Alternatively, all hooks can be run until an error occurs. This boils down to permitting *two* return values, one of which means "I did something, and it was OK" and the other meaning "I did nothing". The first function that returns a value other than one of those two stops the loop, and its return is the return value. Declare these like so:

```
AP_IMPLEMENT_HOOK_RUN_ALL(int, do_something, (request_rec *r, int n), (r, n), O
```

Again, OK and DECLINED are the traditional values. You can use what you want.

Call the hook callers

At appropriate moments in the code, call the hook caller, like so:

```
int n, ret;
request_rec *r;

ret=ap_run_do_something(r, n);
```

Hooking the hook

A module that wants a hook to be called needs to do two things.

Implement the hook function

Include the appropriate header, and define a static function of the correct type:

```
static int my_something_doer(request_rec *r, int n)
{
    ...
    return OK;
}
```

Add a hook registering function

During initialisation, the server will call each modules hook registering function, which is included in the module structure:

```
static void my_register_hooks()
{
    ap_hook_do_something(my_something_doer, NULL, NULL, APR_HOOK_MIDDLE);
}

mode MODULE_VAR_EXPORT my_module =
{
    ...
    my_register_hooks          /* register hooks */
};
```

Controlling hook calling order

In the example above, we didn't use the three arguments in the hook registration function that control calling order. There are two mechanisms for doing this. The first, rather crude, method, allows us to specify roughly where the hook is run relative to other modules. The final argument control this. There are three possible values: `APR_HOOK_FIRST`, `APR_HOOK_MIDDLE` and `APR_HOOK_LAST`.

All modules using any particular value may be run in any order relative to each other, but, of course, all modules using `APR_HOOK_FIRST` will be run before `APR_HOOK_MIDDLE` which are before `APR_HOOK_LAST`. Modules that don't care when they are run should use `APR_HOOK_MIDDLE`. *These values are spaced out, so that positions like `APR_HOOK_FIRST-2` are possible to hook slightly earlier than other functions.*

Note that there are two more values, `APR_HOOK_REALLY_FIRST` and `APR_HOOK_REALLY_LAST`. These should only be used by the hook exporter.

The other method allows finer control. When a module knows that it must be run before (or after) some other modules, it can specify them by name. The second (third) argument is a NULL-terminated array of strings consisting of the names of modules that must be run before (after) the current module. For example, suppose we want `"mod_xyz.c"` and `"mod_abc.c"` to run before we do, then we'd hook as follows:

```
static void register_hooks()
{
    static const char * const aszPre[] = { "mod_xyz.c", "mod_abc.c", NULL };

    ap_hook_do_something(my_something_doer, aszPre, NULL, APR_HOOK_MIDDLE);
}
```

Note that the sort used to achieve this is stable, so ordering set by `APR_HOOK_ORDER` is preserved, as far as is possible.

11.7 Converting Modules from Apache 1.3 to Apache 2.0

This is a first attempt at writing the lessons I learned when trying to convert the `mod_mmap_static` module to Apache 2.0. It's by no means definitive and probably won't even be correct in some ways, but it's a start.

The easier changes ...

Cleanup Routines

These now need to be of type `apr_status_t` and return a value of that type. Normally the return value will be `APR_SUCCESS` unless there is some need to signal an error in the cleanup. Be aware that even though you signal an error not all code yet checks and acts upon the error.

Initialisation Routines

These should now be renamed to better signify where they sit in the overall process. So the name gets a small change from `mmap_init` to `mmap_post_config`. The arguments passed have undergone a radical change and now look like

- `apr_pool_t *p`
- `apr_pool_t *plog`
- `apr_pool_t *ptemp`
- `server_rec *s`

Data Types

A lot of the data types have been moved into the APR[24]. This means that some have had a name change, such as the one shown above. The following is a brief list of some of the changes that you are likely to have to make.

- `pool` becomes `apr_pool_t`
- `table` becomes `apr_table_t`

The messier changes...

Register Hooks

The new architecture uses a series of hooks to provide for calling your functions. These you'll need to add to your module by way of a new function, `static void register_hooks(void)`. The function is really reasonably straightforward once you understand what needs to be done. Each function that needs calling at some stage in the processing of a request needs to be registered, handlers do not. There are a number of phases where functions can be added, and for each you can specify with a high degree of control the relative order that the function will be called in.

This is the code that was added to `mod_mmap_static`:

---

[24]http://apr.apache.org/

```
static void register_hooks(void)
{
    static const char * const aszPre[]={ "http_core.c",NULL };
    ap_hook_post_config(mmap_post_config,NULL,NULL,HOOK_MIDDLE);
    ap_hook_translate_name(mmap_static_xlat,aszPre,NULL,HOOK_LAST);
};
```

This registers 2 functions that need to be called, one in the `post_config` stage (virtually every module will need this one) and one for the `translate_name` phase. note that while there are different function names the format of each is identical. So what is the format?

```
ap_hook_phase_name(function_name, predecessors, successors, position);
```

There are 3 hook positions defined...

- HOOK_FIRST
- HOOK_MIDDLE
- HOOK_LAST

To define the position you use the position and then modify it with the predecessors and successors. Each of the modifiers can be a list of functions that should be called, either before the function is run (predecessors) or after the function has run (successors).

In the `mod_mmap_static` case I didn't care about the `post_config` stage, but the `mmap_static_xlat` **must** be called after the core module had done its name translation, hence the use of the aszPre to define a modifier to the position HOOK_LAST.

Module Definition

There are now a lot fewer stages to worry about when creating your module definition. The old definition looked like

```
module MODULE_VAR_EXPORT module_name_module =
{
    STANDARD_MODULE_STUFF,
    /* initializer */
    /* dir config creater */
    /* dir merger --- default is to override */
    /* server config */
    /* merge server config */
    /* command handlers */
    /* handlers */
    /* filename translation */
    /* check_user_id */
    /* check auth */
    /* check access */
    /* type_checker */
    /* fixups */
    /* logger */
    /* header parser */
    /* child_init */
    /* child_exit */
    /* post read-request */
};
```

The new structure is a great deal simpler...

```
module MODULE_VAR_EXPORT module_name_module =
{
    STANDARD20_MODULE_STUFF,
    /* create per-directory config structures */
    /* merge per-directory config structures  */
    /* create per-server config structures    */
    /* merge per-server config structures      */
    /* command handlers */
    /* handlers */
    /* register hooks */
};
```

Some of these read directly across, some don't. I'll try to summarise what should be done below.

The stages that read directly across :

/* dir config creater */ /* create per-directory config structures */

/* server config */ /* create per-server config structures */

/* dir merger */ /* merge per-directory config structures */

/* merge server config */ /* merge per-server config structures */

/* command table */ /* command apr_table_t */

/* handlers */ /* handlers */

The remainder of the old functions should be registered as hooks. There are the following hook stages defined so far...

ap_hook_pre_config do any setup required prior to processing configuration directives

ap_hook_check_config review configuration directive interdependencies

ap_hook_test_config executes only with -t option

ap_hook_open_logs open any specified logs

ap_hook_post_config this is where the old _init routines get registered

ap_hook_http_method retrieve the http method from a request. (legacy)

ap_hook_auth_checker check if the resource requires authorization

ap_hook_access_checker check for module-specific restrictions

ap_hook_check_user_id check the user-id and password

ap_hook_default_port retrieve the default port for the server

ap_hook_pre_connection do any setup required just before processing, but after accepting

ap_hook_process_connection run the correct protocol

ap_hook_child_init call as soon as the child is started

ap_hook_create_request ??

ap_hook_fixups last chance to modify things before generating content

ap_hook_handler generate the content

ap_hook_header_parser lets modules look at the headers, not used by most modules, because they use `post_read_request` for this

ap_hook_insert_filter to insert filters into the filter chain

ap_hook_log_transaction log information about the request

ap_hook_optional_fn_retrieve retrieve any functions registered as optional

ap_hook_post_read_request called after reading the request, before any other phase

ap_hook_quick_handler called before any request processing, used by cache modules.

ap_hook_translate_name translate the URI into a filename

ap_hook_type_checker determine and/or set the doc type

11.8   Request Processing in the Apache HTTP Server 2.x

> **!** **Warning**
> Warning - this is a first (fast) draft that needs further revision!

Several changes in 2.0 and above affect the internal request processing mechanics. Module authors need to be aware of these changes so they may take advantage of the optimizations and security enhancements.

The first major change is to the subrequest and redirect mechanisms. There were a number of different code paths in the Apache HTTP Server 1.3 to attempt to optimize subrequest or redirect behavior. As patches were introduced to 2.0, these optimizations (and the server behavior) were quickly broken due to this duplication of code. All duplicate code has been folded back into ap_process_request_internal() to prevent the code from falling out of sync again.

This means that much of the existing code was 'unoptimized'. It is the Apache HTTP Project's first goal to create a robust and correct implementation of the HTTP server RFC. Additional goals include security, scalability and optimization. New methods were sought to optimize the server (beyond the performance of 1.3) without introducing fragile or insecure code.

The Request Processing Cycle

All requests pass through ap_process_request_internal() in request.c, including subrequests and redirects. If a module doesn't pass generated requests through this code, the author is cautioned that the module may be broken by future changes to request processing.

To streamline requests, the module author can take advantage of the hooks offered to drop out of the request cycle early, or to bypass core hooks which are irrelevant (and costly in terms of CPU.)

The Request Parsing Phase

Unescapes the URL

The request's parsed_uri path is unescaped, once and only once, at the beginning of internal request processing.

This step is bypassed if the proxyreq flag is set, or the parsed_uri.path element is unset. The module has no further control of this one-time unescape operation, either failing to unescape or multiply unescaping the URL leads to security repercussions.

Strips Parent and This Elements from the URI

All /../ and /./ elements are removed by ap_getparents(). This helps to ensure the path is (nearly) absolute before the request processing continues.

This step cannot be bypassed.

Initial URI Location Walk

Every request is subject to an ap_location_walk() call. This ensures that <LOCATION> sections are consistently enforced for all requests. If the request is an internal redirect or a sub-request, it may borrow some or all of the processing from the previous or parent request's ap_location_walk, so this step is generally very efficient after processing the main request.

translate_name

Modules can determine the file name, or alter the given URI in this step. For example, MOD_VHOST_ALIAS will translate the URI's path into the configured virtual host, MOD_ALIAS will translate the path to an alias path, and if the request falls back on the core, the DOCUMENTROOT is prepended to the request resource.

If all modules DECLINE this phase, an error 500 is returned to the browser, and a "couldn't translate name" error is logged automatically.

Hook: map_to_storage

After the file or correct URI was determined, the appropriate per-dir configurations are merged together. For example, MOD_PROXY compares and merges the appropriate <PROXY> sections. If the URI is nothing more than a local (non-proxy) TRACE request, the core handles the request and returns DONE. If no module answers this hook with OK or DONE, the core will run the request filename against the <DIRECTORY> and <FILES> sections. If the request 'filename' isn't an absolute, legal filename, a note is set for later termination.

URI Location Walk

Every request is hardened by a second ap_location_walk() call. This reassures that a translated request is still subjected to the configured <LOCATION> sections. The request again borrows some or all of the processing from its previous location_walk above, so this step is almost always very efficient unless the translated URI mapped to a substantially different path or Virtual Host.

Hook: header_parser

The main request then parses the client's headers. This prepares the remaining request processing steps to better serve the client's request.

The Security Phase

Needs Documentation. Code is:

```
if ((access_status = ap_run_access_checker(r)) != 0) {
    return decl_die(access_status, "check access", r);
}

if ((access_status = ap_run_check_user_id(r)) != 0) {
    return decl_die(access_status, "check user", r);
}

if ((access_status = ap_run_auth_checker(r)) != 0) {
    return decl_die(access_status, "check authorization", r);
}
```

The Preparation Phase

Hook: type_checker

The modules have an opportunity to test the URI or filename against the target resource, and set mime information for the request. Both MOD_MIME and MOD_MIME_MAGIC use this phase to compare the file name or contents against the administrator's configuration and set the content type, language, character set and request handler. Some modules may set up their filters or other request handling parameters at this time.

If all modules `DECLINE` this phase, an error 500 is returned to the browser, and a "couldn't find types" error is logged automatically.

Hook: fixups

Many modules are 'trounced' by some phase above. The fixups phase is used by modules to 'reassert' their ownership or force the request's fields to their appropriate values. It isn't always the cleanest mechanism, but occasionally it's the only option.

The Handler Phase

This phase is **not** part of the processing in `ap_process_request_internal()`. Many modules prepare one or more subrequests prior to creating any content at all. After the core, or a module calls `ap_process_request_internal()` it then calls `ap_invoke_handler()` to generate the request.

Hook: insert_filter

Modules that transform the content in some way can insert their values and override existing filters, such that if the user configured a more advanced filter out-of-order, then the module can move its order as need be. There is no result code, so actions in this hook better be trusted to always succeed.

Hook: handler

The module finally has a chance to serve the request in its handler hook. Note that not every prepared request is sent to the handler hook. Many modules, such as MOD_AUTOINDEX, will create subrequests for a given URI, and then never serve the subrequest, but simply lists it for the user. Remember not to put required teardown from the hooks above into this module, but register pool cleanups against the request pool to free resources as required.

11.9 How filters work in Apache 2.0

 Warning
This is a cut 'n paste job from an email (<022501c1c529$f63a9550$7f00000a@KOJ>) and
only reformatted for better readability. It's not up to date but may be a good start for further
research.

Filter Types

There are three basic filter types (each of these is actually broken down into two categories, but that comes later).

CONNECTION Filters of this type are valid for the lifetime of this connection. (`AP_FTYPE_CONNECTION`,
`AP_FTYPE_NETWORK`)

PROTOCOL Filters of this type are valid for the lifetime of this request from the point of view of the client, this
means that the request is valid from the time that the request is sent until the time that the response is received.
(`AP_FTYPE_PROTOCOL`, `AP_FTYPE_TRANSCODE`)

RESOURCE Filters of this type are valid for the time that this content is used to satisfy a request. For simple requests,
this is identical to `PROTOCOL`, but internal redirects and sub-requests can change the content without ending
the request. (`AP_FTYPE_RESOURCE`, `AP_FTYPE_CONTENT_SET`)

It is important to make the distinction between a protocol and a resource filter. A resource filter is tied to a specific
resource, it may also be tied to header information, but the main binding is to a resource. If you are writing a filter and
you want to know if it is resource or protocol, the correct question to ask is: "Can this filter be removed if the request
is redirected to a different resource?" If the answer is yes, then it is a resource filter. If it is no, then it is most likely
a protocol or connection filter. I won't go into connection filters, because they seem to be well understood. With this
definition, a few examples might help:

Byterange We have coded it to be inserted for all requests, and it is removed if not used. Because this filter is active
at the beginning of all requests, it can not be removed if it is redirected, so this is a protocol filter.

http_header This filter actually writes the headers to the network. This is obviously a required filter (except in the
asis case which is special and will be dealt with below) and so it is a protocol filter.

Deflate The administrator configures this filter based on which file has been requested. If we do an internal redirect
from an autoindex page to an index.html page, the deflate filter may be added or removed based on config, so
this is a resource filter.

The further breakdown of each category into two more filter types is strictly for ordering. We could remove it, and
only allow for one filter type, but the order would tend to be wrong, and we would need to hack things to make it work.
Currently, the `RESOURCE` filters only have one filter type, but that should change.

How are filters inserted?

This is actually rather simple in theory, but the code is complex. First of all, it is important that
everybody realize that there are three filter lists for each request, but they are all concatenated together. So, the first list is `r->output_filters`, then `r->proto_output_filters`, and finally
`r->connection->output_filters`. These correspond to the `RESOURCE`, `PROTOCOL`, and `CONNECTION`
filters respectively. The problem previously, was that we used a singly linked list to create the filter stack, and
we started from the "correct" location. This means that if I had a `RESOURCE` filter on the stack, and I added a

CONNECTION filter, the CONNECTION filter would be ignored. This should make sense, because we would insert the connection filter at the top of the c->output_filters list, but the end of r->output_filters pointed to the filter that used to be at the front of c->output_filters. This is obviously wrong. The new insertion code uses a doubly linked list. This has the advantage that we never lose a filter that has been inserted. Unfortunately, it comes with a separate set of headaches.

The problem is that we have two different cases were we use subrequests. The first is to insert more data into a response. The second is to replace the existing response with an internal redirect. These are two different cases and need to be treated as such.

In the first case, we are creating the subrequest from within a handler or filter. This means that the next filter should be passed to make_sub_request function, and the last resource filter in the sub-request will point to the next filter in the main request. This makes sense, because the sub-request's data needs to flow through the same set of filters as the main request. A graphical representation might help:

```
        Default_handler --> includes_filter --> byterange --> ...
```

If the includes filter creates a sub request, then we don't want the data from that sub-request to go through the includes filter, because it might not be SSI data. So, the subrequest adds the following:

```
        Default_handler --> includes_filter -/-> byterange --> ...
                                            /
        Default_handler --> sub_request_core
```

What happens if the subrequest is SSI data? Well, that's easy, the includes_filter is a resource filter, so it will be added to the sub request in between the Default_handler and the sub_request_core filter.

The second case for sub-requests is when one sub-request is going to become the real request. This happens whenever a sub-request is created outside of a handler or filter, and NULL is passed as the next filter to the make_sub_request function.

In this case, the resource filters no longer make sense for the new request, because the resource has changed. So, instead of starting from scratch, we simply point the front of the resource filters for the sub-request to the front of the protocol filters for the old request. This means that we won't lose any of the protocol filters, neither will we try to send this data through a filter that shouldn't see it.

The problem is that we are using a doubly-linked list for our filter stacks now. But, you should notice that it is possible for two lists to intersect in this model. So, you do you handle the previous pointer? This is a very difficult question to answer, because there is no "right" answer, either method is equally valid. I looked at why we use the previous pointer. The only reason for it is to allow for easier addition of new servers. With that being said, the solution I chose was to make the previous pointer always stay on the original request.

This causes some more complex logic, but it works for all cases. My concern in having it move to the sub-request, is that for the more common case (where a sub-request is used to add data to a response), the main filter chain would be wrong. That didn't seem like a good idea to me.

Asis

The final topic. :-) Mod_Asis is a bit of a hack, but the handler needs to remove all filters except for connection filters, and send the data. If you are using MOD_ASIS, all other bets are off.

Explanations

The absolutely last point is that the reason this code was so hard to get right, was because we had hacked so much to force it to work. I wrote most of the hacks originally, so I am very much to blame. However, now that the code is right, I have started to remove some hacks. Most people should have seen that the `reset_filters` and `add_required_filters` functions are gone. Those inserted protocol level filters for error conditions, in fact, both functions did the same thing, one after the other, it was really strange. Because we don't lose protocol filters for error cases any more, those hacks went away. The `HTTP_HEADER`, `Content-length`, and `Byterange` filters are all added in the `insert_filters` phase, because if they were added earlier, we had some interesting interactions. Now, those could all be moved to be inserted with the `HTTP_IN`, `CORE`, and `CORE_IN` filters. That would make the code easier to follow.

11.10   Guide to writing output filters

There are a number of common pitfalls encountered when writing output filters; this page aims to document best practice for authors of new or existing filters.

This document is applicable to both version 2.0 and version 2.2 of the Apache HTTP Server; it specifically targets RESOURCE-level or CONTENT_SET-level filters though some advice is generic to all types of filter.

Filters and bucket brigades

Each time a filter is invoked, it is passed a *bucket brigade*, containing a sequence of *buckets* which represent both data content and metadata. Every bucket has a *bucket type*; a number of bucket types are defined and used by the httpd core modules (and the apr-util library which provides the bucket brigade interface), but modules are free to define their own types.

⟹ Output filters must be prepared to process buckets of non-standard types; with a few exceptions, a filter need not care about the types of buckets being filtered.

A filter can tell whether a bucket represents either data or metadata using the APR_BUCKET_IS_METADATA macro. Generally, all metadata buckets should be passed down the filter chain by an output filter. Filters may transform, delete, and insert data buckets as appropriate.

There are two metadata bucket types which all filters must pay attention to: the EOS bucket type, and the FLUSH bucket type. An EOS bucket indicates that the end of the response has been reached and no further buckets need be processed. A FLUSH bucket indicates that the filter should flush any buffered buckets (if applicable) down the filter chain immediately.

⟹ FLUSH buckets are sent when the content generator (or an upstream filter) knows that there may be a delay before more content can be sent. By passing FLUSH buckets down the filter chain immediately, filters ensure that the client is not kept waiting for pending data longer than necessary.

Filters can create FLUSH buckets and pass these down the filter chain if desired. Generating FLUSH buckets unnecessarily, or too frequently, can harm network utilisation since it may force large numbers of small packets to be sent, rather than a small number of larger packets. The section on Non-blocking bucket reads covers a case where filters are encouraged to generate FLUSH buckets.

Example bucket brigade
HEAP FLUSH FILE EOS

This shows a bucket brigade which may be passed to a filter; it contains two metadata buckets (FLUSH and EOS), and two data buckets (HEAP and FILE).

Filter invocation

For any given request, an output filter might be invoked only once and be given a single brigade representing the entire response. It is also possible that the number of times a filter is invoked for a single response is proportional to the size of the content being filtered, with the filter being passed a brigade containing a single bucket each time. Filters must operate correctly in either case.

⚠ An output filter which allocates long-lived memory every time it is invoked may consume memory proportional to response size. Output filters which need to allocate memory should do so once per response; see Maintaining state below.

An output filter can distinguish the final invocation for a given response by the presence of an EOS bucket in the brigade. Any buckets in the brigade after an EOS should be ignored.

An output filter should never pass an empty brigade down the filter chain. To be defensive, filters should be prepared to accept an empty brigade, and should return success without passing this brigade on down the filter chain. The handling of an empty brigade should have no side effects (such as changing any state private to the filter).

How to handle an empty brigade

```
apr_status_t dummy_filter(ap_filter_t *f, apr_bucket_brigade *bb)
{
    if (APR_BRIGADE_EMPTY(bb)) {
        return APR_SUCCESS;
    }
    ....
```

Brigade structure

A bucket brigade is a doubly-linked list of buckets. The list is terminated (at both ends) by a *sentinel* which can be distinguished from a normal bucket by comparing it with the pointer returned by APR_BRIGADE_SENTINEL. The list sentinel is in fact not a valid bucket structure; any attempt to call normal bucket functions (such as apr_bucket_read) on the sentinel will have undefined behaviour (i.e. will crash the process).

There are a variety of functions and macros for traversing and manipulating bucket brigades; see the apr_buckets.h[25] header for complete coverage. Commonly used macros include:

APR_BRIGADE_FIRST(bb) returns the first bucket in brigade bb

APR_BRIGADE_LAST(bb) returns the last bucket in brigade bb

APR_BUCKET_NEXT(e) gives the next bucket after bucket e

APR_BUCKET_PREV(e) gives the bucket before bucket e

The apr_bucket_brigade structure itself is allocated out of a pool, so if a filter creates a new brigade, it must ensure that memory use is correctly bounded. A filter which allocates a new brigade out of the request pool (r->pool) on every invocation, for example, will fall foul of the warning above concerning memory use. Such a filter should instead create a brigade on the first invocation per request, and store that brigade in its state structure.

> **!** It is generally never advisable to use apr_brigade_destroy to "destroy" a brigade unless you know for certain that the brigade will never be used again, even then, it should be used rarely. The memory used by the brigade structure will not be released by calling this function (since it comes from a pool), but the associated pool cleanup is unregistered. Using apr_brigade_destroy can in fact cause memory leaks; if a "destroyed" brigade contains buckets when its containing pool is destroyed, those buckets will *not* be immediately destroyed. In general, filters should use apr_brigade_cleanup in preference to apr_brigade_destroy.

---

[25]http://apr.apache.org/docs/apr-util/trunk/group___a_p_r___util___bucket___brigades.html

Processing buckets

When dealing with non-metadata buckets, it is important to understand that the "`apr_bucket *`" object is an abstract *representation* of data:

1. The amount of data represented by the bucket may or may not have a determinate length; for a bucket which represents data of indeterminate length, the `->length` field is set to the value `(apr_size_t)-1`. For example, buckets of the `PIPE` bucket type have an indeterminate length; they represent the output from a pipe.

2. The data represented by a bucket may or may not be mapped into memory. The `FILE` bucket type, for example, represents data stored in a file on disk.

Filters read the data from a bucket using the `apr_bucket_read` function. When this function is invoked, the bucket may *morph* into a different bucket type, and may also insert a new bucket into the bucket brigade. This must happen for buckets which represent data not mapped into memory.

To give an example; consider a bucket brigade containing a single `FILE` bucket representing an entire file, 24 kilobytes in size:

```
FILE(0K-24K)
```

When this bucket is read, it will read a block of data from the file, morph into a `HEAP` bucket to represent that data, and return the data to the caller. It also inserts a new `FILE` bucket representing the remainder of the file; after the `apr_bucket_read` call, the brigade looks like:

```
HEAP(8K)  FILE(8K-24K)
```

Filtering brigades

The basic function of any output filter will be to iterate through the passed-in brigade and transform (or simply examine) the content in some manner. The implementation of the iteration loop is critical to producing a well-behaved output filter.

Taking an example which loops through the entire brigade as follows:

Bad output filter – do not imitate!

```
apr_bucket *e = APR_BRIGADE_FIRST(bb);
const char *data;
apr_size_t length;

while (e != APR_BRIGADE_SENTINEL(bb)) {
    apr_bucket_read(e, &data, &length, APR_BLOCK_READ);
    e = APR_BUCKET_NEXT(e);
}

return ap_pass_brigade(bb);
```

The above implementation would consume memory proportional to content size. If passed a `FILE` bucket, for example, the entire file contents would be read into memory as each `apr_bucket_read` call morphed a `FILE` bucket into a `HEAP` bucket.

In contrast, the implementation below will consume a fixed amount of memory to filter any brigade; a temporary brigade is needed and must be allocated only once per response, see the Maintaining state section.

Better output filter

```
apr_bucket *e;
const char *data;
apr_size_t length;

while ((e = APR_BRIGADE_FIRST(bb)) != APR_BRIGADE_SENTINEL(bb)) {
   rv = apr_bucket_read(e, &data, &length, APR_BLOCK_READ);
   if (rv) ...;
   /* Remove bucket e from bb. */
   APR_BUCKET_REMOVE(e);
   /* Insert it into  temporary brigade. */
   APR_BRIGADE_INSERT_HEAD(tmpbb, e);
   /* Pass brigade downstream. */
   rv = ap_pass_brigade(f->next, tmpbb);
   if (rv) ...;
   apr_brigade_cleanup(tmpbb);
}
```

Maintaining state

A filter which needs to maintain state over multiple invocations per response can use the ->ctx field of its ap_filter_t structure. It is typical to store a temporary brigade in such a structure, to avoid having to allocate a new brigade per invocation as described in the Brigade structure section.

Example code to maintain filter state

```
struct dummy_state {
   apr_bucket_brigade *tmpbb;
   int filter_state;
   ...
};

apr_status_t dummy_filter(ap_filter_t *f, apr_bucket_brigade *bb)
{

   struct dummy_state *state;

   state = f->ctx;
   if (state == NULL) {

      /* First invocation for this response: initialise state structure.
       */
      f->ctx = state = apr_palloc(f->r->pool, sizeof *state);

      state->tmpbb = apr_brigade_create(f->r->pool, f->c->bucket_alloc);
      state->filter_state = ...;

   }
   ...
```

Buffering buckets

If a filter decides to store buckets beyond the duration of a single filter function invocation (for example storing them in its ->ctx state structure), those buckets must be *set aside*. This is necessary because some bucket types provide buckets which represent temporary resources (such as stack memory) which will fall out of scope as soon as the filter chain completes processing the brigade.

To setaside a bucket, the `apr_bucket_setaside` function can be called. Not all bucket types can be setaside, but if successful, the bucket will have morphed to ensure it has a lifetime at least as long as the pool given as an argument to the `apr_bucket_setaside` function.

Alternatively, the `ap_save_brigade` function can be used, which will move all the buckets into a separate brigade containing buckets with a lifetime as long as the given pool argument. This function must be used with care, taking into account the following points:

1. On return, `ap_save_brigade` guarantees that all the buckets in the returned brigade will represent data mapped into memory. If given an input brigade containing, for example, a `PIPE` bucket, `ap_save_brigade` will consume an arbitrary amount of memory to store the entire output of the pipe.

2. When `ap_save_brigade` reads from buckets which cannot be setaside, it will always perform blocking reads, removing the opportunity to use Non-blocking bucket reads.

3. If `ap_save_brigade` is used without passing a non-NULL `"saveto"` (destination) brigade parameter, the function will create a new brigade, which may cause memory use to be proportional to content size as described in the Brigade structure section.

> ⚠ Filters must ensure that any buffered data is processed and passed down the filter chain during the last invocation for a given response (a brigade containing an EOS bucket). Otherwise such data will be lost.

Non-blocking bucket reads

The `apr_bucket_read` function takes an `apr_read_type_e` argument which determines whether a *blocking* or *non-blocking* read will be performed from the data source. A good filter will first attempt to read from every data bucket using a non-blocking read; if that fails with `APR_EAGAIN`, then send a `FLUSH` bucket down the filter chain, and retry using a blocking read.

This mode of operation ensures that any filters further down the filter chain will flush any buffered buckets if a slow content source is being used.

A CGI script is an example of a slow content source which is implemented as a bucket type. `MOD_CGI` will send `PIPE` buckets which represent the output from a CGI script; reading from such a bucket will block when waiting for the CGI script to produce more output.

Example code using non-blocking bucket reads

```
apr_bucket *e;
apr_read_type_e mode = APR_NONBLOCK_READ;

while ((e = APR_BRIGADE_FIRST(bb)) != APR_BRIGADE_SENTINEL(bb)) {
    apr_status_t rv;

    rv = apr_bucket_read(e, &data, &length, mode);
    if (rv == APR_EAGAIN && mode == APR_NONBLOCK_READ) {

        /* Pass down a brigade containing a flush bucket: */
        APR_BRIGADE_INSERT_TAIL(tmpbb, apr_bucket_flush_create(...));
        rv = ap_pass_brigade(f->next, tmpbb);
        apr_brigade_cleanup(tmpbb);
        if (rv != APR_SUCCESS) return rv;

        /* Retry, using a blocking read. */
        mode = APR_BLOCK_READ;
        continue;
    } else if (rv != APR_SUCCESS) {
        /* handle errors */
    }

    /* Next time, try a non-blocking read first. */
    mode = APR_NONBLOCK_READ;
    ...
}
```

Ten rules for output filters

In summary, here is a set of rules for all output filters to follow:

1. Output filters should not pass empty brigades down the filter chain, but should be tolerant of being passed empty brigades.

2. Output filters must pass all metadata buckets down the filter chain; FLUSH buckets should be respected by passing any pending or buffered buckets down the filter chain.

3. Output filters should ignore any buckets following an EOS bucket.

4. Output filters must process a fixed amount of data at a time, to ensure that memory consumption is not proportional to the size of the content being filtered.

5. Output filters should be agnostic with respect to bucket types, and must be able to process buckets of unfamiliar type.

6. After calling ap_pass_brigade to pass a brigade down the filter chain, output filters should call apr_brigade_cleanup to ensure the brigade is empty before reusing that brigade structure; output filters should never use apr_brigade_destroy to "destroy" brigades.

7. Output filters must *setaside* any buckets which are preserved beyond the duration of the filter function.

8. Output filters must not ignore the return value of ap_pass_brigade, and must return appropriate errors back up the filter chain.

9. Output filters must only create a fixed number of bucket brigades for each response, rather than one per invocation.

10. Output filters should first attempt non-blocking reads from each data bucket, and send a `FLUSH` bucket down the filter chain if the read blocks, before retrying with a blocking read.

11.11 Apache HTTP Server 2.x Thread Safety Issues

When using any of the threaded mpms in the Apache HTTP Server 2.x it is important that every function called from Apache be thread safe. When linking in 3rd party extensions it can be difficult to determine whether the resulting server will be thread safe. Casual testing generally won't tell you this either as thread safety problems can lead to subtle race conditions that may only show up in certain conditions under heavy load.

Global and static variables

When writing your module or when trying to determine if a module or 3rd party library is thread safe there are some common things to keep in mind.

First, you need to recognize that in a threaded model each individual thread has its own program counter, stack and registers. Local variables live on the stack, so those are fine. You need to watch out for any static or global variables. This doesn't mean that you are absolutely not allowed to use static or global variables. There are times when you actually want something to affect all threads, but generally you need to avoid using them if you want your code to be thread safe.

In the case where you have a global variable that needs to be global and accessed by all threads, be very careful when you update it. If, for example, it is an incrementing counter, you need to atomically increment it to avoid race conditions with other threads. You do this using a mutex (mutual exclusion). Lock the mutex, read the current value, increment it and write it back and then unlock the mutex. Any other thread that wants to modify the value has to first check the mutex and block until it is cleared.

If you are using APR[26], have a look at the `apr_atomic_*` functions and the `apr_thread_mutex_*` functions.

errno

This is a common global variable that holds the error number of the last error that occurred. If one thread calls a low-level function that sets errno and then another thread checks it, we are bleeding error numbers from one thread into another. To solve this, make sure your module or library defines _REENTRANT or is compiled with -D_REENTRANT. This will make errno a per-thread variable and should hopefully be transparent to the code. It does this by doing something like this:

```
#define errno (*(__errno_location()))
```

which means that accessing errno will call `__errno_location()` which is provided by the libc. Setting _REENTRANT also forces redefinition of some other functions to their `*_r` equivalents and sometimes changes the common `getc/putc` macros into safer function calls. Check your libc documentation for specifics. Instead of, or in addition to _REENTRANT the symbols that may affect this are _POSIX_C_SOURCE, _THREAD_SAFE, _SVID_SOURCE, and _BSD_SOURCE.

Common standard troublesome functions

Not only do things have to be thread safe, but they also have to be reentrant. `strtok()` is an obvious one. You call it the first time with your delimiter which it then remembers and on each subsequent call it returns the next token. Obviously if multiple threads are calling it you will have a problem. Most systems have a reentrant version of the function called `strtok_r()` where you pass in an extra argument which contains an allocated `char *` which the function will use instead of its own static storage for maintaining the tokenizing state. If you are using APR[27] you can use `apr_strtok()`.

---

[26]http://apr.apache.org/
[27]http://apr.apache.org/

crypt() is another function that tends to not be reentrant, so if you run across calls to that function in a library, watch out. On some systems it is reentrant though, so it is not always a problem. If your system has crypt_r() chances are you should be using that, or if possible simply avoid the whole mess by using md5 instead.

Common 3rd Party Libraries

The following is a list of common libraries that are used by 3rd party Apache modules. You can check to see if your module is using a potentially unsafe library by using tools such as ldd(1) and nm(1). For PHP[28], for example, try this:

```
% ldd libphp4.so
libsablot.so.0 => /usr/local/lib/libsablot.so.0 (0x401f6000)
libexpat.so.0 => /usr/lib/libexpat.so.0 (0x402da000)
libsnmp.so.0 => /usr/lib/libsnmp.so.0 (0x402f9000)
libpdf.so.1 => /usr/local/lib/libpdf.so.1 (0x40353000)
libz.so.1 => /usr/lib/libz.so.1 (0x403e2000)
libpng.so.2 => /usr/lib/libpng.so.2 (0x403f0000)
libmysqlclient.so.11 => /usr/lib/libmysqlclient.so.11 (0x40411000)
libming.so => /usr/lib/libming.so (0x40449000)
libm.so.6 => /lib/libm.so.6 (0x40487000)
libfreetype.so.6 => /usr/lib/libfreetype.so.6 (0x404a8000)
libjpeg.so.62 => /usr/lib/libjpeg.so.62 (0x404e7000)
libcrypt.so.1 => /lib/libcrypt.so.1 (0x40505000)
libssl.so.2 => /lib/libssl.so.2 (0x40532000)
libcrypto.so.2 => /lib/libcrypto.so.2 (0x40560000)
libresolv.so.2 => /lib/libresolv.so.2 (0x40624000)
libdl.so.2 => /lib/libdl.so.2 (0x40634000)
libnsl.so.1 => /lib/libnsl.so.1 (0x40637000)
libc.so.6 => /lib/libc.so.6 (0x4064b000)
/lib/ld-linux.so.2 => /lib/ld-linux.so.2 (0x80000000)
```

In addition to these libraries you will need to have a look at any libraries linked statically into the module. You can use nm(1) to look for individual symbols in the module.

Library List

Please drop a note to dev@httpd.apache.org[29] if you have additions or corrections to this list.

Library	Version	Thread Safe?	Notes
ASpell/PSpell[a] [a]http://aspell.sourceforge.net/		?	
Berkeley DB[a] [a]http://www.sleepycat.com/	3.x, 4.x	Yes	Be careful about sharing a co nnection across threads.
bzip2[a] [a]http://sources.redhat.com/bzip2/index.html		Yes	Both low-level and high-le APIs are thread-safe. Howe high-level API requires thr safe access to errno.
cdb[a] [a]http://cr.yp.to/cdb.html		?	

---

[28]http://www.php.net/
[29]http://httpd.apache.org/lists.html#http-dev

C-Client[a]		Perhaps	c-client uses strtol and gethostbyname which are not thread- on most C library im mentations. c-client's st data is meant to be sha across threads. If strtol and gethostbyname are thread-safe on your c-client *may* be thread-safe
[a]http://www.washington.edu/imap/			
libcrypt[a]		?	
[a]http://www.ijg.org/files/			
Expat[a]		Yes	Need a separate parser insta per thread
[a]http://expat.sourceforge.net/			
FreeTDS[a]		?	
[a]http://www.freetds.org/			
FreeType[a]		?	
[a]http://www.freetype.org/			
GD 1.8.x[a]		?	
[a]http://www.boutell.com/gd/			
GD 2.0.x[a]		?	
[a]http://www.boutell.com/gd/			
gdbm[a]		No	Errors returned via a st gdbm_error variable
[a]http://www.gnu.org/software/gdbm/gdbm.html			
ImageMagick[a]	5.2.2	Yes	ImageMagick docs claim thread safe since version 5 (see Change log[a]).
[a]http://www.imagemagick.org/			[a]http://www.imagemagick.
Imlib2[a]		?	
[a]http://www.enlightenment.org/p.php?p=about/efl&l=en			
libjpeg[a]	v6b	?	
[a]http://www.ijg.org/files/			
libmysqlclient[a]		Yes	Use mysqlclient_r library v ant to ensure thread-safety. more information, please i http://dev.mysql.com/doc/n
[a]http://mysql.com			
Ming[a]	0.2a	?	
[a]http://www.opaque.net/ming/			
Net-SNMP[a]	5.0.x	?	
[a]http://net-snmp.sourceforge.net/			
OpenLDAP[a]	2.1.x	Yes	Use ldap_r library variar ensure thread-safety.
[a]http://www.openldap.org/			
OpenSSL[a]	0.9.6g	Yes	Requires proper usage CRYPTO_num_locks, CRYPTO_set_locking_(CRYPTO_set_id_callb;
[a]http://www.openssl.org/			
liboci8 (Oracle 8+)[a]	8.x,9.x	?	
[a]http://www.oracle.com/			

pdflib[a] [a]http://pdflib.com/	5.0.x	Yes	PDFLib docs claim it thread safe; change indicates it has been tially thread-safe since V1 http://www.pdflib.com/pro family/pdflib/.
libpng[a] [a]http://www.libpng.org/pub/png/libpng.html	1.0.x	?	
libpng[a] [a]http://www.libpng.org/pub/png/libpng.html	1.2.x	?	
libpq (PostgreSQL)[a] [a]http://www.postgresql.org/docs/8.4/static/libpq-threading.html	8.x	Yes	Don't share connections ac threads and watch out crypt() calls
Sablotron[a] [a]http://www.gingerall.com/charlie/ga/xml/p_sab.xml	0.95	?	
zlib[a] [a]http://www.gzip.org/zlib/	1.1.4	Yes	Relies upon thread-safe za and zfree functions Defau to use libc's calloc/free wl are thread-safe.

Chapter 12

Glossary and Index

12.1 Glossary

This glossary defines some of the common terminology related to Apache in particular, and web serving in general. More information on each concept is provided in the links.

Definitions

Access Control The restriction of access to network realms. In an Apache context usually the restriction of access to certain *URLs*.
See: Authentication, Authorization, and Access Control (p. 217)

Algorithm An unambiguous formula or set of rules for solving a problem in a finite number of steps. Algorithms for encryption are usually called *Ciphers*.

APache eXtension Tool (apxs) A perl script that aids in compiling module sources into Dynamic Shared Objects (DSOs) and helps install them in the Apache Web server.
See: Manual Page: `apxs`

Apache Portable Runtime (APR) A set of libraries providing many of the basic interfaces between the server and the operating system. APR is developed parallel to the Apache HTTP Server as an independent project.
See: Apache Portable Runtime Project[1]

Authentication The positive identification of a network entity such as a server, a client, or a user.
See: Authentication, Authorization, and Access Control (p. 217)

Certificate A data record used for authenticating network entities such as a server or a client. A certificate contains X.509 information pieces about its owner (called the subject) and the signing Certification Authority (called the issuer), plus the owner's public key and the signature made by the CA. Network entities verify these signatures using CA certificates.
See: SSL/TLS Encryption (p. 182)

Certificate Signing Request (CSR) An unsigned certificate for submission to a Certification Authority, which signs it with the Private Key of their CA *Certificate*. Once the CSR is signed, it becomes a real certificate.
See: SSL/TLS Encryption (p. 182)

Certification Authority (CA) A trusted third party whose purpose is to sign certificates for network entities it has authenticated using secure means. Other network entities can check the signature to verify that a CA has authenticated the bearer of a certificate.
See: SSL/TLS Encryption (p. 182)

Cipher An algorithm or system for data encryption. Examples are DES, IDEA, RC4, etc.
See: SSL/TLS Encryption (p. 182)

Ciphertext The result after Plaintext is passed through a Cipher.
See: SSL/TLS Encryption (p. 182)

Common Gateway Interface (CGI) A standard definition for an interface between a web server and an external program that allows the external program to service requests. There is an Informational RFC[2] which covers the specifics.
See: Dynamic Content with CGI (p. 226)

Configuration Directive See: Directive

Configuration File A text file containing Directives that control the configuration of Apache.
See: Configuration Files (p. 30)

---

[1] http://apr.apache.org/
[2] http://www.ietf.org/rfc/rfc3875

CONNECT An HTTP method for proxying raw data channels over HTTP. It can be used to encapsulate other proto-cols, such as the SSL protocol.

Context An area in the configuration files where certain types of directives are allowed.
See: Terms Used to Describe Apache Directives (p. 351)

Digital Signature An encrypted text block that validates a certificate or other file. A Certification Authority creates a signature by generating a hash of the *Public Key* embedded in a *Certificate*, then encrypting the hash with its own *Private Key*. Only the CA's public key can decrypt the signature, verifying that the CA has authenticated the network entity that owns the *Certificate*.
See: SSL/TLS Encryption (p. 182)

Directive A configuration command that controls one or more aspects of Apache's behavior. Directives are placed in the Configuration File
See: Directive Index (p. 1030)

Dynamic Shared Object (DSO) Modules compiled separately from the Apache `httpd` binary that can be loaded on-demand.
See: Dynamic Shared Object Support (p. 65)

Environment Variable (env-variable) Named variables managed by the operating system shell and used to store information and communicate between programs. Apache also contains internal variables that are referred to as environment variables, but are stored in internal Apache structures, rather than in the shell environment.
See: Environment Variables in Apache (p. 82)

Export-Crippled Diminished in cryptographic strength (and security) in order to comply with the United States' Export Administration Regulations (EAR). Export-crippled cryptographic software is limited to a small key size, resulting in *Ciphertext* which usually can be decrypted by brute force.
See: SSL/TLS Encryption (p. 182)

Filter A process that is applied to data that is sent or received by the server. Input filters process data sent by the client to the server, while output filters process documents on the server before they are sent to the client. For example, the `INCLUDES` output filter processes documents for Server Side Includes.
See: Filters (p. 100)

Fully-Qualified Domain-Name (FQDN) The unique name of a network entity, consisting of a hostname and a do-main name that can resolve to an IP address. For example, `www` is a hostname, `example.com` is a domain name, and `www.example.com` is a fully-qualified domain name.

Handler An internal Apache representation of the action to be performed when a file is called. Generally, files have implicit handlers, based on the file type. Normally, all files are simply served by the server, but certain file types are "handled" separately. For example, the `cgi-script` handler designates files to be processed as CGIs.
See: Apache's Handler Use (p. 98)

Hash A mathematical one-way, irreversible algorithm generating a string with fixed-length from another string of any length. Different input strings will usually produce different hashes (depending on the hash function).

Header The part of the HTTP request and response that is sent before the actual content, and that contains meta-information describing the content.

.htaccess A configuration file that is placed inside the web tree and applies configuration directives to the directory where it is placed and all sub-directories. Despite its name, this file can hold almost any type of directive, not just access-control directives.
See: Configuration Files (p. 30)

httpd.conf The main Apache configuration file. The default location is `/usr/local/apache2/conf/httpd.conf`, but it may be moved using run-time or compile-time configuration.
See: Configuration Files (p. 30)

HyperText Transfer Protocol (HTTP) The standard transmission protocol used on the World Wide Web. Apache implements version 1.1 of the protocol, referred to as HTTP/1.1 and defined by RFC 2616[3].

HTTPS The HyperText Transfer Protocol (Secure), the standard encrypted communication mechanism on the World Wide Web. This is actually just HTTP over SSL.
See: SSL/TLS Encryption (p. 182)

Method In the context of HTTP, an action to perform on a resource, specified on the request line by the client. Some of the methods available in HTTP are GET, POST, and PUT.

Message Digest A hash of a message, which can be used to verify that the contents of the message have not been altered in transit.
See: SSL/TLS Encryption (p. 182)

MIME-type A way to describe the kind of document being transmitted. Its name comes from that fact that its format is borrowed from the Multipurpose Internet Mail Extensions. It consists of a major type and a minor type, separated by a slash. Some examples are text/html, image/gif, and application/octet-stream. In HTTP, the MIME-type is transmitted in the Content-Type header.
See: mod_mime (p. 704)

Module An independent part of a program. Much of Apache's functionality is contained in modules that you can choose to include or exclude. Modules that are compiled into the Apache httpd binary are called *static modules*, while modules that are stored separately and can be optionally loaded at run-time are called *dynamic modules* or DSOs. Modules that are included by default are called *base modules*. Many modules are available for Apache that are not distributed as part of the Apache HTTP Server tarball. These are referred to as *third-party modules*.
See: Module Index (p. 1025)

Module Magic Number (MMN) Module Magic Number is a constant defined in the Apache source code that is associated with binary compatibility of modules. It is changed when internal Apache structures, function calls and other significant parts of API change in such a way that binary compatibility cannot be guaranteed any more. On MMN change, all third party modules have to be at least recompiled, sometimes even slightly changed in order to work with the new version of Apache.

OpenSSL The Open Source toolkit for SSL/TLS
See http://www.openssl.org/#

Pass Phrase The word or phrase that protects private key files. It prevents unauthorized users from encrypting them. Usually it's just the secret encryption/decryption key used for Ciphers.
See: SSL/TLS Encryption (p. 182)

Plaintext The unencrypted text.

Private Key The secret key in a Public Key Cryptography system, used to decrypt incoming messages and sign outgoing ones.
See: SSL/TLS Encryption (p. 182)

Proxy An intermediate server that sits between the client and the *origin server*. It accepts requests from clients, transmits those requests on to the origin server, and then returns the response from the origin server to the client. If several clients request the same content, the proxy can deliver that content from its cache, rather than requesting it from the origin server each time, thereby reducing response time.
See: mod_proxy (p. 732)

Public Key The publicly available key in a Public Key Cryptography system, used to encrypt messages bound for its owner and to decrypt signatures made by its owner.
See: SSL/TLS Encryption (p. 182)

---

[3]http://ietf.org/rfc/rfc2616.txt

Public Key Cryptography The study and application of asymmetric encryption systems, which use one key for encryption and another for decryption. A corresponding pair of such keys constitutes a key pair. Also called Asymmetric Cryptography.
See: SSL/TLS Encryption (p. 182)

Regular Expression (Regex) A way of describing a pattern in text - for example, "all the words that begin with the letter A" or "every 10-digit phone number" or even "Every sentence with two commas in it, and no capital letter Q". Regular expressions are useful in Apache because they let you apply certain attributes against collections of files or resources in very flexible ways - for example, all .gif and .jpg files under any "images" directory could be written as "`/images/.*(jpg|gif)$`". In places where regular expressions are used to replace strings, the special variables $1 ... $9 contain backreferences to the grouped parts (in parentheses) of the matched expression. The special variable $0 contains a backreference to the whole matched expression. To write a literal dollar sign in a replacement string, it can be escaped with a backslash. Historically, the variable & could be used as alias for $0 in some places. This is no longer possible since version 2.3.6. Apache uses Perl Compatible Regular Expressions provided by the PCRE[4] library. You can find more documentation about PCRE's regular expression syntax at that site, or at Wikipedia[5].

Reverse Proxy A proxy server that appears to the client as if it is an *origin server*. This is useful to hide the real origin server from the client for security reasons, or to load balance.

Secure Sockets Layer (SSL) A protocol created by Netscape Communications Corporation for general communication authentication and encryption over TCP/IP networks. The most popular usage is *HTTPS*, i.e. the HyperText Transfer Protocol (HTTP) over SSL.
See: SSL/TLS Encryption (p. 182)

Server Name Indication (SNI) An SSL function that allows passing the desired server hostname in the initial SSL handshake message, so that the web server can select the correct virtual host configuration to use in processing the SSL handshake. It was added to SSL starting with the TLS extensions, RFC 3546.
See: the SSL FAQ (p. 202) and RFC 3546[6]

Server Side Includes (SSI) A technique for embedding processing directives inside HTML files.
See: Introduction to Server Side Includes (p. 233)

Session The context information of a communication in general.

SSLeay The original SSL/TLS implementation library developed by Eric A. Young

Subrequest Apache provides a subrequest API to modules that allows other filesystem or URL paths to be partially or fully evaluated by the server. Example consumers of this API are DIRECTORYINDEX, MOD_AUTOINDEX, and MOD_INCLUDE.

Symmetric Cryptography The study and application of *Ciphers* that use a single secret key for both encryption and decryption operations.
See: SSL/TLS Encryption (p. 182)

Tarball A package of files gathered together using the `tar` utility. Apache distributions are stored in compressed tar archives or using pkzip.

Transport Layer Security (TLS) The successor protocol to SSL, created by the Internet Engineering Task Force (IETF) for general communication authentication and encryption over TCP/IP networks. TLS version 1 is nearly identical with SSL version 3.
See: SSL/TLS Encryption (p. 182)

---

[4]http://www.pcre.org/
[5]http://en.wikipedia.org/wiki/PCRE
[6]http://www.ietf.org/rfc/rfc3546.txt

Uniform Resource Locator (URL) The name/address of a resource on the Internet. This is the common informal term for what is formally called a Uniform Resource Identifier. URLs are usually made up of a scheme, like `http` or `https`, a hostname, and a path. A URL for this page might be `http://httpd.apache.org/docs/2.4/glossary.html`.

Uniform Resource Identifier (URI) A compact string of characters for identifying an abstract or physical resource. It is formally defined by RFC 2396[7]. URIs used on the world-wide web are commonly referred to as URLs.

Virtual Hosting Serving multiple websites using a single instance of Apache. *IP virtual hosting* differentiates between websites based on their IP address, while *name-based virtual hosting* uses only the name of the host and can therefore host many sites on the same IP address.
See: Apache Virtual Host documentation (p. 114)

X.509 An authentication certificate scheme recommended by the International Telecommunication Union (ITU-T) which is used for SSL/TLS authentication.
See: SSL/TLS Encryption (p. 182)

---

[7]http://www.ietf.org/rfc/rfc2396.txt

12.2 Module Index

Below is a list of all of the modules that come as part of the Apache HTTP Server distribution. See also the complete alphabetical list of all Apache HTTP Server directives (p. 1030) .

See also

- Multi-Processing Modules (MPMs) (p. 80)
- Directive Quick Reference (p. 1030)

Core Features and Multi-Processing Modules

core (p. 354) Core Apache HTTP Server features that are always available

mpm_common (p. 917) A collection of directives that are implemented by more than one multi-processing module (MPM)

event (p. 928) A variant of the WORKER MPM with the goal of consuming threads only for connections with active processing

mpm_netware (p. 931) Multi-Processing Module implementing an exclusively threaded web server optimized for Novell NetWare

mpmt_os2 (p. 933) Hybrid multi-process, multi-threaded MPM for OS/2

prefork (p. 934) Implements a non-threaded, pre-forking web server

mpm_winnt (p. 937) Multi-Processing Module optimized for Windows NT.

worker (p. 939) Multi-Processing Module implementing a hybrid multi-threaded multi-process web server

Other Modules

mod_access_compat (p. 411) Group authorizations based on host (name or IP address)

mod_actions (p. 416) Execute CGI scripts based on media type or request method.

mod_alias (p. 418) Provides for mapping different parts of the host filesystem in the document tree and for URL redirection

mod_allowmethods (p. 424) Easily restrict what HTTP methods can be used on the server

mod_asis (p. 425) Sends files that contain their own HTTP headers

mod_auth_basic (p. 427) Basic HTTP authentication

mod_auth_digest (p. 431) User authentication using MD5 Digest Authentication

mod_auth_form (p. 435) Form authentication

mod_authn_anon (p. 446) Allows "anonymous" user access to authenticated areas

mod_authn_core (p. 449) Core Authentication

mod_authn_dbd (p. 453) User authentication using an SQL database

mod_authn_dbm (p. 456) User authentication using DBM files

mod_authn_file (p. 458) User authentication using text files

mod_authn_socache (p. 460) Manages a cache of authentication credentials to relieve the load on backends

mod_authnz_fcgi (p. 463) Allows a FastCGI authorizer application to handle Apache httpd authentication and authorization

mod_authnz_ldap (p. 470) Allows an LDAP directory to be used to store the database for HTTP Basic authentication.

mod_authz_core (p. 488) Core Authorization

mod_authz_dbd (p. 496) Group Authorization and Login using SQL

mod_authz_dbm (p. 500) Group authorization using DBM files

mod_authz_groupfile (p. 503) Group authorization using plaintext files

mod_authz_host (p. 505) Group authorizations based on host (name or IP address)

mod_authz_owner (p. 508) Authorization based on file ownership

mod_authz_user (p. 510) User Authorization

mod_autoindex (p. 511) Generates directory indexes, automatically, similar to the Unix ls command or the Win32 dir shell command

mod_buffer (p. 523) Support for request buffering

mod_cache (p. 524) RFC 2616 compliant HTTP caching filter.

mod_cache_disk (p. 539) Disk based storage module for the HTTP caching filter.

mod_cache_socache (p. 543) Shared object cache (socache) based storage module for the HTTP caching filter.

mod_cern_meta (p. 547) CERN httpd metafile semantics

mod_cgi (p. 549) Execution of CGI scripts

mod_cgid (p. 552) Execution of CGI scripts using an external CGI daemon

mod_charset_lite (p. 554) Specify character set translation or recoding

mod_data (p. 557) Convert response body into an RFC2397 data URL

mod_dav (p. 558) Distributed Authoring and Versioning (WebDAV[8]) functionality

mod_dav_fs (p. 561) Filesystem provider for MOD_DAV

mod_dav_lock (p. 562) Generic locking module for MOD_DAV

mod_dbd (p. 563) Manages SQL database connections

mod_deflate (p. 568) Compress content before it is delivered to the client

mod_dialup (p. 574) Send static content at a bandwidth rate limit, defined by the various old modem standards

mod_dir (p. 575) Provides for "trailing slash" redirects and serving directory index files

mod_dumpio (p. 580) Dumps all I/O to error log as desired.

mod_echo (p. 582) A simple echo server to illustrate protocol modules

mod_env (p. 583) Modifies the environment which is passed to CGI scripts and SSI pages

---

[8]http://www.webdav.org/

mod_example_hooks (p. 585) Illustrates the Apache module API

mod_expires (p. 587) Generation of `Expires` and `Cache-Control` HTTP headers according to user-specified criteria

mod_ext_filter (p. 590) Pass the response body through an external program before delivery to the client

mod_file_cache (p. 594) Caches a static list of files in memory

mod_filter (p. 597) Context-sensitive smart filter configuration module

mod_headers (p. 605) Customization of HTTP request and response headers

mod_heartbeat (p. 611) Sends messages with server status to frontend proxy

mod_heartmonitor (p. 612) Centralized monitor for mod_heartbeat origin servers

mod_http2 (p. 614) Support for the HTTP/2 transport layer

mod_ident (p. 618) RFC 1413 ident lookups

mod_imagemap (p. 620) Server-side imagemap processing

mod_include (p. 624) Server-parsed html documents (Server Side Includes)

mod_info (p. 637) Provides a comprehensive overview of the server configuration

mod_isapi (p. 640) ISAPI Extensions within Apache for Windows

mod_lbmethod_bybusyness (p. 644) Pending Request Counting load balancer scheduler algorithm for MOD_PROXY_BALANCER

mod_lbmethod_byrequests (p. 645) Request Counting load balancer scheduler algorithm for MOD_PROXY_BALANCER

mod_lbmethod_bytraffic (p. 647) Weighted Traffic Counting load balancer scheduler algorithm for MOD_PROXY_BALANCER

mod_lbmethod_heartbeat (p. 648) Heartbeat Traffic Counting load balancer scheduler algorithm for MOD_PROXY_BALANCER

mod_ldap (p. 649) LDAP connection pooling and result caching services for use by other LDAP modules

mod_log_config (p. 661) Logging of the requests made to the server

mod_log_debug (p. 667) Additional configurable debug logging

mod_log_forensic (p. 669) Forensic Logging of the requests made to the server

mod_logio (p. 671) Logging of input and output bytes per request

mod_lua (p. 673) Provides Lua hooks into various portions of the httpd request processing

mod_macro (p. 700) Provides macros within apache httpd runtime configuration files

mod_mime (p. 704) Associates the requested filename's extensions with the file's behavior (handlers and filters) and content (mime-type, language, character set and encoding)

mod_mime_magic (p. 717) Determines the MIME type of a file by looking at a few bytes of its contents

mod_negotiation (p. 721) Provides for content negotiation (p. 68)

mod_nw_ssl (p. 725) Enable SSL encryption for NetWare

mod_privileges (p. 726) Support for Solaris privileges and for running virtual hosts under different user IDs.

mod_proxy (p. 732) Multi-protocol proxy/gateway server

mod_proxy_ajp (p. 759) AJP support module for MOD_PROXY

mod_proxy_balancer (p. 768) MOD_PROXY extension for load balancing

mod_proxy_connect (p. 772) MOD_PROXY extension for CONNECT request handling

mod_proxy_express (p. 773) Dynamic mass reverse proxy extension for MOD_PROXY

mod_proxy_fcgi (p. 776) FastCGI support module for MOD_PROXY

mod_proxy_fdpass (p. 779) fdpass external process support module for MOD_PROXY

mod_proxy_ftp (p. 780) FTP support module for MOD_PROXY

mod_proxy_html (p. 783) Rewrite HTML links in to ensure they are addressable from Clients' networks in a proxy context.

mod_proxy_http (p. 789) HTTP support module for MOD_PROXY

mod_proxy_scgi (p. 791) SCGI gateway module for MOD_PROXY

mod_proxy_wstunnel (p. 794) Websockets support module for MOD_PROXY

mod_ratelimit (p. 795) Bandwidth Rate Limiting for Clients

mod_reflector (p. 796) Reflect a request body as a response via the output filter stack.

mod_remoteip (p. 797) Replaces the original client IP address for the connection with the useragent IP address list presented by a proxies or a load balancer via the request headers.

mod_reqtimeout (p. 801) Set timeout and minimum data rate for receiving requests

mod_request (p. 803) Filters to handle and make available HTTP request bodies

mod_rewrite (p. 804) Provides a rule-based rewriting engine to rewrite requested URLs on the fly

mod_sed (p. 818) Filter Input (request) and Output (response) content using sed syntax

mod_session (p. 820) Session support

mod_session_cookie (p. 827) Cookie based session support

mod_session_crypto (p. 830) Session encryption support

mod_session_dbd (p. 834) DBD/SQL based session support

mod_setenvif (p. 839) Allows the setting of environment variables based on characteristics of the request

mod_slotmem_plain (p. 843) Slot-based shared memory provider.

mod_slotmem_shm (p. 844) Slot-based shared memory provider.

mod_so (p. 845) Loading of executable code and modules into the server at start-up or restart time

mod_socache_dbm (p. 847) DBM based shared object cache provider.

mod_socache_dc (p. 848) Distcache based shared object cache provider.

mod_socache_memcache (p. 849) Memcache based shared object cache provider.

mod_socache_shmcb (p. 850) shmcb based shared object cache provider.

mod_speling (p. 851) Attempts to correct mistaken URLs by ignoring capitalization, or attempting to correct various minor misspellings.

mod_ssl (p. 853) Strong cryptography using the Secure Sockets Layer (SSL) and Transport Layer Security (TLS) protocols

mod_status (p. 891) Provides information on server activity and performance

mod_substitute (p. 893) Perform search and replace operations on response bodies

mod_suexec (p. 896) Allows CGI scripts to run as a specified user and Group

mod_unique_id (p. 897) Provides an environment variable with a unique identifier for each request

mod_unixd (p. 899) Basic (required) security for Unix-family platforms.

mod_userdir (p. 902) User-specific directories

mod_usertrack (p. 904) *Clickstream* logging of user activity on a site

mod_version (p. 907) Version dependent configuration

mod_vhost_alias (p. 909) Provides for dynamically configured mass virtual hosting

mod_watchdog (p. 913) provides infrastructure for other modules to periodically run tasks

mod_xml2enc (p. 914) Enhanced charset/internationalisation support for libxml2-based filter modules

12.3 Directive Quick Reference

The directive quick reference shows the usage, default, status, and context of each Apache configuration directive. For more information about each of these, see the Directive Dictionary (p. 351) .

The first column gives the directive name and usage. The second column shows the default value of the directive, if a default exists. If the default is too large to display, it will be truncated and followed by `"+"`.

The third and fourth columns list the contexts where the directive is allowed and the status of the directive according to the legend tables below.

`/AcceptFilter protocol accept_filter`		s	C
Configures optimizations for a Protocol's Listener Sockets		p. 356	
`AcceptPathInfo On|Off|Default`	Default	svdh	C
Resources accept trailing pathname information		p. 357	
`AccessFileName filename [filename] ...`	.htaccess	sv	C
Name of the distributed configuration file		p. 358	
`Action action-type cgi-script [virtual]`		svdh	B
Activates a CGI script for a particular handler or content-type		p. 416	
`AddAlt string file [file] ...`		svdh	B
Alternate text to display for a file, instead of an icon selected by filename		p. 513	
`AddAltByEncoding string MIME-encoding [MIME-encoding] ...`		svdh	B
Alternate text to display for a file instead of an icon selected by MIME-encoding		p. 513	
`AddAltByType string MIME-type [MIME-type] ...`		svdh	B
Alternate text to display for a file, instead of an icon selected by MIME content-type		p. 514	
`AddCharset charset extension [extension] ...`		svdh	B
Maps the given filename extensions to the specified content charset		p. 707	
`AddDefaultCharset On|Off|charset`	Off	svdh	C
Default charset parameter to be added when a response content-type is `text/plain` or `text/html`		p. 358	
`AddDescription string file [file] ...`		svdh	B
Description to display for a file		p. 514	
`AddEncoding encoding extension [extension] ...`		svdh	B
Maps the given filename extensions to the specified encoding type		p. 707	
`AddHandler handler-name extension [extension] ...`		svdh	B
Maps the filename extensions to the specified handler		p. 708	
`AddIcon icon name [name] ...`		svdh	B
Icon to display for a file selected by name		p. 515	
`AddIconByEncoding icon MIME-encoding [MIME-encoding] ...`		svdh	B
Icon to display next to files selected by MIME-encoding		p. 515	
`AddIconByType icon MIME-type [MIME-type] ...`		svdh	B
Icon to display next to files selected by MIME content-type		p. 516	
`AddInputFilter filter[;filter...] extension [extension] ...`		svdh	B
Maps filename extensions to the filters that will process client requests		p. 708	
`AddLanguage language-tag extension [extension] ...`		svdh	B
Maps the given filename extension to the specified content language		p. 709	
`AddModuleInfo module-name string`		sv	E
Adds additional information to the module information displayed by the server-info handler		p. 639	
`AddOutputFilter filter[;filter...] extension [extension] ...`		svdh	B
Maps filename extensions to the filters that will process responses from the server		p. 709	
`AddOutputFilterByType filter[;filter...] media-type [media-type] ...`		svdh	B
assigns an output filter to a particular media-type		p. 601	
`AddType media-type extension [extension] ...`		svdh	B
Maps the given filename extensions onto the specified content type		p. 710	
`Alias URL-path file-path|directory-path`		sv	B
Maps URLs to filesystem locations		p. 419	
`AliasMatch regex file-path|directory-path`		sv	B
Maps URLs to filesystem locations using regular expressions		p. 419	
`Allow from all|host|env=[!]env-variable [host|env=[!]env-variable] ...`		dh	E
Controls which hosts can access an area of the server		p. 412	
`AllowCONNECT port[-port] [port[-port]] ...`	443 563	sv	E
Ports that are allowed to CONNECT through the proxy		p. 772	

`AllowEncodedSlashes On|Off|NoDecode` Determines whether encoded path separators in URLs are allowed to be passed through	Off	sv p. 359	C
`AllowMethods reset|HTTP-method [HTTP-method]...` Restrict access to the listed HTTP methods	reset	d p. 424	X
`AllowOverride All|None|directive-type [directive-type] ...` Types of directives that are allowed in `.htaccess` files	None (2.3.9 and lat +	d p. 359	C
`AllowOverrideList None|directive [directive-type] ...` Individual directives that are allowed in `.htaccess` files	None	d p. 361	C
`Anonymous user [user] ...` Specifies userIDs that are allowed access without password verification		dh p. 447	E
`Anonymous_LogEmail On|Off` Sets whether the password entered will be logged in the error log	On	dh p. 447	E
`Anonymous_MustGiveEmail On|Off` Specifies whether blank passwords are allowed	On	dh p. 448	E
`Anonymous_NoUserID On|Off` Sets whether the userID field may be empty	Off	dh p. 448	E
`Anonymous_VerifyEmail On|Off` Sets whether to check the password field for a correctly formatted email address	Off	dh p. 448	E
`AsyncRequestWorkerFactor factor` Limit concurrent connections per process		s p. 929	M
`AuthBasicAuthoritative On|Off` Sets whether authorization and authentication are passed to lower level modules	On	dh p. 427	B
`AuthBasicFake off|username [password]` Fake basic authentication using the given expressions for username and password		dh p. 428	B
`AuthBasicProvider provider-name [provider-name] ...` Sets the authentication provider(s) for this location	file	dh p. 429	B
`AuthBasicUseDigestAlgorithm MD5|Off` Check passwords against the authentication providers as if Digest Authentication was in force instead of Basic Authentication.	Off	dh p. 429	B
`AuthDBDUserPWQuery query` SQL query to look up a password for a user		d p. 454	E
`AuthDBDUserRealmQuery query` SQL query to look up a password hash for a user and realm.		d p. 455	E
`AuthDBMGroupFile file-path` Sets the name of the database file containing the list of user groups for authorization		dh p. 501	E
`AuthDBMType default|SDBM|GDBM|NDBM|DB` Sets the type of database file that is used to store passwords	default	dh p. 456	E
`AuthDBMUserFile file-path` Sets the name of a database file containing the list of users and passwords for authentication		dh p. 457	E
`AuthDigestAlgorithm MD5|MD5-sess` Selects the algorithm used to calculate the challenge and response hashes in digest authentication	MD5	dh p. 432	E
`AuthDigestDomain URI [URI] ...` URIs that are in the same protection space for digest authentication		dh p. 432	E
`AuthDigestNonceLifetime seconds` How long the server nonce is valid	300	dh p. 432	E
`AuthDigestProvider provider-name [provider-name] ...` Sets the authentication provider(s) for this location	file	dh p. 433	E
`AuthDigestQop none|auth|auth-int [auth|auth-int]` Determines the quality-of-protection to use in digest authentication	auth	dh p. 433	E
`AuthDigestShmemSize size` The amount of shared memory to allocate for keeping track of clients	1000	s p. 433	E
`AuthFormAuthoritative On|Off` Sets whether authorization and authentication are passed to lower level modules	On	dh p. 440	B
`AuthFormBody fieldname` The name of a form field carrying the body of the request to attempt on successful login		d p. 440	B
`AuthFormDisableNoStore On|Off` Disable the CacheControl no-store header on the login page	Off	d p. 440	B
`AuthFormFakeBasicAuth On|Off` Fake a Basic Authentication header	Off	d p. 441	B
`AuthFormLocation fieldname` The name of a form field carrying a URL to redirect to on successful login		d p. 441	B
`AuthFormLoginRequiredLocation url` The URL of the page to be redirected to should login be required		d p. 441	B
`AuthFormLoginSuccessLocation url` The URL of the page to be redirected to should login be successful		d p. 442	B

Directive	Default	Context	Module	Page
`AuthFormLogoutLocation uri` The URL to redirect to after a user has logged out		d	B	p. 442
`AuthFormMethod fieldname` The name of a form field carrying the method of the request to attempt on successful login		d	B	p. 442
`AuthFormMimetype fieldname` The name of a form field carrying the mimetype of the body of the request to attempt on successful login		d	B	p. 443
`AuthFormPassword fieldname` The name of a form field carrying the login password		d	B	p. 443
`AuthFormProvider provider-name [provider-name] ...` Sets the authentication provider(s) for this location	file	dh	B	p. 443
`AuthFormSitePassphrase secret` Bypass authentication checks for high traffic sites		d	B	p. 444
`AuthFormSize size` The largest size of the form in bytes that will be parsed for the login details		d	B	p. 444
`AuthFormUsername fieldname` The name of a form field carrying the login username		d	B	p. 445
`AuthGroupFile file-path` Sets the name of a text file containing the list of user groups for authorization		dh	B	p. 503
`AuthLDAPAuthorizePrefix prefix` Specifies the prefix for environment variables set during authorization	AUTHORIZE_	dh	E	p. 479
`AuthLDAPBindAuthoritativeoff|on` Determines if other authentication providers are used when a user can be mapped to a DN but the server cannot successfully bind with the user's credentials.	on	dh	E	p. 479
`AuthLDAPBindDN distinguished-name` Optional DN to use in binding to the LDAP server		dh	E	p. 479
`AuthLDAPBindPassword password` Password used in conjuction with the bind DN		dh	E	p. 480
`AuthLDAPCharsetConfig file-path` Language to charset conversion configuration file		s	E	p. 480
`AuthLDAPCompareAsUser on|off` Use the authenticated user's credentials to perform authorization comparisons	off	dh	E	p. 481
`AuthLDAPCompareDNOnServer on|off` Use the LDAP server to compare the DNs	on	dh	E	p. 481
`AuthLDAPDereferenceAliases never|searching|finding|always` When will the module de-reference aliases	always	dh	E	p. 481
`AuthLDAPGroupAttribute attribute` LDAP attributes used to identify the user members of groups.	member uniquemember +	dh	E	p. 482
`AuthLDAPGroupAttributeIsDN on|off` Use the DN of the client username when checking for group membership	on	dh	E	p. 482
`AuthLDAPInitialBindAsUser off|on` Determines if the server does the initial DN lookup using the basic authentication users' own username, instead of anonymously or with hard-coded credentials for the server	off	dh	E	p. 482
`AuthLDAPInitialBindPatternregex substitution` Specifies the transformation of the basic authentication username to be used when binding to the LDAP server to perform a DN lookup	(.*) $1 (remote use +	dh	E	p. 483
`AuthLDAPMaxSubGroupDepth Number` Specifies the maximum sub-group nesting depth that will be evaluated before the user search is discontinued.	10	dh	E	p. 484
`AuthLDAPRemoteUserAttribute uid` Use the value of the attribute returned during the user query to set the REMOTE_USER environment variable		dh	E	p. 484
`AuthLDAPRemoteUserIsDN on|off` Use the DN of the client username to set the REMOTE_USER environment variable	off	dh	E	p. 484
`AuthLDAPSearchAsUser on|off` Use the authenticated user's credentials to perform authorization searches	off	dh	E	p. 485
`AuthLDAPSubGroupAttribute attribute` Specifies the attribute labels, one value per directive line, used to distinguish the members of the current group that are groups.		dh	E	p. 485
`AuthLDAPSubGroupClass LdapObjectClass` Specifies which LDAP objectClass values identify directory objects that are groups during sub-group processing.	groupOfNames groupO +	dh	E	p. 486
`AuthLDAPUrl url [NONE|SSL|TLS|STARTTLS]` URL specifying the LDAP search parameters		dh	E	p. 486
`AuthMerging Off | And | Or` Controls the manner in which each configuration section's authorization logic is combined with that of preceding configuration sections.	Off	dh	B	p. 491
`AuthName auth-domain` Authorization realm for use in HTTP authentication		dh	B	p. 450
`AuthnCacheContext directory|server|custom-string` Specify a context string for use in the cache key		d	B	p. 461

`AuthnCacheEnable`		s	B
Enable Authn caching configured anywhere		p. 461	
`AuthnCacheProvideFor authn-provider [...]`		dh	B
Specify which authn provider(s) to cache for		p. 462	
`AuthnCacheSOCache provider-name[:provider-args]`		s	B
Select socache backend provider to use		p. 462	
`AuthnCacheTimeout timeout (seconds)`		dh	B
Set a timeout for cache entries		p. 462	
`<AuthnProviderAlias baseProvider Alias> ...` `</AuthnProviderAlias>`		s	B
Enclose a group of directives that represent an extension of a base authentication provider and referenced by the specified alias		p. 451	
`AuthnzFcgiCheckAuthnProvider provider-name|None option ...`		d	E
Enables a FastCGI application to handle the check_authn authentication hook.		p. 468	
`AuthnzFcgiDefineProvider type provider-name` `backend-address`		s	E
Defines a FastCGI application as a provider for authentication and/or authorization		p. 469	
`AuthType None|Basic|Digest|Form`		dh	B
Type of user authentication		p. 451	
`AuthUserFile file-path`		dh	B
Sets the name of a text file containing the list of users and passwords for authentication		p. 458	
`AuthzDBDLoginToReferer On|Off`	Off	d	E
Determines whether to redirect the Client to the Referring page on successful login or logout if a `Referer` request header is present.		p. 498	
`AuthzDBDQuery query`		d	E
Specify the SQL Query for the required operation		p. 499	
`AuthzDBDRedirectQuery query`		d	E
Specify a query to look up a login page for the user		p. 499	
`AuthzDBMType default|SDBM|GDBM|NDBM|DB`	default	dh	E
Sets the type of database file that is used to store list of user groups		p. 501	
`<AuthzProviderAlias baseProvider Alias` `Require-Parameters> ... </AuthzProviderAlias>`		s	B
Enclose a group of directives that represent an extension of a base authorization provider and referenced by the specified alias		p. 492	
`AuthzSendForbiddenOnFailure On|Off`	Off	dh	B
Send '403 FORBIDDEN' instead of '401 UNAUTHORIZED' if authentication succeeds but authorization fails		p. 492	
`BalancerGrowth #`	5	sv	E
Number of additional Balancers that can be added Post-configuration		p. 738	
`BalancerInherit On|Off`	On	sv	E
Inherit ProxyPassed Balancers/Workers from the main server		p. 738	
`BalancerMember [balancerurl] url [key=value [key=value` `...]]`		d	E
Add a member to a load balancing group		p. 738	
`BalancerPersist On|Off`	Off	sv	E
Attempt to persist changes made by the Balancer Manager across restarts.		p. 739	
`BrowserMatch regex [!]env-variable[=value]` `[[!]env-variable[=value]] ...`		svdh	B
Sets environment variables conditional on HTTP User-Agent		p. 839	
`BrowserMatchNoCase regex [!]env-variable[=value]` `[[!]env-variable[=value]] ...`		svdh	B
Sets environment variables conditional on User-Agent without respect to case		p. 840	
`BufferedLogs On|Off`	Off	s	B
Buffer log entries in memory before writing to disk		p. 664	
`BufferSize integer`	131072	svdh	E
Maximum size in bytes to buffer by the buffer filter		p. 523	
`CacheDefaultExpire seconds`	3600 (one hour)	svdh	E
The default duration to cache a document when no expiry date is specified.		p. 529	
`CacheDetailHeader on|off`	off	svdh	E
Add an X-Cache-Detail header to the response.		p. 529	
`CacheDirLength length`	2	sv	E
The number of characters in subdirectory names		p. 540	
`CacheDirLevels levels`	2	sv	E
The number of levels of subdirectories in the cache.		p. 540	
`CacheDisable url-string | on`		svdh	E
Disable caching of specified URLs		p. 529	
`CacheEnable cache_type [url-string]`		svd	E
Enable caching of specified URLs using a specified storage manager		p. 530	

Directive	Default	Context	Status	Page
`CacheFile file-path [file-path] ...` Cache a list of file handles at startup time		s	X	p. 595
`CacheHeader on|off` Add an X-Cache header to the response.	off	svdh	E	p. 531
`CacheIgnoreCacheControl On|Off` Ignore request to not serve cached content to client	Off	sv	E	p. 532
`CacheIgnoreHeaders header-string [header-string] ...` Do not store the given HTTP header(s) in the cache.	None	sv	E	p. 532
`CacheIgnoreNoLastMod On|Off` Ignore the fact that a response has no Last Modified header.	Off	svdh	E	p. 533
`CacheIgnoreQueryString On|Off` Ignore query string when caching	Off	sv	E	p. 533
`CacheIgnoreURLSessionIdentifiers identifier [identifier] ...` Ignore defined session identifiers encoded in the URL when caching	None	sv	E	p. 534
`CacheKeyBaseURL URL` Override the base URL of reverse proxied cache keys.	http://example.com	sv	E	p. 534
`CacheLastModifiedFactor float` The factor used to compute an expiry date based on the LastModified date.	0.1	svdh	E	p. 535
`CacheLock on|off` Enable the thundering herd lock.	off	sv	E	p. 535
`CacheLockMaxAge integer` Set the maximum possible age of a cache lock.	5	sv	E	p. 535
`CacheLockPath directory` Set the lock path directory.	/tmp/mod_cache-lock +	sv	E	p. 536
`CacheMaxExpire seconds` The maximum time in seconds to cache a document	86400 (one day)	svdh	E	p. 536
`CacheMaxFileSize bytes` The maximum size (in bytes) of a document to be placed in the cache	1000000	svdh	E	p. 540
`CacheMinExpire seconds` The minimum time in seconds to cache a document	0	svdh	E	p. 536
`CacheMinFileSize bytes` The minimum size (in bytes) of a document to be placed in the cache	1	svdh	E	p. 541
`CacheNegotiatedDocs On|Off` Allows content-negotiated documents to be cached by proxy servers	Off	sv	B	p. 723
`CacheQuickHandler on|off` Run the cache from the quick handler.	on	sv	E	p. 536
`CacheReadSize bytes` The minimum size (in bytes) of the document to read and be cached before sending the data downstream	0	svdh	E	p. 541
`CacheReadTime milliseconds` The minimum time (in milliseconds) that should elapse while reading before data is sent downstream	0	svdh	E	p. 541
`CacheRoot directory` The directory root under which cache files are stored		sv	E	p. 542
`CacheSocache type[:args]` The shared object cache implementation to use		sv	E	p. 544
`CacheSocacheMaxSize bytes` The maximum size (in bytes) of an entry to be placed in the cache	102400	svdh	E	p. 544
`CacheSocacheMaxTime seconds` The maximum time (in seconds) for a document to be placed in the cache	86400	svdh	E	p. 544
`CacheSocacheMinTime seconds` The minimum time (in seconds) for a document to be placed in the cache	600	svdh	E	p. 545
`CacheSocacheReadSize bytes` The minimum size (in bytes) of the document to read and be cached before sending the data downstream	0	svdh	E	p. 545
`CacheSocacheReadTime milliseconds` The minimum time (in milliseconds) that should elapse while reading before data is sent downstream	0	svdh	E	p. 545
`CacheStaleOnError on|off` Serve stale content in place of 5xx responses.	on	svdh	E	p. 537
`CacheStoreExpired On|Off` Attempt to cache responses that the server reports as expired	Off	svdh	E	p. 537
`CacheStoreNoStore On|Off` Attempt to cache requests or responses that have been marked as no-store.	Off	svdh	E	p. 538
`CacheStorePrivate On|Off` Attempt to cache responses that the server has marked as private	Off	svdh	E	p. 538
`CGIDScriptTimeout time[s|ms]` The length of time to wait for more output from the CGI program		svdh	B	p. 552

Directive / Description	Default	Context	Status
`CGIMapExtension cgi-path .extension` Technique for locating the interpreter for CGI scripts		dh p. 362	C
`CGIPassAuth On|Off` Enables passing HTTP authorization headers to scripts as CGI variables	Off	dh p. 362	C
`CharsetDefault charset` Charset to translate into		svdh p. 555	E
`CharsetOptions option [option] ...` Configures charset translation behavior	ImplicitAdd	svdh p. 555	E
`CharsetSourceEnc charset` Source charset of files		svdh p. 555	E
`CheckCaseOnly on|off` Limits the action of the speling module to case corrections	Off	svdh p. 851	E
`CheckSpelling on|off` Enables the spelling module	Off	svdh p. 851	E
`ChrootDir /path/to/directory` Directory for apache to run chroot(8) after startup.		s p. 899	B
`ContentDigest On|Off` Enables the generation of `Content-MD5` HTTP Response headers	Off	svdh p. 362	C
`CookieDomain domain` The domain to which the tracking cookie applies		svdh p. 904	E
`CookieExpires expiry-period` Expiry time for the tracking cookie		svdh p. 905	E
`CookieName token` Name of the tracking cookie	Apache	svdh p. 905	E
`CookieStyle Netscape|Cookie|Cookie2|RFC2109|RFC2965` Format of the cookie header field	Netscape	svdh p. 905	E
`CookieTracking on|off` Enables tracking cookie	off	svdh p. 906	E
`CoreDumpDirectory directory` Directory where Apache HTTP Server attempts to switch before dumping core		s p. 917	M

`CustomLog file|pipe format|nickname [env=[!]environment-variable|`
`expr=expression]`
Sets filename and format of log file
		sv
		p. 664
			B

`Dav On|Off|provider-name` Enable WebDAV HTTP methods	Off	d p. 560	E
`DavDepthInfinity on|off` Allow PROPFIND, Depth: Infinity requests	off	svd p. 560	E
`DavGenericLockDB file-path` Location of the DAV lock database		svd p. 562	E
`DavLockDB file-path` Location of the DAV lock database		sv p. 561	E
`DavMinTimeout seconds` Minimum amount of time the server holds a lock on a DAV resource	0	svd p. 560	E
`DBDExptime time-in-seconds` Keepalive time for idle connections	300	sv p. 565	E
`DBDInitSQL "SQL statement"` Execute an SQL statement after connecting to a database		sv p. 565	E
`DBDKeep number` Maximum sustained number of connections	2	sv p. 566	E
`DBDMax number` Maximum number of connections	10	sv p. 566	E
`DBDMin number` Minimum number of connections	1	sv p. 566	E
`DBDParams param1=value1[,param2=value2]` Parameters for database connection		sv p. 566	E
`DBDPersist On|Off` Whether to use persistent connections		sv p. 567	E
`DBDPrepareSQL "SQL statement" label` Define an SQL prepared statement		sv p. 567	E
`DBDriver name` Specify an SQL driver		sv p. 567	E
`DefaultIcon url-path` Icon to display for files when no specific icon is configured		svdh p. 516	B

Directive / Description	Default	Context	Status	Page
`DefaultLanguage language-tag` Defines a default language-tag to be sent in the Content-Language header field for all resources in the current context that have not been assigned a language-tag by some other means.		svdh	B	p. 711
`DefaultRuntimeDir directory-path` Base directory for the server run-time files	DEFAULT_REL_RUNTIME +	s	C	p. 363
`DefaultType media-type|none` This directive has no effect other than to emit warnings if the value is not `none`. In prior versions, DefaultType would specify a default media type to assign to response content for which no other media type configuration could be found.	none	svdh	C	p. 363
`Define parameter-name [parameter-value]` Define a variable		svd	C	p. 364
`DeflateBufferSize value` Fragment size to be compressed at one time by zlib	8096	sv	E	p. 571
`DeflateCompressionLevel value` How much compression do we apply to the output		sv	E	p. 571
`DeflateFilterNote [type] notename` Places the compression ratio in a note for logging		sv	E	p. 571
`DeflateInflateLimitRequestBody value` Maximum size of inflated request bodies		svdh	E	p. 572
`DeflateInflateRatioBurst value` Maximum number of times the inflation ratio for request bodies can be crossed		svdh	E	p. 572
`DeflateInflateRatioLimit value` Maximum inflation ratio for request bodies		svdh	E	p. 573
`DeflateMemLevel value` How much memory should be used by zlib for compression	9	sv	E	p. 573
`DeflateWindowSize value` Zlib compression window size	15	sv	E	p. 573
`Deny from all|host|env=[!]env-variable [host|env=[!]env-variable] ...` Controls which hosts are denied access to the server		dh	E	p. 413
`<Directory "directory-path"> ... </Directory>` Enclose a group of directives that apply only to the named file-system directory, sub-directories, and their contents.		sv	C	p. 364
`DirectoryCheckHandler On|Off` Toggle how this module responds when another handler is configured	Off	svdh	B	p. 575
`DirectoryIndex disabled	local-url [local-url] ...` List of resources to look for when the client requests a directory	index.html	svdh	B	p. 576
`DirectoryIndexRedirect on	off	permanent	temp	seeother	3xx-code` Configures an external redirect for directory indexes.	off	svdh	B	p. 577
`<DirectoryMatch regex> ... </DirectoryMatch>` Enclose directives that apply to the contents of file-system directories matching a regular expression.		sv	C	p. 366
`DirectorySlash On|Off` Toggle trailing slash redirects on or off	On	svdh	B	p. 577
`DocumentRoot directory-path` Directory that forms the main document tree visible from the web	"/usr/local/apache/ +	sv	C	p. 367
`DTracePrivileges On|Off` Determines whether the privileges required by dtrace are enabled.	Off	s	X	p. 727
`DumpIOInput On|Off` Dump all input data to the error log	Off	s	E	p. 580
`DumpIOOutput On|Off` Dump all output data to the error log	Off	s	E	p. 581
`<Else> ... </Else>` Contains directives that apply only if the condition of a previous <IF> or <ELSEIF> section is not satisfied by a request at runtime		svdh	C	p. 367
`<ElseIf expression> ... </ElseIf>` Contains directives that apply only if a condition is satisfied by a request at runtime while the condition of a previous <IF> or <ELSEIF> section is not satisfied		svdh	C	p. 368
`EnableExceptionHook On|Off` Enables a hook that runs exception handlers after a crash	Off	s	M	p. 918
`EnableMMAP On|Off` Use memory-mapping to read files during delivery	On	svdh	C	p. 368
`EnableSendfile On|Off` Use the kernel sendfile support to deliver files to the client	Off	svdh	C	p. 369
`Error message` Abort configuration parsing with a custom error message		svdh	C	p. 370
`ErrorDocument error-code document` What the server will return to the client in case of an error		svdh	C	p. 370

`ErrorLog file-path|syslog[:facility]` Location where the server will log errors	logs/error_log (Uni +	sv p. 372	C
`ErrorLogFormat [connection|request] format` Format specification for error log entries		sv p. 372	C
`Example` Demonstration directive to illustrate the Apache module API		svdh p. 586	X
`ExpiresActive On|Off` Enables generation of `Expires` headers	Off	svdh p. 588	E
`ExpiresByType MIME-type <code>seconds` Value of the `Expires` header configured by MIME type		svdh p. 588	E
`ExpiresDefault <code>seconds` Default algorithm for calculating expiration time		svdh p. 589	E
`ExtendedStatus On|Off` Keep track of extended status information for each request	Off[*]	s p. 374	C
`ExtFilterDefine filtername parameters` Define an external filter		s p. 592	E
`ExtFilterOptions option [option] ...` Configure MOD_EXT_FILTER options	NoLogStderr	d p. 593	E
`FallbackResource disabled	local-url` Define a default URL for requests that don't map to a file		svdh p. 578	B
`FileETag component ...` File attributes used to create the ETag HTTP response header for static files	MTime Size	svdh p. 375	C
`<Files "filename"> ... </Files>` Contains directives that apply to matched filenames		svdh p. 376	C
`<FilesMatch regex> ... </FilesMatch>` Contains directives that apply to regular-expression matched filenames		svdh p. 376	C
`FilterChain [+=-@!]filter-name ...` Configure the filter chain		svdh p. 602	B
`FilterDeclare filter-name [type]` Declare a smart filter		svdh p. 602	B
`FilterProtocol filter-name [provider-name] proto-flags` Deal with correct HTTP protocol handling		svdh p. 603	B
`FilterProvider filter-name provider-name expression` Register a content filter		svdh p. 603	B
`FilterTrace filter-name level` Get debug/diagnostic information from MOD_FILTER		svd p. 604	B

`ForceLanguagePriority None|Prefer|Fallback`
`[Prefer|Fallback]`
Action to take if a single acceptable document is not found
	Prefer	svdh
		p. 723
			B

`ForceType media-type|None` Forces all matching files to be served with the specified media type in the HTTP Content-Type header field		dh p. 377	C
`ForensicLog filename|pipe` Sets filename of the forensic log		sv p. 670	E
`GprofDir /tmp/gprof/|/tmp/gprof/%` Directory to write gmon.out profiling data to.		sv p. 378	C
`GracefulShutdownTimeout seconds` Specify a timeout after which a gracefully shutdown server will exit.	0	s p. 918	M
`Group unix-group` Group under which the server will answer requests	#-1	s p. 899	B
`H2Direct on|off` H2 Direct Protocol Switch	on (for non TLS)	sv p. 614	E
`H2MaxSessionStreams n` Maximum number of active streams per HTTP/2 session.	100	sv p. 615	E
`H2MaxWorkerIdleSeconds n` Maximum number of seconds h2 workers remain idle until shut down.	600	s p. 615	E
`H2MaxWorkers n` Maximum number of worker threads to use per child process.		s p. 615	E
`H2MinWorkers n` Minimal number of worker threads to use per child process.		s p. 615	E
`H2SerializeHeaders on|off` Serialize Request/Resoonse Processing Switch	off	sv p. 616	E
`H2SessionExtraFiles n` Number of Extra File Handles	5	sv p. 616	E
`H2StreamMaxMemSize bytes` Maximum amount of output data buffered per stream.	65536	sv p. 617	E

`H2WindowSize bytes`	65536	sv	E
Size of Stream Window for upstream data.		p. 617	
`Header [condition] add|append|echo|edit|edit*|merge|set|setifempty|unset|note`		svdh	E
`header [[expr=]value [replacement] [early|env=[!]varname|expr=expression]]`			
Configure HTTP response headers		p. 607	
`HeaderName filename`		svdh	B
Name of the file that will be inserted at the top of the index listing		p. 516	
`HeartbeatAddress addr:port`		s	X
Multicast address for heartbeat packets		p. 611	
`HeartbeatListenaddr:port`		s	X
multicast address to listen for incoming heartbeat requests		p. 612	
`HeartbeatMaxServers number-of-servers`	10	s	X
Specifies the maximum number of servers that will be sending heartbeat requests to this server		p. 612	
`HeartbeatStorage file-path`	logs/hb.dat	s	X
Path to store heartbeat data		p. 613	
`HeartbeatStorage file-path`	logs/hb.dat	s	X
Path to read heartbeat data		p. 648	
`HostnameLookups On|Off|Double`	Off	svd	C
Enables DNS lookups on client IP addresses		p. 378	
`IdentityCheck On|Off`	Off	svd	E
Enables logging of the RFC 1413 identity of the remote user		p. 618	
`IdentityCheckTimeout seconds`	30	svd	E
Determines the timeout duration for ident requests		p. 618	
`<If expression> ... </If>`		svdh	C
Contains directives that apply only if a condition is satisfied by a request at runtime		p. 379	
`<IfDefine [!]parameter-name> ... </IfDefine>`		svdh	C
Encloses directives that will be processed only if a test is true at startup		p. 379	
`<IfModule [!]module-file|module-identifier> ...`		svdh	C
`</IfModule>`			
Encloses directives that are processed conditional on the presence or absence of a specific module		p. 380	
`<IfVersion [[!]operator] version> ... </IfVersion>`		svdh	E
contains version dependent configuration		p. 907	
`ImapBase map|referer|URL`	http://servername/	svdh	B
Default base for imagemap files		p. 622	
`ImapDefault error|nocontent|map|referer|URL`	nocontent	svdh	B
Default action when an imagemap is called with coordinates that are not explicitly mapped		p. 623	
`ImapMenu none|formatted|semiformatted|unformatted`	formatted	svdh	B
Action if no coordinates are given when calling an imagemap		p. 623	
`Include file-path|directory-path|wildcard`		svd	C
Includes other configuration files from within the server configuration files		p. 381	
`IncludeOptional file-path|directory-path|wildcard`		svd	C
Includes other configuration files from within the server configuration files		p. 382	
`IndexHeadInsert "markup ..."`		svdh	B
Inserts text in the HEAD section of an index page.		p. 517	
`IndexIgnore file [file] ...`	"."	svdh	B
Adds to the list of files to hide when listing a directory		p. 517	
`IndexIgnoreReset ON|OFF`		svdh	B
Empties the list of files to hide when listing a directory		p. 518	
`IndexOptions [+|-]option [[+|-]option] ...`		svdh	B
Various configuration settings for directory indexing		p. 518	
`IndexOrderDefault Ascending|Descending`	Ascending Name	svdh	B
`Name|Date|Size|Description`			
Sets the default ordering of the directory index		p. 521	
`IndexStyleSheet url-path`		svdh	B
Adds a CSS stylesheet to the directory index		p. 522	
`InputSed sed-command`		dh	X
Sed command to filter request data (typically `POST` data)		p. 819	
`ISAPIAppendLogToErrors on|off`	off	svdh	B
Record `HSE_APPEND_LOG_PARAMETER` requests from ISAPI extensions to the error log		p. 642	
`ISAPIAppendLogToQuery on|off`	on	svdh	B
Record `HSE_APPEND_LOG_PARAMETER` requests from ISAPI extensions to the query field		p. 642	
`ISAPICacheFile file-path [file-path] ...`		sv	B
ISAPI .dll files to be loaded at startup		p. 642	
`ISAPIFakeAsync on|off`	off	svdh	B
Fake asynchronous support for ISAPI callbacks		p. 643	

Directive	Default	Context	Status
`ISAPILogNotSupported on|off` Log unsupported feature requests from ISAPI extensions	off	svdh p. 643	B
`ISAPIReadAheadBuffer size` Size of the Read Ahead Buffer sent to ISAPI extensions	49152	svdh p. 643	B
`KeepAlive On|Off` Enables HTTP persistent connections	On	sv p. 382	C
`KeepAliveTimeout num[ms]` Amount of time the server will wait for subsequent requests on a persistent connection	5	sv p. 382	C
`KeptBodySize maximum size in bytes` Keep the request body instead of discarding it up to the specified maximum size, for potential use by filters such as mod_include.	0	d p. 803	B
`LanguagePriority MIME-lang [MIME-lang] ...` The precendence of language variants for cases where the client does not express a preference		svdh p. 724	B
`LDAPCacheEntries number` Maximum number of entries in the primary LDAP cache	1024	s p. 654	E
`LDAPCacheTTL seconds` Time that cached items remain valid	600	s p. 655	E
`LDAPConnectionPoolTTL n` Discard backend connections that have been sitting in the connection pool too long	-1	sv p. 655	E
`LDAPConnectionTimeout seconds` Specifies the socket connection timeout in seconds		s p. 655	E
`LDAPLibraryDebug 7` Enable debugging in the LDAP SDK		s p. 656	E
`LDAPOpCacheEntries number` Number of entries used to cache LDAP compare operations	1024	s p. 656	E
`LDAPOpCacheTTL seconds` Time that entries in the operation cache remain valid	600	s p. 656	E
`LDAPReferralHopLimit number` The maximum number of referral hops to chase before terminating an LDAP query.		dh p. 657	E
`LDAPReferrals On|Off|default` Enable referral chasing during queries to the LDAP server.	On	dh p. 657	E
`LDAPRetries number-of-retries` Configures the number of LDAP server retries.	3	s p. 657	E
`LDAPRetryDelay seconds` Configures the delay between LDAP server retries.	0	s p. 658	E
`LDAPSharedCacheFile directory-path/filename` Sets the shared memory cache file		s p. 658	E
`LDAPSharedCacheSize bytes` Size in bytes of the shared-memory cache	500000	s p. 658	E
`LDAPTimeout seconds` Specifies the timeout for LDAP search and bind operations, in seconds	60	s p. 658	E
`LDAPTrustedClientCert type directory-path/filename/nickname [password]` Sets the file containing or nickname referring to a per connection client certificate. Not all LDAP toolkits support per connection client certificates.		dh p. 659	E
`LDAPTrustedGlobalCert type directory-path/filename [password]` Sets the file or database containing global trusted Certificate Authority or global client certificates		s p. 659	E
`LDAPTrustedMode type` Specifies the SSL/TLS mode to be used when connecting to an LDAP server.		sv p. 660	E
`LDAPVerifyServerCert On|Off` Force server certificate verification	On	s p. 660	E
`<Limit method [method] ... > ... </Limit>` Restrict enclosed access controls to only certain HTTP methods		dh p. 383	C
`<LimitExcept method [method] ... > ... </LimitExcept>` Restrict access controls to all HTTP methods except the named ones		dh p. 384	C
`LimitInternalRecursion number [number]` Determine maximum number of internal redirects and nested subrequests	10	sv p. 384	C
`LimitRequestBody bytes` Restricts the total size of the HTTP request body sent from the client	0	svdh p. 384	C
`LimitRequestFields number` Limits the number of HTTP request header fields that will be accepted from the client	100	sv p. 385	C
`LimitRequestFieldSize bytes` Limits the size of the HTTP request header allowed from the client	8190	sv p. 386	C
`LimitRequestLine bytes` Limit the size of the HTTP request line that will be accepted from the client	8190	sv p. 386	C

`LimitXMLRequestBody bytes`	1000000	svdh	C
Limits the size of an XML-based request body		p. 387	
`Listen [IP-address:]portnumber [protocol]`		s	M
IP addresses and ports that the server listens to		p. 919	
`ListenBacklog backlog`		s	M
Maximum length of the queue of pending connections		p. 920	
`ListenCoresBucketsRatio ratio`	0 (disabled)	s	M
Ratio between the number of CPU cores (online) and the number of listeners' buckets		p. 920	
`LoadFile filename [filename] ...`		sv	E
Link in the named object file or library		p. 846	
`LoadModule module filename`		sv	E
Links in the object file or library, and adds to the list of active modules		p. 846	
`<Location "URL-path|URL"> ... </Location>`		sv	C
Applies the enclosed directives only to matching URLs		p. 387	
`<LocationMatch regex> ... </LocationMatch>`		sv	C
Applies the enclosed directives only to regular-expression matching URLs		p. 389	
`LogFormat format|nickname [nickname]`	`"%h %l %u %t \"%r\" +`	sv	B
Describes a format for use in a log file		p. 665	
`LogIOTrackTTFB ON|OFF`	OFF	svdh	E
Enable tracking of time to first byte (TTFB)		p. 672	
`LogLevel [module:]level [module:level] ...`	warn	svd	C
Controls the verbosity of the ErrorLog		p. 389	
`LogMessage message [hook=hook] [expr=expression]`		d	X
Log user-defined message to error log		p. 667	
`LuaAuthzProvider provider_name /path/to/lua/script.lua function_name`		s	X
Plug an authorization provider function into MOD_AUTHZ_CORE		p. 689	
`LuaCodeCache stat|forever|never`	stat	svdh	X
Configure the compiled code cache.		p. 689	
`LuaHookAccessChecker /path/to/lua/script.lua hook_function_name [early|late]`		svdh	X
Provide a hook for the access_checker phase of request processing		p. 690	
`LuaHookAuthChecker /path/to/lua/script.lua hook_function_name [early|late]`		svdh	X
Provide a hook for the auth_checker phase of request processing		p. 690	
`LuaHookCheckUserID /path/to/lua/script.lua hook_function_name [early|late]`		svdh	X
Provide a hook for the check_user_id phase of request processing		p. 691	
`LuaHookFixups /path/to/lua/script.lua hook_function_name`		svdh	X
Provide a hook for the fixups phase of a request processing		p. 691	
`LuaHookInsertFilter /path/to/lua/script.lua hook_function_name`		svdh	X
Provide a hook for the insert_filter phase of request processing		p. 692	
`LuaHookLog /path/to/lua/script.lua log_function_name`		svdh	X
Provide a hook for the access log phase of a request processing		p. 692	
`LuaHookMapToStorage /path/to/lua/script.lua hook_function_name`		svdh	X
Provide a hook for the map_to_storage phase of request processing		p. 693	
`LuaHookTranslateName /path/to/lua/script.lua hook_function_name [early|late]`		sv	X
Provide a hook for the translate name phase of request processing		p. 693	
`LuaHookTypeChecker /path/to/lua/script.lua hook_function_name`		svdh	X
Provide a hook for the type_checker phase of request processing		p. 694	
`LuaInherit none|parent-first|parent-last`	parent-first	svdh	X
Controls how parent configuration sections are merged into children		p. 695	
`LuaInputFilter filter_name /path/to/lua/script.lua function_name`		s	X
Provide a Lua function for content input filtering		p. 695	
`LuaMapHandler uri-pattern /path/to/lua/script.lua [function-name]`		svdh	X
Map a path to a lua handler		p. 696	
`LuaOutputFilter filter_name /path/to/lua/script.lua function_name`		s	X
Provide a Lua function for content output filtering		p. 696	

`LuaPackageCPath /path/to/include/?.soa`		svdh	X
Add a directory to lua's package.cpath		p. 697	
`LuaPackagePath /path/to/include/?.lua`		svdh	X
Add a directory to lua's package.path		p. 697	
`LuaQuickHandler /path/to/script.lua hook_function_name`		sv	X
Provide a hook for the quick handler of request processing		p. 698	
`LuaRoot /path/to/a/directory`		svdh	X
Specify the base path for resolving relative paths for mod_lua directives		p. 698	
`LuaScope once|request|conn|thread|server [min] [max]`	once	svdh	X
One of once, request, conn, thread – default is once		p. 698	
`<Macro name [par1 .. parN]> ... </Macro>`		svd	B
Define a configuration file macro		p. 702	
`MaxConnectionsPerChild number`	0	s	M
Limit on the number of connections that an individual child server will handle during its life		p. 920	
`MaxKeepAliveRequests number`	100	sv	C
Number of requests allowed on a persistent connection		p. 391	
`MaxMemFree KBytes`	2048	s	M
Maximum amount of memory that the main allocator is allowed to hold without calling `free()`		p. 921	
`MaxRangeOverlaps default | unlimited | none |` `number-of-ranges`	20	svd	C
Number of overlapping ranges (eg: `100-200,150-300`) allowed before returning the complete resource		p. 391	
`MaxRangeReversals default | unlimited | none |` `number-of-ranges`	20	svd	C
Number of range reversals (eg: `100-200,50-70`) allowed before returning the complete resource		p. 391	
`MaxRanges default | unlimited | none | number-of-ranges`	200	svd	C
Number of ranges allowed before returning the complete resource		p. 392	
`MaxRequestWorkers number`		s	M
Maximum number of connections that will be processed simultaneously		p. 921	
`MaxSpareServers number`	10	s	M
Maximum number of idle child server processes		p. 935	
`MaxSpareThreads number`		s	M
Maximum number of idle threads		p. 921	
`MaxThreads number`	2048	s	M
Set the maximum number of worker threads		p. 932	
`MemcacheConnTTL num[units]`	15s	sv	E
Keepalive time for idle connections		p. 849	
`MergeTrailers [on|off]`	off	sv	C
Determines whether trailers are merged into headers		p. 392	
`MetaDir directory`	.web	svdh	E
Name of the directory to find CERN-style meta information files		p. 547	
`MetaFiles on|off`	off	svdh	E
Activates CERN meta-file processing		p. 548	
`MetaSuffix suffix`	.meta	svdh	E
File name suffix for the file containing CERN-style meta information		p. 548	
`MimeMagicFile file-path`		sv	E
Enable MIME-type determination based on file contents using the specified magic file		p. 720	
`MinSpareServers number`	5	s	M
Minimum number of idle child server processes		p. 935	
`MinSpareThreads number`		s	M
Minimum number of idle threads available to handle request spikes		p. 922	
`MMapFile file-path [file-path] ...`		s	X
Map a list of files into memory at startup time		p. 595	
`ModemStandard V.21|V.26bis|V.32|V.92`		d	X
Modem standard to simulate		p. 574	
`ModMimeUsePathInfo On|Off`	Off	d	B
Tells MOD_MIME to treat `path_info` components as part of the filename		p. 712	
`MultiviewsMatch Any|NegotiatedOnly|Filters|Handlers` `[Handlers|Filters]`	NegotiatedOnly	svdh	B
The types of files that will be included when searching for a matching file with MultiViews		p. 712	
`Mutex mechanism [default|mutex-name] ... [OmitPID]`	default	s	C
Configures mutex mechanism and lock file directory for all or specified mutexes		p. 392	
`NameVirtualHost addr[:port]`		s	C
DEPRECATED: Designates an IP address for name-virtual hosting		p. 395	
`NoProxy host [host] ...`		sv	E
Hosts, domains, or networks that will be connected to directly		p. 739	

`NWSSLTrustedCerts filename [filename] ...`		s	B
List of additional client certificates		p. 725	
`NWSSLUpgradeable [IP-address:]portnumber`		s	B
Allows a connection to be upgraded to an SSL connection upon request		p. 725	
`Options [+|-]option [[+|-]option] ...`	FollowSymlinks	svdh	C
Configures what features are available in a particular directory		p. 395	
`Order ordering`	Deny,Allow	dh	E
Controls the default access state and the order in which ALLOW and DENY are evaluated.		p. 413	
`OutputSed sed-command`		dh	X
Sed command for filtering response content		p. 819	
`PassEnv env-variable [env-variable] ...`		svdh	B
Passes environment variables from the shell		p. 583	
`PidFile filename`	logs/httpd.pid	s	M
File where the server records the process ID of the daemon		p. 922	
`PrivilegesMode FAST|SECURE|SELECTIVE`	FAST	svd	X
Trade off processing speed and efficiency vs security against malicious privileges-aware code.		p. 727	
`Protocol protocol`		sv	C
Protocol for a listening socket		p. 396	
`ProtocolEcho On|Off`	Off	sv	X
Turn the echo server on or off		p. 582	
`Protocols protocol ...`	http/1.1	sv	C
Protocols available for a server/virtual host		p. 397	
`ProtocolsHonorOrder On|Off`	On	sv	C
Determines if order of Protocols determines precedence during negotiation		p. 397	
`<Proxy wildcard-url> ...</Proxy>`		sv	E
Container for directives applied to proxied resources		p. 740	
`ProxyAddHeaders Off|On`	On	svd	E
Add proxy information in X-Forwarded-* headers		p. 741	
`ProxyBadHeader IsError|Ignore|StartBody`	IsError	sv	E
Determines how to handle bad header lines in a response		p. 741	
`ProxyBlock *|word|host|domain [word|host|domain] ...`		sv	E
Words, hosts, or domains that are banned from being proxied		p. 742	
`ProxyDomain Domain`		sv	E
Default domain name for proxied requests		p. 742	
`ProxyErrorOverride On|Off`	Off	svd	E
Override error pages for proxied content		p. 742	
`ProxyExpressDBMFile <pathname>`		sv	E
Pathname to DBM file.		p. 774	
`ProxyExpressDBMFile <type>`		sv	E
DBM type of file.		p. 774	
`ProxyExpressEnable [on|off]`		sv	E
Enable the module functionality.		p. 775	
`ProxyFtpDirCharset character set`	ISO-8859-1	svd	E
Define the character set for proxied FTP listings		p. 782	
`ProxyFtpEscapeWildcards [on|off]`		svd	E
Whether wildcards in requested filenames are escaped when sent to the FTP server		p. 782	
`ProxyFtpListOnWildcard [on|off]`		svd	E
Whether wildcards in requested filenames trigger a file listing		p. 782	
`ProxyHTMLBufSize bytes`		svd	B
Sets the buffer size increment for buffering inline scripts and stylesheets.		p. 783	
`ProxyHTMLCharsetOut Charset	*`		svd	B
Specify a charset for mod_proxy_html output.		p. 784	

`ProxyHTMLDocType HTML|XHTML [Legacy]`
OR
`ProxyHTMLDocType fpi [SGML|XML]`
Sets an HTML or XHTML document type declaration.
		svd
		
		p. 784
			B

`ProxyHTMLEnable On|Off`	Off	svd	B
Turns the proxy_html filter on or off.		p. 785	
`ProxyHTMLEvents attribute [attribute ...]`		svd	B
Specify attributes to treat as scripting events.		p. 785	
`ProxyHTMLExtended On|Off`	Off	svd	B
Determines whether to fix links in inline scripts, stylesheets, and scripting events.		p. 785	
`ProxyHTMLFixups [lowercase] [dospath] [reset]`		svd	B
Fixes for simple HTML errors.		p. 786	

`ProxyHTMLInterp On|Off` Enables per-request interpolation of PROXYHTMLURLMAP rules.	Off	svd p. 786	B
`ProxyHTMLLinks element attribute [attribute2 ...]` Specify HTML elements that have URL attributes to be rewritten.		svd p. 786	B
`ProxyHTMLMeta On|Off` Turns on or off extra pre-parsing of metadata in HTML <head> sections.	Off	svd p. 787	B
`ProxyHTMLStripComments On|Off` Determines whether to strip HTML comments.	Off	svd p. 787	B
`ProxyHTMLURLMap from-pattern to-pattern [flags] [cond]` Defines a rule to rewrite HTML links		svd p. 787	B
`ProxyIOBufferSize bytes` Determine size of internal data throughput buffer	8192	sv p. 743	E
`<ProxyMatch regex> ...</ProxyMatch>` Container for directives applied to regular-expression-matched proxied resources		sv p. 743	E
`ProxyMaxForwards number` Maximum number of proxies that a request can be forwarded through	-1	sv p. 744	E

`ProxyPass [path] !|url [key=value [key=value ...]]`
`[nocanon] [interpolate] [noquery]`
Maps remote servers into the local server URL-space
		svd
		
		p. 744
			E

`ProxyPassInherit On|Off` Inherit ProxyPass directives defined from the main server	On	sv p. 752	E
`ProxyPassInterpolateEnv On|Off` Enable Environment Variable interpolation in Reverse Proxy configurations	Off	svd p. 752	E
`ProxyPassMatch [regex] !|url [key=value [key=value ...]]` Maps remote servers into the local server URL-space using regular expressions		svd p. 752	E
`ProxyPassReverse [path] url [interpolate]` Adjusts the URL in HTTP response headers sent from a reverse proxied server		svd p. 753	E

`ProxyPassReverseCookieDomain internal-domain public-domain`
`[interpolate]`
Adjusts the Domain string in Set-Cookie headers from a reverse- proxied server
		svd
		
		p. 754
			E

`ProxyPassReverseCookiePath internal-path public-path`
`[interpolate]`
Adjusts the Path string in Set-Cookie headers from a reverse- proxied server
		svd
		
		p. 754
			E

`ProxyPreserveHost On|Off` Use incoming Host HTTP request header for proxy request	Off	svd p. 755	E
`ProxyReceiveBufferSize bytes` Network buffer size for proxied HTTP and FTP connections	0	sv p. 755	E
`ProxyRemote match remote-server` Remote proxy used to handle certain requests		sv p. 755	E
`ProxyRemoteMatch regex remote-server` Remote proxy used to handle requests matched by regular expressions		sv p. 756	E
`ProxyRequests On|Off` Enables forward (standard) proxy requests	Off	sv p. 756	E
`ProxySCGIInternalRedirect On|Off|Headername` Enable or disable internal redirect responses from the backend	On	svd p. 792	E
`ProxySCGISendfile On|Off|Headername` Enable evaluation of *X-Sendfile* pseudo response header	Off	svd p. 792	E
`ProxySet url key=value [key=value ...]` Set various Proxy balancer or member parameters		d p. 757	E
`ProxySourceAddress address` Set local IP address for outgoing proxy connections		sv p. 757	E
`ProxyStatus Off|On|Full` Show Proxy LoadBalancer status in mod_status	Off	sv p. 757	E
`ProxyTimeout seconds` Network timeout for proxied requests		sv p. 758	E
`ProxyVia On|Off|Full|Block` Information provided in the `Via` HTTP response header for proxied requests	Off	sv p. 758	E
`ReadmeName filename` Name of the file that will be inserted at the end of the index listing		svdh p. 522	B
`ReceiveBufferSize bytes` TCP receive buffer size	0	s p. 923	M
`Redirect [status] URL-path URL` Sends an external redirect asking the client to fetch a different URL		svdh p. 420	B
`RedirectMatch [status] regex URL` Sends an external redirect based on a regular expression match of the current URL		svdh p. 421	B

`RedirectPermanent URL-path URL`	svdh	B
Sends an external permanent redirect asking the client to fetch a different URL	p. 422	
`RedirectTemp URL-path URL`	svdh	B
Sends an external temporary redirect asking the client to fetch a different URL	p. 422	
`ReflectorHeader inputheader [outputheader]`	svdh	B
Reflect an input header to the output headers	p. 796	
`RemoteIPHeader header-field`	sv	B
Declare the header field which should be parsed for useragent IP addresses	p. 798	
`RemoteIPInternalProxy proxy-ip|proxy-ip/subnet|hostname` ...	sv	B
Declare client intranet IP addresses trusted to present the RemoteIPHeader value	p. 798	
`RemoteIPInternalProxyList filename`	sv	B
Declare client intranet IP addresses trusted to present the RemoteIPHeader value	p. 799	
`RemoteIPProxiesHeader HeaderFieldName`	sv	B
Declare the header field which will record all intermediate IP addresses	p. 799	
`RemoteIPTrustedProxy proxy-ip|proxy-ip/subnet|hostname` ...	sv	B
Declare client intranet IP addresses trusted to present the RemoteIPHeader value	p. 800	
`RemoteIPTrustedProxyList filename`	sv	B
Declare client intranet IP addresses trusted to present the RemoteIPHeader value	p. 800	
`RemoveCharset extension [extension]` ...	vdh	B
Removes any character set associations for a set of file extensions	p. 713	
`RemoveEncoding extension [extension]` ...	vdh	B
Removes any content encoding associations for a set of file extensions	p. 713	
`RemoveHandler extension [extension]` ...	vdh	B
Removes any handler associations for a set of file extensions	p. 714	
`RemoveInputFilter extension [extension]` ...	vdh	B
Removes any input filter associations for a set of file extensions	p. 714	
`RemoveLanguage extension [extension]` ...	vdh	B
Removes any language associations for a set of file extensions	p. 715	
`RemoveOutputFilter extension [extension]` ...	vdh	B
Removes any output filter associations for a set of file extensions	p. 715	
`RemoveType extension [extension]` ...	vdh	B
Removes any content type associations for a set of file extensions	p. 715	
`RequestHeader add|append|edit|edit*|merge|set|setifempty|unset header [[expr=]value [replacement] [early|env=[!]varname|expr=expression]]`	svdh	E
Configure HTTP request headers	p. 609	
`RequestReadTimeout [header=timeout[-maxtimeout][,MinRate=rate] [body=timeout[-maxtimeout][,MinRate=rate]`	sv	E
Set timeout values for receiving request headers and body from client.	p. 801	
`Require [not] entity-name [entity-name]` ...	dh	B
Tests whether an authenticated user is authorized by an authorization provider.	p. 492	
`<RequireAll>` ... `</RequireAll>`	dh	B
Enclose a group of authorization directives of which none must fail and at least one must succeed for the enclosing directive to succeed. p. 494		
`<RequireAny>` ... `</RequireAny>`	dh	B
Enclose a group of authorization directives of which one must succeed for the enclosing directive to succeed.	p. 494	
`<RequireNone>` ... `</RequireNone>`	dh	B
Enclose a group of authorization directives of which none must succeed for the enclosing directive to not fail.	p. 495	
`RewriteBase URL-path`	dh	E
Sets the base URL for per-directory rewrites	p. 805	
`RewriteCond TestString CondPattern`	svdh	E
Defines a condition under which rewriting will take place	p. 805	
`RewriteEngine on|off` off	svdh	E
Enables or disables runtime rewriting engine	p. 810	
`RewriteMap MapName MapType:MapSource`	sv	E
Defines a mapping function for key-lookup	p. 811	
`RewriteOptions Options`	svdh	E
Sets some special options for the rewrite engine	p. 812	
`RewriteRule Pattern Substitution [flags]`	svdh	E
Defines rules for the rewriting engine	p. 813	
`RLimitCPU seconds|max [seconds|max]`	svdh	C
Limits the CPU consumption of processes launched by Apache httpd children	p. 398	
`RLimitMEM bytes|max [bytes|max]`	svdh	C
Limits the memory consumption of processes launched by Apache httpd children	p. 398	

`RLimitNPROC number|max [number|max]`		svdh	C
Limits the number of processes that can be launched by processes launched by Apache httpd children		p. 399	
`Satisfy Any|All`	All	dh	E
Interaction between host-level access control and user authentication		p. 415	
`ScoreBoardFile file-path`	logs/apache_runtime +	s	M
Location of the file used to store coordination data for the child processes		p. 923	
`Script method cgi-script`		svd	B
Activates a CGI script for a particular request method.		p. 417	
`ScriptAlias URL-path file-path|directory-path`		sv	B
Maps a URL to a filesystem location and designates the target as a CGI script		p. 422	
`ScriptAliasMatch regex file-path|directory-path`		sv	B
Maps a URL to a filesystem location using a regular expression and designates the target as a CGI script		p. 423	
`ScriptInterpreterSource Registry|Registry-Strict|Script`	Script	svdh	C
Technique for locating the interpreter for CGI scripts		p. 399	
`ScriptLog file-path`		sv	B
Location of the CGI script error logfile		p. 550	
`ScriptLogBuffer bytes`	1024	sv	B
Maximum amount of PUT or POST requests that will be recorded in the scriptlog		p. 551	
`ScriptLogLength bytes`	10385760	sv	B
Size limit of the CGI script logfile		p. 551	
`ScriptSock file-path`	cgisock	s	B
The filename prefix of the socket to use for communication with the cgi daemon		p. 553	
`SecureListen [IP-address:]portnumber Certificate-Name [MUTUAL]`		s	B
Enables SSL encryption for the specified port		p. 725	
`SeeRequestTail On|Off`	Off	s	C
Determine if mod_status displays the first 63 characters of a request or the last 63, assuming the request itself is greater than 63 chars.		p. 400	
`SendBufferSize bytes`	0	s	M
TCP buffer size		p. 924	
`ServerAdmin email-address|URL`		sv	C
Email address that the server includes in error messages sent to the client		p. 400	
`ServerAlias hostname [hostname] ...`		v	C
Alternate names for a host used when matching requests to name-virtual hosts		p. 401	
`ServerLimit number`		s	M
Upper limit on configurable number of processes		p. 924	
`ServerName [scheme://]fully-qualified-domain-name[:port]`		sv	C
Hostname and port that the server uses to identify itself		p. 401	
`ServerPath URL-path`		v	C
Legacy URL pathname for a name-based virtual host that is accessed by an incompatible browser		p. 402	
`ServerRoot directory-path`	/usr/local/apache	s	C
Base directory for the server installation		p. 403	
`ServerSignature On|Off|EMail`	Off	svdh	C
Configures the footer on server-generated documents		p. 403	
`ServerTokens Major|Minor|Min[imal]|Prod[uctOnly]|OS|Full`	Full	s	C
Configures the `Server` HTTP response header		p. 404	
`Session On|Off`	Off	svdh	E
Enables a session for the current directory or location		p. 824	
`SessionCookieName name attributes`		svdh	E
Name and attributes for the RFC2109 cookie storing the session		p. 828	
`SessionCookieName2 name attributes`		svdh	E
Name and attributes for the RFC2965 cookie storing the session		p. 828	
`SessionCookieRemove On|Off`	Off	svdh	E
Control for whether session cookies should be removed from incoming HTTP headers		p. 828	
`SessionCryptoCipher name`		svdh	X
The crypto cipher to be used to encrypt the session		p. 831	
`SessionCryptoDriver name [param[=value]]`		s	X
The crypto driver to be used to encrypt the session		p. 831	
`SessionCryptoPassphrase secret [ secret ... ]`		svdh	X
The key used to encrypt the session		p. 832	
`SessionCryptoPassphraseFile filename`		svd	X
File containing keys used to encrypt the session		p. 833	
`SessionDBDCookieName name attributes`		svdh	E
Name and attributes for the RFC2109 cookie storing the session ID		p. 836	
`SessionDBDCookieName2 name attributes`		svdh	E
Name and attributes for the RFC2965 cookie storing the session ID		p. 836	

`SessionDBDCookieRemove On|Off`	On	svdh	E
Control for whether session ID cookies should be removed from incoming HTTP headers		p. 837	
`SessionDBDDeleteLabel label`	deletesession	svdh	E
The SQL query to use to remove sessions from the database		p. 837	
`SessionDBDInsertLabel label`	insertsession	svdh	E
The SQL query to use to insert sessions into the database		p. 837	
`SessionDBDPerUser On|Off`	Off	svdh	E
Enable a per user session		p. 837	
`SessionDBDSelectLabel label`	selectsession	svdh	E
The SQL query to use to select sessions from the database		p. 838	
`SessionDBDUpdateLabel label`	updatesession	svdh	E
The SQL query to use to update existing sessions in the database		p. 838	
`SessionEnv On|Off`	Off	svdh	E
Control whether the contents of the session are written to the *HTTP_SESSION* environment variable		p. 824	
`SessionExclude path`		svdh	E
Define URL prefixes for which a session is ignored		p. 824	
`SessionHeader header`		svdh	E
Import session updates from a given HTTP response header		p. 825	
`SessionInclude path`		svdh	E
Define URL prefixes for which a session is valid		p. 825	
`SessionMaxAge maxage`	0	svdh	E
Define a maximum age in seconds for a session		p. 826	
`SetEnv env-variable [value]`		svdh	B
Sets environment variables		p. 583	
`SetEnvIf attribute regex [!]env-variable[=value]` `[[!]env-variable[=value]] ...`		svdh	B
Sets environment variables based on attributes of the request		p. 840	
`SetEnvIfExpr expr [!]env-variable[=value]` `[[!]env-variable[=value]] ...`		svdh	B
Sets environment variables based on an ap_expr expression		p. 842	
`SetEnvIfNoCase attribute regex [!]env-variable[=value]` `[[!]env-variable[=value]] ...`		svdh	B
Sets environment variables based on attributes of the request without respect to case		p. 842	
`SetHandler handler-name|None`		svdh	C
Forces all matching files to be processed by a handler		p. 404	
`SetInputFilter filter[;filter...]`		svdh	C
Sets the filters that will process client requests and POST input		p. 405	
`SetOutputFilter filter[;filter...]`		svdh	C
Sets the filters that will process responses from the server		p. 405	
`SSIEndTag tag`	"->"	sv	B
String that ends an include element		p. 632	
`SSIErrorMsg message`	"[an error occurred +	svdh	B
Error message displayed when there is an SSI error		p. 633	
`SSIETag on|off`	off	dh	B
Controls whether ETags are generated by the server.		p. 633	
`SSILastModified on|off`	off	dh	B
Controls whether `Last-Modified` headers are generated by the server.		p. 633	
`SSILegacyExprParser on|off`	off	dh	B
Enable compatibility mode for conditional expressions.		p. 634	
`SSIStartTag tag`	"<!-#"	sv	B
String that starts an include element		p. 634	
`SSITimeFormat formatstring`	"%A, %d-%b-%Y %H:%M +	svdh	B
Configures the format in which date strings are displayed		p. 635	
`SSIUndefinedEcho string`	"(none)"	svdh	B
String displayed when an unset variable is echoed		p. 635	
`SSLCACertificateFile file-path`		sv	E
File of concatenated PEM-encoded CA Certificates for Client Auth		p. 858	
`SSLCACertificatePath directory-path`		sv	E
Directory of PEM-encoded CA Certificates for Client Auth		p. 858	
`SSLCADNRequestFile file-path`		sv	E
File of concatenated PEM-encoded CA Certificates for defining acceptable CA names		p. 858	
`SSLCADNRequestPath directory-path`		sv	E
Directory of PEM-encoded CA Certificates for defining acceptable CA names		p. 859	
`SSLCARevocationCheck chain|leaf|none`	none	sv	E
Enable CRL-based revocation checking		p. 859	

`SSLCARevocationFile file-path` File of concatenated PEM-encoded CA CRLs for Client Auth		sv p. 860	E
`SSLCARevocationPath directory-path` Directory of PEM-encoded CA CRLs for Client Auth		sv p. 860	E
`SSLCertificateChainFile file-path` File of PEM-encoded Server CA Certificates		sv p. 860	E
`SSLCertificateFile file-path` Server PEM-encoded X.509 certificate data file		sv p. 861	E
`SSLCertificateKeyFile file-path` Server PEM-encoded private key file		sv p. 862	E
`SSLCipherSuite cipher-spec` Cipher Suite available for negotiation in SSL handshake	DEFAULT (depends on ⊦	svdh p. 862	E
`SSLCompression on|off` Enable compression on the SSL level	off	sv p. 865	E
`SSLCryptoDevice engine` Enable use of a cryptographic hardware accelerator	builtin	s p. 865	E
`SSLEngine on|off|optional` SSL Engine Operation Switch	off	sv p. 865	E
`SSLFIPS on|off` SSL FIPS mode Switch	off	s p. 866	E
`SSLHonorCipherOrder on|off` Option to prefer the server's cipher preference order	off	sv p. 866	E
`SSLInsecureRenegotiation on|off` Option to enable support for insecure renegotiation	off	sv p. 867	E
`SSLOCSDefaultResponder uri` Set the default responder URI for OCSP validation		sv p. 867	E
`SSLOCSPEnable on|off` Enable OCSP validation of the client certificate chain	off	sv p. 867	E
`SSLOCSPOverrideResponder on|off` Force use of the default responder URI for OCSP validation	off	sv p. 868	E
`SSLOCSPResponderTimeout seconds` Timeout for OCSP queries	10	sv p. 868	E
`SSLOCSPResponseMaxAge seconds` Maximum allowable age for OCSP responses	-1	sv p. 868	E
`SSLOCSPResponseTimeSkew seconds` Maximum allowable time skew for OCSP response validation	300	sv p. 869	E
`SSLOCSPUseRequestNonce on|off` Use a nonce within OCSP queries	on	sv p. 869	E
`SSLOpenSSLConfCmd command-name command-value` Configure OpenSSL parameters through its *SSL_CONF* API		sv p. 869	E
`SSLOptions [+|-]option ...` Configure various SSL engine run-time options		svdh p. 870	E
`SSLPassPhraseDialog type` Type of pass phrase dialog for encrypted private keys	builtin	s p. 871	E
`SSLProtocol [+|-]protocol ...` Configure usable SSL/TLS protocol versions	all -SSLv3 (up to 2 +	sv p. 872	E
`SSLProxyCACertificateFile file-path` File of concatenated PEM-encoded CA Certificates for Remote Server Auth		sv p. 873	E
`SSLProxyCACertificatePath directory-path` Directory of PEM-encoded CA Certificates for Remote Server Auth		sv p. 873	E
`SSLProxyCARevocationCheck chain|leaf|none` Enable CRL-based revocation checking for Remote Server Auth	none	sv p. 873	E
`SSLProxyCARevocationFile file-path` File of concatenated PEM-encoded CA CRLs for Remote Server Auth		sv p. 874	E
`SSLProxyCARevocationPath directory-path` Directory of PEM-encoded CA CRLs for Remote Server Auth		sv p. 874	E
`SSLProxyCheckPeerCN on|off` Whether to check the remote server certificate's CN field	on	sv p. 875	E
`SSLProxyCheckPeerExpire on|off` Whether to check if remote server certificate is expired	on	sv p. 875	E
`SSLProxyCheckPeerName on|off` Configure host name checking for remote server certificates	on	sv p. 875	E
`SSLProxyCipherSuite cipher-spec` Cipher Suite available for negotiation in SSL proxy handshake	ALL:!ADH:RC4+RSA:+H +	svdh p. 876	E

Directive / Description	Default	Context	Status
`SSLProxyEngine on|off` SSL Proxy Engine Operation Switch	off	sv p. 876	E
`SSLProxyMachineCertificateChainFile filename` File of concatenated PEM-encoded CA certificates to be used by the proxy for choosing a certificate		s p. 876	E
`SSLProxyMachineCertificateFile filename` File of concatenated PEM-encoded client certificates and keys to be used by the proxy		s p. 877	E
`SSLProxyMachineCertificatePath directory` Directory of PEM-encoded client certificates and keys to be used by the proxy		s p. 877	E
`SSLProxyProtocol [+|-]protocol ...` Configure usable SSL protocol flavors for proxy usage	all -SSLv3 (up to 2 +)	sv p. 878	E
`SSLProxyVerify level` Type of remote server Certificate verification	none	sv p. 878	E
`SSLProxyVerifyDepth number` Maximum depth of CA Certificates in Remote Server Certificate verification	1	sv p. 878	E
`SSLRandomSeed context source [bytes]` Pseudo Random Number Generator (PRNG) seeding source		s p. 879	E
`SSLRenegBufferSize bytes` Set the size for the SSL renegotiation buffer	131072	dh p. 880	E
`SSLRequire expression` Allow access only when an arbitrarily complex boolean expression is true		dh p. 880	E
`SSLRequireSSL` Deny access when SSL is not used for the HTTP request		dh p. 882	E
`SSLSessionCache type` Type of the global/inter-process SSL Session Cache	none	s p. 883	E
`SSLSessionCacheTimeout seconds` Number of seconds before an SSL session expires in the Session Cache	300	sv p. 884	E
`SSLSessionTicketKeyFile file-path` Persistent encryption/decryption key for TLS session tickets		sv p. 884	E
`SSLSessionTickets on|off` Enable or disable use of TLS session tickets	on	sv p. 885	E
`SSLSRPUnknownUserSeed secret-string` SRP unknown user seed		sv p. 885	E
`SSLSRPVerifierFile file-path` Path to SRP verifier file		sv p. 885	E
`SSLStaplingCache type` Configures the OCSP stapling cache		s p. 886	E
`SSLStaplingErrorCacheTimeout seconds` Number of seconds before expiring invalid responses in the OCSP stapling cache	600	sv p. 886	E
`SSLStaplingFakeTryLater on|off` Synthesize "tryLater" responses for failed OCSP stapling queries	on	sv p. 886	E
`SSLStaplingForceURL uri` Override the OCSP responder URI specified in the certificate's AIA extension		sv p. 886	E
`SSLStaplingResponderTimeout seconds` Timeout for OCSP stapling queries	10	sv p. 887	E
`SSLStaplingResponseMaxAge seconds` Maximum allowable age for OCSP stapling responses	-1	sv p. 887	E
`SSLStaplingResponseTimeSkew seconds` Maximum allowable time skew for OCSP stapling response validation	300	sv p. 887	E
`SSLStaplingReturnResponderErrors on|off` Pass stapling related OCSP errors on to client	on	sv p. 887	E
`SSLStaplingStandardCacheTimeout seconds` Number of seconds before expiring responses in the OCSP stapling cache	3600	sv p. 888	E
`SSLStrictSNIVHostCheck on|off` Whether to allow non-SNI clients to access a name-based virtual host.	off	sv p. 888	E
`SSLUserName varname` Variable name to determine user name		sdh p. 888	E
`SSLUseStapling on|off` Enable stapling of OCSP responses in the TLS handshake	off	sv p. 889	E
`SSLVerifyClient level` Type of Client Certificate verification	none	svdh p. 889	E
`SSLVerifyDepth number` Maximum depth of CA Certificates in Client Certificate verification	1	svdh p. 890	E
`StartServers number` Number of child server processes created at startup		s p. 925	M

`StartThreads number`		s	M
Number of threads created on startup		p. 925	
`Substitute s/pattern/substitution/[infq]`		dh	E
Pattern to filter the response content		p. 893	
`SubstituteInheritBefore on|off`	off	dh	E
Change the merge order of inherited patterns		p. 894	
`SubstituteMaxLineLength bytes(b|B|k|K|m|M|g|G)`	1m	dh	E
Set the maximum line size		p. 895	
`Suexec On|Off`		s	B
Enable or disable the suEXEC feature		p. 900	
`SuexecUserGroup User Group`		sv	E
User and group for CGI programs to run as		p. 896	
`ThreadLimit number`		s	M
Sets the upper limit on the configurable number of threads per child process		p. 925	
`ThreadsPerChild number`		s	M
Number of threads created by each child process		p. 926	
`ThreadStackSize size`		s	M
The size in bytes of the stack used by threads handling client connections		p. 926	
`TimeOut seconds`	60	sv	C
Amount of time the server will wait for certain events before failing a request		p. 406	
`TraceEnable [on|off|extended]`	on	sv	C
Determines the behavior on `TRACE` requests		p. 406	
`TransferLog file|pipe`		sv	B
Specify location of a log file		p. 666	
`TypesConfig file-path`	conf/mime.types	s	B
The location of the `mime.types` file		p. 716	
`UnDefine parameter-name`		s	C
Undefine the existence of a variable		p. 407	
`UndefMacro name`		svd	B
Undefine a macro		p. 702	
`UnsetEnv env-variable [env-variable] ...`		svdh	B
Removes variables from the environment		p. 584	
`Use name [value1 ... valueN]`		svd	B
Use a macro		p. 703	
`UseCanonicalName On|Off|DNS`	Off	svd	C
Configures how the server determines its own name and port		p. 407	
`UseCanonicalPhysicalPort On|Off`	Off	svd	C
Configures how the server determines its own port		p. 408	
`User unix-userid`	#-1	s	B
The userid under which the server will answer requests		p. 900	
`UserDir directory-filename [directory-filename] ...`		sv	B
Location of the user-specific directories		p. 902	
`VHostCGIMode On|Off|Secure`	On	v	X
Determines whether the virtualhost can run subprocesses, and the privileges available to subprocesses.		p. 728	
`VHostPrivs [+-]?privilege-name [[+-]?privilege-name] ...`		v	X
Assign arbitrary privileges to subprocesses created by a virtual host.		p. 729	
`VHostGroup unix-groupid`		v	X
Sets the Group ID under which a virtual host runs.		p. 729	
`VHostPrivs [+-]?privilege-name [[+-]?privilege-name] ...`		v	X
Assign arbitrary privileges to a virtual host.		p. 730	
`VHostSecure On|Off`	On	v	X
Determines whether the server runs with enhanced security for the virtualhost.		p. 730	
`VHostUser unix-userid`		v	X
Sets the User ID under which a virtual host runs.		p. 731	
`VirtualDocumentRoot interpolated-directory|none`	none	sv	E
Dynamically configure the location of the document root for a given virtual host		p. 911	
`VirtualDocumentRootIP interpolated-directory|none`	none	sv	E
Dynamically configure the location of the document root for a given virtual host		p. 911	
`<VirtualHost addr[:port] [addr[:port]] ...> ...` `</VirtualHost>`		s	C
Contains directives that apply only to a specific hostname or IP address		p. 408	
`VirtualScriptAlias interpolated-directory|none`	none	sv	E
Dynamically configure the location of the CGI directory for a given virtual host		p. 912	
`VirtualScriptAliasIP interpolated-directory|none`	none	sv	E
Dynamically configure the location of the CGI directory for a given virtual host		p. 912	

`WatchdogInterval number-of-seconds`	1	s	B
Watchdog interval in seconds		p. 913	
`XBitHack on|off|full`	off	svdh	B
Parse SSI directives in files with the execute bit set		p. 635	
`xml2EncAlias charset alias [alias ...]`		s	B
Recognise Aliases for encoding values		p. 915	
`xml2EncDefault name`		svdh	B
Sets a default encoding to assume when absolutely no information can be automatically detected		p. 915	
`xml2StartParse element [element ...]`		svdh	B
Advise the parser to skip leading junk.		p. 916	

www.ingramcontent.com/pod-product-compliance
Lightning Source LLC
LaVergne TN
LVHW060134070326
832902LV00018B/2796